To Kara McGee —
Wonderful P.A. who works
with one my favorite
providers on earth, Dr.
Michelle Ogle —
With gratitude

POSITIVE

One Doctor's Personal Encounters
with Death, Life, and
the US Healthcare System

MICHAEL SAAG, MD

GREENLEAF
BOOK GROUP PRESS

Published by Greenleaf Book Group Press
Austin, Texas
www.gbgpress.com

Distributed by Greenleaf Book Group LLC

For ordering information or special discounts for bulk purchases, please contact Greenleaf Book Group LLC at PO Box 91869, Austin, TX 78709, 512.891.6100.

Design and composition by Greenleaf Book Group LLC
Cover design by Greenleaf Book Group LLC
Cover images:
©iStockphoto.com/enjoynz/ enjoy industries; ©iStockphoto.com/Hocus Focus Studio

Publisher's Cataloging-In-Publication Data
Saag, Michael S.
   Positive : one doctor's personal encounters with death, life, and the US healthcare system / Michael Saag.—1st ed.
   p. ; cm.
   Issued also as an ebook.
   ISBN: 978-1-62634-064-0
   1. Saag, Michael S. 2. Physicians—United States—Biography. 3. Medical care—United States. 4. AIDS (Disease)—Patients—United States. I. Title.
R154.S22 A3 2014
610/.92   2013948287

Part of the Tree Neutral® program, which offsets the number of trees consumed in the production and printing of this book by taking proactive steps, such as planting trees in direct proportion to the number of trees used: www.treeneutral.com

Printed in the United States of America on acid-free paper

13 14 15 16 17 18   10 9 8 7 6 5 4 3 2 1

TreeNeutral®

First Edition

For those we might have saved yesterday, if only we'd had more knowledge. And for those we could have saved today, if only we'd had more courage.

CONTENTS

Acknowledgments

I feel sorry for the aspiring young doctors who are assigned to me as residents and house staff; they have to put up with my nonsense and pretend to enjoy it. At the outset of our time together, I always say to them with mock gravity, "I will give you my three rules for survival as a physician, and a fourth rule for when you're on service with me.

"Rule One: Treat every patient as if every one were a family member. Every one of them deserves the best you have to give.

"Rule Two: Be honest, especially with yourself. Don't bullshit yourself or pretend you know something you don't, because that's when you'll make a mistake and people will get hurt.

"Rule Three: Have fun. The practice of medicine should be a joy, and if you aren't having fun, you've either picked the wrong specialty or you're morbidly depressed.

"And the fourth rule, specifically for when you're working on my service: No matter what, *it's all about me.*"

After listening with extreme earnestness to my first three rules, the newbies hear Rule Four and crack up. They exhale and relax—and, sometimes, they get my point: that this life is *never* all about any one of us. It's about teamwork toward a common goal.

It's also true of this book.

After years of threatening to write a book, I never would have gotten off the dime to do it without the support of two people: my cousin and inspiration Mary Fisher, and my longtime adviser and friend, A. James Heynen.

Mary has shown me, through her example, that living courageously and with purpose, we can all make a difference and that *everything* is possible—including writing a book. Mary has been with me through the past twenty years of my professional journey, as a patient. She's heard me marvel at the advances we have made on the science front; she's listened when I despaired at barriers interfering with making the science come to life in practice.

Jim Heynen is my guardian angel. His "day job" is as an organizational consultant, but for me, he is my lead sounding board and "life coach." I am very grateful to both of them for helping to convince me that a book in this area was needed, and for encouraging me to keep pushing until it was done.

Patty Edmonds has served as my lead editor for this project. While I have written many grants and manuscripts for publication in the scientific literature, I have never attempted the type of writing required for telling a story in a book. Patty led me gently into this new world and helped me find my voice. I am forever grateful to her for her patience, honesty, impeccable journalism, professionalism, and soul!

A huge shout-out goes collectively to my colleagues, my fellow providers and fellow investigators, locally, nationally, and around the world. As I have said to most of them while I was writing this book, "Any one of you could have written your story and it would be just as compelling." Each one of us took care of too many patients to count who touched our lives, moved us to tears, and inspired us to do our best to bring HIV/AIDS under control. The work we did at the University of Alabama at Birmingham (UAB) was directly connected to clinics and labs around the world, each of us doing our part to contribute to solving the mystery of this horrific disease that rudely roared into our consciousness in the early 1980s. This is especially true regarding my colleagues at the 1917 Clinic, several of whom are profiled in this book. Jim Raper is a consummate leader who puts his soul into his work, as well as his heart. Malcolm Marler brought GRACE to the clinic, both literally and figuratively. And the many, many coworkers, physicians, nurse practitioners, nurses, social workers, pharmacists, receptionists, lab technicians, psychologists, counselors, clergy, and medical records and administrative staff, all of whose collective intellect, insights, wisdom, generosity, honesty, tireless effort, and heart—always heart—are constant inspirations. Especially while writing about these folks, I've seen again how their heart has eased the pain of the collective losses we all experienced over the years. Thank you.

At the risk of leaving out some key colleagues and collaborators, I am compelled to mention several collaborators and friends who enabled me to have success both as an investigator and as a provider. Paul Volberding and his San Francisco colleagues' vision for a comprehensive HIV outpatient clinic that merged the best in science, clinical medicine, and heart into a single center set the stage for our clinic, and many, many others, to become complete medical "homes" for patients with HIV and their families. Paul's vision has served me well over my entire career, and he has been a "consultant" to me on many topic areas, ranging from which professional opportunities to engage in to which shoes to buy while in Italy!

Paul could not have set up Ward 86 as completely as he did without the support of Merle Sande. I met Merle through Paul, and Merle took me on as one of his own. Even though I never worked at San Francisco General Hospital or UCSF, Merle always treated me as if I was one of his faculty members, creating many opportunities for me over the years. I am grateful to him.

Although similar in age to me, George Shaw and Beatrice Hahn are my primary mentors in all things related to basic science. My formative years in their lab had everything to do with my decision to become involved in AIDS medicine. They made it fun, exciting, and productive. Their collective intellect and intuition is as strong as any I've ever encountered in science, but their generosity is really what sets them apart. I cannot imagine more generous mentors, and I have tried to emulate them in my relationships with the investigators and house staff I mentor.

Donna Jacobsen and my fellow board members of the International Antiviral Society-USA have provided remarkable insight into the ways of the world, especially related to what true continuing medical education is and what it takes to do it right. I am grateful for their guidance as I navigated the turbulent waters generated at the interface of education and indoctrination. Thanks to them for the way forward.

The University of Alabama at Birmingham has been a magical place to work. There is a can-do, entrepreneurial spirit there that I have not seen at any other academic institution. As is evident throughout this book, I was afforded opportunities very early in my career that would not have happened elsewhere solely because UAB and its leaders focus on ideas, not on the age of the person who brings the idea forward. In particular, my distinguished mentors, Drs. Claude Bennett, Bill Dismukes, and Glenn Cobbs, are special beyond words. George Karam, a close friend and colleague, has likened mentorship to parenting: "You give unconditionally to those who you mentor with the hope your guidance will help your 'offspring' become all they can be, without any expectation of payment or recognition in return." My mentors are the embodiment of this ideal and I am grateful for their vision, insight, and encouragement over the years. And I am grateful to the many visionary leaders and colleagues at UAB—Joe Volker, Tinsley Harrison, Dick Hill, Scotty McCallum, Jim Pitman, Bill Koopman, John Durant, John Kirklin, Ray Watts, Dick Marchase, and Rich Whitley—who created a nurturing environment in which I could thrive. I am privileged to have worked at UAB for over thirty years.

William Osler, the legendary physician who set the tone for modern American medicine, once said, "He who studies medicine without books sails an uncharted sea, but he who studies medicine without patients does not go to sea at all." I could not have gained the insights I have regarding the practice of medicine without the patients for whom I have been privileged to provide care, as well as their families. Over the years I strived to give my best effort, and in return they put their trust in me. I learned, and continue to learn, from every patient I see. And my obligation is to take this collective knowledge and use it for the benefit of the next patient I'll see. My experience learning from and with so many patients in need is what motivated me to write this book. To all of them, my heartfelt gratitude.

To the activists, who spurred us all on to do better even when we thought we were doing our best, my thanks. Larry Kramer, Martin Delaney, Dawn Averitt-Bridge, and countless others are all heroes who saved the lives of millions around the world through their impatience grounded in grief. And a very special thanks to Tom Blount, a quiet warrior whose grace, intellect, generosity, and heart made so much happen for so many, including me.

Finally, to my family, whose love and support over the years has enabled me to do what I do every day. Some of their stories are highlighted in the book, others are not. My extended Weil family in Birmingham, especially my mother-in-law, Pat Weil, and my late father-in-law, Leonard, who supported Amy through all the days and nights I was consumed with my work. My mom, Elaine Koppel Saag, has provided steadfast support; I hope the pages within the book do justice to her hard work. Eddie Saag, my father, was and remains my rock, laying out the principles for leading a good and fun-loving life. My sisters, Terry and Barbara, along with their husbands, Gary and Greg, have always been there for me and sustained a "functional" family dynamic. Our oldest son, Andy, and his wife, Brittany, have brought joy to us every day. They have both been great editors for the book. Harry, our middle son, has played a key role as a sounding board for me while I formulated ideas for this book. His insights and groundedness are invaluable. Julie, our daughter and youngest, is pure joy. She lights up a room with her sunshine at all times.

And Amy, my wife of thirty-six years . . . there is a place in heaven for you, simply for being who you are.

My heartfelt thanks to everyone for putting up with my nonsense and quirks over the years, especially during the time I spent pulling this book together. Without that ongoing support, none of this would have happened.

Note to Readers

I use patient stories as case examples to illustrate key messages throughout the book and to create authenticity. I very carefully chose among thousands of patient stories. Due to US privacy laws, some of the stories have been "de-identified" for those cases in which I was unable to obtain patient permission.

I thank the patients and their family members for sharing their stories through this book. I am very grateful for their generosity and their spirit of helping to shine a light on the struggles in the war on AIDS and our daily wrestling with the US healthcare system. Thank you for being who you are and making a difference.

Chapter 1

MAGICAL THINKING

I don't remember the airline or the destination. It was one of thousands of forgettable flights I've boarded in the past thirty years, a conglomerated blur of conferences and lectures and interviews and research meetings, patients, family, and students, all mingled with exhaustion and illness and hope. I'm pretty sure I was in an aisle seat toward the back because my upgrade didn't come through. I know that I was on my way to give a lecture and that I had one tedious task to do in-flight: reviewing the biography that would be used to introduce me.

If you are a would-be comic—which I am—you can read only so many straitlaced descriptions of yourself before you're itching to punch things up. The introduction that had been sent for my approval, like most of them, dutifully listed the basics: He teaches medicine, he does research, he runs a clinic. Held an endowed chair here, published papers there, distinguished this and honorary that. It was all very suitable for your typical medical audience: suitable, and boring. I sounded boring. I felt boring.

To break the monotony, I thought that I might incorporate a few more facts. "Dr. Michael Saag tells long stories that he finds charming, and he makes short movies in his spare time." Or, "He's known to burst abruptly into song—generally a Broadway show tune or a Marx Brothers classic—with no provocation, and to perform lustily in inappropriate settings, sometimes on key." Perhaps even "When not engaged in HIV/AIDS research, Dr. Saag is a part-time barber." (I do cut my sons' hair in our home's basement salon, which is complete with a lighted barber pole and posted Shoppe Rules. Rule no. 6: "Mirrors are not allowed in the Shoppe at any time.")

I've amused myself on more than one occasion with strategies by which to jazz up these introductions. But one reason would-be comics are "would-be" is that they lack courage. I've never dared do it. I've considered replacing my straight lecture with a mix of lecture-and-shtick, half research and half jokes, just to see if anyone notices. More recently, I've fantasized about supplanting my scholarly lecture with a full-throated rant about the failures of the US healthcare system—not particularly funny, perhaps, but certainly less boring.

For pre-scripted introductions, I always stop short and just edit what they sent me. I sink Walter Mitty-like into my airline seat, playing only the role of the tired, overbooked nomad I have become, and I do the minimum necessary to keep the introduction honest. Okay, it's accurate if uninteresting: check. I skim the packet for place and time of lecture: check. I take one more look at my balanced, benign lecture: in order, check.

Typically, this is the moment when—despite my best intentions of grabbing a beer or a nap—I let myself wander off into almost-thought. I try to recall why I went into medicine: what motivated or deluded me, what I imagined and expected. I think about how, over three decades of unparalleled advances in science and healing, so much about practicing medicine seems to have gotten worse. Medical professionals' time with patients has decreased while the workload has increased. The cost of patient care has risen by almost every measure, while insurers appear to profit more and help less. On any given day, I'm barely holding it together enough to see patients, write proposals, attend university meetings, guide research, teach, mentor, and spend a few minutes with my wife. When the children were younger, I swear that my daughter used to call me "Uncle Dad." And I'm not uncommon. I'm typical of the women and men in my field.

By the time I've ruminated my way to this lament, I no longer feel like a comic. I'm now a critic, or maybe the author of a scathing op-ed. What infuriates me is that America is so rich in medical know-how, human resources, technology, and good will that, with relatively few adjustments, it could be home to the best healthcare in the world. *Could be.*

I have a speech I give mostly while holding the steering wheel. It's all about how to make American healthcare the envy of the world. I give it while driving to the clinic early in the morning, before the frustrations of the day have brought me down. If I'm still delivering my masterpiece as I pull into the parking lot outside the lab, I already know what my team of colleagues would say if they heard my brilliance: "Mike's got his magical thinking going today." I see Bonnie's rolling eyes and Jim's knowing grin as they catch me at it. Only when I exasperate them beyond all human limits do they actually say what they otherwise merely think: "You're pretending that the impossible is within reach, Mike, and that because you can imagine it, it'll happen. Life and medicine don't work that way. Stop it!"

I like magical thinking. I grew up in a family that saw magic in the "sixth sense" of my great-aunt Florence, fondly regarded as the family's good witch. She was a southern lady in touch with another world, with an inexplicable knack for foreseeing or affecting events. She accepted this reality as happily as she responded to the only name by which the adults ever referenced her, "Flo Honey" pronounced as one word: Flohoney.

Throughout my medical career, colleagues have complained—sometimes in colorful terms—that it would take a magician to pull off the goals I set for our work together. Maybe. But my reigning belief is that aiming high is reasonable, even fun. Saying we're going to achieve what hasn't been achieved before is a perfect objective for research; otherwise, why do it? Saving a life that would otherwise be lost is a mandatory hope for a physician. Looking to change a procedure that doesn't work, or a policy that results in patients dying—this isn't "magic." It's necessary. It's why we're here. It's what gives us meaning.

Maybe I whine about prespeech introductions because they make me feel like everything's been done that's going to be done, at least by me. "Dr. Saag has published . . . taught . . . participated . . . led . . ." My life is recast in the past tense. And the script of my life is converted to a fairy tale because no one wants to tell the unvarnished truth: "Dr. Saag has embarrassed himself as he's failed . . . stumbled . . . ignored . . . whined . . ." In fact, I don't live in the past, and my past is as littered with false starts as it is with happy out-comes. Research isn't a steady march to genius; it's a trial-and-error process that frustrates your best guesses and only occasionally rewards your instincts.

In the end, the achievements and the flops add up to what's been done. What I'd really like to think is that we stand on what we've done to reach for what's ahead, that the past is only our footstool. And what this does for me—this "standing on the shoulders of our past" thinking—is launch me out of the here-and-now and into the world as it should be. Once there, I look around, smile, and say to myself, "Yeah, this is right. This is what we should be doing. This is it." When I return from such visits and share my convictions about what I've seen, that's when my colleagues' eyes start rolling.

During my thirty years slugging it out in the US medical system, all sorts of things I believed to be certainties have turned out not to be even close. I went to the University of Alabama at Birmingham (UAB) expecting to become a cardiologist, and instead I stumbled into an entirely differ-ent specialty, infectious diseases. I imagined settling into a private practice where work hours would leave time for friends, football, a marriage, and a family. My imagination had not factored in the events of June 5, 1981, when the US Centers for Disease Control reported eight cases of unusual opportunistic infections in gay men, and I happened to be where that mat-tered. In time, the "gay cancer" first described came to be known as Acquired Immune Deficiency Syndrome, caused by the Human Immunodeficiency Virus. I couldn't then have imagined that brawling with HIV and knocking out AIDS would become my life's passion.

Months passed, then years, and with time I found myself chasing an elusive cure—or, if not a cure, at least something to slow the suffering and dying—all the while watching as the pandemic killed people I'd come to know and love. What we needed to do, it seemed to me, was so clear, so simple: We just needed to stop the virus. If we knew how to stop the virus, we could stop the terror, the wasting, the dying.

Thirty-some years later I think I was right about what needed to be done in an ideal sense: The virus should be stopped. By now, science has given us the tools to stop the virus. But in the real world where my patients live and my colleagues work, medicine hasn't been able to end the plague, because knowing how to keep someone alive doesn't necessarily or magically morph into public policy that keeps them alive. They don't *need* to die of a disease we can manage, but they do. They've been dying for more than thirty years. They are dying as I write this sentence. They'll die before you finish reading this page.

I came into medicine believing that we—my fellow professionals and I—would care for people based on need, not on finance or public opinion. I was wrong. I came in believing that drug companies developed drugs to help people, independent of what the market would support. Wrong. I thought health insurance companies felt a responsibility to provide just as much benefit for their policyholders as for their shareholders. Wrong again. I originally suffered something more than magical thinking; I was possessed by naïveté.

Over the years, the naïve elements in my thinking have largely been beaten out of me. I've been schooled as a witness to withering illness and excruciating death, some as an immediate consequence of policies intended only to save money, not lives. I've been disciplined by caring for hundreds—perhaps by now it's thousands—of people dying of a disease that their insurers balk at covering and their parents dare not mention to friends. In my world, when we're winning, we're still going broke. And when we're losing, our patients are treated like twenty-first-century lepers: Their family puts "cancer" in the obituary because they don't want the shame of saying plainly that my patient died of AIDS.

If I've lost my innocence, I still haven't lost my optimism. Even in the darkest corners of the AIDS pandemic, I've seen flickers of the coherent, compassionate medical system that all of us want and deserve.

It isn't only in my Walter Mitty world that I see colleagues' heroism, patients revived, and hope justified. I've seen ordinary people put their lives on hold and come together to advocate and care for those who suffer, as well as to bury those who die. They did it without asking who would pay. They only wanted the suffering to stop and, when it could only be stopped by death, they—we—leaned on each other until the grieving eased.

I've watched parents (especially mothers), partners, and spouses care for those who are dying, compensating for their lack of medical training with the incredible power of love. They gave up sleep and sometimes careers, risked their own financial ruin, and devoted themselves to another human being who was dying. It didn't get them bonus points or angel's wings; it got them exhaustion. And sometimes, I've seen people do it twice.

I've seen the stinginess of institutions overcome by the self-sacrifice of individual nurses, passionate social workers, devoted admissions staff, and honest doctors. I've seen patients, medical professionals, and community advocates bound by such commitment to one another that they're not just what industry jargon calls a "medical home"—they're a bona fide *medical neighborhood.*

When I rehearse all of this, even in the back of a stuffy jetliner, I'm pulled back toward the reality that healing is possible. I may have boarded the flight with my optimism running on fumes, but remembering these remarkable colleagues revives me. It's why I keep packing up my magical thinking and getting on these planes: to lobby the policymakers, to give pep talks to fellow researchers, to teach new generations of practitioners. It's why I gather stories from America's medical neighborhoods and share them in my lectures, my movies—and now, for the first time, in a book.

Riding airplanes, I've met a lot of people who genuinely believe that America is well served by the existing healthcare system. If that's really been their experience, then as Carol Linn (one of my nurses) would say, "Bless their hearts." But if their granddaughter contracts cystic fibrosis and they are short of cash; if their son is diagnosed with diabetes and they had saved money by buying a low-cost insurance plan; if they become unemployed and uninsured and suffer the usual fate encountered by those ineligible for Medicare—for these, my nurse reserves another saying: "God help 'em." They are, whether they know it or not, on their way to bankruptcy.

What makes magic "magic" is doing a trick that everyone knows has to be a trick; it's impossible. No one can drive a sword through an occupied box and not hit some flesh and bone. Nobody can levitate on cue or draw rabbits from empty hats. But when we see with our eyes what we know with our brains isn't possible, we ooh and aah and call it magic.

The real magicians, it turns out, are the insurance companies and politicians who claim that we have "the best healthcare system in the world" right here in the U. S. of A. This is where we should be oohing and aahing. The magic is that some of us believe this! My nonmagical thinking reminds me that in fact, the United States has an infant mortality rate twice as high as that of Sweden and Germany, as well as a maternal mortality rate twice as high as the United Kingdom's and seven times higher than Australia's. Is it "best" to rank far behind other developed nations, such as Japan and Denmark, in physician visits per capita? Or well behind France or Switzerland in per capita days of hospital treatment? If America's system really was the best, would a US patient facing renal failure be one-half to one-third less likely to get a kidney transplant than a patient in Spain or Canada? The magicians have convinced us that we're best. We're not.

Here's an item that someone in my audience always believes I've made up; it's too outlandish to be true. Sorry, but it *is* true: Two-thirds of personal bankruptcies in the United States are precipitated by medical bills that can't be paid, even among those *with insurance*. In fact, most of the bankruptcies occur among those who have health insurance. There just wasn't enough insurance.

The US healthcare system is far and away the globe's leader in one category: cost. Americans' average per-person cost for healthcare each year? Nearly $8,000, compared to less than $5,000 for our neighbors across the border in Canada. Those out-of-pocket payments you cough up for care? They're two or three times what your German or French counterparts pay. And the procedures and drugs you need to maintain your health, everything from a heart bypass to a dose of cholesterol-lowering medicine to a doctor's office visit? They're more expensive—usually significantly more—in the United States than in other developed countries. Even an insurance trade association's survey of medical services and products around the globe concludes that US costs sit atop every major category measured in every single developed nation. To add insult to injury, as the cost of US healthcare keeps escalating, the dollars are increasingly going into corporate profits, not into the pockets of patients, families, or caregivers.

As out of whack as this is, the most maddening truth about our healthcare system is that despite my zany magical thinking, we don't need magic to fix it. Providing affordable, appropriate care to all Americans is not at all impossible. It's unquestionably within reach. Unquestionably. No magical thinking needed. A common sense application of what we already know can get us there.

Every second of every hour of every day, the leadership of the United States chooses not to do it, and we all participate with them in their decision. We choose not to save that child's life or that woman's eye or that man's career or that family's future. The choice is made before the child or the woman shows up for care, because they show up too late, owing to lack of access to care. We who know better go mute when the syndicate dominated by insurance lobbyists and those elected on their money obscure the truth. We make these choices quietly, so no one quite notices. We use fancy language—try "cost prioritization" or "resource allocation"—to obscure the harsh truth: We are choosing who gets treatment and who gets ignored, who will live and who will die, not by virtue of their illness but on the grounds of what insurance they have (or don't have) and what annual income they can confirm (or can't). These factors control access.

Honestly, this is not magical thinking. It isn't whining about our past or lamenting our present. It's the unhappy and unnecessary truth. For those who think otherwise, well, "bless their hearts."

And for those who are already learning these truths through experience? "God help 'em."

Chapter 2

GROWING UP

At my birth in 1955, my solidly Jewish mother exclaimed, "A boy! He'll be *a doctor!*" I don't actually remember it very well, but I respect my mother and trust her account.

Even if this is an American stereotype, my mother couldn't imagine a goal higher or an achievement greater than producing a doctor. It wasn't about being Jewish; it was about making a difference in the lives of others. She never doubted this was my lot in life, and my father never questioned it (or her, on much of anything). For all my interest in music and film, as well as my abiding claim that I was meant to be in theater, I never really doubted it either.

Knowing the career lurking in my future, I took special note when, around the age of four, I was marched into the office of one of Louisville's finest pediatricians. I didn't care much for the antiseptic smell of the place. His paternalist tone—"Well, young man, let's take that shirt off"—made me skeptical. And when he pulled out needles, swabbed the business end with alcohol, and wiped my arm with the same swab, I could see what was coming. He turned his back for a moment and I was gone, past the receptionist desk, out the front door, and up a tree two blocks away.

Sitting in that tree and watching my mother walk beneath me, first in one direction and then the other, calling my name, I knew the truth. She had otherwise been a good mother, but on this score she'd been mistaken.

The last thing I wanted to be was a doctor. Who would want to spend his life pulling kids out of trees? Let one of my know-it-all older sisters be the stupid doctor. I liked movies. I had inherited the Switow family passion for film. Take me out of the tree and give me a cushioned seat, a bag of popcorn, and a darkened theater—was this too much to ask? Even now, remembering it, it makes sense to me.

I'm convinced that our family's movie-loving gene came from my great-grandfather, the source of my first name, Michael ("Grandpa") Switow. He died in 1940, a decade and a half before I was born. But I've always felt a spiritual connection to him, as if my destiny ran on from his. I've learned all that I could about him. Though a stroke at age seventy left his left side paralyzed, his memory and sharp wit were intact, and he spent the next few months dictating his life's story to his secretary. The memoir remains one of my family's most cherished possessions, although my grandmother Lela, Michael's second daughter, handed down this review of her father's book: "Half of these stories are true—we just don't know which half!"

His name was Michael Switofsky when, at sixteen, he left his family, his friends, and his village in northern Russia. Unwilling to be drafted into the army of a country that persecuted Jews, he escaped to Austria and, after hard months doing odd jobs in abject poverty, stowed away on an ocean-going freighter bound for the United States. He landed in New York Harbor in winter 1878, joined other Jewish immigrants of that era on Manhattan's Lower East Side, and tried to survive as a street peddler. Lonely and broke, he soon headed south and west, doing odd jobs, construction, manual labor, selling whatever he could barter along the way, and living briefly in small communities in the Midwest before moving on to the next town. Along the way, he developed the three rules of business that he would preach for the rest of his life, with enough people remembering the sermon for it to be handed down from generation to generation:

- Rule #1: Never buy retail;
- Rule #2: Always negotiate with the boss (not some middle-manager who couldn't close the deal); and
- Rule #3: Always work on OPM—(that is, Other People's Money).

I've always assumed that creatively applying his third rule is what caused him to leave most towns so abruptly.

In the boisterous, swaggering river town of St. Louis, Missouri—a place that swarmed with merchants, drifters, gamblers, and women of leisure—Michael met Annie Tuval, who was none of these things. Michael had learned that selling neckties—"one for a dime, three for a quarter"—would earn him more money in a day than digging ditches did in two weeks. Annie motivated him to sell. He travelled through neighboring states building up a dowry and returned to St. Louis in 1892 to ask Annie's father for her hand in marriage. They wed later that same year.

Annie didn't like the sound of Switofsky, so after she took Michael's name she had it shortened to Switow. Annie's relatives were in the candy business; soon, so was Michael Switow, learning to make hard candies, saltwater taffy, and other confections. By the time their brood was complete—two older girls and three younger boys—the Switows were running a modestly successful candy store in Jeffersonville, Indiana, just across the Ohio River from Louisville, Kentucky.

But Michael had bigger dreams. In 1893, he had attended the Chicago World's Fair where he and the rest of America got the first glimpses of new wonders such as Cracker Jack, the Ferris wheel, and Thomas Edison's Kinetoscope for viewing moving pictures. Magic! Instantly, the man for whom I was later named visited the future and saw how much more candy he could sell if he converted the confectionary store into a makeshift movie theater at night. By 1908 he was showing silent movies there, often with piano accompaniment supplied by him or his son, Harry—later known by all in my family as Papaharry.

The movie house was such a hit that Michael set about opening theaters in small towns throughout the region. Even during the Great Depression, his businesses thrived as people struggling to survive found a nickel's worth of escape in the latest serial or feature film. In an earlier generation, Sam Clemens had made a living by having Mark Twain describe the era, the people, and the fantasies of the day; in his own day, Michael Switow could make a dime selling it all in a darkened theater, along with some popcorn and candy.

When Michael and Annie's second daughter, Lela, married David

Sagaloski in 1920, she must have loved his work ethic. Dave ran a furniture store by day, a twenty-four-hour diner called Pappy's Restaurant at night, and in between managed a farm that grew produce for the restaurant and popcorn for the Switows' theaters. What Lela did not like was Dave's bulky surname. She figured out that if she shortened the name and added a second "a," her family would be listed first on the "S" page of Louisville's phone book. And with that, the Sagaloskis became the Saags. My father, Eddie, born in 1924, was the middle of three Saag sons.

As a youngster, my father loved his visits to Grandpa Switow's theaters. On a good Sunday afternoon, they might hit three or four as they sped over the Kentucky and Indiana highways that connected the small-town cinemas. (When he thought I was old enough to hear it, one of my dad's favorite stories from those Sundays was of Grandpa arriving at a theater with a tremendous need to relieve himself. Since the women's restroom was on the first floor and the men's was in the basement, Grandpa strode into the women's restroom and was doing what he needed to do when the manager rushed in, shouting, "No, no, Mr. Switow—this is for the ladies!" Grandpa looked down, nodded, and said over his shoulder, "You got that right, Cal.")

Eddie Saag was a hard worker and bright, but by his own account was never much of a student. He frittered away a year in college before World War II summoned, and he became a demolition specialist in the Army Corps of Engineers. While serving in France in 1944, a bomb Eddie was defusing detonated. The episode earned him the Purple Heart and a reputation for quiet strength. I don't remember a single moment in my entire life in which I questioned either my father's courage or his devotion to me and our family.

Once back in America, Eddie took a shine to a teenager playing basketball in the alley between his family's house and hers. Elaine Koppel was five years his junior, and the last thing her overprotective father wanted was for some returning veteran to court his daughter. But Eddie won Elaine's heart, and in June 1948 they were married. A workaholic like his dad, Eddie worked three jobs. He did whatever needed doing at Pappy's Restaurant. He managed a drive-in for M. Switow & Sons, the growing chain of indoor and outdoor theaters run by his grandfather and uncles Sam, Fred, and Harry.

And he worked at Saag Brothers, a construction company he founded with his brother Henry. Meanwhile, Elaine raised their three children. First came daughter Terry, the straight-arrow overachiever. Next came Barbara, creative and rebellious. And then there was me, the tree climber, Michael the Second.

As the baby of the family, the only boy, and the first male Saag grandchild, I led a charmed life. By the time I was five, I was allowed to put on "work clothes" and tag along with Dad to the construction sites. I would sit proudly at his side as the construction team pored over blueprints and site plans. And then I would do whatever I could to get as dirty as possible so that by day's end I'd wear proof that I'd been working. At some sites, I would get to deliver the last few whacks of the hammer to nails driven by the lead carpenter, Loggie. So far as I knew, Loggie had no last name, and neither did John or Guy the Painter. They all had nicknames: Filthy McNasty, Gantze Macher (Yiddish for "big shot"), Good-for-Nothing, Jack, Cadillac.

By age eight, I was working at a Switow drive-in theater, selling tickets in the box office before the movies started and manning the concession stand at intermission. I watched the same movies night in and night out, becoming a student of film without the bother or tuition of enrollment. At the end of the night, while Dad and the concession stand manager were reconciling the books, I was sent out to "clear the arena."

Clearing the arena consisted of walking up to the cars still parked in the back row after the last movie had finished, standing on my tiptoes, shining a flashlight through the fogged up windows, and telling the surprised patrons, clad and unclad alike, "Time to go home!" I could have begun practicing then the line I would later perfect with patients after a physical exam, "You can put your clothes back on now"—although the gravel parking lot was a little less clinical.

By the time I was eleven, I'd been promoted to movie marketing. Sort of. The first of the so-called "spaghetti Westerns," *A Fistful of Dollars*, was to open at the Kentucky Theatre on 4th Street in downtown Louisville. The afternoon before the premiere showing, I was in my great-uncle Sam Switow's office above the theater, filling up hundreds of balloons that would be pushed off the marquee in just a few hours. As part of the promotion, while most of the balloons were empty, some of them had cash stuffed in them—mostly one-dollar bills, a few fives, tens, and twenties. One balloon contained a Ben Franklin, a crisp hundred-dollar bill.

At one point, Sam looked up from his desk to see me still furiously tying off balloons using fingers that had grown raw. He asked me what I wanted to be when I grew up. I told him I wasn't sure. He then asked me if I was a son of a bitch, and I told him, no, I wasn't. "Well, then," he declared, "you shouldn't go into business, because the only person who makes it in business is the son of a bitch who is a bigger son of a bitch than the other son of a bitch!"

I can't remember if I replied, but I know what I was thinking: *Guess I won't be going into business.*

That same year, I traveled with Dad to Shelbyville, Indiana, to help at an outdoor theater called the Starlite Drive-In. To run a sewage line to the Starlite, we needed to cross under a nearby highway, and that meant narrowing traffic to a single lane. The first few days in Shelbyville I was the flagman, stopping traffic in one direction and admitting it from the other. But after days of watching Cadillac, John, and others perform what looked like a much more interesting task, I asked: Could I be the jackhammer guy?

The next thing I knew, I was trying to hang on to a seventy-five-pound jackhammer as its body slammed a metal blade into simmering asphalt fifty times a second. Success was chiefly a matter of holding on, and I was too frightened to let go, too embarrassed to fail. So I rode that ear-shattering, body-snapping machine for an hour, and then another; I held on until the end of the day. I had never exerted such energy, nor had I ever felt such pain. But at day's end, Uncle Harry and Dad took me back to the motel, handed me a Falls City beer, and said, "If you work like a man, you can drink like a man." I was hot, tired, dirty, and on top of the world. I was a man.

Then came summer 1968, the summer of the assassinations: first Dr. King and then Robert Kennedy. Each death, and both deaths, reverberated through Louisville in a way I still struggle to describe. Temperamentally as well as geographically, Louisville was nearer to Ohio than to Mississippi, not really in the South but not entirely in the North. The assassinations sent shock waves through my hometown. The birthplace of Cassius Clay—later transformed by events and by choice into Muhammad Ali—erupted in riots.

Buildings burned. Cars were overturned and shops looted. Anarchy reigned. The fabric of our nation and our city had been torn once again, ripped by the still unfinished business of the American Revolution and the Civil War.

Within my family, and for me, the reaction was deeply personal. Ours was a joyfully Jewish household, whether we were singing the ancient Shabbat blessing around the dinner table or belting out bawdy songs with Uncle Harry at the piano. I never felt overtly discriminated against for being Jewish, though I sometimes felt singled out—like when I had to be excused from eighth-grade football practices to attend bar mitzvah classes, and the coach described it as "your day to go to Jew School." But after the assassinations, with those two strong voices against bigotry silenced, I was left feeling vulnerable and alone, wondering, "Who's next?"

American Jews had always been in kindred spirit with the oppressed, especially the oppressed in black America. I now know that a large number of the Freedom Riders in the early 1960s were Jews. Rabbis across the country and especially in the Deep South spoke out early, forcefully, and often against racial segregation and bigotry. (Rabbi Milton Grafman of Birmingham's Temple Emanu-El, my religious home in Birmingham, was among the loudest and most influential of those voices, a tradition maintained by our current rabbi, Jonathan Miller.) When racists planted bombs at Birmingham houses of worship, it was not only in predominantly black churches. Birmingham historian Solomon Kimerling records that five years before four young black girls died in a bomb blast at the 16th Street Baptist Church, an even larger bomb had been planted at Birmingham's Temple Beth-El, but it was discovered before it was detonated.

I mourned the deaths of Bobby and Martin as if sitting shiva for my own kin. There was new poignancy to the Torah portion I was preparing for my bar mitzvah: the last verses of the thirty-second book of Deuteronomy, where God tells Moses he may glimpse the Promised Land but will not reach it himself. I've never been depressive; in fact, I've occasionally been found obnoxiously cheerful. But the deaths of King and Kennedy sobered me. It may have been the first time I saw the dark side of the world in such a way that I felt it, deep inside of me.

And it wasn't just me; the spring of '68 reached all the way into our kitchen. We were both Jewish and fiercely, proudly American. Our family marched behind a decorated-veteran father who had gone to war willingly and come home gratefully. By working hard, keeping our noses clean, and treating other people fairly, we believed good things would happen; that was the American Dream, and we were just going about the business of achieving it. But so was Dr. King; so was Bobby Kennedy. We felt their losses like a blow to the nation's creed as well as our own. I wrote their spirit into my Torah speech, insisting that even when our goals seem hopelessly out of reach, we must keep trying to get there. It didn't seem like magic then; it just seemed right.

It was a lot to think about during the sweltering days on the construction site. Nearly thirteen and big for my age, I had a job digging postholes with a heaving, greasy auger on the back of an ancient, yellow Case tractor. Hilton "Pitt" Pitcock drove the tractor, positioning the auger above the spot where I was to guide it down, hold it true, and make sure the result was a clean hole where a drive-in movie speaker post would be placed. It had to be eighteen inches in diameter and four and a half feet deep to hold the concrete and steel needed to build the South Park Drive-In Theatre on National Turnpike in Louisville.

A leather-skinned chain smoker whose squint reminded me of Clint Eastwood's, Pitt was respectful because he knew I could be his boss one day. But he cut me no slack. If I signaled "thumbs up" before pulling my head clear after inspecting the hole, the auger would roar out of the ground looking for me. I can still taste the blood in my mouth from the two times I recklessly held up my thumbs and Pitt pulled that lever early. I don't think he did damage intentionally, but neither do I think he was watching out for me as if I were a child.

After a particularly long and hot June day, I was amazed to find myself still unbloodied when Pitt called out, "Quittin' time." I was wearing more dirt than cloth. Red dust saturated every pore of my body, but we had dug 185 postholes in one day, a construction crew record that may still stand. Pitt squinted at me over his half-finished unfiltered Camel and muttered, "You did good, Mike." I still consider it one of the highest compliments I have ever received. I wish I could put it on my office wall next to my diplomas and professional tributes. "You did good, Mike." Some days I still want to believe it.

The construction trailer had air conditioning, and Dad and Uncle Harry were indulging themselves in that luxury. They handed me my Falls City beer. I tried to stretch the ache out of my back, studied the dirt that shrouded me, sucked down that icy beer, and thought to myself, *I don't want to do this the rest of my life.* I wasn't cut out for construction. I wasn't enough of a son of a bitch for business. I was back to the career options I had contemplated as a runaway kid in a tree: movies, or medicine—or maybe, somehow, both.

Chapter 3

THAT YOU, PITT?

ost of the friends who graduated with me from Louisville's Ballard High School were headed to one of Kentucky's state universities, or maybe to Indiana University two hours away. I wanted to go somewhere I could enjoy a little more distance and anonymity, as well as get a good education—meaning that I could have fun without having instant reports filed with my folks via hometown friends. Armed with my 8mm movie camera and the earnings from my summer jobs, I headed for New Orleans and Tulane University, which took me in as a would-be chemistry major and premed student.

I was grateful: Tulane exceeded my criteria for excellence and distance. My mother was giddy; this fulfilled step two in the three-step tribute as "he wants to be a doctor" slid into "my son's studying to be a doctor" (which would ultimately morph into "My Son, The Doctor").

During my sophomore year, I became friends with a slender, shapely, dark-haired Tulane freshman with a stunning smile and incredible mind. Amy Weil was dating her hometown sweetheart, who had decided to go to the University of Florida. This left her going out at Tulane with several guys just casually; I loved watching her roll her eyes, giving each of them grief for their lame attempts to woo her. I elbowed my way into her social circle, where I worked, hard, to become her confidante and friend. When trouble brewed in her long-distance relationship with the Florida Gator, she sought my advice; when he wanted more, I was clearly opposed. By the time I started my junior year, I was in love.

In fact, Amy and I had much in common. We both were born into spirited Jewish clans. Our families owned remarkably similar businesses: Hers ran an electrical supply company in Birmingham, and my dad purchased a lighting distribution company with proceeds he made from the sale of the movie theaters. Both Amy and I enjoyed socializing, thought having a sense of humor mattered, studied hard, and wanted eventually to have a family. We also both felt strongly about making a contribution in the world. While I hoped to do that as a doctor, Amy was studying to be a teacher. We were and have remained idealists and in love.

Among the sweet gifts Amy brought to me was this: She laughed at my jokes. When I sang songs, instead of suggesting an improved key—say, the one in which the music might have originally been cast—she tapped out the rhythm on the table top. If I tried a dance routine, she'd giggle and dance next to me. When I recited long passages from classic Marx Brothers movies, she was the perfect audience of one, applauding when I delivered (however lamely) the punch line. And when I told her I was making a movie, she cared.

With my acceptance into medical school and Amy a year away from graduating from Tulane, it was time to talk about marriage. From my college philosophy class, I remembered Aristotle's contention that true friendship presents the option of viewing the world through two sets of eyes. I asked myself, "Is this the person whose eyes I want to see the world with, for the rest of my days?" My answer was an unqualified yes. I didn't see any advantage to waiting a year or two to marry; if this was the right person, waiting meant missing out.

Amy and I were married in Birmingham on a stormy summer night in July 1977, under a chuppah we shared with Rabbi Henry Bamberger. Temple Emanu-El's rabbi at the time, Rabbi Bamberger made the night memorable by somehow relating marriage to Atlanta Braves baseball. I've never been able to reconnect the two, or explain how he did it, but he pulled it off to everyone's delight.

After a brief honeymoon, we moved to my hometown, Louisville, where Amy finished her degree in elementary education while I started medical school. I've never regretted the decision to return home and attend the University of Louisville, although I'd been accepted at other medical schools with more prestigious names and bigger reputations. Maybe it was the lessons I'd learned while riding a jackhammer or digging postholes, but I couldn't help noticing that the cost of one semester at any of the fancy schools was about equal to all four years at U of L. The thought of explaining such lofty costs to my father made me itch: I couldn't think of a single good reason to tax my savings, my parents, and my government in order to have a famous name on my diploma. (As it turned out, the choice was not only prudent but hugely beneficial. I received gifts of faculty interest and personal attention at Louisville that I would never have enjoyed in one of America's more famous "doctor factories.")

The next decision was a tougher one: What kind of doctor did I want to be, and why? I spent most of medical school going over the options. Because my mother greatly admired a hometown surgeon, Norton Waterman, she had always hoped that surgery would be my specialty. But I had at best marginal interest in cutting bodies open and having people's lives so literally in my two hands. I wasn't keen on having to report to work every day at 5:00 a.m. And I didn't like the brevity of the surgeon-patient relationship: Surgeons were forever saying good-bye to patients, even those they cured.

I also ruled out oncology for fear that I would feel useless and hopeless treating so many terminal patients. And I steered away from pediatrics because I did not think I could stand kids dying and feeling the pain of the bereaved parents, especially the moms. (I could not have imagined, at that time, the reality that I and so many other HIV docs would confront in the eighties and nineties: so many terminal patients, so many of them little more than children, and so many bereaved moms and dads.)

By the start of my senior year, I'd decided to do internal medicine with the ultimate goal of being a cardiologist. In the vast and complex medical universe of thirty years ago, cardiology was a discipline that made sense to me: There was a pump, there was blood flow, there was resistance and pressure. But even as I made that choice, running through my head was the siren song of the classmates who chose radiology: *C'mon, Mike, join us! Civilized hours, fantastic pay . . .*

The fall of my senior year I snagged a role I'd coveted for four years: co-chair of the Skit Night show that the medical school staged every December. The show gave would-be doctors a chance to flaunt our nonmedical talents in wicked parodies that we wrote and performed. By tradition, after all the silly skits, the finale would be a sentimental slide show of pictures taken over the previous four years, usually set to sappy music (think: *The Way We Were*).

If I hate anything more than sappy music, it's a photo-montage slide show set to sappy music. So I proposed we do what I considered a much more suitable finale: a movie-quality music video set to The Beatles' classic "A Day in the Life" from their 1967 album *Sgt. Pepper's Lonely Hearts Club Band*. I wound up being the chief cinematographer, director, producer, film editor, and projectionist. From the start, I could see each scene of the 4-minute-48-second movie in my mind:

> *I read the news today oh, boy*
> *About a lucky man who made the grade . . .*

A student—played by my classmate Bruce Tasch, now a psychiatrist in Louisville—is seen opening his acceptance letter to medical school. *That's how it starts*, I thought. *You take these incredibly creative, diverse, interesting people, and then you put them on a conveyor belt of endless, mindless classes out of which they all tumble, at the far end, stamped into precisely the same form.*

> *And though the news was rather sad*
> *Well, I just had to laugh . . .*

In the second year, the medical student faces more courses, more pressures. At the end of that year—when he's supposed to be ready to go on the wards and see patients—the film shows him flipping out while observing a grisly procedure in the ER, reeling down the hospital halls, and winding up spinning dizzily in a graveyard.

And then he's in his third year:

> *Woke up, fell out of bed*
> *Dragged a comb across my head*
> *Found my way downstairs and drank a cup*
> *And looking up, I noticed I was late*
> *Found my coat and grabbed my hat . . .*

But instead of making the bus, he's at the hospital making rounds

> *. . . in seconds flat.*
> *Found my way upstairs and had a smoke*
> *And somebody spoke and I went into a dream . . .*

In the fourth year, and the movie's final scenes, the medical student dreams that he's lying on the lawn of a big mansion, wearing his white coat and wondering how he got there. Patient-like wraiths appear out of the mist, and they do to the student doctor what he's been doing to patients—inserting tubes and catheters and worse. "Hold that position, please." "This will sting a little." "Cough." He awakens from the dream as the soundtrack moans,

> *I'd love to turn . . . you . . . on . . .*

Against a montage of *LIFE* magazine photos of major events in my generation's life from 1955 to 1981, the music crescendos and builds. After four years, we medical students finally are coming off the conveyor belt, molded into what we are supposed to be. The last chord resonates as the newly minted doctor, wearing his white coat and carrying his black bag, walks into the sunset.

I wasn't trying to be outrageous or shocking. I was just following my gut instinct about what would make a good movie. But sometimes, as my fellow director Frank Capra once said, "A hunch is creativity trying to tell you something."

The Monday evening before Skit Night, I completed the final edits. I threaded the film onto the reels of the projector to watch the newly completed movie for the first time. As I turned the projector on, the bulb blew, and when I reached in to remove it, the metal spring that held the bulb in place sliced my left index finger. "Is there a doctor in the house?" The humor wasn't that keen, and my finger hurt like sin. I grabbed a gauze pad, wrapped the wound as best I could, and hoped the bleeding would stop before I needed to actually get stitches. While waiting for the blood to stop splashing on the floor, I turned on the television.

At the moment the bulb had popped in Louisville—December 8, 1980—John Lennon was being fatally shot by a deranged fan on the Upper West Side of New York City. I had always felt psychically or spiritually connected to Lennon. I was injured, and he wounded fatally, as I finished my cautionary tale mocking the choice for a life of conformity. As I tried to screen the film for the first time, the brilliant nonconformist on its soundtrack was silenced.

Parallel and perhaps paranormal things like this have happened throughout my life. My great-aunt Florence (Flohoney, the family's benevolent witch) called such incidents *beshert*. Loosely translated, *beshert* means something that is fated, preordained, destined for the one who experiences it. Sort of a Yiddish cousin of magical thinking.

Beshert experiences aren't the sort of thing I include in conference presentations or scholarly journals. I'm not embarrassed by them, exactly, but neither do I know quite what to say or do about them. They leave me feeling there's something special going on. It's not being charmed or invincible; if there's one thing medicine shakes out of you early, it's the youthful sense of indestructibility. But a *beshert* experience leaves me a little silent, vaguely feeling that something uncommon is expected of me, or maybe that I'm called to a special duty or role. If this is delusional, fine; it's been a useful delusion.

Skit Night went on as scheduled the weekend after John Lennon's death, and we dedicated the movie ("A Day in the Life") to his memory. Sappy as it may sound now, I was not the only one who wept while watching and listening.

Leaving med school for residency, I wanted both a specialty and an institution full of possibility, a place where I could do uncommon things. I interviewed at six internal medicine residency programs, but the one that stood out above the rest was the program at the University of Alabama at Birmingham Hospitals and Clinics. Though barely forty years old, UAB had one of the most respected training programs in internal medicine anywhere in the United States, competing well with Duke, Vanderbilt, Emory, and other southern medical-program powerhouses.

At UAB, I was instantly impressed with the charming, bespectacled Alabama native who interviewed me. Bill (William E.) Dismukes was the newly appointed director of UAB's house staff training program. He'd been educated in the finest programs in the East, then returned to build research capacity at UAB. There he came to be recognized as one of the world's experts in the treatment of fungal infections, particularly cryptococcal meningitis, a type of fungal meningitis that would later loom large in the world of AIDS and, therefore, my career. Magic.

UAB had a great cardiology program, inspiring leaders, and a wonderful house staff. On "Match Day," when I opened the envelope to learn which of the schools I wanted had also wanted me, I was elated to see that I had matched in UAB's internal medicine program. I was on the road to becoming another bald, Jewish cardiologist—precisely what the world needed.

Birmingham offered me an education and brought Amy back to her hometown and her parents, sister, and two brothers. Amy had a native's knowing love of the city. My first glimpse of Birmingham had been in news photographs from the desegregation battles of the 1950s and '60s: snarling dogs, brutal sheriffs, and fire hoses unleashed on schoolchildren asking to be treated as human beings. Before we headed to Birmingham, I had to make peace with that history.

I'm not black and did not suffer those dogs, those police clubs, or those fire hoses. Blacks in America have always had the harder road to travel, forced to pay the cost of slavery, Jim Crow lynchings, and segregated institutions. But I am Jewish, and I know something about discrimination and socially sanctioned evil. From childhood, I remember my grandparents explaining to me in whispers why some people we knew had hidden their lineage, and why others wore tattooed numbers on their forearms.

Silently renewing my opposition to all forms of enslavement, hatred, and inequality, I moved with Amy to Birmingham. I embraced as if it were my own "Letter from Birmingham Jail," in which the Rev. Dr. Martin Luther King explained that "I am in Birmingham because injustice is here." I began the journey from my own self-righteousness over Birmingham's history to the discovery of my own ignorant biases and prejudices.

Just a few days after we landed in Birmingham, on June 5, 1981, the US Centers for Disease Control reported eight cases of unusual opportunistic infections that were occurring in gay men in Los Angeles and New York City. If I read or heard the news report on that day, I scarcely noticed it in the excitement of moving and my anxiety about surviving my internship year.

During my first six months at UAB, I rotated through three facilities: the University Hospital, the Veterans Administration (VA) hospital associated with it, and the Cooper Green Hospital, which served the indigent population of Jefferson County. Like most cocksure new docs, I thought I was prepared to practice. But I was completely unprepared for how differently medicine was practiced at these three locations. And so began my earliest education in just how separate-and-unequal American healthcare could be.

The VA rotation was first. Patients there were mostly middle-aged to elderly men with chronic medical conditions, and I'll never forget one who greeted me on the sweltering day I started. He was sitting in his wheelchair in a shady spot by the hospital entrance, wearing a brown seersucker robe. For a brief moment, perhaps because of the heat of the day and the memory it evoked, I thought the patient was my old construction boss, Pitt. His skin was as leathery, his eyes were the same squinting blue, and in his right hand was a smoking, unfiltered Camel cigarette.

It wasn't Pitt, but it could have been. Just beneath his Adam's apple was a permanent tracheostomy, a metal plate with a hole in the center, held in place by a green nylon ribbon. There were deep purple ink lines on his neck, roughly box shaped, to help the oncology technician aim the radiation equipment being used to treat his throat cancer. As I approached him, he lifted the Camel to his "trach" opening with tobacco-stained fingers. *Feeding the monster that's killing him,* I thought. He took a deep drag through the tiny metal opening in his throat, and as he exhaled a gust of blue-gray smoke, his eyes met mine and he nodded. I swear it felt like Pitt saying, "Hey, Mike, welcome to your new job."

At the VA, the government paid the bills as thanks for the veterans' service to country. The place wasn't luxurious, but we could mostly get the patients what they needed, if only by slogging through a lot of paperwork. During each of my early rotations, partly to keep my sanity and partly just to have fun, I wrote parody songs with a new set of lyrics for what I experienced each week. The song from the VA was set to the tune of "In the Navy" by Village People, and its opening verse featured that memorable patient:

At the VA
You can get an even break
At the VA
You can smoke right through your trach
At the VA
Everybody cleans their plate, at the VA

Next rotation: University Hospital, so new and well appointed compared to the VA that it felt like moving from Dogpatch to Beverly Hills. Providers from around the region sent patients with unusual diseases to University for evaluation, and fewer than 10 percent of them arrived without health insurance. Thanks to an abundance of resources and staff, the patients there generally received timely, top-notch care.

Then came Cooper Green, a hospital established to serve Jefferson County's uninsured patients. The same residents and many of the same attending (senior) physicians who worked at University and VA also saw patients at Cooper Green, so there was little difference in medical providers. There was a big difference, however, in ancillary support services and the overall patient experience. Most everything at Cooper Green happened in slow motion: The lab work came back slower, the X-rays took longer. And the patients—on average, lower income and less well educated—showed up for care much later in the course of their illnesses. Because these folks had avoided seeking medical care for as long as they could, the severity of their condition was striking, especially compared to what I saw at University. Ulcers were bigger, heart failure more severe, tumors more advanced.

Patients came late to Cooper Green for all kinds of reasons: the hassle of getting off work or finding transportation, no primary care physician to refer them, no habit within their family of seeking early or preventive care.

But I quickly learned that the chief reason patients arrived at Cooper Green long after they had first begun battling symptoms, months after they'd first felt the lump or spotted the blood, was dollars and cents. They saw doctors, hospitals, and clinics as just another source of bills that they had no money to pay. Many of them came from generations of families who might have valued hard work more than education, who had limited finances but a strong sense of decency, for whom incurring a debt you could not pay was shameful. It wasn't that they were cheap or that they "didn't know any better." The truth is that they often knew the risks they were taking with their own lives, but they did not want to suffer the shame of unpaid bills.

The staff at Cooper Green did its best to explain to them that they could seek care and then hope that the slow-moving state benefits system would declare them "medically indigent" and not required to pay. But the sound of it, "medically indigent," was insulting. And what if the bills arrived before that ruling, or if they somehow weren't eligible for free care? Rather than risking it, they stayed away, using home remedies that included heavy doses of prayer and blind hope. When it became clear that the symptoms were not reversing, they came reluctantly (and usually at night) to our emergency room. By then, for so many, the time when we might have arrested their disease was long past.

For most of my residency, I divided my time between the three different worlds of these hospitals. When I was at University Hospital, the faces and lessons of the Cooper Green and VA rotations never quite left me. To this day, I remember the fifty-six-year-old black grandmother who collapsed at home and was brought to the Cooper Green ER on a Friday night. The woman's head CT showed a massive bleed in her brain, the result of years of untreated high blood pressure. There was nothing that could be done. We put her in a private room with the head of the bed elevated.

I had been up the whole night before, and I looked it in my blood-stained scrubs and vomit-smeared sneakers. When I went in to check on the woman before going home, it was just the two of us in the room. She looked peaceful, almost dead. I leaned in to see if she was breathing. As I positioned my head above hers, her jaw suddenly snapped, forcing her teeth together in a loud "whack." I leaped backward, shaking.

After about twenty seconds, I cautiously eased back to the bedside. She hadn't awakened. That jarring jaw snap was some sort of reflex—that was the medical explanation, I told myself. But in spiritual terms, I felt like she was telling me, "Back off, Sonny. I'm here because your system failed. And it's far too late for you to do anything about it." She was dead the next morning.

The man outside the VA, the apparition of Pitt? He has become, for me, the face of medical need, the patient who has only the US healthcare system standing between him and disaster. He took up residence in my cerebral cortex where, as it turned out, he never left. Decades later, he's still shoving that Camel through the slot in his shiny metal plate directly into my brain stem.

Chapter 4

BIRMINGHAM TO PARIS

Midway through my second year of training at UAB, I was asked to report to the office of the chairman of the department of medicine. I made a quick mental inventory of sins that might have been reported, expecting to be called on the carpet. Might someone have taken offense at the parody I wrote about my University Hospital rotation (to the tune of "Let It Snow")?

Oh the weather outside is frightful
And the patients so . . . "delightful"?
What the hell am I doing here?
Get me beer, get me beer, get me beer!

It turned out I wasn't in trouble. The recently appointed chairman, Dr. J. Claude Bennett, had me summoned so he could ask if I'd accept the honor of serving as a chief medical resident (CMR). The answer to his offer was, of course, *yes*. This meant that after the standard three years of residency, I would stay for a fourth, helping him and Dr. Dismukes run the internal medicine residency program. I called it my "remedial" year of training, and it turned out to be a pivotal time and role.

I'd arrived at UAB with my sights set on cardiology. Within weeks, I was having reservations. The more I experienced, the more I doubted that I'd made a wise choice. It seemed as if every question about treating a heart patient got the same answer—"We're going to catheterize him." In reality, thirty years ago this was often the right diagnosis and proper treatment. Even then, I wasn't arguing about the science. But a lifetime devoted to giving the same answer to every question and performing the same procedure day after day held no appeal.

While my enthusiasm for cardiology was fading, I'd begun to explore a field that I'd earlier dismissed: infectious disease. Part of my attraction to ID was the breadth and unpredictability of the field. It covered everything from mutant cancers to bugs from Tanzania. While many of the mainstay diseases were historic and heavily studied—malaria, for example—other diseases were little more than an accumulation of observed symptoms compiled into a "syndrome" without a known cause. Truly weird things popped up from places I couldn't spell, odd fevers in Central Africa and strange maladies known mostly off the coast of Madagascar. By its very nature, working in ID meant that you were in research, since much of what you were trying to identify and remedy came to you in the form of uncertain diagnoses and improbable, perhaps even unheard of, illnesses. If the practice of cardiology seemed utterly predictable, life amid infectious diseases seemed brilliantly unpredictable.

(And predictions being made in the ID field added a whole other layer of interest. Just a bit later, in April 1984, America's Health and Human Services Secretary Margaret Heckler held a press conference to announce that Dr. Robert Gallo of the National Cancer Institute had found the virus that causes AIDS. At that event, Heckler postulated that a vaccine against AIDS might be produced within two years. I distinctly remember listening to that and thinking, *Madame Secretary, what planet are you on?* I had seen Heckler's boss, President Reagan, take a medical issue seriously: In 1982, when seven people died after taking cyanide-laced Tylenol, the world stopped and the US government went into crisis mode, searching relentlessly for the culprit. By the time of Heckler's press conference, some 5,000 people had died of AIDS, and the president appeared not to have noticed. He hadn't even said the word "AIDS" in public, a fact made even more inconceivable by the fact that many of his former colleagues in the film-making business were directly affected, if not infected, by the AIDS virus. The Reagan administration's strikingly different responses to seven Tylenol deaths and 5,000 AIDS deaths was a huge source of anger among AIDS activists. I never understood how President Reagan could remain silent on events that were having such a profound effect on the nation publicly and on him privately.)

Knowing the field would never be boring, I opted for ID.

There was also an additional lure to ID at UAB: the faculty. Dr. C. Glenn Cobbs, a onetime Marine who studied at Princeton and Harvard, started as the first director and lone faculty member of UAB's ID division. At the end of his internship at UAB, Cobbs was hand-selected by Tinsley Harrison, the venerable chair of medicine at UAB and lead editor of the famous *Harrison's Textbook of Medicine*, to study ID at New York's Cornell University and bring his knowledge back to UAB. Upon his return, Cobbs—methodically, persistently, and with the patience of a researcher and the persuasive capacity of a car salesman—built the division into a powerhouse. Kirk Avent, a talented clinician-educator, was hired first. Then he attracted Bill Dismukes, who was known as "one of the world's top disease sleuths" and who had trained in the prestigious Epidemiology Intelligence Service at the US Centers for Disease Control and Prevention. They worked with Claude Bennett, the chair of microbiology and namesake for the Dreyer-Bennett Hypothesis, a breakthrough in the understanding of genetic coding. These men were not only stars in the UAB faculty; they were household names in the global ID and microbiology community.

ID guaranteed a career with plenty of Sherlock Holmes to it, unraveling mysteries and pursuing the unknown. It seemed as if this field would satisfy my altruism as well as my intellect: I could solve the mystery of a disease and then hand my patients the cure. This made sense to me. This was worth climbing out of the tree for.

But I hadn't banked on being chief medical resident. Typically, faculty members select as the CMR a candidate intent on an academic career. I still aimed to go into private practice ID and had no intention of staying in academia. But I loved teaching, found great joy in patient care, and figured

I could use the extra year provided by my CMR appointment to have fun, as well as to hone skills.

Claude Bennett, who had moved from chair of microbiology to become the chair of medicine, took great pride in grooming his CMRs for academic medicine. He saw their "extra year" as a warm-up for inspiring work to be done as junior faculty in his institution. CMRs were, in Bennett's way of thinking, prefaculty. So it was no surprise when I learned that as a required part of my CMR duties, I'd accompany Bennett to an annual meeting of the American Society of Clinical Investigation (ASCI) in Washington, D.C.

Attending that May 1985 meeting felt like the academic-medicine equivalent of attending the Academy Awards. I was starstruck at the eminences gathered there: editors I knew as names on major medical textbooks, authors of landmark papers that had shaped my training. Though I could easily have become a gawker on the sidelines, Claude—we were on a first-name basis now—was generous about making introductions. I was particularly taken by Dr. George Shaw, a young investigator from the National Cancer Institute whom Claude had just recruited to come to UAB.

George Meade Shaw was raised on a farm near Logan, Ohio. He sped through an MD-PhD degree program in five years followed by an internal medicine residency, and then he landed a postdoctoral fellowship position at the National Cancer Institute, in Dr. Gallo's laboratory, as part of his training to become an oncologist. George went to Gallo's lab to study HTLV-I, which was known to cause diseases including T-cell leukemia/lymphoma syndrome, a rare cancer of the immune system's own cells. But while George was working there, others in Gallo's lab discovered that a cousin retrovirus, HTLV-III, was the cause of AIDS.

My meeting with George lasted only two or three minutes. But George immediately came to mind two months later when, on my first day working in UAB's ID clinic, I met a thirty-four-year-old patient from a small town in Alabama. It was the moment in which academic research and real-world healing, sterile laboratories and crowded emergency rooms, came together for me.

The woman, a schoolteacher, was twenty-one when she married her husband. She said that he had been her only sexual partner, and I believed her. They had two children, ages eight and twelve. In May 1985, as she had done every six months for as long as she could remember, the teacher donated blood at her local blood bank. But this time, a month after her blood donation, she received a letter from the Red Cross informing her that the HTLV-III test they had performed on her blood came back positive. (The Red Cross first began testing the nation's blood supply for HTLV-III in May 1985.) The test finding meant that the teacher was infected with the AIDS virus.

The teacher was adamant that she had never, ever, received a blood transfusion. She'd never used intravenous drugs, or any drugs for that matter. She had not had unprotected sex with multiple partners. Nonetheless, when her family-practice doctor repeated the tests—a commonly used test called ELISA (enzyme-linked immunosorbent assay) and a more complex, confirming test called the Western Blot—they were both positive. By all criteria, the teacher was infected with the AIDS virus.

Thinking her virus must have come from her husband, the physician called him in and checked his blood, but he tested negative. As if her physical future—in the mid-1980s, AIDS meant guaranteed suffering and death—were not enough to cause panic, the emotional and marital stress was almost beyond measure. How could she be dying if he was healthy, unless she had been untruthful? And if she had been truthful and faithful, how was this possible? Their physician was baffled by her diagnosis and referred her to UAB. She was mine.

She arrived an hour early for her morning appointment, red-eyed from crying and desperate for answers. Through tears, she grilled me: Her hairdresser was gay, could she have gotten it from him? Did the experts really know *all* the ways the AIDS virus was transmitted? I felt like a poseur, trying to answer her questions as an "expert" with so little ID training under my belt. But after listening intently, I reached three conclusions:

(1) This didn't make sense;

(2) Either the tests were wrong or the experts were wrong; and

(3) I couldn't work this out without some help.

While the teacher waited in the exam room, I went down the hall and telephoned George Shaw, who had by now relocated to UAB.

I started to thank George for taking my call, but he graciously cut me off and dove straight into the case. He grilled me about the teacher's story: Was I *sure* she had no other exposures? No other partners? No injections? No forgotten blood transfusions, perhaps blotted out by anesthesia when she delivered her two children? Ultimately, we agreed: This required further testing. He suggested I draw as much blood as I safely could and bring it to his lab immediately.

I wonder if it sounded as dramatic as it felt—like a scene in a movie—when I counseled the teacher about what came next. I told her I was working with one of the world's top experts in AIDS who had been in the laboratory where the virus was discovered. I tried to sound reassuring when I said something like, "We'll get to the bottom of this." Then I took enough of her blood to fill twenty tubes, gave her a hug good-bye, and headed across the street to George's laboratory, the vials bulging in the pockets of my white coat.

George and I prepared a dozen of the tubes to ship to colleagues for simultaneous testing. Four tubes to Mika Popovic in Gallo's lab. Four tubes to Wade Parks, an AIDS pediatrician and virologist in Miami. Four tubes to Judy Britz at one of the companies that manufactured the then-new "AIDS test" used by the Red Cross. From the remaining eight tubes of blood, we placed some in vials to preserve at -70 and -150 degrees centigrade—George's farsighted choice, and my first recognition that stored specimens might have value one day. With the remaining samples, we ran our own tests.

The way AIDS tests work is not by looking for the virus itself but by looking for the antibodies directed against the virus. In ELISA, the patient's blood is placed in a laboratory vessel where AIDS antibodies will bond to a test medium and show up a certain color under a laser beam. If that test is positive, the costlier Western Blot may be done for confirmation. It uses a different test medium and process to get more detailed results.

In George's lab, we repeated the ELISA and Western Blot tests that had been done by the Red Cross. Both were positive. But when we did a more specific radioimmunoassay, a more sensitive test for specific antibodies, it came out negative. The culture results from Mika Popovic and Wade Parks both returned negative, no HTLV-III identified. Through multiple studies, Judy Britz found no HTLV-III specific antibodies—but she did find some antibodies in the patient's blood that "cross-reacted" with a substance in the standard assays and created *the appearance* of AIDS antibodies.

The first person I needed to talk to was my patient. To save her a trip back to Birmingham, I immediately called her and did my best to explain the good news. I listened as she exploded in tears. Sobbing into the phone, she asked if I was absolutely sure. I said yes, and explained briefly what we just had discovered about the tests.

What we had learned thanks to one woman's agonizing experience was a critical discovery: the first known false-positive Western Blot test for the AIDS virus. For my rural Alabama patient, the discovery meant that a death sentence had been commuted, a marriage spared, and a life continued. The teacher was not infected and was at no special risk for AIDS. Of broader importance to the scientific and medical communities wrestling with the virus, the discovery meant that our testing measures, while very good, were not perfect and were subject to error on rare occasion. "False positives" was a way of saying "not true."

At that moment, I would have done almost anything to spare another person that teacher's ordeal. The one thing we could do, George observed, was to write up the case as soon as possible in order to alert colleagues to the possibility of false-positive Western Blots. As George and I worked with Judy Britz on the manuscript, we agreed that publication in the *New England Journal of Medicine* would have the greatest impact. To improve our chances of quickly getting into that prestigious journal, we decided to submit the story as a "Letter to the Editor" responding to previous articles on AIDS testing.

There was one hitch: The journal's policy for letters was to list no more than two authors' names. Though I argued that he had played the lead role in this discovery, George insisted that the two author names be Judy's and mine. In an academic world where whose name is listed on a publication can make the difference between promotion and demotion, between getting a prestigious and funded chair or getting no recognition at all, George said, "Leave me off." In that one, self-effacing act, I glimpsed the professional commitment and personal selflessness that I associate with George to this day.

The journal published the letter, and we heard from other ID docs who thanked us for the discovery. I was realizing my dream of becoming a medical sleuth: Mike Saag plays Sherlock Holmes. Though I did not recognize it at the time, this episode and the publication of our letter marked my formal career pivot into academic medicine and AIDS research. Before, I had dabbled; with this, I was committed. It was one of my life's charmed moments, owing less to me than to a true AIDS pioneer, George Shaw, a stellar researcher and extraordinarily good man.

By the time George had earlier arrived in Robert Gallo's famed laboratory, researchers around the world were searching in earnest for the cause of the mysterious immunodeficiency syndrome. Since that first report by the US Centers for Disease Control in June 1981, more and more American patients, mostly gay men, were coming into hospitals in major urban centers with unusual infectious diseases, including *pneumocystis carinii* pneumonia (PCP), *Toxoplasma gondii* encephalitis, Cytomegalovirus retinitis and colitis, Mycobacterium avium complex sepsis and end organ disease, and *Cryptococcus neoformans* meningitis. Within a year, the Latin names were common parlance in America's gay community. Men with no medical training would whisper "pneumocystis" and know its meaning; even casual conversations in San Francisco coffee shops were laced with "cryptococcus" and a description of the drug regimen that had been prescribed.

Patients were presenting with unusual cancers seldom seen in the young. Some had rare types of lymphoma in the brain; others had Kaposi's sarcoma, a highly vascular tumor in the skin and internal organs, typically seen only in older men of Mediterranean descent. Each of these disorders occurred in situations where the severe weakening of the immune system gave the pathogens and tumors the opportunity to flourish, so they were called "opportunistic" infections and malignancies. But why was this happening? There had to be something *causing* the immune systems of these patients to be so impaired.

In Los Angeles where four of the first cases of PCP were described, a young immunology fellow at UCLA looked for clues by running some blood through a new piece of lab technology. Dr. Michael Gottlieb drew blood from each of the initial patients and ran it through a Fluorescent Antibody Cell Sorter (FACS) machine, which quantitates how many immune system cells and which types are present. Among the T-lymphocytes, there are CD4 cells (so-called Helper T-cells) that orchestrate an efficient immune response to infections and tumors, as well as CD8 cells (so called Suppressor T-cells) that cool off the immune response and/or kill other T-cells as part of the cellular immune response. Normally, there are more Helper (CD4) T-cells than Suppressor (CD8) T-cells in a ratio of up to 2:1. The FACS machine counts and gives a readout of the number of cells per microliter (abbreviated as *ul*); a healthy patient typically has a CD4 count between 500 and 1500 cells/*ul* and a CD8 count of roughly half of that value.

These numbers are important to understanding what happened next. When Gottlieb ran the blood from patients with opportunistic infections at UCLA through the FACS machine, he could barely detect *any* CD4 cells. It appeared that one patient had ten CD4 cells/*ul* and another had three. Imagining that there was some error in the equipment or his procedure, Gottlieb ran the tests again. And again. Always, the results came up the same. What he'd discovered was evidence demonstrating the degree of immunosuppression, and he'd given us a standard by which to measure this suppression. For the first time, we realized that the virus was not only damaging the immune system; the virus was erasing it, explaining instantly how such opportunities existed for strange cancers and insidious infections.

Work done by investigators from the US Centers for Disease Control has largely been unheralded, but it was no less heroic than Gottlieb's. Men and women, young and old, sleepless and committed—they descended on the medical centers in Los Angeles and New York, San Francisco and Miami, Chicago and Atlanta, looking for common threads in the stories of the patients struggling to stay alive while suffering indignities and pain. Following standard epidemiologic methodology but working at a furious pace, they gathered findings on patients and grouped the findings into constellations that formed a case definition of the new disease, or "syndrome." Since all of the initially reported cases of the illness appeared to be in homosexual men, and since the widespread epidemic in the heterosexual communities of Africa and Asia had not yet been identified, the first name given in the United States was Gay-Related Immunodeficiency Syndrome, or GRID.

Patients who met criteria for GRID were interviewed over and over to learn their background, their behaviors, their potential exposures. Where did they travel? What food did they eat? What water did they drink? Who did they have sex with? What sexual practices did they engage in? What recreational drugs did they take? When had they first felt ill?

Some patterns emerged quickly. Most of the men had engaged in receptive rectal intercourse. Many had used recreational drugs, including amyl nitrite, so-called "poppers," that users inhaled during sex to enhance orgasm. What in these two things, if anything, could cause AIDS?

In the space of one year, we watched an epidemic take shape, and it was breathtaking. Obviously, countless patients were never seen; they died in places and with diagnoses that went unnoticed. But within six months of the initial findings in June 1981, about 100 patients had been identified; a year later, the number was at least ten times higher, more than 1,000. During the day, those of us working with patients would say to ourselves, "Maybe the thing will plateau with this round of infections." At night, alone with our thoughts, we worried that the truth might be the opposite: Perhaps this was only the beginning. Perhaps the epidemic would swell to tens of thousands, then hundreds of thousands, then millions. But these were merely fears. What we absolutely knew was that to be infected, to have GRID, was to bear a death sentence. And death by GRID—death by AIDS—was not an easy passing.

As the CDC teams crisscrossed the country pressing for more data, more information, more knowledge, it soon became clear that this new syndrome was striking more than gay men. Others arriving at hospitals with unusual opportunistic infections included heroin-addicted patients who were not gay, hemophiliacs who had received multiple blood transfusions, and, most strangely, immigrants from Haiti, most of them living in New York. (It was later discovered that in Haiti, a vacation destination for gay men from the United States, commercial sex was a common way for folks to make extra money.) For a brief period, the illness became known as the "4-H Syndrome," for homosexuals, hemophiliacs, heroin users, and Haitians.

By the end of 1982, it was clear that there was no causal link between being gay and being infected; the virus was as happy infecting straight people as gay. We needed, as quickly as possible, to dissociate the illness from our own mistaken assumptions. (Retrospectively, we now know that the "gay" assumption proved to be the most damaging over the long term, and it may still be the greatest contributor to risk.) We moved to the term the CDC had adopted: Acquired Immune Deficiency Syndrome, or AIDS.

Within the first year of the burgeoning epidemic, attention began to swing toward the nation's blood supply. If hemophiliacs were coming down with AIDS, were they being infected via blood they were being given? Or might it be in the equipment used to draw blood or infuse it? Or could it be in one of the commonly used cleaning agents? Or maybe it was transmitted through touching someone with the disease? What seems clear now was not at all clear then, in the heat and fear of the moment. Epidemiologists looked at other possibilities: Could an unusual side effect from "poppers" (amyl nitrate) be responsible? Some labs explored other possibilities including Epstein-Barr Virus, the agent that causes mononucleosis, but found nothing that would cause the immune deficiency.

Within months, a few laboratories that were exploring infectious causes began to focus on retroviruses. Most infectious agents reproduce in the same way human cells do: by copying DNA into RNA and then into proteins. Retroviruses, discovered in the late 1960s by Howard Temin and David Baltimore, go in the opposite direction: They start by copying RNA into DNA in a backwards or "retro" direction using a unique enzyme, reverse transcriptase (that is, transcribing in the opposite direction of normal cells). Gallo initially suspected a retrovirus he had discovered, HTLV-I, but the tests for that agent didn't support this hypothesis.

At the Pasteur Institute in Paris, Luc Montagnier and Françoise Barré-Sinoussi were also focusing on a retroviral etiology. They had some initial signals of the presence of reverse transcriptase in tissue cultures of lymph nodes taken from AIDS patients, but strangely, the cells died too quickly to confirm the initial findings. In Gallo's lab, however, Phil Markham and

Mika Popovic began replenishing the tissue cultures with freshly stimulated lymphocytes every other day and were able to demonstrate that there was indeed a retrovirus in the tissue culture. At roughly the same time, the French group obtained electron microscopy images of a typical retrovirus budding from the surface of the cells in tissue culture. Two teams of scientists working intensely on two continents were finally able to explain the cause of the syndrome.

Though George Shaw had initially worked on HTLV-I in Gallo's lab, he shifted focus to HTLV-III. He then became the first investigator to describe the presence of the virus in the brain and to link this finding to the dementia exhibited by many patients with late-stage AIDS.

A few months after George and I had partnered on the Alabama teacher's case, George asked me to meet him in the University Hospital cafeteria. It was one of the few free moments I had in long days of training on hospital ID rounds, learning how to treat patients with all types of infections: bacterial, fungal, parasitic, viral.

As we chatted over french fries, George asked me, "Do you plan to do any research during your fellowship?"

I was a little surprised; I thought he knew. "Sure, I am working with Dr. Dismukes on studies of new drugs to treat fungal infections."

George dipped a fry in ketchup and said, without looking up, "That's great, but I mean lab research."

I told him I had worked in the lab in both college and medical school. It was my way of saying "been there, done that," and dismissing the idea.

George smiled knowingly, took time to down two more fries, then drew a sharp distinction. A student doing "research" in someone else's lab is basically a technician, he said. If I did lab research as a postdoctoral fellow, I would have a say in what experiments were run and ultimately get to develop projects of my own. As a student, I was watching research; as a postdoc fellow, I would *do* it.

Well! The idea of doing research in a lab had never occurred to me. I was focused on being a physician, not a lab researcher, and the notion that I might do both was as foreign as Tranquility Base. But I admired George enormously, and I had learned so much from him in the lab on the schoolteacher's case that his proposal was instantly appealing. Why not give the lab a spin? After all, when I returned to Louisville to make a career in private practice—as I still fully intended to do—I wasn't likely to get the chance again to do research.

"So, interested in the lab?"

I dipped a fry of my own and heard someone say yes. The voice was mine. Magic.

On January 2, 1986, I showed up in George's laboratory—or rather, the laboratory he shared with the formidable Beatrice Hahn. A native of Munich, Germany, Beatrice had worked with George in Gallo's lab and came to UAB when he did. Once the AIDS virus was discovered, Beatrice was the first person in the world to clone and sequence it, which is why the original sequence's name, BH10, includes Beatrice Hahn's initials.

I didn't need a microscope to see how my two lab mentors differed. George was easily knocked off task, and still is today, if asked a question that strikes his fancy. Beatrice was then and remains always on point, intensely focused, strong willed. If asked to take on projects not directly related to her research, she has no problem saying no or some variant of no often peppered with expletives. George has described Beatrice as "right 95 percent of the time, and when she is right, she is absolutely right." He did not mention the rest of the story: She may not be particularly merciful to those who are wrong. Beatrice does her work as if lives depend on it; she takes it seriously. If you have other priorities, she has some language she'll share with you, but no time.

On my first day in their lab, George showed me how to run a test called a Southern Blot. The test detects DNA in much the same way that a Western Blot detects antibodies. But that day, I had the sense that this test might also be used to detect something else: my seriousness, aptitude, and precision in the lab. I watched George meticulously prepare the buffers, materials, sponges, and nitrocellulose paper required to do the Southern Blot. I took copious notes. Working with cells from a patient infected with HTLV-III, we were seeking an answer to a critical question: How many different viruses exist in any AIDS patient?

Step one in the Southern Blot is to extract from the cells their DNA, which contains genetic material from the virus. Next, the extracted DNA is treated with enzymes that cut it into fragments at particular locations in its coding, much as scissors might cut a string of soft spaghetti. Then, using test agents and electrical current, the fragments are run through a gel that separates them by size, "denatured" from the usual double strand into a single-strand state and transferred to nitrocellulose paper. The paper is incubated with radioactively labeled virus fragments that bond tightly and specifically to any denatured HTLV-III virus present on the paper. It is then washed, dried, and, in a darkroom, placed into a cassette containing X-ray film. The next morning the film is developed, and any fragments of viral DNA show up as dark bands at specific locations, depending on how many times the DNA was cut by the enzymes. When the test is done properly, it will show the distinct characteristics of the individual's virus, as unique to that patient as his or her fingerprint.

I realized immediately that this type of lab work was like gourmet cooking: There were techniques, a recipe, and a final product that could be utterly ruined by imprecision. It took two weeks for me to become comfortable performing the Southern Blot test. Once George was sure I was competent, he handed me a small vial containing clear, viscous fluid and said, "Here's your project." He might as well have said, "Here's your future."

I stared at the vial and the three letters on its label: RJS. It was DNA dissolved in water, taken from a patient who was diagnosed when the army started giving all active military personnel the new AIDS test. The R was for Redfield, a physician at Walter Reed Army Hospital. The J and S were the initials of Dr. Redfield's patient—a guy who, before joining the army, had worked in a Los Angeles bath house in the late 1970s and early 1980s.

The medical file that came with the vial included a sexual history, in which JS estimated that he had had sex with . . . *more than 1,500 different partners.* (So much for maintaining professional composure: My jaw dropped at that number.) Sex was a fringe benefit of JS's job at the bath house, where men came to have anonymous, typically anal or oral sex. The file said JS's "record" was forty different partners in one night.

In their heyday, the bath houses were notorious breeding grounds for sexually transmitted diseases. During the time JS worked there, it's likely that at least half of the patrons were already infected with the AIDS virus. If JS had unprotected sex with more than 700 different AIDS-infected partners, the question we were asking in the lab was: Could he have been "super-infected" with different strains of the virus? We knew already that each person's virus was relatively unique in genetic sequence. My mission was to see what JS's virus looked like and whether there were viruses from other partners present.

I meticulously prepared all of the reagents, making sure all the enzymes I would use were fresh from previously unopened vials. I paid such attention to every detail at each step of the procedure that just preparing the Southern Blot took most of the day. My last step was to place the dried, radiolabeled paper into the X-ray cassette and leave it in a -70 degree freezer overnight to facilitate a clean signal.

The next morning, I removed the cassette from the freezer, let it thaw for an hour, and took it to the darkroom. As I stood on the other side of the developer waiting for the processed film to appear, I was anxious but mostly excited. My first real experiment, in a modern lab, doing cutting-edge work on an emerging epidemic. By now, it wasn't just an epidemic; it was also JS. Already I was experiencing what it meant to be researcher and physician, to focus my mind simultaneously and intensely on an epidemic and a patient.

The film dropped into the tray with a little clunk. I picked it up and placed it on the lighted view box. I was pleased with the technical outcome: The bands were crisp and well defined, almost handsome. But there were too many of them; way too many. The virus is 9,000 base pairs, or 9 kilobases (kb), long. No matter how many fragments result from cutting by an enzyme, they should add up to 9 kb. But I had fragment totals adding up to two and three times that. Something was wrong. I went to see George.

Maybe George's contact lenses had been bothering him. He was wearing his glasses instead, and his eyes looked red. I handed him the film from my experiment. He held it up toward the fluorescent ceiling light, at arm's length from his thick-lensed glasses, and stared. And stared. And stared. During maybe four minutes of staring, I don't think he blinked once. Without looking away from the blot, he began pelting me with questions: Which vial of RJS DNA did I use? Which pipette tips? Where did I get them? Whose buffers did I use? Which enzymes? Were they fresh or previously opened? Did anyone else touch the DNA or my vials at any time during the procedure? The questions went on for ten or fifteen minutes, but for me it felt like hours. I wasn't even thinking about what these test results might mean if they were accurate because I was so busy thinking that if they were *not* accurate, I must have screwed up.

George called Beatrice in from her office and showed her the blot. She looked at it briefly, then looked at me and said what I'd been thinking, in her own saltier version: "You must have [screwed] it up." George came to my defense, saying that he had grilled me on the technique and that I seemed to have done it properly. "Well, repeat it," Beatrice said, and walked out.

Sweating, I went back into the lab. I carefully looked over my notes, trying to see what I had done wrong. I remade all the chemical buffers, paying extra attention to measuring precisely. I double-washed every one of the containers they were prepared in. I used a new set of enzymes, fresh. And I repeated the experiment, paying absolute heed to every detail at every step.

When I showed up the next morning to pull my cassette from the freezer, George was in the lab staring at a Southern Blot film on the light box. He was wearing the same clothes as the day before and still wearing his glasses. Impossible as it would have seemed the previous morning, his eyes were even redder now. The blot on the light box looked like the one I had run the day before—but the handwriting on its label was George's. He had stayed up all night, again, repeating the experiment I had done.

I went to my bench, retrieved the film from my second try on my first experiment, and held it next to George's film. They were identical; my result was the same as George's.

This was not a screwup. It was a breakthrough.

Typically, when someone is infected with a microorganism, all the bugs are genetically identical because they emerge from the same clone. It isn't possible for them to be otherwise. For example, if someone has a staph infection, the first bacteria that led to the infection is genetically identical to the billionth bacteria that grows in the infected wound. What George and I had uncovered, aided by Beatrice's indelicate direction, was that what we assumed to be true was *not* true. The certainty of a staph organism was not a certainty for the AIDS virus. Here, as the disease progressed and the virus replicated, we were finding more of what was genetically not-the-same.

AIDS patients are initially infected with one particular clone known as the "wild-type" of the virus, and in the early stage of infection, hundreds of billions of viruses are produced that remain identical to it. Then, as the host's immune system begins to recognize that it has been infected and responds to the virus, mutants emerge that are highly related to but genetically distinct from the original infecting virus. The virus irritates the body, and the body responds by attacking the virus (immunity); under attack, the virus mutates, changes its character to escape the immune response. A deadly game of cat and mouse.

Clever virus? Not really, just prolific. When describing the virus to the general public I sometimes tell audiences, "The virus is like most men—all it wants to do is survive and replicate!" Women get it immediately; men just look at me dumbfounded.

Compared to most viruses, the AIDS virus replicates so often, so quickly, that the probability of a mutation emerging is vastly amplified. This change occurs because the virus's way of replicating is inherently error prone. Each time the virus reproduces its genetic material, it uses the reverse transcriptase (RT) enzyme to make a copy of itself. RT is a sloppy enzyme, making at least one error in every 3,000 to 4,000 base pairs. Since the AIDS virus is 9,000 base pairs long, that means on average one to three errors each time the virus replicates. When the immune system begins to respond to the initial wild-type virus, one of the new copies of the virus—formed, by chance, with an error or two—suddenly has a growth advantage over the wild-type virus now spotted and being attacked by the body. What had been the mutant begins to emerge as the predominant species. Darwinism, survival of the fittest, operating at warp speed. For the duration of the infection this process continues, resulting in dozens of unique but highly genetically related viruses.

That is what I had detected with my Southern Blot experiment, and that is what George had confirmed when he duplicated my work: The simultaneous presence of multiple viruses that were highly related to the virus that initially infected JS, but definitely distinct. Such a swarm of variant viruses is called a quasi-species—and we had discovered the quasi-species nature of the AIDS virus.

This nature explains why drug resistance can so easily (and rapidly) emerge when the anti-HIV drugs are not potent enough to fully suppress replication. Naturally occurring errors that spontaneously appear can, by chance, lead to a virus that is not inhibited by the antiviral drug. All of the susceptible viruses are suppressed, but the resistant virus, unaffected by the drugs, survives, then overgrows the wild-type and becomes the predominant virus in the quasi-species. (Our finding all those years ago also has had profound implications for the development of an AIDS vaccine: If there are dozens of viruses in one person's bloodstream, how do we create a vaccine that can protect against the transmission of *all* of them? It's a tall order that we're still trying to overcome.)

My dream of solving mysteries in ID medicine had just been realized, in spades. The ramifications of our Southern Blot results had critical ripple effects. With this discovery, we had played a role in a drama of global proportions, the race to understand AIDS. Each step forward in that race put us closer to offering hope where it mattered most: in the hospital rooms of our HIV patients.

Already then I was beginning to carry those patients with me into the lab, and when I moved to their bedsides I hauled the lab in with me. A researcher and a physician are different. I understood that. But the two roles were occupied by one person: me. What I increasingly realized was that my work in the lab—everyone's work in every lab—was the only hope for patients I knew not just as initials on a vial of fluid but by name, face, family, history, gifts, character, and fear. The virus wasn't just a virus; it was an enemy. My patients weren't just patients; they were David and "Jamie," "Kevin" and Ed, Michael and Brian.

My wife, Amy, has a favorite story about me from that era—and when I say "favorite," I mean she loves to tell it on me as a loving but pointed reminder of how engrossed in work I can become. As she tells it, "One night when Andy was a toddler and Harry just a baby, Mike came home late at night. When he came in, I saw something in his hand as he headed for the kitchen.

"I said, 'Michael, what did you just do?' And he said, 'I had to put something in the freezer.' And I said, 'What was it?' And he said, 'A vial.' Of course I asked, 'A vial of what?' And he said, 'A vial of infected blood.' [Pause] 'But it's triple-wrapped.' And I said, 'I don't give a damn if it's quadruple-wrapped, you don't ever bring home infected blood and stick in it my freezer!'"

While I'm sure that I've committed other work-obsessed infractions since then, I never repeated that one. But it *was* triple-wrapped.

In the weeks that followed our initial discovery, Beatrice, George, and I fleshed out our findings. We evaluated the genetic fingerprints of other patients and confirmed our original finding: All patients with established infection are walking around with a quasi-species of viruses. At the end of January 1986, I submitted an abstract of our work to the 2nd International AIDS Conference. The abstract was accepted for presentation at the conference, to be held in June—in Paris.

I had never thought much about the ladder-climbing in the medical profession; my attitude was that if you do good work, good things will happen. I was already having that experience: Good things *were* happening as if by magic.

In the wake of the discovery of which I'd been a part, it was as if I had climbed aboard a rocket ship. It felt like I was strapped in the capsule on top of the giant Atlas 2 booster rocket I'd watched lift off as a kid. I was blasting off, pulling about 4 Gs and hoping for weightlessness. I didn't exactly know how I got there and didn't know how I was going to land, but it was one wild ride.

When my feet finally touched ground, I was in Paris on the summer solstice, June 21, 1986. I was so excited to be on my first trip to Europe that I couldn't sleep on the flight from Atlanta to Charles de Gaulle Airport. My eyes in Paris had taken on the hue of George's eyes in the lab, but I remember everything about our early-morning arrival at the Hotel Franklin Roosevelt in Paris's 8th arrondissement. We emerged from the cab to hear a man on the hotel balcony yelling, "Be-a-trice! Be-a-trice! Be-a-trice!" Raoul, a high school friend of Beatrice who was now a chef in St. Tropez, had come to Paris to meet her and be our tour guide.

As quickly as I could drop my luggage in my room and grab my Super 8 movie camera, we were off. I almost always set my movies to music I select after I shoot the footage. But from the moment I got on the plane in Atlanta, I knew this movie's soundtrack would be Gershwin's "An American in Paris"—and as we walked toward the Champs-Élysées, I could hear its opening stanzas in cadence with my steps. It was magical.

For six hours, we toured famous French landmarks and I shot film, going through three reels that first day. It was an unseasonably warm day, so when we stopped for a bistro lunch, I gulped a little food and washed it down with the chilled Beaujolais that Raoul ordered. When we were done, I tried standing up. Nothing. I couldn't feel my legs or feet. The wine, the excitement, the wine, the jet lag, and the wine sent me to bed for the rest of the day.

At 9:30 p.m., I woke to a chorus of horns playing—I swear—in the cadence of "An American in Paris." *Beep, beep, beep! Honk, honk, honk!* As Parisian motorists celebrated the French soccer team's World Cup quarterfinals victory over perennial powerhouse Brazil, George, Beatrice, Raoul, and I explored the Technicolor whirl of the Left Bank. We ate and drank, mingled with soccer fans, and applauded performances of the annual Fête de la Musique street music festival. By the time we called it a night, the Metro was closed and no cabs were in sight, so we walked weary miles to find our hotel.

At 6:00 a.m. I fell back into bed, ending one of the most exhilarating and surreal days of my life. I now wonder if it's true that, falling asleep, I heard Flohoney telling me: *You belong here, Michael. Stick with AIDS.*

Chapter 5

THE 1917 CLINIC

I f we are lucky, at least once in life we experience what Plato called "clear light"—a moment in which something powerful occurs, we see it whole in all its dimensions and meaning, and we understand it completely.

I've always thought that I lived by luck or magic as much as by skill and effort. But while I was a medical student looking at all the optional career paths, I felt stuck. No single road seemed to lead to everything I thought I needed to be both useful and challenged. I found much that I loved in ID, in the lab and the hospital; I didn't want to give up research or the practice of medicine. But neither did I really see a career path forward. Then in January 1987, in a dusty conference room unlikely to host any great dreams, I experienced clear light. I knew my place in the medical world. It was not a delusion, and it's unfolded precisely as I saw it: my profession, my practice, my place.

The challenge of the moment, in 1987, was the realization that I wasn't going to "find" what I had just experienced. My place was clear, but did not yet exist. I'd have to build it myself.

I entered medical school fully intending to be the surgeon who'd fulfill my mother's ambition for me. Over the next nine years, I changed my mind about surgery; chose cardiology and then discarded it; fell into ID more than chose it, and set course for a comfortable life of ID private practice that never happened.

One of my favorite teachers in medical school was Dr. Julio Melo, a Colombian-born ID specialist who for years was hailed as one of Louisville's top physicians in his field. Julio wasn't just a good doctor; he was a good person. At the start of my second year of ID fellowship, I received a call from Julio asking me if I wanted to join him in his practice. No financial buy in; just start working with him as an equal partner. The thought of going home to Louisville, working with one of my favorite physicians, practicing ID in collaboration with many physicians I had known when I was growing up, was hugely attractive. Julio and I agreed I could start in summer 1987. It was my dream come true.

But at the same time I was accepting Julio's kindness in Louisville, my life was heading everywhere *except* Louisville. Making two discoveries in the UAB lab with George Shaw and publishing them in *NEJM* and *Nature*. Presenting findings at the International AIDS Conference (and making my movie) in Paris. Thriving under the mentorship of Bill Dismukes, who wanted me to be assistant chief of the medical service at the Veterans Administration hospital and help run the UAB house staff training program— a truly tempting prospect, since I loved teaching. I was torn between the opportunities. On Labor Day weekend 1986, I went to Louisville to visit with Julio.

I'm glad I'm writing, because when I try to tell this story face-to-face, I usually choke up.

I planned to meet Julio after Sunday morning rounds at one of the three hospitals his one-man practice served. A few minutes after nine, Julio half-staggered into the doctor's lounge, looking as tired and overworked as he was. *This guy needs a partner*, I thought. Feeling guilty even to raise it, I told him my dilemma. I wanted to be his partner in Louisville, but I felt drawn to the lab and patients at UAB. Without hesitation, Julio said, "Mike, there's nothing better than academic medicine. You owe it to yourself to give it a shot."

What my mother now says she actually ordained at my birth was not merely that I would be a doctor but that I'd be a "doctor's doctor," someone whose opinion other physicians would seek on their most difficult cases. Infectious diseases was a perfect specialty for this, as ID cases are often the most difficult to sort out. Working with Julio, one of the most respected physicians in town, would seal the deal. I would become a pillar in the Louisville medical community and the favored son of the Louisville Jewish community. Didn't I owe it to my mother to grant her the dream of "my son the doctor" coming home?

You owe it to yourself to give it a shot.

In his unflinching and unselfish response, Julio liberated me to be whatever I wanted to be, my mother's dreams notwithstanding. Had Julio been caring even a little for himself, he'd have talked me out of it. I'd have listened to his trusted counsel. But he didn't. On the contrary, he started me thinking full-bore about staying in Birmingham and in academia, a life vision I'd never really imagined.

I knew that I could stay in the lab doing research with George and Beatrice—a comfortable situation, like a water-skier traveling in the boat's wake. But I'd increasingly realized that I would miss the patients. I loved the interaction with those who came for healing; I loved them not just as "cases" but as confidantes, teachers, friends, partners. The lab was a place to seek knowledge, but the interaction with patients was where the knowledge mattered most. But I'd never imagined a way to stay in the lab *and* be deeply engaged with patients.

The same time I was being redirected by Julio, an abstract I'd worked on with George was accepted for presentation at a December 1986 hematologists' meeting in San Francisco, six months past Paris. Hematology didn't much interest me, but a few days in San Francisco did. San Francisco General Hospital (SFGH) had perhaps the most respected AIDS outpatient clinic anywhere, Ward 86. In 1983, when their team had opened the nation's first dedicated AIDS inpatient ward, within days it was fully occupied. They were working at the epicenter of the disaster. In a fearful, stricken city, SFGH stood like a lighthouse in a hurricane.

After giving my talk, I spent a day at the hospital with doctors such as the late and still grieved Merle Sande and the brilliant and very much alive Paul Volberding. They'd led the shock troops trying to counter the virus that had attacked the city so ruthlessly. In my mind, I still see their clinic's "war room" where patients were tracked on a huge whiteboard filled with names. In the upper right-hand corner of the board, someone had drawn a beatific, beaming sun. Carefully lettered under it was a list—often a long list—of the patients who had died that week. It reminded me of TV news scenes when I was growing up in the 1960s, with Walter Cronkite reporting the weekly death numbers from Vietnam.

I was at SFGH for one day. I visited with as many staff members as I could find, including Donald Abrams, Connie Wofsy, Phil Hopewell, John Stansell, Michael Clement, John Mills, Mark Jacobson, Julie Gerberding, Allison Moed, and Grace Lusby, stealing precious moments from their intense care for patients. Over and over I asked them the same question—"If you were starting over from scratch, how would you design an AIDS clinic?"—and I took pages and pages of notes. The knowledge was precious. The experience of those people was unforgettable.

I flew back to Birmingham with a notebook full of suggestions, a new model for clinical care and caregivers, and no clear plan of action. The notes wound up in a pile on my desk as patient files began to accumulate. As if overnight, we were facing our own AIDS onslaught. From New York, San Francisco, Atlanta, and elsewhere, people with AIDS-related illnesses were returning home to die in places like Montgomery, Selma, Huntsville, and Dothan (population 125,000), all places that looked to Birmingham for AIDS relief. Local doctors, unprepared to manage patients' grim, end-state conditions, offered what words of comfort they could and sent their patients to our ER. If they arrived alive, we'd admit them to our hospital and, ideally, offer stabilization and perhaps improvement. But once they were able to be discharged, what could we do? Send them back home? Within days they'd have new symptoms no happier than those they'd suffered earlier, and they'd be heading back to Birmingham. We were running a boomerang business in an epidemic where everyone was dying.

UAB had no outpatient facility, no home healthcare resources, no way to take care of these folks. What we had were some indescribably committed team members who made up for lack of resources with an abundance of courage, intelligence, commitment, and faith. What I'd seen in SFGH

I now saw all around me. Overworked and underpaid colleagues cobbled together solutions. Some HIV patients needed blood transfusions and IV medication infusions that took hours to administer; we had nowhere for them to sit or lie while being infused. Jim Raper, head nurse of the emergency department and trauma center, opened clinical space in the University emergency department every night when it was less busy so that we could treat these people. No available staff to work odd hours, weekends, holidays? No problem. Jim Raper came in himself to administer the treatments. As we sat together between charts and coffee one hushed overnight shift, while patients slept as their treatments progressed, Jim told me his remarkable life story.

Raised in northeastern Ohio with five brothers and sisters, Jim spent most summers working on a North Carolina farm for his grandfather, who had fathered twenty children. "Grandpa Raper dedicated his life to running his farm, raising his family, and bringing them through the Depression," Jim told me with obvious pride. "He knew what hard work was all about, but he made work fun." Even as a youngster, Jim loved the feeling of being part of a group effort and making things run smoothly. Long before he'd graduated high school he was as dependable as any adult, rising before dawn to milk cows, doing chores, and going to bed in the dark once the livestock were fed. But as a gay youth who sensed the need to one day live openly, "I knew I wasn't going to end up living on a farm and having a family," Jim said.

Although Jim dreamed of becoming a physician, his family couldn't spare money for college, let alone medical school. A high school teacher Jim knew suggested he get a nursing degree while working to pay for it. So for four years, Jim spent his days studying nursing at Ohio's Kent State University while working forty hours a week on overnight shifts as a hospital emergency room orderly.

With his nursing degree in hand, Jim joined the US Army Nurse Corps, hoping to see the world. He got as far as Huntsville, Alabama, and a posting at the Redstone Arsenal. During three years of active duty, he worked as head nurse of the base hospital's emergency room while earning a master's degree in nursing at the University of Alabama at Huntsville. Near the end of his assignment, Jim met Steve, a music teacher and high school band director who was tall, athletic, handsome, and nine years Jim's senior. After a few months of courting, the two were a couple. In spring 1983, Jim moved to be with Steve in Birmingham, and he applied for work at UAB.

To call Jim's first UAB job a trial by fire is probably an understatement. As assisting head nurse for the cardiovascular operating room, Jim worked for Dr. John W. Kirklin, an honest-to-God medical giant. At the Mayo Clinic in the '50s and later as surgery department chairman at UAB, Kirklin revolutionized cardiovascular surgery. He developed and refined the heart-lung machine and used it in the world's first series of open-heart operations.

Kirklin was as exacting as he was brilliant. Some found him hard, perhaps impossible, to satisfy. I know excellent team members who couldn't survive more than a month working with Kirklin. Jim Raper worked with him for three years. Asked about what it was like, Jim says simply that Kirklin was "intense." When UAB needed a new head nurse for its emergency department and trauma center, Kirklin suggested Jim. By promoting Jim for that post, Kirklin brought into my circle a gift I desperately needed and still value beyond words. Jim Raper pursued treatment and resources for our HIV patients anywhere and in any way he could, and he was soon a key partner for all my patient work.

We knew all-night workarounds in the ER and other "solutions" carved out of desperation wouldn't be sufficient for long. The need was growing, the hospital was searching for a sustainable way to treat people with AIDS, and I remembered the notes from San Francisco buried somewhere on my desk.

On a Thursday afternoon in February 1987, I settled into room 229, a book-lined conference room that doubled as the ID library at the Tinsley Harrison Research Tower, named for the Alabamian who was a twentieth-century pioneer in internal medicine. I remember the silence and the dusty-library smell. I remember taking out my SFGH notes, a yellow legal pad, and a blue ink pen. I started writing and instantly felt as if I needed not to guide the pen, but just to stay out of the way of whatever force was forming the words.

Three hours later—though it seemed, at the time, like fifteen minutes—I had completed a detailed proposal for a UAB AIDS clinic.

Its first few pages made my case. UAB already was doing top-notch infectious disease research, as good as anywhere in the world. We already were seeing patients in great need and, given what we knew and could project about the epidemic, this was just the beginning. Nowhere else in Alabama could you find the capacity or the will to handle what was coming, I wrote. Without brandishing the words "moral imperative," I made it clear that I believed this was a state university's duty. UAB couldn't run away from AIDS. We needed to get out in front, quickly, so we would be ready when it arrived in full force.

Then I described a clinic that could do this, incorporating the best practices I'd seen at SFGH. It would be built around a five-fold mission: patient care, social services support, medical provider education, community outreach, and research. Though all five were needed, what would be critical—and new—would be combining two of them, the patient care and the research. Since this is such a new disease, I argued, every patient could be followed carefully, as if "on study." In the past I'd seen how research impacted patients; here I argued that every patient was research. Best of all, it wasn't mere rhetoric. It was necessary, and it was true.

Treating every patient as a research subject would mean entering the data on each patient into a database and following them over time. Since drugs to treat HIV effectively were scarce, we would enroll as many patients as possible into clinical trials of new medications, cutting-edge therapies to which they never would have access otherwise. With this approach, we'd be giving them state-of-the-art treatment, advancing our knowledge as we studied the outcomes—and, not incidentally, paying our bills with money the drug companies would give us to run the trials.

(Pharmaceutical financing was critical to our model, as most of our patients would have neither money nor insurance to cover their care. So long as there were sufficient research dollars to funnel into patient care, we would be financially sustainable. For years, research dollars hid the real cost of treatment and allowed us to avoid the hard realities that insurers were unreliable, public funds were limited, and patients who are agonizingly sick and sliding toward death are, among other things, not inexpensive. We didn't worry about America's healthcare system because research money made us an exception to most of the rules.)

Under the proposal, UAB's clinic would open with two assets the SFGH staff said they wished they had: a database to capture every scrap of information on every patient, and a specimen repository to preserve blood samples. We knew many of our patients would die before we fully understood the disease killing them. But with the contents of the database and repository—in a sense, their bequest to the AIDS fight—we could conduct research and quickly apply what we learned to other patients' treatment.

I gave the yellow pad to a colleague who typed the proposal (and corrected my spelling, which is lousy to this day). Then I sent it off to the chair of medicine, J. Claude Bennett, with a request for an appointment to discuss it.

An affable man with a gray goatee and a penetrating gaze, Claude was a brilliant scientist: His name was attached to research breakthroughs on genetic coding for protein structure, gene splicing, and monoclonal antibodies. Claude had known me from the time I'd been his chief resident, when he'd encouraged my interest in research, but I suspect he still considered my overture pretty brazen.

I walked into his office prepared for battle and began my pitch. I hadn't gone three minutes when Claude motioned for me to stop. "We need to do this," he said in his calm, matter-of-fact way, and he proceeded to explain how the university planned to bring me on faculty and provide clinic space and start-up staff. His parting words to me were "Just try not to run in the red."

And there it was, like magic. A state-sponsored university in Birmingham, Alabama—this city not long removed from turning dogs on protesters—would create a clinic for the AIDS patients just launching their own civil rights crusade. A second-year ID fellow had asked the big boss for an AIDS clinic and received a yes in three minutes. Within months, we were underway. How could I *not* believe in magical thinking?

The hospital operated its internal medicine residents' clinic in a freestanding building located at 1917 Fifth Avenue South. Nestled under the looping exit ramp of a parking garage, it still makes me think of Alvy Singer, Woody Allen's character in the movie *Annie Hall*, whose house sits beneath a roller coaster track at Coney Island. The schedule for internal medicine residents left the facility open Thursday and Friday afternoons. To start, UAB administrators said we could have the space for those two half days plus the services of nurses already on the clinic staff. Given the stigma surrounding the disease, I didn't want people to call it "The AIDS Clinic" because I feared terrorizing neighbors and making patients reluctant to come in. I named it for the street address: the 1917 Clinic. (When asked about the name over the years, I've been known to say we were commemorating the launch of the Bolshevik Revolution; occasionally, I've been believed.)

Colleagues already working in HIV/AIDS clinics had warned me, "There's no good way to say, 'You're positive'"—no way to give a patient that AIDS test result without it sounding like a death sentence. I understood how they felt, standing there as supposed healers yet having to admit: *We cannot heal you of this.* But I had one advantage most full-time clinicians didn't: I was also continuing to work in the lab, where a game-changing discovery might be unimagined one minute and under the microscope the next. I spent one hour with despairing patients but the next on promising science. For me, the lab offset the despair of patients while the patients instilled passion in the lab. I settled on my own way to tell patients their tests results: "You're HIV-positive—*and there are a lot of things we can do.*"

On January 28, 1988, a quiet, chilly Thursday afternoon, we saw our first eight patients at the 1917 Clinic. Word spread, we picked up steam, and some 100 patients entered treatment in our first nine months. Nearly all who came stayed for as long as we could keep them alive. We loaded all their information into our new database on a bare-bones computer that I kept at home. We preserved their blood samples in our repository, using a confidential numeric coding system to link patients to specimens, a system that I have kept to this day.

The AIDS care that physicians Sande, Volberding, and their colleagues pioneered at SFGH took a "holistic approach" and acted as a "medical home" before either of those terms became healthcare clichés. To recreate that atmosphere at the 1917 Clinic, we borrowed liberally from their approach. Staffers were trained to be respectful and knowledgeable about the gay community from which so many patients came. Gay and straight community volunteers served as "clinic hosts," making patients and their loved ones feel welcome, guiding them to resources, and offering a shoulder to cry on or a hug to bring comfort. Some days, our waiting room felt like a group therapy session.

The first few weeks were bumpy. Waiting times were long because so many patients were sick and had complex medical histories. Social services were critical for nearly every patient, particularly those needing to learn how to access medications. Home-based IV medicines were almost indescribably complicated to administer and therefore difficult to get right. And coordination between the providers taking care of patients in the hospital with those of us providing care in the clinic was particularly challenging.

I remember the day an ambulance pulled up to the clinic's only public entrance. Its attendants unloaded a patient who was more dead than alive and proceeded to roll his stretcher through the middle of our packed waiting room. Relatives who'd brought in other patients nearly gagged. The place fell so silent that you could almost hear the other patients thinking, "That's going to be me soon . . ."

We changed protocols after this fiasco so that ambulances could only bring patients through a back door off an alley. But it was a cosmetic fix, because in those early days every patient, and every person who held the patient's hand as he or she checked in, soon knew that a diagnosis with AIDS was tantamount to a death sentence.

I remember thinking, when I was a fifth grader, that all the great issues facing America—especially race relations—would be settled by the time I was grown. Not so, it turned out. My great issue would be HIV/AIDS, a scientific enigma and medical impossibility wrapped in cultural judgments and social stigma. My goal would be to make a university research-and-treatment center number one in tackling it—something the state would be proud of, like it was proud of 'Bama or Auburn being number one in football.

I didn't care whether others thought I was delusional or given to magical thinking. I didn't care, because I had held test tubes holding the secrets that could bring life, and I'd held too many hands of dying patients. In the 1917 Clinic, I had found not just a career but a cause. This mattered.

Chapter 6

FACES

I suspect that some people in the 1917 Clinic waiting room the day the EMTs wheeled in our cadaver patient still remember the moment. They recall looking away in an effort to show respect or offer the dying some dignity, or feeling a panic that tore at their soul. Most could not help but look past the taut arms of the stretcher-bearers and into the patient's gaunt face.

A first glance is mere curiosity—what stops us when we drive past a car accident. Then comes some engagement: *Do I know him? Is he breathing?* Within seconds comes recognition and understanding. We know where we are, what we're seeing, what it means. In the faces of the suffering, those who already had tested positive see a reflection of themselves and their future. For those infected with the virus, caring for infected loved ones was once described as "looking-glass love." They saw what was ahead for them in every fever, every open sore, every form of torment. Most of them loved well enough to continue providing care despite their own illness.

For clinicians fighting the disease, the faces we saw became our reason to press on. Every face came with a name, and every name came with a story of love and courage, pain and staggering loss.

There is a power in dying that deeply affects most of us who care for patients with end-stage illness. To see them and hear them and hold them is to know: There's no time to waste. There are no second tries. There is only the best shot we can take, however long the odds. When it doesn't work, there's frustration and anger, sometimes guilt or self-blame, almost always a searing grief—and grief morphs into the energy that drives us back into the search.

Before we opened the doors of the 1917 Clinic to a flood of HIV-infected people, I had experienced healthcare and AIDS mostly as two separate interests or communities, two different worlds. Healthcare was about science and specialization, clinical precision and discovery in spotless labs and certified wards. AIDS was about the streets, gritty and tough, about patients who presented in our waiting rooms so late in their illness that most of what we had to offer was sympathy and a bit of palliative support. Our outreach staff came back with reports from apartments where sick friends cared for even sicker friends, where they'd noticed a mortuary phone number scribbled on a sticky note.

For me, AIDS was also my introduction to vast numbers of gay men, many of whom had become dead to their families when they explained ("came out") their sexual orientation. Now they were dying again.

I was a straight, married, Jewish doctor in a mostly Christian, socially conservative state, in a country whose president knowingly went years refusing to publicly speak the name of the disease that was killing my patients. Even through the rosy glow of my optimism and with funding still arriving from our research grants, I was seeing more and more what didn't work in American healthcare. I was struggling to ensure care for my patients, many of them social and religious outcasts who viewed the medical establishment with skepticism because the gay community historically—and many of my new patients personally—had encountered layers of refusal built on stigma and shame when seeking medical care.

As the virus spread, the government's faltering willingness to recognize the epidemic bred new suspicions in the gay community. Rumors and ignorance took the place of science and medicine. Suspicions easily gave rise to fear, and fear bred anger—anger that their lives were being cut short (most were in their twenties and thirties), anger that their doctors seemed powerless, anger that the nation didn't seem to care. They heard the whispers—"They're getting what they deserve"—and the sermons about God's justice being delivered through the plague.

In a sense, I was drawn to the crisis precisely because it was a crisis. I wanted to fix it. I wanted to do what wasn't being done. Each morning I rallied my team, most of whom had no more experience in such chaos than I. Each day that we could keep patients alive was such a cause for celebration that we turned that quest into a clinic mantra: "Birthdays are our business." And each night, I would slump into my office chair or trudge toward home wondering, *What the hell am I doing here? In the ungodly confusion of this crisis, what role can I play?* Slowly, I was coming to realize that I was neither Sherlock Holmes nor Superman.

At best, I hoped to alter my patients' place on a sort of spectrum of mortality. In the early years of the epidemic, we only imagined that there was a bright end of the spectrum where patients would survive AIDS altogether. In the meantime, we fought like mad cats to keep patients in the middle range of the spectrum, where they were responding to treatment and enjoying months or years of health before the disease overtook them. The reality was that we spent a lot of time at the dark end of the spectrum where patients died swift, hard deaths following slow, brutalizing sickness.

I entered medicine to be a healer, but in the early days at the 1917 Clinic, it sounded hollow to call myself that. I was trained to cure, but I had no cure for AIDS. I was trained to fix, but I couldn't fix these patients. I was grasping for whatever I could do for them, their parents, their spouses and lovers. It was not in my makeup to quit: "Finish what you start," my dad always commanded. You keep pushing, you figure something out, you find some magical solution—or else you get beaten.

So I stayed, and some remarkable, tireless, committed colleagues stayed with me. On difficult days, we did get beaten; on even more days, we *felt* beaten. But we didn't quit. We joined our patients' support teams, if they had one. Their lovers (who often were already our patients too) became our friends; their mothers became our colleagues. While maintaining our role as a clinic and not just a hospice, we also embraced the goal of assuring our patients comfort and dignity through their lives and at their deaths. At some ill-defined but obvious point, we reached a fork in the road where I became less a doctor and more a rabbi, when the clinic staff and I stopped pushing the medical and switched to the spiritual. Instead of trying to get someone well, we would just try to ease their way, whatever that meant and whatever it took.

———

Ed had lived in San Francisco in the early 1980s and worked as a waiter and part-time chef. What he could do with food was magic.

Like so many other residents of the neighborhood called the Castro, he was diagnosed with the gay plague and suffered illnesses that became known as AIDS's calling cards: Kaposi's sarcoma, then *pneumocystis* pneumonia. Ed became my patient at the 1917 Clinic in spring 1988 after moving back to Alabama to be closer to his family.

Ed was a bearded, lean guy whose eyes brimmed with intelligence and humor. He claimed that years of frustrated idealism had left him a cynic, but I could see he still held on to his idealism as intensely as he held on to life itself. His dry wit was endearing, and the food he created was seductive.

Ed was one of the first patients in Birmingham to take azidothymidine (AZT), on which so many hopes were pinned in those years. The drug was initially developed at the National Cancer Institute (NCI) in 1964 as an anticancer agent. At that time—only sixteen years after the discovery of DNA—researchers hoped that by mimicking the normal building blocks of DNA (nucleosides), the drugs would confuse the replication process and hinder cancer cell growth.

Like most of the "nucleoside inhibitors" developed as anticancer agents in the 1960s and 1970s, AZT didn't work so well against cancer and was put on the shelf. When HIV was discovered as the cause of AIDS, researchers at Burroughs Wellcome (BW), working in concert with Sam Broder and his colleagues at the NCI, determined that AZT was one of several nucleoside drugs that had activity against HIV. The first Phase II study conducted by BW showed that the drug dramatically reduced mortality from AIDS over six to twelve months compared to a placebo. In 1987, the drug was the first to be approved in the United States for use against AIDS.

Within the early-epidemic national AIDS community, led mostly by gay artists and activists, original expectations for AZT were unrealistically high. Words like "solution" yielded to words like "cure." It was the first and therefore the best hope at the time, and hope—desperation?—soared beyond the bounds of either science or common sense.

In those days, AZT had to be taken every four hours *around the clock*. Side effects were common, the result of the drug inhibiting replication of *normal* cells as well as the virus. Ed experienced most of them: nausea, profound anemia, fatigue, and neuropathy (pain, burning, tingling, and numbness, especially in the hands and feet). And yet he still managed to work as a chef and server at A Social Affair, a Birmingham caterer that I often hired to provide food for department events. The consummate "foodie," Ed delighted in sharing his culinary specialties and expertise. He even managed to teach a kitchen amateur like me a few things, such as when to cook with olive oil instead of the butter I had favored since my undergraduate days in New Orleans.

Ed loved life even more than he loved food, and he was determined to sample both for as long as possible. Even when a medication made him violently ill, he kept taking it; like most patients at that time, he kept telling himself he could stand it until a better treatment came along. In Ed's mind, a better drug—or even "the cure"—was always just around the corner. He kept that sunny outlook even as his white blood cell count tumbled lower and lower, a complication of AZT treatment. With no white blood cells, he would have no ability to fight even a common cold, let alone more serious ailments.

Things seemed hopeful heading into the holidays at the end of 1990. We'd kept Ed alive for another season of office parties where the star of the catered tables was his signature bruschetta topped with sun-dried tomatoes and cream cheese. Christmas Day found my family and me in Atlanta for the bris of my eight-day-old nephew, Alec. Conducting a Jewish ritual circumcision on Christmas played right into my warped sense of humor—and so, in my best Santa Claus voice, I greeted all the relatives with a hearty "Merry Bris-mas! Merry Bris-mas!"

Somewhere midcelebration, a call came from Birmingham. A tearful hospital colleague told me that Ed had just died. He'd been found by a fast-moving bloodstream infection that his compromised immune system couldn't fight off. One moment I was laughing at my Bris-mas joke; the next, I was yanked off the mountaintop.

Without explanation to anyone, I went out for a walk to compose myself. When I returned to the family gathering—surrounded by generations of loved ones, from baby Alec to his grandparents and great-uncles—I could not get my mind off Ed. How many Christmases and christenings and bar mitzvahs, birthdays and weddings and anniversaries, had AIDS stolen from him and his loved ones by taking him so soon? How many Eds were already in our system, and how many more were waiting, too frightened to come for testing and discover that they were HIV-positive?

Beneath these questions loomed a larger one that I resolutely pushed from my mind. If it dared rise to my consciousness, I'd slap it away again. This time, it came up full throttle: How many more losses like this could I handle?

———

Susan Wilder certainly didn't need to work at the 1917 Clinic. She "came from means," as my parents' generation would say: Her husband was a successful businessman, and they lived in an old-money hamlet south of Birmingham. Susan's four children were in high school and college when she decided she wanted to do more than volunteer work. So she went back to school and got her degree in social work, for which her quick mind and big heart were ideally suited.

The first social worker hired at the 1917 Clinic, Susan was a child of the sixties who continued to live out that generation's rhetoric about service to humanity. She wore her shoulder-length, dark hair loose around her still-girlish face. With her upbeat, can-do attitude, Susan was one of the most positive people with whom I ever worked.

Each workday, Susan drove to the clinic from her tidy suburb to help AIDS patients manage their decidedly untidy lives. She counseled the twenty-something Caribbean man with a student visa who was facing the prospect of returning home with HIV and without vital medications.

For the sixty-something farmer who got the virus from a blood transfusion and was extremely hard of hearing, Susan would shout out medical information, including explicit safe-sex guidance that made others giggle or blush. When a fifty-something construction worker and former IV drug user was dying, Susan somehow got him into perhaps the only local nursing home that would take a patient with AIDS, and then helped train the staff there that gave him end-of-life care. (In thanks, the man bequeathed Susan his prized possession, the Bible he'd been given in his twelve-step recovery program.)

Early in 1989, a thirty-year-old woman named "Jamie" came to the 1917 Clinic with needle-tracked arms, a relentless *pneumocystis* pneumonia cough, and a new baby girl. Susan instantly took to Jamie and, to this day, when she talks about Jamie, her voice takes on a motherly tenderness.

As Susan tells the story, "Jamie had lived a very tough life. She was intelligent and wellspoken, and she told me she had come from a fairly well-to-do family in New York City. She rebelled and ran away from home, and she was on the streets at about age thirteen or fourteen. Her parents disowned her and she never saw them again. She panhandled and got into prostitution and drugs. She hooked up with this guy and got pregnant, decided to have the baby, and the two of them moved south and wound up in Birmingham. After Jamie had the baby and she and her daughter were diagnosed with HIV, the baby ended up in the hospital in intensive care and the guy disappeared.

"Jamie was so proud of the baby. She was trying to make changes in her life; she would show up for her clinic appointments, so appreciative of anything we did for her. It was devastating to her that the baby was sick. Jamie couldn't stand going to the hospital and seeing the baby suffering with all the tubes and wires attached to her. She hated going by herself, so I'd go with her.

"The baby didn't live very long. When she died, Jamie was devastated. There was no money to bury her, but I called around, and a lovely local funeral home donated a service. They set out chairs and put on recorded music, and there was a tiny white casket. The only people there besides Jamie were Dr. Saag, our clinic nurse coordinator, and me. It was heart-wrenching, but Jamie was so thankful.

"With the baby gone, Jamie stopped taking her medicine. She stopped coming to the clinic regularly, and then she just disappeared. About a year later, I got a call from a doctor at a New York City hospital. Jamie had had my card, with the clinic's phone number, in her pocket when she collapsed on the street. She later died in the hospital, and the doctor was calling to ask me if there were any family members who could bury her. I couldn't help because she never even told me her family name. So she was buried in a pauper's grave.

"Jamie had tried to do the right thing," Susan concluded, "but she was just so lost. The drugs kept getting in her way."

Burnout runs rampant among AIDS medicine professionals, which Susan knew both from professional training and personal experience. To help her 1917 Clinic colleagues fight that, she used to invite us to her lovely home for pool parties, croquet matches, food and drink, and sing-alongs.

Susan had been a clinic mainstay for nearly six years when, one day in 1994, her husband, Geoff, died of a heart attack while jogging. Someone had to step in and run the family business; Susan did, even though it meant leaving the clinic.

The only reason I could abide the worst times—watching helplessly as patients died and loved ones grieved—was because I worked with colleagues who were beyond imagination. The people who've worked in the 1917 Clinic, Susan among them, are angels in this world. And through the decades in this work, I've seen that *every* clinic, in *every* community, is filled with angels like Susan and our team. They are living proof of something we all want to believe: that when horrific events occur, good people do good things simply for goodness' sake. What lies beyond magic is, I think, miracle.

———

Through decades of losing patients, I've grieved with their spouses, lovers, siblings, children—but I have felt the most profound pain for their parents. I'm sure my pain relates in some ways to the fact that I'm a parent myself. If I imagine what it would mean for Amy or me to hold Harry or Andy or Julie as they took a last breath, I am beyond distraught—it's agony even as imagination. As my kids would say, "I can't even go there."

Looking into the faces of the dying patients' parents—especially the mothers—is what tears me up the most. They're losing a son or daughter and, as if that were not horrible enough, they're losing them to a horrendous, stigmatized disease. For parents still in denial about a sexual orientation or lifestyle that may have opened the door to the virus, standing at their child's deathbed represents proof positive of truths they long avoided. The suffering is incomparable, but so is the love.

When parents are racked by the pain of losing their child, I encourage our staff to be there for them, to offer support and strength. If we can stay composed while they are in agony, that can be helpful. But when we who've tried to sustain that life watch it finally flicker out, we also grieve. When the parents weep, there is no sin in weeping with them. A collective, sobbing hug may be what enables us all to go on.

I remember nothing about "Kevin's" father except that he never came along for Kevin's clinic visits. But I have clear memories of his mother, "Margaret," who brought Kevin in when he was so limp and depleted he could barely stand. Though he was only in his late twenties, months of wasting and fevers had left Kevin looking much older to me. But by the way Margaret gazed at him, it was clear she still saw the slight, sweet southern boy she had always known.

It being autumn and us living in Alabama, I made some idle comment on the seasonal preoccupation, Crimson Tide football. Kevin perked up appreciably. He was a huge 'Bama fan, his mother said; though he never had been able to spare the money to attend a game in person, he never missed a game on TV.

Kevin's chart showed that almost every form of treatment had been thrown at him and still he was failing, his blue eyes sunken and his face starkly pale against his dark hair. I remember thinking: *What do we have to lose? Maybe he has adrenal insufficiency. Let's try a course of steroids; it might work.* I gave Margaret a prescription for him and asked them to come back in a week.

A week later, it was as if we had flipped a switch. Kevin was like a new man, striding into my office unassisted and wrapping me in a big hug. "I can't believe this; it's like you gave me my life back!" he crowed.

While he was regarding me as a miracle worker, I knew that the steroid booster effect would last only so long, a few months at best. I figured, while he was feeling so good, I'd show him the real deal on miracles. I knew he was pining to attend a Crimson Tide game, and I knew people who knew people. So we arranged two tickets for Kevin and Margaret in seats just behind the Alabama bench with a great view of the sidelines action as well as the game. On a glorious November day, surrounded by more than 70,000 other rabid fans, Kevin watched the Tide roll to a 37–14 victory. He showed up to his next visit still elated and brought me a souvenir, a Crimson Tide baseball cap.

After a few stable weeks, Kevin's health took a nosedive. I had no bullets left in the gun, nothing more to try. When they came back to the clinic for what I expected would be the last time, Margaret felt it too. She let go of Kevin's hand long enough to rise and give me a long, wordless hug.

Kevin faded in and out, and was spared knowing that his team lost to Miami in the Sugar Bowl on New Year's Day. But through it all, Margaret was steadily at his bedside, and somehow I'm sure that was what Kevin knew.

I still have Kevin's crimson hat hanging in a place of honor in my office.

———

Every day, it seemed, another UAB colleague learned of an acquaintance, friend, or relative who had been diagnosed HIV-positive. But for one of us, the epidemic hit particularly close to home.

In 1989, Jim Raper's partner, Steve, came down with pneumonia. Before Jim and Steve became a couple, Steve had been with a partner who later died of complications from AIDS. "So we kind of knew what was happening," even before Steve tested positive for the virus in 1989, Jim says now.

Jim took a position as a night shift nursing department administrator so he could have days with Steve and continue his doctoral studies in nursing service administration (the man is indefatigable). Steve was enrolled in clinical trials right away, but "there really wasn't much medicine at that point," as Jim recalls. "There was AZT, which Steve took. And he took what was then an experimental drug, didanosine or DDI, which had to be chewed, two tablets twice a day, and they tasted absolutely horrific. But Steve used to say he'd eat shit on a Ritz cracker if he thought it would keep him alive."

As an "AIDS doc," I was a walking pharmacy. If *this* didn't work with a patient, maybe *that* would. They'd be on a promising protocol for a week, everything would collapse, and I'd be ready with a new option, a small adjustment, a big change—until I was out of options, and they were out of luck. Needless to say, I developed a special bond with patients who were enrolled in the drug trials. Life was a drug train, and we rode it together.

As an extra safeguard for their privacy, many of these patients entered trials under code names. We had a "Peter Pan" who was hardly a small child in tights. We had a "Roy Rogers" with neither hat nor horse. And we had a "Pearly James"—quite a name, especially for a man—who never will be forgotten at the clinic.

Pearly's case was typical of the roller-coaster rides endured as we sought drug combinations that had efficacy against the virus without poisonous side effects for the patient. He was enrolled in a clinical trial to compare results from monotherapy, a single AIDS medication, to those from dual therapy, a two-drug regimen. When his CD4 count dipped below 500, crossing the border from healthy to unhealthy, we started him on DDI. Six months later, the protocol dictated that we add AZT—to which Pearly was totally intolerant. His red blood cell count rapidly plunged so low that we wanted to give him a blood transfusion, which he refused even though many days he was so weak that he could barely walk a few yards without rest.

Hoping for the best, we stopped the AZT and substituted a drug in the same class, stavudine. Pearly's health rebounded; his CD4 count rose to the 700s and stayed there.

Amid all the dying and all the failure that it represented, amid all the struggle to keep team morale high and desperation low, I can't tell you how badly we all needed Pearly James.

————

Even sitting on a clinic examination table in a drab medical gown, Michael had presence. While I put him through the paces of a routine physical exam, he sat up perfectly straight, as if his spine and head were suspended from a string somewhere in the ceiling. When I had him follow my finger with his eyes and my hand swept to the left and to the right, his eyes moved but his body stayed perfectly still, as if frozen in a pose. Thanks to years of ballet training, Michael was the most graceful, physically poetic individual I'd ever met.

In New York City, Michael had danced with such prestigious troupes as the Joffrey Ballet and the National Ballet Company. By late 1987, progressive fatigue and shortness of breath forced Michael off the stage. He and his partner, Evan, moved to Birmingham, aiming to teach dance. Evan took up teaching, but Michael's shortness of breath got worse until he wound up in the emergency room with a diagnosis of *pneumocystis* pneumonia. He was started on anti-*pneumocystis* therapy and breathing treatments, but his condition worsened. He was transferred to the intensive care unit and put on a mechanical ventilator.

Anyone who's had that experience—a machine breathing for you but never quite relieving the feeling that you're gasping for air—knows that one day on a ventilator can feel like a week. Ventilators are a way to keep someone alive, but barely. Michael was, in fact, on the ventilator for nearly six weeks. Most of that time he was totally paralyzed by Pavulon, the drug we administered to keep muscle contractions from interfering with the ventilation.

After Michael rebounded and we got him off the ventilator, we discussed the experience. The man who had flown onstage, who had soared above the symphony and heard thunderous ovations, admitted that it had been difficult to be totally aware of what was going on around him yet unable to move, with a tube down his throat and the perpetual sensation of breathlessness. I asked him how he got through six weeks of this normally intolerable process. His response floored me.

Michael had asked the nurses to tell him every morning when it was 5:30 a.m., the time his day would have begun in his New York City apartment. As soon as the nurses gave the word, Michael began imagining himself performing his old morning routine. He visualized it all in timed detail: He'd slowly get up, then do stretches, then go to the dance studio—and there, rehearse every step of every dance routine he ever had performed. In that hospital bed he was prone and intubated, but in his mind, he was performing intricate, athletic choreography for hours at a time. As the ventilator pumped out twenty breaths per minute, Michael used its cadence as his metronome. He would "dance" a certain number of steps per breath for an *andante* number, then twice that many for an *allegro* piece. While the medical team was tending to his body, Michael was sustaining his spirit.

We became dear friends, Michael and I. As most patients did, he responded very well to AZT initially. His p24 antigen—the crude marker we used then to gauge the amount of virus in the bloodstream—fell to undetectable levels. Michael regained enough strength to dance again for his own pleasure, though not professionally. When he developed anemia (another common AZT side effect), we tried a new drug called erythropoietin, a naturally occurring blood hormone that stimulates the production of red blood cells in the bone marrow. He did well with it and required fewer blood transfusions to keep his blood count in a reasonable range.

One day in fall 1991, when he had been my patient for about four years, Michael came to the clinic with abdominal pain and fever. His CD4 count, which the AZT initially kept fairly high, had dropped into the teens. I feared that the cause was mycobacterium avium complex (MAC), an opportunistic infection common among people with profound immune deficiency from HIV. We admitted Michael to the hospital for a workup; his mother, Peggy, with whom I also had become close, traveled from their native Louisiana to be with him and Evan.

By Michael's third day in the hospital, his abdominal pain was severe. I suggested a procedure that might help us diagnose and relieve it. But Michael had decided, with his partner's and his mother's blessing: no procedure. No more was to be done.

I ordered extra morphine to ease Michael's pain and sat at his bedside for the last time. How utterly cruel, I thought: After he willed himself to live for all those weeks on the ventilator, now he's going to die, and we won't even know the cause. I apologized to Michael for that—and without hesitation, he said that if it would help us treat others in the future, he'd gladly give permission for us to do an autopsy. He said it without emotion; I cannot even remember it that way.

Michael's death was peaceful. The following day, the autopsy showed the cause of his pain was an intestine so riddled with MAC infection that it had telescoped in on itself and become obstructed. We did not know this possibility before; Michael's autopsy equipped us to quickly recognize and manage it in future cases.

To the last, Michael made the most of his artistic calling. In life, he had delighted audiences with that exquisitely honed dancer's body. In death, he gave us what was left of it for the benefit of others.

———

I met Carol Ann Linn in 1987 when I was an ID fellow at UAB and she was a nurse working for the American Red Cross. We put together a week-long crash course for police and other first responders, "AIDS 101," to bring them up to speed on everything from the needs of HIV/AIDS patients to the safety of the US blood supply. The thirty-something mother of two sons, Carol had a sweet temper and a gentle Alabama accent, and people took to her immediately. While I went on to run the 1917 Clinic, Carol moved among nursing jobs, including at UAB.

In 1994, when I needed a nurse to fill a temporary position, Carol got the assignment and joined the ranks of our staff heroes. To this day, Carol plays down her role: "Because I was coming off several years as a psychiatric nurse, the 1917 Clinic patients knew more than I did about HIV treatment. It was their life, they ate and slept and breathed it, so if I didn't know something, they were more than happy to fill me in. They were just eager for any healthcare provider that was willing to work with them; I had never been in a setting where the patients so valued the staff."

I'll say what Carol is too modest to say. The patients also valued her for the same reasons I did, and still do: She is a generous, caring person and a gifted, conscientious nurse. When her temporary assignment was nearly done, I asked if she would come to work at the clinic long term, and she turned me down. Sweet but steely, she noted that our clinic staffers worked ridiculous hours "and you don't even pay well." I came up with a pay increase, and that helped her explain her decision to others. But more than anything, Carol joined the clinic—and is still there, nearly two decades later—because she cares so much about the patients.

On Carol's desk sits a picture of a movie-star-handsome young man in a tuxedo. That's Andy, one of the first patients Carol worked with at the clinic. He was about ten years older than Carol's own firstborn, and it's literally true that Carol and Andy became as close as family. You can hear it in the way she tells his story in her soft drawl:

"Andy was the kindest person you'd ever meet. Everyone in the clinic, including other patients, loved him; he was a social butterfly. Several years before I met him in 1995, Andy and his partner, 'Boyd,' decided they wanted to have a child. So they found a surrogate, Boyd donated the sperm, and they had a son, 'Ned.'

"By the time of Ned's fifth birthday, they wanted to have a swimming pool party for him. Andy had developed a Kaposi's sarcoma (KS) lesion on his shin, but he was not going to let that stop him. He got a waterproof Batman tattoo and put it over the lesion so it wouldn't interfere with his son's party.

"Andy never complained. Even though he was doing everything we asked as far as HIV medications, the KS progressed, and soon it was rampant. There was some on his face, on his chest and back. From his waist down, it was just solid lesions. He ended up having his scrotum removed, having skin grafts on his penis, and he got lots of infections on his legs. As the KS progressed it robbed his skin and muscles of their blood supply, and the tissue died. At the clinic, when he walked in the door, people could smell the rotting flesh. At first, when they didn't know he was hearing them, other patients would say, 'What is that stench?!' But after they realized, they did everything they could not to hurt his feelings. And when he would come in for me to do his chemotherapy infusion, we would spray a citrus cleaner on paper towels and use a desktop fan to blow that citrus smell out toward the waiting room in order to cut down on the odor, so he wouldn't offend others.

"With all this progression of the KS came horrible, horrible pain. Andy developed such a high tolerance for the pain medications that we had to adjust them every month. I remember one night when Andy was in the hospital, Dr. Saag was not on service, and I was not on call but had left my pager on, just in case. Andy paged me saying he was in such unbearable pain that he wished he was dead, but the doctors at the hospital would not increase the dose. They didn't know his case and what a high tolerance he had developed to the pain medications, and they were afraid that giving him more could kill him.

"I went in to the hospital and talked to the staff, but they said they could not prescribe more. So I paged Dr. Saag, who was at home with his family, and he said, 'I'll be right there.' I went back to the clinic and got Andy's medication records, and Dr. Saag was able to show the records to the hospital team and persuade them to increase the dose.

"After the medication was administered and Andy's pain started to ease, he asked Dr. Saag to sit on one side of his bed and me to sit on the other. He wanted us to stay awhile and pray with him. He prayed that if it was God's will, he would live through the night, but if not, he would not be in pain anymore."

Andy survived that crisis, and a few more. Carol was relentless about finding ways to help him deal with the KS and the pain. When Ned had a baseball game, Carol would go to the ball field with Andy to help manage his wounds and dressings and wheelchair. When Andy attended the 1917 Clinic's annual spiritual retreat at a national park an hour away from Birmingham, Carol went with him, "and while the other people were doing sports or crafts, we would do his IV medication," she recalls, as if there were nothing extraordinary about that.

What Carol did find extraordinary was Andy's ability to live so joyfully in spite of everything. "One night while we were at the retreat, he called home and asked Boyd if he could say goodnight to Ned, but Ned was already asleep. So he asked Boyd to hold the phone by Ned's face so that Andy could just listen to him breathe. And when Andy got off the phone, his face was so full of love, and he said, 'Carol, isn't that the sweetest sound in the world, when your baby is sleeping soundly?'

"Andy was a good father, a good partner, a good son, and a good friend. And he was a good patient, no matter how the disease ravaged him."

Andy died April 14, 1998, during a brutal season for the clinic: A lot of patients were developing resistance to the only drugs we had for them, and within a matter of a few weeks, fifteen or sixteen had died. "It was really hard on the staff," Carol says now, "because it was the first time in years when we had had that many patients dying."

Carol still talks by phone occasionally with Andy's parents. When she calls, Carol says, Andy's mother still cries with fresh grief "even though he's been gone now for so many years."

Carol still keeps Andy's photo on her desk, she says, because "he was just a special guy, and he made me understand what's important. For Andy, what was important was the here and now, and living your life to the fullest you could live it."

Carol still kids me about something I said when I hired her. She was fretting that she hadn't started an IV in a while, and I said, "Carol, I can teach a monkey how to start an IV—but what you have can't be taught." She can joke all she wants about the first half of that statement; I hope she knows the truth in the second half of it.

Carol stayed at the clinic even when a loved one accused her of having "a death wish" because she worked with AIDS patients. Carol stayed at the clinic even though, when other parents learned where she worked, many wouldn't sit with her at their kids' ballgames or let her sons sleep over. Carol has stayed at the clinic through the years as our caseload has changed from mostly well-educated, often well-off people who could champion their own needs to people with less knowledge and significantly fewer resources to bring to the fight.

"So many of our patients now have little or no support system," she says, "but they can always talk to me. I don't always know what we'll be able to do. But I always say, 'Tell me what you need.'"

———

"David" was striding through an East Coast airport wearing his airline pilot's uniform on his way to captain a flight. Partway down the concourse, he could not catch his breath. After an examination revealed *pneumocystis* pneumonia (PCP), David retired from the airline. He moved home to Tuscaloosa to work as a private pilot and live with his mother, "Eva."

David was among the first patients at the 1917 Clinic. He became a

friend and also served as my unofficial mentor and guide to the gay community, a population from which I drew many of my patients but about which
I was largely ignorant. I knew that some of us were straight and some of us
were gay, but it had never meant much to me. David changed that.

Because he knew I meant well, David patiently answered my questions,
including some that I now realize may have seemed daft. I distinctly remember the moment when I hit him with that clueless-straight-guy classic: "So,
David, when did you know you were gay?" He smiled knowingly, paused,
and said, "Mike, I'll answer your question, but first I want you to answer
mine: When did you know you were straight?"

By answering in that way, David might have been gently mocking me—
and I definitely felt my face redden. But mostly, he was trying to help me
understand, honestly and viscerally. He followed up with this: "Let's say
you're walking down a street and it's just you, looking straight ahead. On
the left side of the street is Christie Brinkley, on the right side of the street is
Tom Selleck, and they're both naked. Who will you look at?" We each knew
the answers—ours, and each other's—without saying a word.

"None of us gets taught this," he said, looking at me kindly. "It's who
we are."

I got it. And I so appreciated David's ability to explain things, to serve as
an interpreter among the various professional and cultural groups in which
he and I both moved, that I recruited him for that role repeatedly. A former
Navy fighter pilot, David was a natural in social settings, a handsome, com-
pact man with a gregarious nature and a gift for public speaking.

As David continued to battle the PCP, hospitals in some of the hardest-
hit cities—Los Angeles, San Francisco, New York—began offering patients
a new therapy: inhaled pentamidine, an infection-fighting agent delivered
via a costly nebulizer apparatus. David was a candidate for the therapy, as
were a number of other patients at our clinic, which was then about a year
old. But our shoestring operation didn't have the money for the equipment to offer pentamidine. So when some patients who wanted the treatment threatened to march on the clinic to protest us not providing it, I was
beside myself.

I vented my frustration to David: "What the f—? I don't want news cameras covering protests outside this clinic, showing every bigot in the state where it is!" I could see how well this was going to go down in the dean's office. Besides, I had self-righteousness on my side: "We set up this damned clinic for these patients when they were outcasts, and now they're marching on me, on us? We are the *last* people on earth they should be marching on!"

Patiently, David talked me down. "You don't understand, Mike; it's not about you. They respect you. They like you. They like the clinic. But they're terrified and desperate and dying, and they've got to do something. It's the white coat they're marching on. It's the Establishment, which you represent, like it or not."

When I first conceived of an AIDS clinic and did the math about the burgeoning epidemic, it was scary how many patients would need care. Knowing that the 1917 Clinic couldn't serve them all, I devised training sessions for other providers called "What Every Physician Should Know about HIV." The training was offered at gatherings of primary care physicians, medical association meetings, and hospital grand rounds. Basically it was me with a microphone, posing my questions and the audience's questions to a patient with HIV—very often, David. Audiences were rapt as he described his background, including his hitch as a military fighter pilot, and his life since contracting the virus. He wasn't shy about nosy questions or squeamish about clinical ones. He never lapsed into self-pity. Only occasionally would he tear up when speaking of friends whom AIDS had claimed; by then, many of the rest of us were too teary-eyed to notice.

I never will forget the end of one session when, before an audience of 500 physicians at the State Medical Association's annual meeting in Montgomery, I asked David if he had any parting message. "We live in a very religious society," he observed, "and most of the people in this part of the country believe strongly in Jesus Christ. If anybody was to ask me how to find Jesus, I would say, 'You can find him at the University Hospital every day, on the sixth floor, providing care for the AIDS patients there. That's where Jesus lives.'"

In fall 1989, when David was fighting a third episode of PCP, we got him into a study for a potent new drug. In his case, it was too potent; the drug killed off so many of the infectious microorganisms so fast that David's lungs became inflamed and further compromised. As he struggled to breathe, we put him in the ICU with a mask to deliver more oxygen.

Nowadays, when we use that potent drug on PCP patients, we know to administer steroids in advance to protect the lungs against inflammation. In David's day, we didn't know that—that, and so much more.

David had made his wishes clear: "No more ventilators, Mike." No putting him on a breathing machine when he became unable to breathe for himself—and we both knew that time might be near. Before departing for Louisville to spend Thanksgiving with family, I looked in on David and found him sitting up in bed in the ICU wearing a full oxygen mask that covered most of his face. Knowing he couldn't speak through the mask, I said a few words and gave him a wave. David raised a gaunt arm and flashed me a thumbs-up sign. At that moment, I could see him in his flight suit, in his F-14 cockpit, in the clouds. On his last mission.

Two days later, the hospital telephoned me at my parents' home. I knew it was news about David, so I took the call in the back of the house, where my relatives wouldn't see me sobbing.

I suppose it's a confession of some kind that, as a straight, happily married man, I want the world to hear me say I really loved David. Love is the only right term. He was a great guy. All these years later, when I think of him, I wonder "what if?" What if David, and others like him, could have held on for another five years? What if the triple-drug cocktail we call HAART (highly active antiretroviral therapy) had been developed sooner? What if my progress in the lab had been faster, or if I had worked harder or smarter?

Then, I swear, I actually hear David's voice: "Mike, it's not about you."

Of course that's right. It isn't about caregivers torturing ourselves with "what if" questions. It's about doing the best we can do for patients, whatever that is at the time. In David's time, while we were doing the best we could do, he and hundreds of thousands of others died.

What's most tortuous for me when I remember David is that, years after we lost him, the US healthcare system is so, so far from doing the best we can do for other patients. We are failing, knowingly failing, and we seem unable to stop the failure. Perhaps this, too, is not about me. But I take it personally, with the same intensity I feel when I say, slowly and deliberately and without reservations: I loved David.

———

"Jacob" was the first Jew I took care of who had HIV. We connected through that shared identity, that sense of being *lonsman*, the Yiddish term for a member of our tribe. Jacob was a gay man in his early thirties from a family of modest means. He had thinning reddish brown hair that flowed down below his collar, and he wore wire-rim glasses that gave him a kind of hippie-intellectual look. Jacob was energetic, fun to be around, and constantly in and out of medical peril for the nearly five years that I knew him.

Just weeks after he was found to be HIV-positive and diagnosed with PCP, Jacob was started on AZT. He developed profound anemia; eventually, we pulled him back from that brink with blood transfusions. He then developed mycobacterium avium complex, which ultimately spread throughout his body. For the last year of his life, we could not get his CD4 count above single digits. Through it all, Jacob's loved ones were wonderfully supportive and engaged in his care. If I saw Jacob in the hospital, odds are I also would see one or more parents, siblings, rabbis, and friends from the local synagogue he attended.

One day late in another of Jacob's lengthy hospital stays, I was making rounds trailed by a half dozen house staff and medical students. I asked them to wait at the door as I entered Jacob's room. What I saw was a tableau an old master could have composed for a painting called *The Death Watch*. The light fell just so across the bed and the still, white-faced figure in it. The mother, father, brother, and sister-in-law hovered at the bedside, leaning in with grim, watchful faces; their rabbi stood in the background providing moral support.

I could not spare Jacob's relatives this grief, and I did not want to intrude on it. But they motioned me to come nearer, so I did, as the students looked in from the doorway. I walked to the foot of the bed and stood with them in silence.

Knowing that the family was hanging on every spike and dip of the EKG monitor as if it could be Jacob's last heartbeat, I reached over and disconnected the monitor. I had seen too many instances where, after a patient died, the heart still might tick a random beat that would make the family think the patient had come back to life. I didn't want Jacob's loved ones to experience that horror on top of what they were experiencing already.

I knew there were no words, but I could not help trying. "I'm so sorry," I said, and my voice cracked. "I'm so sorry there was nothing more I could do."

I imagine they said something, but I was beyond hearing. I hugged Jacob's father, I hugged his mother, and I rested a trembling hand briefly on Jacob's forehead. Then I walked out of his room and down the hall a few paces before I collapsed against a wall, fighting sobs. I raised a hand to the medical students, signaling them to give me a minute.

I didn't feel embarrassed about them seeing me cry, but I didn't want to go on with rounds until we discussed it. We found a small conference room, and as best I can remember, I told them something like this:

"What you just witnessed is what being a physician is all about. Nobody is going to teach you that you should let yourself feel like this. You'll probably hear the opposite—that you should keep a 'clinical distance' and find ways to protect yourself from feeling. That it will cloud your judgment or make you seem weak or less professional.

"That's bullshit. If you don't let yourself feel this, you're missing out on what really matters. You want to be a healer? This is the cost. This is the essence of what we do."

———

When I talk about my patients who died, I don't always choke up. But more often than not, I do.

When one of my patients dies, it's failure, it's loss, it's injustice. It's anger about the lost potential of a talented young person and frustration that I couldn't do more—that my magical thinking didn't turn into magical healing, that I couldn't will this to come out differently. I am so invested in that patient's survival that when he or she dies—and if it's unprofessional to admit this, too bad—a part of me dies, too.

This feeling is not unique to me. I see it in almost every qualified HIV provider, the nurses, the social workers, the nurse practitioners, the doctors. When we provide care to someone, it's a partnership, often a very urgent and heartfelt one. When we don't succeed, we forfeit our partner. It is a cruel loss, especially when experienced over and over.

I know the passage of time is supposed to diminish grief, but for me it also compounds the loss. This isn't the kind of loss you feel when a colleague is leaving or when you suffer a professional or political setback; I can cope with those. This is a sense of enormous, collective loss; the almost unfathomable loss of the potential of all these people whose lives ended so prematurely. What would they have done? What could they have been? How much might they have achieved for themselves and for others? The empty spaces where the rest of their lives should have been—this is, to me, the enduring tragedy of AIDS.

What motivates me not only to stay within the healthcare system but to seek its change is here. What drives me is the truth I heard myself say in the wake of Jacob's death: This is the essence of what we do. Any system that puts profits ahead of lives has no right to use the term "healthcare." That it would actually be *less* costly, regardless of the illness they face, to treat people early and well is a stinging irony. That we would tolerate such suffering, turn a blind eye to such dying, is obscene.

Chapter 7

BEYOND THE CLINIC

S ome people claim to have photographic memories. I would say I have a cinematic memory. When I witness something that seems impor- tant, my brain retains it with all the action and detail—the setting, the players, the dialogue—of a pivotal movie scene.

I've captured these kinds of memories while attending International AIDS Conferences. From the 1986 Paris meeting, for example, I remember the conference room, the wallpaper, the speaker's lilting accent as I heard the new term being used: in French, Virus Immunodéficitaire Humain and its three-letter abbreviation, pronounced vay-ee-ahsh. This was a far cry from the inaccurate pejoratives of GRID and 4-H Syndrome, names implying that only some cursed fraction of us were at risk. Now the virus that causes AIDS should be known officially and worldwide as HIV, leaving no doubt about who was vulnerable: *humans*. Period.

The next year, the conference was in Washington, D.C., at the hotel nick- named the "Hinckley Hilton" after would-be assassin John Hinckley shot President Reagan there in 1981. I remember taking my seat in the cavern- ous Hilton ballroom, about ten rows from the dais and surrounded by a Who's Who of AIDS research scientists. To address this august gathering, the Reagan administration had sent the sitting vice president, George Her- bert Walker Bush.

To welcome the vice president, protesters from ACT UP were outside the hotel venting their frustration at what their official statements called the US government's "lack of interest and leadership in the AIDS crisis." The organization—full name, AIDS Coalition To Unleash Power—had formed in New York City a few months earlier under the leadership of playwright and gay activist Larry Kramer. In 1982, Larry had founded a pioneering AIDS service organization, Gay Men's Health Crisis (GMHC). But Larry soon split with that group over the more political, confrontational approach he deemed necessary to overcome what he saw as inaction and apathy about the disease. Whether I heard him on a loudspeaker at a protest or saw his words shouting from a printed page, the blunt phrases Larry used ring in my memory: "People are DYING! What are you DOING?" "This is a plague! And all of you are treating it like another day at the office!" "Maybe if you were infected with the virus you would feel and act differently!" "Stop farting around and GET TO WORK!" But his f-word wasn't "farting."

The language on the streets became more raw and the protesters' expressions got more furious with every week that passed as their friends died of AIDS and their president could not bring himself to say the word within range of a microphone. The Reagan administration was seen by many in the AIDS community as not only disinterested but perhaps secretly pleased to see the population shrinking. After all, their demographic—chiefly, young, gay, urban males—were not likely to vote the GOP's way. Less than twenty years after the police raid and resulting riots at New York City's Stonewall Inn marked the birth of gay rights activism, the movement was still young and largely unrecognized. At the time, I was typical of Americans who knew all about KKK bombings and Dr. King's famous speech, but had no clear memory of the Stonewall riots and no particular sympathy for gay rights. Sitting inside the Hinckley Hilton, I was just beginning to understand why protesters, fearful and in pain, were willing to entertain even incredible rumors about AIDS, such as the claim that government agents had planted the virus to kill off gays. Very slowly, it was dawning on me.

Inside the ballroom, the audience was not patients or protesters, but physicians and scientists. When Mr. Bush rose to speak, I'm sure he expected a polite welcome, and he got it: Most of the audience stood and applauded.

But then, as people began settling back into their seats, about a third of the audience remained standing.

In a silent wave of motion that swept across the ballroom, those who remained standing turned 180 degrees, putting their backs to Bush. And for the duration of his remarks—maybe twenty minutes—they held that stance, obviously according to a plan (though one that no one had mentioned to me). From where I sat, the vice president looked visibly shaken, as if he didn't know what to do with this proper, prestigious, professional crowd's act of defiance. I was impressed with the resourcefulness of my colleagues who'd found a way to say to the vice president, *We're turning our backs on you like your administration has turned its back on us and our patients.*

My head was still spinning from that event when I squeezed into a conference room with an overflow crowd. Sitting cross-legged on the floor in front of the chairs, I craned my neck to see the speaker's presentation— and almost drooled over the possibilities. A Cetus Corporation biochemist named John Sninsky was explaining innovations in polymerase chain reaction (PCR) which made it possible to isolate a DNA sequence and copy it a virtually infinite number of times. As I scribbled numbers from his talk, all I could think was: This could transform the way our lab looks at the AIDS virus.

With PCR, we could accurately *quantify* the amount of virus in the bloodstream. Think what that would mean: We could tell how much virus was present and follow the actual *activity* of drugs. (Sninsky's colleague, Kary Mullis, who invented the PCR technique, would win the Nobel Prize for his achievement, and his discovery would form the foundation for UAB's later work on quantitative PCR.) After the session, when I asked Sninsky if the PCR might be used to quantitate the amount of virus in the bloodstream, he said no, because the PCR technology was so sensitive that even slight variations in the test processes might lead to wild overestimation or underestimation of the number of viruses present. My enthusiasm was undiminished. Magical thinking had been inspired.

A year after Washington, in 1988, the conference was in Stockholm. There, I first saw the term protease inhibitor, the experimental drug that could prevent an already-infected cell from producing more copies of itself by inhibiting the enzyme responsible for the maturation of the virus into an infectious particle. I also saw a shift in focus from pure science to more patient-centered concerns: For the first time, the conference hosted a display of the Names Project AIDS Quilt, by then grown to more than 8,000 panels commemorating lives lost. I hadn't been taking care of patients long enough to see names of any of them on the quilt, but I remember vividly the grief on the faces of dozens of providers as they recognized the name of one of their own. I was seeing quilt panels; they were seeing faces.

In the United States in 1988, the federal government mailed 107 million homes an educational pamphlet, "Understanding AIDS." The government also named a brilliant and dedicated physician, Anthony Fauci, to be acting director of the National Institutes of Health's new Office of AIDS Research. And to support research on the virus, NIH set up seven Centers for AIDS Research at universities around the country, including one at UAB. What finally moved the US political establishment to take these fairly ordinary steps? For those who were counting, it was 82,362 cases of AIDS reported nationwide—and 61,816 recorded AIDS-related deaths. And at the end of the year, the presidential vote count sent George H. W. Bush to the White House, bringing with him a tradition of silence on AIDS steadily maintained by his boss, The Great Communicator.

Even in the thick of the epidemic, I saw physicians and scientists making gains against the virus, and that kept my natural optimism afloat. But as for the politicians and power brokers, the opinion makers and influential institutions—that was another story. I spent much of my life wanting to think the best of people in such positions of stature. But time and again, what these "leaders" did and said about HIV/AIDS—or, more often, what they *didn't* do or say—knocked the rose-colored glasses off my face.

I never wanted to believe the bitter joke that one of life's great lies is, "Hello, I'm from the government, and I'm here to help you." I was raised by a man who'd bent over an explosive device and won a Purple Heart. He came home grateful to be an American, and he taught his children why gratitude was appropriate. I preferred to think that if America's politicians and public servants fully understood the HIV/AIDS crisis and what they could do to help arrest it, they would embrace new strategies as a civic and moral duty.

I wasn't quite as idealistic as Jimmy Stewart's character in the classic movie *Mr. Smith Goes to Washington*—but I was close.

Dr. Saag Goes to Washington was my personal miniseries. Several times when I was planning to be in Washington, D.C., for medical events, I requested meetings with US House and Senate members, chiefly those from Alabama and those assigned to committees governing healthcare policy. The research we were doing at UAB was yielding lots of new information about what worked (and what didn't work) in HIV/AIDS treatment and prevention. We were one of the seven outposts in which funds were being invested and on which hopes were being hung. I felt certain that our findings could help Congress craft more effective policy and get the most bang for each federal buck spent on the crisis. I went to Capitol Hill knowing that if they knew what we knew, they'd do things differently.

A time or two, an actual lawmaker stepped into one of the meetings ever so briefly to say hello or to pose for a "grip-and-grin" photograph shaking hands with me. But more frequently on these appointments, I never saw the elected representative. I shared my research findings with legislative aides, many of whom appeared to have little knowledge of the field and even less real interest. My overwhelming impression was that the meetings were designed not to inform the lawmaker but to appease me, a constituent with too many titles after my name to be ignored completely.

At the same time, some lawmakers' staff aides did seem to take the information I offered them seriously. They took notes and asked follow-up questions. One aide, who had worked in medicine before joining a Senate staff, surprised me with this statement: "Do you know how refreshing this is, a doctor who walks in the door and has data to back up what he's advocating?" No, actually, I didn't know. I'd never imagined that coming prepared to back my case with facts would make me an outlier on the Hill.

After each Hill visit, I saw the situation more clearly. All day every day, legislators get requests to do things from people who have powerful constituencies, favors to trade, money to donate, votes to leverage. Some of those people, like me, bring data and ask for time to argue their cases. If lawmakers and their aides tried to listen to even a fraction of those who petition them, they'd be utterly overwhelmed. So they book their meetings and formulate their positions based on some combination of interest, obligation, and partisanship. And then they go into session with fellow lawmakers knowing full well that having fact-based positions matters far less than having a majority.

During one of my Capitol Hill visits, I was attending several events with a friend I'd made, a onetime member of the US House of Representatives. He'd retired at age fifty and had gone into the private sector. He was a moderate, Heartland Republican who told me he'd originally come to Congress bursting with energy and altruism. He'd left Congress voluntarily after romping to huge majorities in every election; in the end, he'd served most of two decades. He'd been out of Congress about five years when, one sunny morning, we entered the imposing Rayburn House Office Building together. I was still chatting to him when I realized he wasn't next to me; he'd lagged behind, clinging to the hallway wall. His face was blanched as if he had turned suddenly ill.

I went back and asked, "Are you okay?" He looked at me, drew a long breath, and said as he stared down the long hallway, "I'd forgotten how much I hated it."

By "it," he meant the polarization and frustration, the grandstanding and self-serving pettiness that ultimately drove him out of politics. He'd arrived decades earlier, enthusiastic about conversations with those who agreed with him and those who didn't. He'd expected a single mission focused on serving the American people. He had come with the same naïveté that I'd brought on my first visit. And when he chose not to run for reelection in the mid-1990s, he made his decision based on his own private grief that "we can't serve others anymore because we're all so focused on our own positions. We live in stalemate defending our own egos and blaming the other side for stalemate."

After our event in the Rayburn Building, my friend took me to the south wing of the Capitol to have lunch in the members' dining room. He introduced me to some members he used to serve with, including one lawmaker who was almost his political opposite: a very liberal Democrat from an urban East Coast district. I had barely told that lawmaker what I did for a living when he launched into a rant about his own work: How he had gone into politics to get things done, to help people, to make a difference. How he felt stymied at every turn by the opposition party, by the bureaucracy, by the status quo.

I tried to keep a composed, "clinical distance" expression on my face as he spoke—but I was floored. My first thought was: *This guy doesn't know me from Adam, but he's so frustrated that he's pouring his heart out to me like I'm his psychotherapist!* And my next thought was: *This has got to be one of the most dysfunctional places on earth.*

That second thought has stayed with me to this day. Making healthcare work better for all Americans would be a tall order even for a bold, collaborative Congress. But we don't have one of those. What we have now is a gridlocked, slur-slinging Congress that earns record low public approval ratings: In a February 2012 Gallup poll, just one in ten Americans approved of the job Congress was doing. Asked to rank their preferences among a variety of objects in 2013, Americans ranked cockroaches as preferable to Congress.

Even its own members call the legislative branch dysfunctional: That's the word Maine Republican Senator Olympia Snowe used in announcing she would leave the Senate in 2012 after eighteen years of service. "The political paralysis has overtaken the environment to the detriment of the good of this country," Snowe told an interviewer. "We are not working out issues anymore. We are working on a parallel universe, with competing proposals, up or down votes . . . That's not how our founding fathers envisioned the United States Senate and the overall Congress."

On healthcare issues, I'm one of many Americans who see Washington politics as part of the problem. But, on the flip side, I am *not* expecting politicians to devise the solution, certainly not single-handedly. From the beginning of the HIV/AIDS crisis, our stigmatized, isolated patients could not count on any institutional deliverer stepping in to speak for them, to nurse them, to insure them. In the early days, it was hard to find people even to clean up after them: At San Francisco General and other hospitals, laundry room workers would burn AIDS patients' linens that they were too afraid to wash. So one of the earliest lessons of the HIV/AIDS fight was to cast a wide net for allies at all levels—to cultivate awareness, understanding, and support among community, charitable, and religious groups, as well as civic and political organizations.

For my part, seeking allies in Birmingham, I went straight to the top: my father-in-law. Leonard Weil, a respected local leader, generously gave me introductions to a broad range of community and benevolent groups. I also put out feelers to representatives of faith communities. Surely we could count on help from Christians, Jews, and others whose scriptures talk at length about ministering to the sick?

Leonard Weil was sitting on the dais to provide my introduction and for moral support when I addressed a luncheon meeting of the Downtown Rotary Club of Birmingham in spring 1992, more than a decade into the American epidemic. In preparing my remarks, I had wondered: What could I tell these people in twenty minutes to both educate them about HIV/ AIDS and build support for the 1917 Clinic's work? I showed my slides of pie charts and reeled off the statistics. I noted that, starting in 1986, AIDS had become the number one killer of men ages 20–44. When I finished, audience members were silent.

In my audience that day, unknown to me, was Ed Dixon. Retired after a successful career at an international construction company, Ed ran a family foundation that made grants to the community, and he was active in his church, Vestavia Hills Methodist. A few days after the luncheon, Ed telephoned me, introduced himself, and asked one question: "Dr. Saag, what do you think is the most important thing that could be done that isn't already being done to stop the epidemic?"

After thinking for a few minutes, I told Ed I thought it was essential to help parents talk frankly to their children about sex and AIDS, which would demystify the subject and help the youngsters protect themselves. I wondered aloud whether local churches might spearhead such an effort, and Ed responded with glee: "I can't believe you suggested that!" In the 1960s and 1970s, Ed had helped lead a church movement to share information and reduce stigma associated with cancer. He was eager to spearhead a similar effort focused on AIDS—and his foundation would provide starter funding for it. It was one of those moments when a Jew sees real evidence for a Christian miracle.

From the Dixon Foundation funding, I carved out money to hire a full-time chaplain whose role would be to ignite a movement among church leaders in the community. The idea was to launch the initiative with a half-day retreat that would make the case to the clergy. Surely they would "get it" and join with us in partnership on this issue.

Ultimately, this led to one of those odd bounces of fate that my family so loves. In spring 1993, as I was pulling together the agenda for the retreat, I reconnected with a third cousin I barely knew—and who would become both my patient and one of my staunchest allies in the fight against HIV/AIDS.

Mary Fisher is the granddaughter of Papaharry and Flohoney Switow, the great-uncle and great-aunt who had been like an extra set of grandparents to me. Mary's mother, Marjorie Switow, had grown up in Louisville in our rowdy, extended family. Marjorie's first husband had left her to raise two young children on her own, Mary and her brother, Phillip. Mutual friends subsequently introduced Marjorie to Max Fisher, an accomplished business-man and Republican Party leader from Michigan. In 1953, Marjorie mar-ried Max and moved her children from Louisville to Detroit for a new life with their adoptive father.

As the decades passed, I'd see Mary occasionally at family events and was generally aware of her life's course: growing up in affluence, graduating from a fine prep school, working as a television producer and then as the first female "advance man" at the White House during the presidency of Michi-gan's Gerald R. Ford. After both Ford and Mary had left the White House, she pursued a promising art career, married a fellow artist, and began to raise two sons with him in Florida.

I did not know in July 1991 that her marriage had faltered, a mean divorce had occurred, and Brian, by then her ex-husband, had called to tell her that he'd tested positive for HIV. When Mary went in for testing, she learned that she also had been infected (although, fortunately, her sons were not). In the following months, Mary's mother Marjorie quietly sought my counsel, which I gladly shared. I knew Mary's treatment was in the hands of superb physicians and I wanted to respect her privacy, so I never contacted Mary myself.

I watched with pride in early 1992 as Mary went public with her status in an interview with newswoman Diane Sawyer and became an advocate for

AIDS awareness and prevention. She delivered, and epitomized, a message that was hugely important: *If a straight, white, suburban, Republican mom could get the AIDS virus, so could you.*

In the summer of that presidential election year, the Democrats featured AIDS activists in primetime speeches at their nominating convention. That put pressure on Republicans planning their convention, and they offered a speaking slot to Mary. On my television screen the night of August 19, she looked small, fragile, and lovely behind the podium in the cavernous Houston hall, her blonde hair perfect and a red AIDS ribbon glittering on the collar of her dress.

The earlier days of the convention had been full of divisive rhetoric. In what came to be known as "the 'culture war' speech," commentator Pat Buchanan declared that the debate over social and religious issues amounted to a "war going on in our country for the soul of America."

Perhaps convention organizers thought that because Mary was a longtime member of the GOP fold, her remarks would echo the party orthodoxy. But in a breathtaking, historic speech, Mary did something much bolder. She challenged Republicans "to take a public stand no less compassionate than that of the president and Mrs. Bush," who had been personally supportive of Mary, her sons, and Marjorie and Max. Then Mary spoke to all the rest of America—to those touched, and to those as yet untouched, by the virus:

"To the millions of you who are grieving, who are frightened, who have suffered the ravages of AIDS firsthand: Have courage and you will find comfort," she said. "To the millions who are strong I issue the plea: Set aside prejudice and politics to make room for compassion and sound policy."

The speech vaulted Mary to the forefront of AIDS activism and made her a star of the speaking circuit. Though I still feared breaching her privacy by calling, I really wanted to tell her how much I admired what she was doing. And then came the perfect excuse: Cathy Friedman, a friend from Birmingham's Temple Emanu-El, wanted Mary to speak there. Could I relay the invitation? The timing was ideal: I could invite her to speak at the temple, and also at our AIDS clergy retreat.

When I telephoned Mary, she was so eager and gracious that we immediately began thinking bigger. Rather than bring her to Birmingham for those two events, we would organize a whole weekend. Soon, she was booked to speak at events for caregivers, physicians, and local churches. She ultimately would give three sermons: at Temple Emanu-El, at Ed Dixon's mostly white and suburban Vestavia Hills Methodist church, and at the historic, mostly black 16th Street Baptist Church on the thirtieth anniversary of the bombing that killed four little girls attending Sunday school.

"Awed" is not too strong a word for how Mary and I felt to be at that church on that anniversary, her to speak and me just to attend. If some Americans remained unmoved when black men were lynched by white-robed Klansmen, none could ignore the murder of four daughters dressed in their Sunday best that fateful morning in September 1963. The bombing was a watershed event in the civil rights movement, the moment when a critical mass of national media, northerners and southerners alike, finally rallied to the cause.

The pastor at 16th Street, the Rev. Christopher Hamlin, was brave to invite Mary on two counts. A white woman taking the pulpit on that hallowed day wasn't received well by some parishioners. And black churches generally found it difficult to discuss AIDS given religious taboos about sexuality and drug use. The congregation for Mary's sermon was not large, but those in attendance heard a soul-stirring sermon. Mary titled it "To Rise from the Ashes," in honor of the parents who pulled their slain daughters from the bombed-out church and the congregation that struggled to rebuild it. Mary preached on the Old Testament story of Job, who had also wound up in the ash heap, a "blameless and upright man" struck by plague after plague. She likened Job's plight to the congregation's grief at the bombing deaths, and to her own agony when she learned she was infected. At these times, she said, it's worth remembering that even Job doubted God's presence.

"In the months that followed my diagnosis," Mary told the congregation, "I found out where God was. He was there. He was there more surely than the virus itself, giving my life new purpose and new meaning. . . ."

> Where was God when the bomb tore apart the bodies of children and adults? He was there, in the ashes, waiting to comfort those who mourned. . . . He was there in the hours of

rebuilding, turning anger to commitment. . . . He was there when Dr. Martin Luther King—standing over the small, white coffins—promised a day when these children would look down on a nation of brotherhood. . . He was there when you, the members of this church, built not a tombstone remembering human agony but a temple dedicated to human freedom. . . .

If you listen today as AIDS pilgrims march by this rebuilt sanctuary, you will hear the same question whispered there. The million and a half or two million Americans headed toward a withering, wasting death are haunted by the question: 'Where is God?' The time is long overdue for those who claim to be washed in God's grace to demonstrate that grace—by reaching out to those who suffer, by demanding justice, by pouring out compassion. By going into the streets and carrying the pilgrims home to God when they've grown too weak to walk.

I do not believe that some of us are less than human for the color of our skin or for the virus in our veins, because I believe we are all God's children. Therefore, when justice rolls down like a river, it will wash not only the back of the slave who did not ask for his beating but also the fevered brow of the patient who did not ask for his virus.

Mary's sermon culminated in an utterly personal plea. "You do not contract this disease by loving us, or by comforting us, or by taking up the cry for justice. When this service has ended, you may avoid me or embrace me; you may shun me or you may hug me. Neither can give you AIDS, but one can give me comfort. . . ."

After the service, the scene in the church foyer spoke volumes about the congregation's pain and Mary's gift for sharing it. I was assigned to get Mary to her next event on time and was about to tell her we had to go. But before I could reach Mary, one of the church ladies approached her; I gave them a moment to share a short, quiet conversation and then a heartfelt hug. As that parishioner left, I again tried to approach—but then another woman engaged Mary in the same way and, after her, several more. They formed a silent circle around where Mary stood, each waiting her turn at a discreet distance. Then, one by one, they came, they spoke, they hugged and sometimes wept.

After the fifth or sixth person had been with Mary, I'd drawn close enough to overhear a few words. "I lost my son to AIDS," one whispered to Mary. Another said, in a hushed voice that only Mary and I could hear, "I lost my brother." They had been suffering in silence, not daring to tell other congregants how their loved ones died.

When Mary and I discussed the scene afterward, we reflected on AIDS's terrible power to isolate—but also recognized that isolation is a side effect less of the virus than of our culture. What is a church or synagogue supposed to be, if not a community where people can share their burdens and sorrows? The experience made me more grateful than ever for Mary's presence at the last event of the weekend, the kickoff of our project to train more Birmingham clergy to do HIV/AIDS education.

As 1993 ended, the plague had been roaring for a dozen years, and yet so many cultural, political, and religious institutions were still looking away. Just when I needed an antidote to encroaching cynicism, I met Malcolm Marler—on Christmas Eve, no less, in a twist of timing worthy of Frank Capra's film *It's a Wonderful Life*.

Maintaining a proud and much-joked-about tradition among Jewish physicians, I had volunteered to staff the clinic on December 24 (before taking my family out for a Chinese-restaurant dinner) so my Christian coworkers could be with their families. Patient appointments were light that afternoon, so I had time to interview a candidate for the clinic chaplaincy. In came Malcolm, a strapping Selma native with an easy laugh and a long church pedigree.

Malcolm's dad and granddad each spent fifty years as pastors in the Baptist church, in which Malcolm was raised, trained, and ordained. He also served as a youth minister in the Presbyterian Church and a pastoral minister in the United Church of Christ before joining the Episcopal Church. Malcolm had been away from Alabama for a couple of decades, but he wanted to move back from the East Coast to be close to his dad, who was ailing. Years later, Malcolm described our Christmas Eve meeting this way:

"Mike has this way of telling stories. In the first ten minutes after we met, he built a bridge from his Jewish tradition to my Baptist tradition, and from then on we just walked back and forth on that bridge all day long. I left that interview three hours later thinking to myself, 'That's somebody I want to work with.'"

When Malcolm described himself as "a child of God who is trying to find his way," that put him in step with almost every soul in the clinic. I offered him the job and was thrilled when he took it. But some of Malcolm's East Coast friends had misgivings, he later confided: "When I told them I was moving to Birmingham to be a chaplain at an AIDS clinic and try to help churches reach out to AIDS patients, they said to me, 'You've lost your mind.'"

In no time, Malcolm launched a program he called GRACE, an acronym for Giving and Receiving AIDS Compassionate Education. He invited groups of clergy, lay leaders, and members from area churches to attend "Friday Morning GRACE," weekly trainings where they could learn about the disease and about how to provide practical, emotional, and spiritual support to AIDS-affected people. To make it clear that we really were all in this together, Malcolm's customary greeting to his trainees went something like this: "Isn't it amazing that a physician who happens to be Jewish got together with a businessman who happens to be Methodist, and the two of them convinced a state-run university hospital system to hire a Baptist minister to reach out to people with HIV/AIDS and to all of you?"

Malcolm ran the GRACE program on what he called "the Head, Heart, and Feet model." He filled his recruits' heads with sound scientific information about HIV/AIDS that they could relay to their congregations. He softened their hearts by arranging interviews and meetings at the clinic in which patients shared their life stories. The program's last element was its most important: "feet," Malcolm's shorthand for concrete, specific action. What were the church personnel going to do with the knowledge and empathy they had just gained?

What many churches did was form support teams that adopted clinic patients as their team "friends." The volunteers' service to the friends could be anything from driving them to a doctor's visit or helping with prescriptions to providing creature comforts. The learning and personal bonds that developed were what made these teams so successful. When an affluent church adopted one of our desperately poor patients, I remember thinking that it would be interesting to see if they could relate. For all that the church might have showered on that woman, what she told them she really wanted was some home cooking. And so, most Sundays, the church team would prepare collard greens and grits and deliver them to the woman's threadbare home. To her, it was manna from heaven. To me it was proof that sometimes, "the best healthcare" is less about cost than about kindness.

Malcolm's work was not incidental to what we were doing; it was essential. We saw the consequences in patients' lives and health. But after a couple of years of building alliances with local faith communities, we still had no black churches participating in the GRACE program or other clinic outreach efforts. We figured that if we could get one high-profile black pastor to work with us, others might follow. And so Malcolm and I asked for a meeting with a legendary Alabama reverend. I knew the pastor by reputation, as a contemporary of Dr. King and the Rev. Joseph Lowery of the Southern Christian Leadership Conference. I also knew that two of the pastor's sons had died in our hospital of AIDS-related illnesses—but that when he preached their funerals, no cause of death was mentioned.

On the appointed day, we knocked at the door of the parsonage. The pastor's wife led us to a modest sitting room where the pastor welcomed us and asked what he could do for us. We explained the GRACE project and how important it was to gain church support in Alabama's black communities where the epidemic was surging. The pastor, a burly man, was known for his rafter-shaking preaching voice. But he lowered it almost to a whisper when he said, "I need to tell y'all something. Here's how black folk think about AIDS: Nobody wants to hear about it. It's just more bad news. We fought through slavery, we fought through segregation, we fought through the civil rights struggle. Then just as we're coming out of all that, here comes AIDS. We just can't handle it. It's too much."

He must have seen the disbelief on our faces. So the pastor tried again, and this time his voice was edged with pain. "The best way I can explain what you're up against is to give you a story. You know my sons died of AIDS. You know I buried them. After we lost our first son, our second son came to me and he told me that he had the virus. I spent a month or two thinking about how on earth I could tell my wife this. I figured we would need some time alone to discuss it."

He paused to draw a long breath, remembering. "We were going to be driving from Mobile to Birmingham, about a five-hour drive. I waited until about twenty minutes into the drive, as we had crossed the bridge coming out of Mobile, and I said to my wife, 'Dear, I am so sorry to tell you this: Our other son has been diagnosed with AIDS.' And immediately she put her hand up and she said to me, 'STOP. Stop. I do not want to hear anything about that.' And for the next four and a half hours, we rode in silence."

Malcolm and I told the pastor we understood—but we had to do something; we had to try to reach his community. Wasn't there anything he felt he could do to help us? "No," he said. "I'm sorry, I can't help you."

In a way, the pastor's story has a redemptive ending. Not long before his death, I'm pretty sure I saw him at an Alabama AIDS walk. From where I was, though, it was hard to tell where he was standing: with the activists, or on the sidelines. That's often how it was when we looked for powerful allies in the fight to stop AIDS. On any given day, community leaders might give the impression of standing with us, yet never quite make good. And whether they were with us or not, our burdens at the clinic didn't change: same big caseload, same small budget. But I've always wanted to believe that the experience of being a grieving parent had touched the powerful pastor, and that he stood with the activists in the end.

My tireless friend Malcolm kept running those GRACE trainings—for groups of twenty people, twelve people, or even six—almost every week for the better part of three years. The result was that by 1996, more than 100 support teams were operating in the greater Birmingham area. Then, as Malcolm recalls it: "Because the new medications were really helping patients, I began getting calls from our support teams saying, 'Malcolm, we don't think the friend we've sponsored needs us any more; he's getting better. What should we do?' My answer to that was: 'First, throw a party to celebrate this with your support team and your friend. After you throw the party, ask around and find someone else who's sick, start caring for them, and we'll get back to you.'" At the same time, Malcolm recalls, "We also began getting calls from congregations around the country asking how they could start this kind of program."

So Malcolm came to me to discuss what he called "our good problems": that some local AIDS patients no longer needed as much GRACE team support, and that other congregations wanted our help creating support team programs for a range of health needs. Malcolm wanted to be sure I didn't think he had forgotten his job description. "Mike," he said, "you hired me to be a chaplain in an AIDS clinic and reach out to our local community. Is it really okay if now I'm going out to teach people to create support teams not just for HIV/AIDS patients but for people with Alzheimer's and diabetes and cancer?"

I thought for a matter of seconds before answering him: "Malcolm, it's just perfect." As we took this model nationwide, we would not only be training faith communities to meet the real health needs of their neighborhoods. We also would be mainstreaming the discussion of HIV/AIDS—wrapping it right in with all the other conditions for which teams would extend sympathy and support.

The national Support Team Network was born. By 2006, Malcolm reckoned that the program had conducted 125 conferences in 37 states, training more than 5,000 participants who went on to establish more than 10,000 support teams. "We didn't have the staff to keep a good count of everything that developed," he admitted. "We just threw the training out there like handfuls of seeds, and a lot of them sprouted." Malcolm Appleseed.

In the evolving world of HIV/AIDS medicine, our goal always has been to make the most out of whatever we have. When faced with a challenge that seems insurmountable, we just go after it. We search for solutions; sometimes we find them, sometimes we don't. The only failure would be in not trying, in not doing everything humanly possible to get the best outcomes most of the time for the most patients possible.

And that, in my opinion, is how we ought to be approaching our whole healthcare system. We need never to let the system's flaws defeat us without making a full-out effort. And by "we," I mean all the providers, all the patients, all the insurers—every player in every part of the US healthcare system, in every zip code in the United States.

Despite more than because of my experiences on Capitol Hill, I'm convinced our legislative leaders have a critical and reforming role to play. Even when tangled in drama that seems mostly of their own making, they have the power of policy and the power of funding. There will be situations where we lose, but we have to keep believing that something will happen—some magic—and we will achieve what we're aiming for. We're going to get there, somehow, because we can't afford not to.

At risk of sounding preachy: The important word in what we'll achieve is WE. If this debate becomes about me or you, as opposed to about us, we've already failed. How healthcare is planned, delivered, funded, and improved cannot be about the individual. It must be about the collective, the community. The neighborhood.

Chapter 8

A BAD MODEL

I was born into a medical system where, when the bratty young patient ran off and climbed a tree, the friendly pediatrician coaxed him down and still had time to do an exam.

I graduated from medical school into a terrifying pandemic with no proven approaches to diagnosis, treatment, or prevention—so we improvised, learned as we went, and buried too many good people while working to save others.

I chose to be a bench researcher as well as a bedside physician, believing that both roles would equip me to help patients. It soon became clear that what my patients really needed me to be was a teammate—that is, a partner with them and the other healthcare players in their orbit.

After years of working on those partnerships, here's what I have concluded: When America's healthcare practitioners put our heads together with our patients and their loved ones and their payers (usually, insurers), patient care can almost always be made more efficient, appropriate, and costeffective.

But, too often, we haven't pulled together. We've treated each other like strangers—or worse, like rivals or nuisances or patsies. Our systems are designed too much for profits and not enough for patients; we've blamed each other for what doesn't work instead of working as neighbors to fix the problems. When attitudes like ours harden into policy, you get the kind of healthcare system America has today: wasteful, shortsighted, disorganized, ineffective. And the nightmare of trying to sustain good health in this system can be summed up in two words:

Ticket, please.

America's healthcare system is designed for the person who has the ticket. In an ideal world, every one of us has some form of payment that is our ticket into the system. But the first problem becomes clear at the turnstile where folks should come in: There's no single ticket. There's a vast menu of tickets, all the different types of insurance and noninsurance with all their different coverages and noncoverages, requirements, and rules. It's almost like Disney World: many different tickets, A through E, but only the prized E tickets would get you through waiting lines and onto the best rides.

In the United States, almost all of the elderly are insured through the Medicare program. The adequacy of Medicare coverage is debatable, but breadth of coverage is impressive. About 56 percent of the nonelderly—in other words, half of the rest of us—"received health coverage as a benefit through either their own or a family member's job" in 2011, according to the Kaiser Family Foundation (KFF), a nonpartisan and highly trusted source for health policy research and analysis. Another 6 percent purchased insurance on their own, KFF says, while about 20 percent had coverage through public programs for those with disabilities and/or very low incomes, such as Medicaid and CHIP (the Children's Health Insurance Program).

In the grand American traditions of free-market competition and "more is better" philosophy, we've been told that having lots of different insurance options is a virtue. In fact, in my opinion, having many options produces very little benefit and a great deal of misunderstanding, chaos, and inequity.

Despite all my years dealing intimately with healthcare and insurance, I struggled to help my daughter recently as she chose among her new employer's coverage options. Each one of us who is fortunate enough to be employed has to pick our ticket—that is, choose or design an insurance plan—based on information that most of us find insufficient and confusing. This dental coverage or that vision coverage? High deductible or low deductible? Most of us see a chunk of change going out the door every month for something that we're not happy to buy but afraid to do without. So when we're not sure what we're buying, we tend to choose the ticket that costs us the least up front. The A ticket instead of the E ticket, at least if we're paying for it.

And we don't know if we've chosen the right ticket until we have to use it. After you've actually needed your ticket and learned about its effectiveness, you generally cannot change or replace it.

So you have a health need, you walk in the door of a doctor's office, clinic, or ER, and you show your ticket. You hear, "You have a $30 copay." Or, "Your deductible is $1,000." Or, the most dreaded of responses, "We don't honor that here."

During the annual "open enrollment season" for insurance, you have a chance to switch to some other kind of ticket that might better serve your needs. But how do you know whether to change, or what to change to? What if you plan your coverage around your conditions and your health today, and then next month you are diagnosed with some new condition or your health takes a nosedive?

None of us fully grasps how screwedup The System is until we have to use it and find ourselves saying, "Oh no, I was sure I was covered for *that*—you mean I'm not?" Or, "All these years I've been paying and it can't get me what I need now?" How about "My child needs this $100,000 treatment to stay alive, but I don't have the $20,000 that's our portion to pay." In each of these circumstances and more, what we want to scream is:

"I HAVE A TICKET! CAN'T YOU HEAR ME?
WHY ISN'T THIS WORKING?"

That's the situation for the lucky ones, the ticket holders. What about the people who *don't* have a ticket? According to KFF, roughly 48 million Americans—about 18 percent of the population—did not have health insurance in 2011. These people know two things about The System: that it dispenses incredibly expensive care, and that it regards them as third-class citizens. As a result, these people try to avoid The System at any cost. So they go to the doctor only when they absolutely must, when a lump or pain or cough has become so bad that they can no longer stand it. Had they come in sooner, the disease might have been arrested. When they show up late with advanced disease, most are told that there's a small chance of recovery—but they'll still get a big bill. For them, bankruptcy looms, and what they are unable to pay is added to the cost of our care. The System gets its money one way or the other.

Here are three quick stories from a recent tour of duty I had on the general medical service at University Hospital that highlight the role tickets play and their unintended consequences:

- "Nancy" is a thirty-something woman who has a severe, unusual autoimmune disorder that is tough to control. Her disease was no longer responding to steroids and some other medications, and she needed a new, expensive, powerful anti-inflammatory drug that had to be given by injection twice a day. The new drug could be given as an outpatient, but her insurance company refused to pay for it, and she made too much money to be eligible for the compassionate use program by the company that made the drug. Her rheumatologist admitted her to my inpatient service in the hospital to ensure that she could get the medicine. On her second hospital day I received a call from the insurance company saying there was no indication for admission to the hospital and that she would get a bill for the hospital stay. Here is a woman who had "good insurance," a nice ticket, but it didn't cover what she needed when she needed it.

- "Butch" is a fifty-two-year-old man who was admitted to our team for evaluation of chest pain. His symptoms had started six weeks earlier, occurred every third or fourth day, and were very typical of angina, or chest pain from coronary artery disease. He had a strong family history of heart disease; his father had died of a heart attack at age forty-seven. I asked him, "When you had the chest pain, what did you think it was?" He replied, "I thought it was my heart. I thought I might be having a heart attack." I said, "So, your dad died from a heart attack and you thought you were having one two to three times per week for six weeks before you got brought in for evaluation. Why did you wait so long to be seen?" "I didn't have health insurance," was his response.

- "Corey" is a forty-nine-year-old man with very aggressive high blood pressure, which led to several "ministrokes" that muddied his thinking and made it difficult for him to keep up with his medicines. He had four recent admissions for what I call "HIBGIA" (the most common diagnosis known to man): "Had it Before, Got it Again," where his blood pressure on admission was 260/140 because he couldn't keep up with his complicated blood pressure regimen. I knew we couldn't send him home again to live by himself, and he had no family who could take him in. A boarding house would be ideal, but he had no income and no health insurance, and no boarding house or nursing home would take him. So he stayed on my service in perpetuity, taking up a bed in the hospital so that we could give him oral blood pressure medications. On one of our call nights I took a call from a physician at a sixty-bed rural hospital who wanted to transfer a thirty-four-year-old woman; she had had a fever for over eight days and he couldn't find a cause. I wanted to accept the patient in transfer, but UAB hospital was on "bed diversion," meaning there were no beds available to accept transfer patients. The hospital was full. So I had to turn down the transfer for someone who happened to have insurance (a ticket) because some (at least one) of our beds were occupied by people we couldn't discharge owing to our inability to find an appropriate place for them to go.

As a provider, it is my job to care for people; as a *provider,* I don't care if they have great insurance, meager insurance, or no insurance. But The System cares a lot. The System says to people without tickets, "We'll take care of you if we have to, but we don't want to. You're going to cost us money." To me, you're a patient. To The System, you're a pariah.

Say a fire destroys your home and you come to the hospital with life-threatening burns but no health insurance. Your care becomes a battle between the provider who says, "I'm going to care for this burn patient" and The System that says, "Man, these burn patients who don't have insurance are costing us a fortune." Then The System says, "In order to pay for this uninsured burn patient, we're going to increase the charges to the patients who have tickets." The insurance companies fully understand this. Their policyholders are being overcharged, but they have room to make adjustments that protect their profits. And if the policyholders pushed back too hard, The System (mostly hospitals and their owners, including investors, universities, and religious communities) would rebel or go bankrupt, thereby ending the gravy train for insurance companies.

This opaque "cost shifting" is an accepted way of life in US healthcare, and a huge contributor to the chaos, inefficiencies, and high overhead within the current system. And it is barely understood, it seems, by most of the public and the public's elected officials, who continue to believe that "if everyone has access, someone needs to pay." What do folks think is happening today? Last night when the impoverished and uninsured mother showed up at the ER with her cough and her child's pneumonia, who paid? We did. All of us who are insured, who pay taxes, who give contributions, who are Americans: We paid. We pay now, and a huge share of what we pay goes not to healing but to profits for those who live off the healthcare system, especially insurers.

For years, Drs. Steffie Woolhandler and David Himmelstein of Harvard University have studied healthcare financing and policy. Their research found that not only is America's $7,500 per capita healthcare cost much higher than in many other developed nations, but a stunning $2,000 of that per capita cost—more than a quarter—is eaten up by overhead. Since their research data is a few years old and all the cost trends are up, the healthcare and overhead costs are almost certainly higher by now.

Even though we pay more for healthcare than is necessary, some of America's ticket holders still manage to get by. But even Americans with tickets do not always get by. They impoverish their families trying to pay their medical bills. In other nations of the developed world, from Great Britain and Japan to Switzerland and Canada, you don't have citizens going bankrupt because of medical bills. But in the United States, with its supposed "best healthcare system in the world," nearly two-thirds of all personal bankruptcies are associated with healthcare debt, according to research Woolhandler and colleagues published in 2009.

What's more, a shocking three-fourths of those who declare a medical-related bankruptcy have health insurance.

The cost of care was an issue for Brian, a patient referred to me after he sought emergency room treatment. Had he not been worried about the cost, Brian would have seen a doctor when his headaches first progressed from bad to worse. But let me back up.

I met Brian and his partner, Joe, not long after they moved from Southern California to Auburn, Alabama. Brian was an artist, a bohemian who worked construction and retail jobs to pad his income from selling paintings and drawings. Joe had just completed his PhD and postdoctoral fellowship in plant biology, and he had been offered an assistant professorship in Auburn University's department of botany. While neither Brian nor Joe had ever *conceived* of living in the southern United States, they moved enthusiastically. Teaching at a major university was not only Joe's dream job, but it meant steady income and health insurance—a ticket!

Joe's ticket, however, was not transferable to Brian. Gay men did not, and in many places today still do not, have partner benefits. So before the couple left California, Brian bought an independent health insurance policy. The $800 monthly premium took a big bite out of Brian's earnings, so to help, Joe paid most of it. Despite the policy's cost and its high deductible for hospitalizations, Brian figured it was an adequate safety net for someone like him who'd always been very healthy.

Brian and Joe were still settling into their new home in Auburn when Brian's headaches began. They started at the base of his skull and were dramatically more painful whenever he coughed or sneezed—"like the top of my head would blow off," Brian reported. These are the classic symptoms of what Brian later was confirmed to have, cryptococcal meningitis. "Crypto" is caused by a fungal organism in the environment that most of us can breathe into our lungs without being harmed, thanks to our normal immune systems. If the immune system is impaired as it can be by HIV, the organism sets up shop. Then it causes pneumonia or, more often, infection and inflammation of the meninges, the layer of protective tissue that surrounds the brain. Inside the skull, spinal fluid bathes the brain and creates a cushion between it and the meninges. A healthy person's body creates about 500 milliliters of spinal fluid a day and reabsorbs the same amount, maintaining an even exchange of fluid. But crypto meningitis impairs that reabsorption so that the fluid accumulates in the skull, causing increases in intracranial pressure (ICP) that, if not relieved, can have devastating effects on the brain. To describe the pain associated with this as a "headache" is like thinking of a nuclear bomb as a firecracker.

On top of the headaches, Brian began experiencing confusion, impaired vision, and loss of hearing. On a Friday in early November 1988, Joe took Brian to the emergency department in Auburn, where he was seen by Dr. Allen Graves, once an infectious disease fellow at UAB. By that time, the rising ICP had rendered Brian blind and deaf, and the only way to get to the bottom of his condition was to perform multiple procedures, including a lumbar puncture. The procedure, commonly known as a spinal tap, is uncomfortable for some patients, excruciating for others.

For someone unable to hear or see, I can only imagine that it would be terrifying to be held tight and still by strangers' hands, then poked in the lower spine with a needle. But the procedure was essential, both to collect cerebrospinal fluid for analysis and to lower the pressure in Brian's skull. On the manometer used to measure ICP, a normal measurement is 50–100 mm of fluid. Brian's initial tap exceeded 550 mm, the highest reading on the instrument.

Allen transferred Brian to my care, and I was at the UAB hospital on Saturday afternoon when he arrived. He was on an ambulance stretcher, writhing back and forth, fighting the restraints the attendants placed on his arms and legs to keep him from hurting them or himself. Joe was at Brian's side, stroking his hand and speaking soothingly, but Joe's reassurance literally fell on deaf ears. It was an agonizing sight.

The subsequent taps we performed lowered the pressure in Brian's head enough that his confusion cleared and his hearing was partly restored. Once we could communicate with him and explain what was happening, Brian was able to relax and to talk about what he had been through. In his pain and confusion, he had imagined that he was being kidnapped and his captors had put something over his head so he couldn't see or hear. But he could certainly *feel*, and when Allen stuck the needle in his back, he was sure he was being tortured!

Brian's vision never returned—a profound loss for a man so passionate about making art. But we got the meningitis under control with medication, and after a few weeks of recovery, he was discharged from the hospital and went home to Auburn. Every two weeks, Joe would bring Brian back to Birmingham for another spinal tap as part of a study protocol he was on. On every visit, Brian arrived with a smile on his face and headphones on his ears. Though he regained only partial hearing after the crypto, Brian could hear recordings if he turned the volume up high. He especially loved listening to tapes of the 1960s TV sitcom *The Andy Griffith Show* because in his mind, he could "see" the episodes that he had loved watching as a child.

Brian had suffered what few of us will ever suffer, and he responded by creatively adapting and demonstrating an unquenchable spirit. Despite everything thrown at him—the painful procedures, the HIV diagnosis, the dismal future, the hearing and vision loss—he retained his zest for life.

I love humor and I bring it into my practice to a degree some find "unprofessional." Tough. It works for me, and it seems to work for most patients. Brian—half-deaf, blind, body being punctured in the name of research and facing a prognosis of greater difficulties ahead—was a total comedian who would match me joke for joke.

One week, Brian came to his clinic visit with a little something extra. When I pulled up his shirt to do the tap, on his spine where the needle would go was a sticker, burnt orange and navy blue. It was the logo of the Auburn University Tigers, the football archrivals of my cherished Crimson Tide. We both laughed until we could hardly breathe.

For Christmas 1989, about a year after Brian's transfer to UAB, he and Joe brought me a flat, rectangular present wrapped in holiday paper. It was a chalk drawing Brian had done for me since losing his sight. He had drawn a colorful tree, with a hand above it holding a watering can. On the water pouring from the can, he had scrawled "LIFE," and next to the hand, "DR. SAAG." The inscription at the bottom read, "Merry Christmas, Dr. Saag. Thanks for saving my life."

I hugged Brian and Joe as I thanked them, tearfully. In that moment, I really felt like American medicine was doing something right. We'd bought time for Brian, and he was a living gift to each of us.

But "bought" is the right word, because Brian's reprieve came at a price. Unable to work as he did before he lost his sight, Brian's income consisted of the $500 a month he received in Social Security disability. That princely sum, in the state of Alabama, made him too well-off to get insurance through

Medicaid; it was "above the threshold." So he clung to his existing health insurance policy although, in the year since the crypto diagnosis, the premium had soared from $800 a month to $1,200 a month. We'd found ways to treat his illness, but we were back to the same issue that had originally delayed Brian's entry into treatment: the high cost of healthcare.

In 2010, "the United States spent about $7,500 per capita on health care compared to an average of $3,300 in other rich countries," according to Gary Burtless, a senior fellow at the Brookings Institution, a nonprofit public policy research organization in Washington, D.C.

"If the nation obtained better-than-average health outcomes in exchange for its much-higher-than-average health spending, we would have little reason to complain," Burtless added on the Brookings website. "However, there is almost no evidence US health outcomes are better than those in other rich countries. A variety of statistics on mortality and morbidity suggest outcomes may be worse in this country than they are elsewhere."

This, in my estimation, is why The System stinks. In one of the most medically sophisticated nations on earth, I cannot accept the idea that we can't do any better.

While I'm railing against Washington, D.C., and our elected leaders, I will admit that many of them have tried. "The country has been on the verge of national health reform many times," says a KFF research report. But for the better part of a century, under both Republican and Democratic administrations, efforts to improve healthcare access, quality, and affordability have gone down to defeat repeatedly. According to the KFF report:

- President Franklin Roosevelt tried. In his first term, the panel FDR appointed to devise national old age and unemployment benefits was also considering a healthcare and health insurance program. But the American Medical Association (AMA) opposed such a program, claiming it would restrict doctors' freedom and earnings. Rather than jeopardize his entire proposal, FDR left major healthcare reform out of the Social Security Act, which passed easily in 1935. Later in FDR's presidency, when the health coverage idea was raised again, the opposition had grown to include business groups and "the emerging private health insurance industry," says the KFF report.

- President Harry Truman tried. A key part of his Fair Deal agenda was "a single insurance system that would cover all Americans with public subsidies to pay for the poor," says the KFF report. Truman was elected in 1948 after making national healthcare a campaign issue, but couldn't get it passed. Union support was split, given the offer of employer-paid healthcare by General Motors and other big corporations. The AMA and business leaders tarred national healthcare as "socialized medicine." And southern lawmakers fought it, lest a federal role interfere with the racial segregation still practiced in hospitals in their states.

- President John Kennedy tried to get hospital coverage for seniors passed in 1962, but opponents defeated it. After Kennedy's assassination and President Lyndon Johnson's landslide election in 1964, Johnson made Medicare health coverage for seniors the cornerstone of his "Great Society" program. It passed in July 1965, as did Medicaid health coverage for low-income Americans. But the gap remained, leaving millions of Americans under age sixty-five with no health coverage.

- President Richard Nixon tried. In 1974, he championed a bold health insurance plan that would provide universal coverage, with employers footing part of the cost. Though Nixon nearly rounded up enough support for his plan, the effort was slowed by competition from other lawmakers' proposals, and ultimately it was derailed by the Watergate scandal that forced Nixon's resignation.

And so it went, for decades more. Regardless of the economic times, the rise or fall of the stock market, or the rate of unemployment, the one constant since the mid-1970s has been the relentless rise of healthcare costs. When good healthcare is expensive, higher-income people still can purchase it, but lower-income people can't. Better-quality care generally means better health outcomes. So, to put it bluntly, the Haves can afford more good health than the Have Nots. We buy the better tickets.

This began to change in my corner of the medical world in 1990 when

Congress enacted legislation that was as revolutionary for HIV/AIDS care as the passage of Medicare had been for elder care.

The Ryan White Comprehensive AIDS Resources Emergency (CARE) Act was named for an Indiana youngster who suffered from hemophilia, contracted HIV from a blood transfusion, spent the rest of his life raising awareness and fighting discrimination against people with HIV, and died at age eighteen in the year the act passed. As of this writing, the act has been amended and reauthorized four times, most recently in 2009. Though its full name has changed slightly (the latest version was called the Ryan White HIV/AIDS Treatment Extension Act of 2009), it's generally known simply as Ryan White.

Ryan White helps supplement the cost of care for hundreds of thousands of HIV-infected Americans. In particular, it covers the costs of most medications through the AIDS Drug Assistance Program (ADAP) and outpatient clinic costs through its Part A (supplying funds to the cities hardest hit), Part B (to states), Part C (directly to adult clinics), and Part D (directly to clinics providing care to women and children with HIV).

Among American healthcare consumers overall, there continue to be enormous disparities in healthcare outcomes between the Haves and the Have Nots. With that in mind, consider how remarkable this next statement is: In roughly a dozen years, Ryan White has *virtually eliminated* health outcome disparities among HIV patients (for those who are in care) by supplementing their cost of care.

The practical effect of this was nicely demonstrated in a paper published in 2012 by Richard Moore, Jeanne Keruly, and John Bartlett from Johns Hopkins University. They examined health outcomes among all the patients attending their HIV clinic in East Baltimore and showed that folks with the lowest annual income had *exactly the same outcomes* in terms of life expectancy and virologic success as those with the highest incomes. In almost every other disease condition and clinic across the country, patients with lower incomes uniformly have worse outcomes. For those in care, the health disparities expected with HIV have been mostly eliminated via funding through the Ryan White program.

Ryan White has provided money as a godsend to most AIDS clinics in the country, including the 1917 Clinic. Ever since Dr. Bennett approved the clinic with his terse directive—"just try not to run in the red"—a key part of my job has been finding operating funds. If we're all to keep riding this rocket, it's largely up to me to keep fuel in the engine. From one year to the next, I usually don't know exactly how I'll get it. But I have to figure out something, because as I've come to realize, magical thinking can do little about funding.

When we started the clinic, most of our patients couldn't afford medications, so we put them in drug studies where they could get the newest, best drugs at no cost. We were too busy trying to stem the epidemic to pause and ask the question: How did those drugs get to be so expensive in the first place? Now, we've asked and answered. And in the process, I've pretty much lost my innocence about two of the big-money aspects of drug development: the creating and testing of new drugs, and the marketing of same.

Let's discuss the marketing first, in honor of Howard (Howie) Reiss. Howie was a hustler, but in a good-natured and respectful way. A pharmacist by training, he went into the field of health communications and became a consultant to pharmaceutical companies, helping them strategically position new drugs in the marketplace. Born and raised in Queens, Howie was a quintessential New Yorker: aggressive, witty, and endearing. He was relatively short, a bit overweight, and had a boisterous, infectious laugh.

What's more, Howie was wicked smart. Not just intelligent, but street smart. A survivor. To the "thought leaders"—those physicians and researchers who were labeled by the pharma companies as the ones to whom others listened—he was the consummate gentleman, always attentive, engaging, and encouraging. Fun to be around. To the staff who worked for him, he was sharp, terse, demanding, and impatient. "Fix it, Fax it, FedEx it!" were his frequent orders as problems emerged. He had a way of always getting things done, and done well.

In December 1989, I received a call from Howie inviting me to participate in a "Treatment Workshop" for AZT in San Francisco. He told me I was an "up-and-comer," a gifted teacher he thought explained things well to others, and someone he wanted to promote as a thought leader in the HIV/AIDS arena. I had never met Howie before, but I immediately liked him, partly because he was so complimentary: As a young assistant professor, hearing someone say such nice things about me was attractive, if not intoxicating. There was also an instant connection because Howie was a *lonsman*, a fellow Jew, and he talked about wanting to make a difference.

Howie said he wanted me to be on a panel with MDs whom I admired and who already had become legends in the HIV field: UCSF's Paul Volberding, Margaret Fischl of the University of Miami, Larry Corey of the University of Washington, and Doug Richman of the University of California–San Diego. Howie said that I and another rising investigator, Rob Murphy from Northwestern in Chicago, would be the "new talent" he wanted to develop and give exposure to. And he encouraged me to bring Amy along so that she could enjoy the experience as well. How could I say no to such an invitation?

The meeting was held in the Fairmont Hotel on top of Nob Hill in January 1990. Plane tickets for both Amy and me were provided. When we landed in San Francisco, we were met by a driver holding a sign seeking "Dr. Saag," who then took us to the Fairmont in a stretch limo. Amy looked at me and asked, "What did you do to get this kind of treatment?" I simply shrugged and thought, *Howie sure knows how to take care of his faculty.*

As Amy and I were heading to our room after checking in, we walked by one of the ballrooms, which seemed to have been transformed into a television studio. Always intrigued by anything to do with visual media, I peeked my head in to look around. On risers in front of rows of chairs was a long table covered with blue velvet, with microphones laid out in a row along the tabletop. Three large, studio-quality television cameras were being moved around on casters by crewmembers. Floodlights were being adjusted and sound checks were under way.

Out of the chaos I heard a voice: "Dr. Saag!" A rapidly approaching man stuck out his hand and said, "I'm Howie Reiss. So glad you are here! Nice to meet you—and Mrs. Saag, delighted you could join us." He briefly described the agenda for the weekend: We would rehearse the session tonight and shoot it tomorrow morning. We'd then go by bus to the Napa Valley for a wine tasting and dinner at Tra Vigne, a world-class Italian restaurant. We'd be bused back to the Fairmont Saturday night and depart for home on

Sunday. Amy and I were overwhelmed. As we headed to our suite high in the Fairmont tower, I felt like a rock star.

The panel discussion Saturday morning was moderated by Paul Volberding. We were going to discuss the flow of optimal patient care: how to diagnosis HIV and "stage the infection" (that is, how to tell how far along the patient was in the course of the infection), how and when to treat with antiretrovirals, how to look for and manage the complications of therapy, and what to expect in the long run. The panel was stacked with all these heavy hitters . . . then Rob Murphy and me. Naïvely, I figured that if they asked me to be there, I belonged there. I assumed they simply wanted me to represent what I saw from the trenches of care in Alabama, sort of a reality test of how the clinical trials results were translating into the real world.

I participated with energy and, where possible, with humor. I had done enough television in college to know that nothing is more boring than a bunch of talking heads droning on about a bunch of technical data. I figured I'd take the role of the "color commentator," and it seemed to work. Afterward Howie rushed up to me and said, "You're a natural! We need to do this more often." After the way Amy and I had been treated on the trip, who was I to argue?

In retrospect, that weekend was a turning point in my career. I had a chance to participate in an event with the big names in the field and held my own. More importantly, the social events on Saturday afternoon and evening gave me the chance to really get to know the other faculty members as professionals and as people. I learned about wine from Doug Richman and about the difficulties of performing the first AZT trial from Margaret Fischl; I learned how much I had in common with Paul Volberding—children roughly the same age, a similar sense of humor, and shared values about why we entered medicine. It was the beginning of treasured friendships that continue to today.

I knew that Burroughs Wellcome (BW), the maker of AZT, funded the entire event. Howie explained to me at dinner Saturday night that BW's concept was to educate as many providers about HIV as possible so that they could diagnose more patients and get them started on appropriate medication. A simple statement, and one that seemed logical. But from there on, as I learned and thought more about this realm, it gradually would become less clear-cut.

Howie was employed as a strategic marketing consultant for BW. As such, he would meet frequently with Marty Hunnicutt, the product manager for AZT at BW, to brainstorm how to increase sales of the product. But as Howie phrased it, Marty didn't have to sell AZT; all Marty had to do was sell HIV as a disease that needed to be diagnosed and treated and, since AZT was the only drug on the market at the time, the drug would sell itself. Howie had taken this approach previously when BW launched the drug acyclovir for the treatment of herpes infections. Experts such as Richman and Corey had participated in that launch. Now Howie was expanding his reach and vision into HIV and AZT by nurturing new "talent" such as Rob Murphy and me.

The "sell the disease" approach was a win-win for BW, creating the appearance that the company was engaged and concerned about the epidemic and physician education while, oh by the way, selling their drug. And somehow for us, the "thought leaders," it allowed us to stand apart from the selling of AZT. We were doing what academic physicians are supposed to do—educating—and we were passionate about it. It was a near-perfect marriage of academia and industry, each serving its own interests and thereby serving the other's.

It turns out Howie was well ahead of his time. He was one of the first to pitch selling a disease as a means of creating market share for a new drug product. In his case, he pitched the disease by offering knowledge and continuing medication education to healthcare providers in order to secure market share.

Letting AZT sell itself simply by educating providers about HIV worked well until competition arrived. In 1991 Bristol Myers Squibb's (BMS) drug DDI was approved, followed soon thereafter by DDC (Roche, 1992) and D4T (BMS, 1994). As the field moved from one drug and one company to four drugs made by three companies, the battle over market share began, and the thought leaders were in the middle of the crossfire.

Since HIV was such a youthful field populated by mostly younger investigators, there were only a few key speakers to go around on the lecture circuits. Richman, Fischl, and Volberding were in the highest demand, but all of us were receiving invitations to speak almost daily. The typical road trip consisted of a visit to a major city, where we were picked up at the airport by the local drug rep and maybe his or her regional manager. They escorted us to speak at a series of "grand rounds" at local hospitals and the local medical school. On the ride from venue to venue, the drug rep would give a profile of who the major local treaters were. Often, the manager would chime in with a concern about the need to get this or that "message" to the treaters. The manager's plea might go like this: "Dr. Saag, I am not telling you what to say, but it would really help us out if you could cover the results of study XYZ to emphasize the problems with drug A"—the competitor drug. And the unspoken message was, "We just spent money flying you in and we're paying you $1,000 per lecture, so how about helping us out here?"

Having been raised on the Eddie Saag Code of Honesty Above All, these attempts at influence made me squirm. I felt certain I could resist them and keep my integrity while giving providers information they needed, which was the point. To my mind, my fellow speakers and I were educators. To our audiences, we were experts who could offer the latest data and put them into perspective for use in clinical practice. But to the drug company, we were a marketing tool. Merely by bringing us in, they could get face time with a large number of their area's high-level treaters all in one place, an opportunity they didn't get often. And if Dr. Expert's remarks aligned with what the company wanted the audience to hear, so much the better.

Regardless of which company we were being asked to speak for, my colleagues and I pretty much used the same slides in our presentation and gave the same spiel. In many ways it was like vaudeville; we were on the circuit, telling the same story—and, in my case, the same *shtick*—from town to town. When the drug company reps prompted, the temptation always was there to emphasize the virtues of their drug or linger a bit longer on the adverse effects of the competitor's drug. Try as we might to skirt the sponsoring companies' requests and present a balanced assessment of the drugs, none of us felt good about being treated like a spokesperson.

Frustrated with this state of affairs, Paul Volberding, Doug Richman, and Margaret Fischl came up with an idea. They would found a not-for-profit organization whose mission was to provide unbiased education and drug information to providers in the major US cities where HIV was hitting hardest. It would organize educational events that drug companies would fund—but it would pool funding from multiple companies with competing products, so no single company or donation could influence an event's content. Paul had just stepped down as president of the International AIDS Society (IAS), the Swedish-based entity that sponsors the large annual conferences, and he wanted to create an IAS subsidiary in the United States. By the time the founders learned they could not affiliate the new US nonprofit with the foreign-based entity, they already had named it IAS-USA. The name stuck.

For the IAS-USA's founding executive director, Paul thought of a young, energetic staffer he had met while working with Howie Reiss on an HIV treatment monograph. Donna Jacobsen was born and raised on Long Island. After college she worked in a lab at Memorial Sloan Kettering Hospital in Manhattan until she joined the health communications firm where Howie worked. Donna is a thorough and disciplined executive whose blue eyes narrow with intensity when she discusses projects. She is never intimidated by the medical "big names" who participate in IAS-USA events. She expects them to meet deadlines and do things "the right way," meaning with the highest professional integrity and without commercial bias.

In 1993, I joined the board of directors of the IAS-USA. In that role, I've learned a lot about medical education, including how drug companies used thought leaders—also called Key Opinion Leaders (KOLs)—to market messages that help sell drugs. Here's how it works:

- Every lecture given by any KOL is attended by representatives of each company. They take note of the main message(s) delivered by the presenter and report back to the company's corporate office.

- If the message is favorable to the company's marketing agenda, that company often follows up with invitations for that KOL to speak in additional cities, usually selected based on where their market data indicate they are having sales problems.

- If the message is unfavorable, the company usually sends a high-level regional or national sales manager to meet with the KOL in their office shortly after their lecture. Such a visit starts off with open-ended questions such as, "What do you think about product A?" "How do you think it fits with your current treatment paradigm?" But later the questioning becomes more focused: "We heard you made a comment about Drug A in your lecture at Certain Venue; can you explain what you were thinking?" "Are you aware of this paper with new data about Drug A? What do you think now that you have seen these data?" In essence, their job is to "turn" the KOL away from the negative message to one more favorable to their product.

Using this approach, the companies try to manage the KOLs to help them stay true to the company's strategic sales messaging. "I have total freedom to say whatever I want in any lecture I give," is the retort I hear most when a KOL is asked if there is bias in their presentations. And they're right: Most of them *are* presenting the information they want to present when they lecture. But they usually aren't aware that the company that just asked them to speak at a given meeting has followed their every lecture, creating a dossier on them, and knows precisely what they are likely to say even before they take the podium.

Back in the 1700s and early 1800s, remedies of different sorts were sold by traveling salesmen to a vulnerable public. Their potions were typically extracts from roots or plant leaves, and the concentration of the active ingredient could vary widely from batch to batch, ranging from so high that it was toxic to so low that it had no human effect. To get a handle on these products and the swindlers who peddled them, the 1906 Pure Food and Drug ("Snake Oil") Act was passed requiring "truth in labeling." It led to the establishment of the US Food and Drug Administration (FDA) whose responsibilities include "assuring the safety, efficacy, and security" of drugs and medical devices.

By the time I got involved in drug development research, there were exhaustive federal regulations governing practically everything I do in the clinical lab and everything drug companies do to take candidate drugs from concept through clinical trials to FDA approval. The process goes roughly like this.

Each company developing drugs must first identify a lead candidate or two and assess their activity in the lab. They then must assess the lead drugs' safety, absorption, and elimination in the body to predict the proper dose range; that often starts with animal models before the drugs are introduced into humans. This is a highly creative and expensive, mostly trial-and-error process with vastly more failures than successes. And it's only the first step toward creating a product to be sold; after investing millions, when successful, the company is granted permission to go to the next step and spend more.

At the outset, tens of thousands of compounds are screened for potential medicinal activity. Once a few "hits" are identified, the compound is critically evaluated and the chemists go to work making minor adjustments to its structure to help it be more active, or better used, or more efficiently retained by the body. This iterative process, which can take months or even years, ultimately yields one or more "lead compounds." The process of drug identification, optimization, testing in animals, and all the work prior to testing in humans is called preclinical development. By now, we're spending real money—millions and millions and millions, without (yet) selling a single pill. All the money is going out, and none of it is coming back to the company and its investors.

Next come clinical trials with humans, with risks that warrant big in-surance policies to keep the companies from being bankrupted by a single small error. (Can you spell "thalidomide"?) These are typically divided into four phases. The testing goes from one to the next, and each successive phase involves larger groups of test subjects and helps scientists answer different questions.

- In Phase I studies, small numbers of subjects are given different doses followed by blood draws to assess the drug's safety and its absorption and metabolism in the body. These typically are followed by Phase I(b) studies, which are used as "proof of concept" that the drug is doing what it was designed to do and what it appeared to do in Phase I. If you're counting dollars, your cost dial is spinning.

- In Phase II studies, a greater number of test subjects are given a couple of selected doses to further assess safety and determine relative activity of the drug. More people, more risk, more money.

- Phase III studies then use a "best dose" to see how the drug performs in large numbers of patients. That may include pitting the drug against a placebo in a double-blind study where neither the provider nor the subject knows who is receiving the active drug and who is receiving the inactive but identical-looking placebo. Such Phase III studies are typically called "pivotal" trials, and two of them conducted independently are required to secure FDA approval. Budgets are, by now, enormous.

- Once a drug is approved, postmarketing Phase IV studies are conducted to further define the use of the drug in different patient populations or to help the marketing objectives of the company.

By the time approval is granted, this process has wrung money from companies like water from a soggy washcloth. Costs in the preclinical period can range from $20 million to $150 million. Some compounds are so chemically complex or difficult to synthesize that the scale-up needed for drug production is deemed cost prohibitive, so they are sent back to the chemists for modification. Such obstacles and delays lead to increased costs.

Phase I studies, although intense, require only a few dozen patients treated for a short period of time. Their cost is on the order of *only* $10 million. Usually there are several Phase II trials, each involving from dozens to hundreds of subjects, costing upwards of $100 million. The Phase III studies are the most expensive, involving several hundreds of patients each and costing upwards of $300 million. Once data are generated from the two pivotal trials, the drug company team prepares a dossier of information on the drug to be submitted to the FDA for review and approval. Simultaneously, the company has already begun building or has built plants to produce the drug according to FDA-approved manufacturing practices that ensure each tablet is pure and created to the proper specifications. This effort adds to the expense.

Taken together, the cost of drug development from conception of an idea to the approval of the drug—including the new product launch costs such as marketing and distribution—is approximately $1 billion to $1.5 billion per new drug in today's world.

I am not privy to how drug companies determine the price of their new drugs. I know many factors are involved, including the actual cost of ingredients, competition, need, uniqueness of the product, and the ability of the market to afford the new drug. Having watched the launch of a lot of new drugs since 1987, it appears to me that some sort of formula is used whereby the cost of drug development (say, $1.5 billion) is divided by the estimated number of pills that will be sold in the first eighteen to twenty-four months after the launch. The number of pills is determined by the number of patients estimated to take the drug prescribed, the number of pills per dose, the number of doses per day, and the length of time the drug will need to be taken. Maybe the formula is more sophisticated than this, but it seems almost certain that pricing enables the company to recover its cost of drug development in one or two years after initial release. From that time until the patent for that drug expires—usually twenty years after the company's filing of an Investigational New Drug application with the FDA—each drug is a profit center for its manufacturer. (I do know, for a fact, that if the company makes no profit, its investors get no returns and the company soon disappears.)

Companies can also sell a so-called "off patent" drug; it just will be less lucrative, as it may have competition from generic drugs once the patent expires.

Let's test-drive my imagined formula for recouping drug development costs. Suppose that new Drug X, which cost $1.5 billion to develop and a few cents per pill to manufacture, will be taken by 1 million patients in its first eighteen months on the market. Each of those patients will take four pills a day for thirty days. If the manufacturer of Drug X were to set its per-pill cost using my formula, it would divide $1.5 billion by $4 \times 30 \times 1$ million—and the drug would sell for $12.50 per pill. In the case of drugs used for common diseases, more patients would take the drug and the per-unit cost could be lower. However, for rarer diseases that affect only a few hundred people per year, the per-unit cost could be prohibitively high, on the order of thousands of dollars per dose.

But what a pharmaceutical firm charges also depends on what buyers will pay. Most often, large payers such as insurance companies, large pharmacy chains, and the US government can negotiate bulk rate purchases of medications at some discount off the average wholesale price. That seems fair, right? But typically, the US government does not get as big a discount as do governments in other Western countries. Why? Because most other countries have single-payer healthcare systems that can negotiate for lower, fairer pricing. The US has no single-payer healthcare system, in part because opponents of such systems—many of them heavily funded by lobbyists for drug companies—have fanned opposition to them as "socialized medicine." The result is that the United States and its people end up footing a disproportionate share of the costs of drug discovery and development for the rest of the world. We get stuck with this bill in large part because of our inability to negotiate as a single agent with pharmaceutical companies and our chaotic payer system.

And that, as we say in Yiddish, is the *shanda*—the crying shame. Because we pay disproportionately more for brand-name pharmaceutical drugs, we foot the bill of drug development for the rest of the world. As my colleague James Willig frequently says when there's some burden to be shouldered, "Everybody should bleed a little." In the case of drug development, the United States is hemorrhaging while everyone else reaps the benefits.

Meanwhile in Washington, D.C., the discussion is about budget cuts and fiscal constraint while policies are approved that prevent cost savings. Mistaken thinking is elevated to near insanity in some "austerity proposals" that would call for dramatic, across-the-board cuts, including the R&D budget of the NIH, one of the few drug-development sources where we actually *save* money. No public outcry is mounted because the general public has no sense of how the economics of healthcare research work. Most of us don't know which dollars are costs and which are investments, which save lives and which save dollars. For most of us, it's all just "bloated budget."

In fact, research that yields cures—remember the vial of fluid that was my first lab "project"?—happens largely in places like my medical school at the University of Alabama at Birmingham. We get maybe 10 percent of our budget for faculty from the state, maybe 10 percent from tuition; all of this is fairly fixed and pays for education. But roughly 80 percent of the money that pays medical school research faculty salaries at places like UAB comes from research grants, mostly from federal sources. Without these grant dollars, medical schools and other institutions of higher learning would only have at best one-half to one-fifth of their current faculty available for teaching, and that's if they were teaching full time and doing nothing else. Reductions in this federal research funding would at least weaken today's medical schools. A significant reduction might well destroy medical, dental, and nursing education as it now exists in this country, as well as devastate vital R&D entities such as the NIH. Federal spending in these areas has been flat for the last twelve years and continues to be on the chopping block. These are very, very expensive "savings" because the cost of lost opportunity and real patient care combine to a higher total than the dollars not spent. Every passing year, the costs go higher as the cuts go deeper—like trying to dig your way out of a hole by going deeper and deeper.

As a result, we are—right now, as I write—losing an entire generation of PhD researchers who have no other options for employment. Some aspiring MD researchers may find a way to work as a physician provider, as I did, but will not be able to pursue their interest in research. Just days into 2013, I got an email from a talented, frustrated colleague asking the plaintive question, "*Is research dead?*" He had just heard that a superb young researcher he knew whose grant proposal was at the top of the list at NIH still had not gotten funding.

I had the unhappy task of telling this gifted scientist that until Congress stops its partisan warfare and passes a continuing budget resolution, NIH is unlikely to approve any new funding. And honestly, while I could hope that funding is only delayed, I could offer him no reassurance that it would not be cut, or even eliminated. "Then my lab is dead," responded my colleague, who was counting on a near-term NIH grant to keep a key project afloat. "I already had to let go my best technician . . . I may not have the funds to hold my other lab members, let alone continue my actual research."

This is an emerging national tragedy rapidly, and quietly, approaching the level of a crisis. When our congressional representatives talk about cutting what they call "discretionary spending," they seem not to realize that cuts to NIH and other national science agencies constitute triple whammies. Such cuts restrict the country's scientific advances, deplete faculty at our universities, and risk sacrificing an entire generation of young scientists whom we'll never be able to get back. These are all losses of knowledge; the consequence is loss of life.

Some forecasters believe we're already seeing the cascade effect as the brightest of would-be scientists, seeing how little their nation values them, are pursuing other opportunities.

So someday soon, when Senator Shortsighted's daughter develops a genetically influenced growth disorder and he asks if there's really nothing doctors can do, the truth will be, "You shut down the lab that was within months of finding the answer." And when Representative Heedless wonders why his wife's coughing can't be stopped, and he hears the physician say respiratory syncytial virus, someone should lean in and tell him that we had the science, but he stopped the funding, so knowledge never became cure.

When I get into discussions like this, I remember the scene from the 1976 movie *All the President's Men* where the shadowy source known as Deep Throat told reporter Bob Woodward that to solve the puzzle of the Watergate break-in and cover-up, he should "follow the money." If you look at advances in medicine and healthcare in the last half century and you follow the money, here's what you see:

- Fewer US dollars going to independent scholars doing serious R&D.

- US pharmaceutical firms paying for their R&D predominantly by profiting from US customers because we lack a single-payer system.

- The growth of private health insurance, an industry that barely existed a century ago and today is one of the nation's most powerful and profitable.

I have health insurance. My children are insured. I think of the US insurance industry as no different or more difficult than any business. But the current moneymaking model leaves health insurance's interest competing with the patient's interest before he or she walks through the door. As a for-profit business, an insurance company must do its utmost to make money for its stockholders. Its first obligation is to the people who buy its stock, not the people who buy its insurance. Unhappily, when the insurance "customer" becomes a "patient," he or she turns into a liability whose costs should be minimized to maximize profit for the shareholder.

It's complicated: Retirees are living off dividends paid by insurance companies in whom they've invested. But when the retiree becomes "a patient," her dividend check is best protected if she doesn't cost much.

As investment opportunities, health insurance companies are doing well. Consider this: In the depths of the global recession of 2009, America's five largest for-profit insurers had a combined profit of $12.2 billion, *up 56 percent* over the previous year, according to the advocacy group Health Care for America Now (HCAN). Then consider this: Also in 2009, HCAN reported, while our five big insurers profited handsomely, they also cancelled policies for their costliest patients and raised premiums on other policyholders. Ouch.

When Ben Franklin gave us insurance as a concept, I think he had a fine idea. But if Brother Ben took a hard look at what we have today, I think he'd revolt. In the current system, the companies selling insurance have interests aligned directly with their shareholders (make money) rather than with their patient policyholders (provide care).

There has to be a way to do both. Imagine a health insurance company whose "insureds" were their shareholders. In this model, any *savings* created by the efficient operation of the company would lead to one of two great outcomes for those they insure: lower premiums or enhanced services. In recent years, the shareholders of for-profit insurance companies in the United States have enjoyed annual profits averaging 9–12 percent. Imagine how much improvement in care and health that could buy for America's patients (also known as *us*).

For me, every discussion of healthcare costs comes back to the personal stories of patients—people like Joe and Brian. Throughout the entire course of Brian's illness, Joe stood by his side physically, emotionally, spiritually— and financially. When Brian's insurance proved woefully insufficient, Joe footed the bills, assuming enormous debts on credit cards and other loans. On more than one occasion, he narrowly avoided declaring bankruptcy. To Joe's great credit, he never thought twice about bearing this responsibility for Brian's care. He simply did it because he thought it was the right thing to do. My father would have pronounced him a "good American."

For a while, AZT kept Brian in pretty good shape. For Christmas 1990, his gift to me was a chalk drawing of a big, vivid flower and, for Christmas 1991, a drawing of a bunch of balloons. Then, as with so many patients, the AZT began to fail Brian and opportunistic infections swept in. By summer 1992, we were fighting multiple infections with potent drugs—including one that, with continued use, might have prolonged life but would have caused deafness.

I consulted with Brian, with Joe, and with Brian's mother, Irene, another of the steadfast moms who had been there throughout her son's ordeal. None of us could bear the thought of Brian being plunged into silence again, so that drug was dropped. Brian went home from the hospital in the fall and lived only a week more. Talking on the phone with Joe and Irene after Brian died, it felt as if they were consoling me as much as I was consoling them.

A dozen years after Brian's death, his artwork still hangs in the 1917 Clinic. A dozen years after Brian's death, Joe has only just paid off the last of his healthcare debts.

Chapter 9

"... AND TWELVE HOURS."

can't tell you the patient's name. But I can tell you that because of what
he gave, we made breakthroughs that turned the tide on HIV/AIDS.

On a gray day in January 1986, I was heading to my lab at UAB's
Lyons Harrison Research Building when I met Glenn Cobbs in the hall,
on his way to the VA hospital next door. Glenn, one of my role models in
ID medicine, was known for conducting medical consults on the fly in as
few words as possible. Literally without breaking stride as he passed me,
Glenn announced, "Hey, think a guy over there has acute seroconversion
syndrome, why don't you scope it out, O-kee?" That was it. And really, that's
all he needed to say, because we both knew that when a patient was in that
initial phase of very recent infection, it gave us a unique opportunity to
chronicle how the immune system evolves in response to the virus in the
earliest stages.

To get from my lab to Glenn's patient at the VA was as simple as walking
across a sky bridge connecting the two buildings, a corridor that looked a lot
like the one Don Adams walked down in the opening of one of my favorite
1960s television shows, *Get Smart*. (None of my students today was alive
then; when I try to explain this to them, their eyes glaze over and they look
at their iPhones.)

I introduced myself to Glenn's patient and explained what we thought was going on and why it was so critical that we evaluate him now and each day for the next week. Once he gave informed consent to participate in our ongoing research project, I drew twenty tubes of his blood. I marked them according to our lab's protocol, with a four-letter identifier drawn from a scrambling of the patients initials: WEAU. Back in the lab, I prepared and stored WEAU's blood samples. In coming weeks, I would draw many more, test some immediately, and store the rest for later use.

The patient known as WEAU had been infected with HIV sometime around Thanksgiving 1985; he ultimately died of HIV-related complications in 1991. But through the blood samples he left, WEAU may have contributed more to a quarter century of HIV/AIDS research than any other single human being. WEAU's blood helped George, Beatrice, and me establish the natural evolution of the quasi-species nature of the virus. And that was only the beginning. Based on mostly George and Beatrice's studies, WEAU is a part of more papers in *Science* and *Nature* (two prestigious scientific journals) than any other single individual. Studies using WEAU's blood built our lab's reputation for the kind of quick, solid research that drug companies needed as they worked on new agents that were more potent and better tolerated than the existing drugs.

One drug company that sought us out was Merck, and our first big study with them was hatched—to my great delight—on the outskirts of Walt Disney World, a place known for magic.

Starting in the late 1980s, the pharmaceutical giant Merck had been working on a new drug, a so-called non-nucleoside reverse transcriptase inhibitor. The existing drugs such as AZT and DDI (didanosine) were all nucleosides, false building blocks of viral DNA that, when inserted in the growing DNA chain, shut down replication and blocked further propagation of the virus. The ability of the virus to go from RNA to DNA was done through this new enzyme reverse transcriptase (RT), and the non-nucleoside agents acted by attacking the RT enzyme directly.

Structurally, RT looks like a hand, and the business end of the molecule is in the cleft between the thumb and the index finger. The non-nucleoside drugs inserted themselves precisely into that cleft and blocked the ability of the virus to interact with the RNA to produce a DNA copy. Merck had spent four or five years perfecting their candidate drugs to fit very tightly and specifically into this pocket in order to shut down viral replication with very small quantities of drug.

In January 1991, I got a call from Oscar Laskin, an MD pharmacologist who worked at Merck and had collaborated with Rich Whitley, a world-renowned herpes virologist at UAB. Oscar asked me to meet with him and one of his colleagues, Emilio Emini, to discuss a possible clinical study. Orlando, Florida, was a mutually convenient meeting destination, so in late January, I flew there accompanied by Eric Hunter, an HIV virologist who was the leader of our federally backed Center for AIDS Research program at UAB.

Over dinner, Oscar and Emilio told the development history of their lead compound, L–697,661 (a set of digits I would soon know as well as my own phone number). We began discussing what a trial might look like and the potential questions we might address at a single site study—that is, a study conducted at one location by one group of investigators using a single protocol.

To continue our planning, we drove back to Oscar's hotel, Eric and Oscar in one car and Emilio and me in the other. As Emilio and I talked about our lives in HIV medicine, I was struck by the tall, husky Italian's constant refrain: "I hate this virus!"

Emilio had started working on HIV soon after it was discovered. After identifying a type of protease enzyme called Renin that contributed to high blood pressure, Merck had worked on anti-Renin compounds. And because HIV also had a protease gene that was critical in the ability of the virus to replicate, Emilio had hoped to use discoveries in the anti-Renin arena to create an anti-HIV compound. Up to that point, though, he had been thwarted at every turn—one more reason for his vehement mantra "I hate this virus!"

Oscar was staying at a hotel whose rooms were appointed accordingly: pictures of Daisy and Donald Duck, a bedspread with Mickey Mouse ears, a telephone shaped like Goofy. In this marvelously cartoonish setting, we outlined two concurrent HIV drug studies: one for patients with CD4 counts below 200, with or without a prior opportunistic infection; and another for patients entering treatment earlier with CD4 counts between 200 and

500. Since L–697,661 was in very early stages of development, we wanted to assess the pharmacokinetics—the amount of drug in the bloodstream at different doses, as well as the safety in terms of side effects and the drug's ability to inhibit the virus.

Doing the study only at UAB would keep things simpler in scientific terms but was an ambitious undertaking logistically. Each study would enroll sixty patients, fifteen in an AZT control group and fifteen each in three treatment groups at different doses of the new drug. Each patient would need a prestudy evaluation, a day-of-entry visit, weekly visits for six weeks, a postvisit evaluation—in all, ten visits over ten weeks for 120 patients. Oscar gave me a slightly skeptical look and asked, "Can you guys really enroll that many patients in that period of time with that frequency of visits?"

"Give me a minute," I said, and opened a notebook. I drew a grid charting how many patients we would see over the ten-week period. By the end of the period, the numbers were staggering: We would be seeing over 100 patients per week! I remember looking at my completed graph, then at the Goofy telephone, the Mickey Mouse bedspread, and the Daisy portrait. I said to Oscar, "No problem, we can do it"—because at that moment all I could think was, *If Disney could turn swampland into parks that get 50 million visitors a year, I can handle 120 patients on a study.*

Oscar looked at Emilio and said, "Okay, we can do this, but don't mess it up. A lot is riding on this."

On the way back to Birmingham, Eric finally asked, "So, Mike, you can do this?" I didn't hesitate. "We don't have a choice." Eric thought for a moment and said, "Yes, but what's your Plan B?" I told the truth: "Plan B is for Plan A to work."

We couldn't fit a study of this magnitude into the 1917 Clinic on Fifth Avenue South, so I called Claude Bennett, explained the importance of the study, and asked if we could have some additional space. When Claude's facilities team identified an entire suite of unused clinic space in a UAB building, empty and waiting for us, we couldn't believe our luck. I hired two new research nurses and a new data manager. We had the new research clinic operational in less than two weeks.

There weren't enough existing patients at the 1917 Clinic to fill the study in the timeframe Oscar and Emilio set, and that worried me. But I knew that others were in touch with patients desperate for such opportunities—and that's how I came to know Martin Delaney and Tom Blount.

A San Francisco native and a onetime Jesuit seminarian, Marty Delaney became involved in the quest for better HIV/AIDS drugs in the early 1980s when several of his friends were fighting the virus. In 1985 Marty founded an organization called Project Inform (PI) to keep patients and the affected community aware of new developments in the fight against AIDS. Though it started out locally, PI quickly became a national clearinghouse for patients desperate for information on treatments that could prolong their lives. PI offered basic information about the virus, HIV tests, where to go to get the best care in a given neighborhood or city, and what treatments were available. For the more sophisticated, Marty and his team kept abreast of the latest drugs in development, where the drugs were active in clinical trials, and how to access the drugs via companies' compassionate use programs. When those programs weren't available, PI helped patients form "buyers' clubs" to purchase drugs across the border or overseas. Marty and PI laid the foundation for what became a community-based HIV research movement, helping patients argue for and gain access to promising medications in a variety of ways, including through studies like ours.

One of Marty's close friends was Tom Blount, a tall, soft-spoken gentleman with a goatee and wire-rimmed spectacles. Tom's family owned a prosperous construction business in Montgomery, and he certainly had the intellect and drive to lead it, had he wished to. Instead, Tom, an architect, settled in Atlanta with his longtime partner, Jim Straley, a landscape architect and graduate student. Tom has a heart bigger than Texas and is one of the most generous men I've ever met. In the late 1980s, when the AIDS epidemic hit Atlanta hard, Tom tested negative, Jim tested positive—and Tom set out to do everything he could to help Jim and others fight the virus.

By 1991, Tom had helped establish a buyers' club in Atlanta called AIDS Treatment Initiatives, which had linked up with like-minded organizations in other cities, including Marty Delaney's group in San Francisco. The clubs helped patients who couldn't afford new medicines on the market and connected patients to the compassionate use programs that drug companies often set up prior to their product's FDA approval for sale in the United States. When Tom invited me to speak at an Atlanta forum, word quickly spread that Birmingham's 1917 Clinic was gaining access to new drugs that might be able to treat HIV much better than AZT or any of the existing agents.

Within days our phone lines were overwhelmed with calls, and I realized I had a different problem: We were going to have *too many* interested patients. We finally settled on a ratio of two outside patients allowed to enter for each one who came from the Birmingham area.

Some who applied were naïve to therapy. Others had been on AZT in the past and were failing. Among those was Tom Blount's partner, Jim Straley. At the Atlanta forum, Tom had confided that Jim was exhausting his available options. I had urged Tom to bring Jim to Birmingham for evaluation in our new study, and Jim was one of the first people enrolled.

With the Atlanta recruits, the study quickly filled. While it was stressful to enroll all these patients and have them return to Birmingham every week for a study visit, the patients were so motivated that very few ever missed an appointment, much less a dose of medicine.

To clinicians like me, providing access to studies was a reprieve from helplessness. I'd had my fill of hand-holding, hugging sobbing mothers at the bedside, choking back my own tears. Against the darkness of death, science represented light, progress, hope. There was no better tonic for my pain than negotiating a new trial to come to our clinic, then offering spots in the study to patients desperately clinging onto life. For activists like Marty Delaney and Tom Blount, advancing access to drugs was more than a tonic; it was an urgent mission and cause. AIDS Treatment Initiatives, Project Inform, and other groups like them around the country helped legions of HIV-positive people become informed and militant about access to medications.

In addition to Jim Straley, several patients whose situations I knew well were in the L–697,661 study: Harry Wingfield, a songwriter and musician who had been fired from his job in UAB's theater department when his HIV-positive status became known; Alan Woelhart, an artist, actor, and foundry worker whose partner was one of the clinic nurses helping us run the drug trial; and the 1917 Clinic patient code-named Pearly James. As the study went forward, Emilio or Oscar flew to Birmingham almost every week to check on our progress, underscoring the critical nature of this study to Merck's development plans. They'd gambled that I could deliver, even though I'd never done anything like this before. It was a bit scary but mostly exhilarating to know that several years before it would be on the market, we were able to offer our patients one of the newest and most promising agents.

How promising? In the first week of therapy, as we looked at the information for all 120 patients, we saw that the amount of virus in their bloodstream dropped by anywhere from ten- to one hundredfold. Unfortunately, by week six, for the majority of them the virus had returned to the level that was present at baseline. Through this study, we discovered that this non-nucleoside agent had worked just as expected of a potent inhibitor of HIV in the first couple of weeks. But more importantly, the study also told us that when we came at the virus with only one agent at a time, the virus basically laughed at us—it quickly mutated into a form that was resistant to the drug. (Later experiments looking at the actual clonal analysis told us that resistant viruses were appearing within two days of exposure and took over the entire population of viruses within fourteen to twenty-eight days.)

The study results made our course clear: We would need a "cocktail" of multiple agents used simultaneously to successfully suppress the virus. One agent at a time wasn't going to cut it. George and I wrote up the original draft of the study, and the team from Merck provided expert assistance in writing the manuscript with us. We submitted the article to the *New England Journal of Medicine*, where it was ultimately published. We finished the manuscript sitting at Beatrice's grandmother's dining room table, the same table where we wrote the original quasi-species paper published in *Nature*— our good luck table.

Weeks later, we were at the same table discussing how quickly the virus had reversed our success and spiked back up. "You know," I said to George, "the viral replication must be pretty rapid. We really should put that into the paper." He agreed, and the final paragraph of our paper may have been the most important:

> The rapidity with which resistant viral populations were
> selected reflects a previously unsuspected dynamism of HIV–1
> in vivo. Although there has been a growing appreciation that

microbiologic latency of HIV–1 in vivo does not exist, our study suggests an even higher rate of ongoing replication . . . than previously appreciated.

Unfortunately, we weren't clever enough at that moment to focus on the critical next question: "Just *how* rapid?"

Fast-forward to Thursday, June 11, 1992. The phone rang at my hospital desk at one o'clock in the afternoon. I remember it so clearly because events triggered by that call would change the course of AIDS medicine and my life in it.

"Hi, I'm Jeff Lifson," said the caller, identifying himself as a scientist working at Genelabs Technologies in Redwood City, California. Jeff said a mutual colleague of ours, Rich Whitley, "told me that you had a specimen repository that had historically collected specimens from 1987 forward on a large number of patients." I responded, "That's correct." Jeff then said, "I want to tell you about a new test we have that can quantitate the amount of virus in the bloodstream though PCR. Do you have a minute?" I responded, "Absolutely."

Ever since I had heard biochemist John Sninsky's presentation on polymerase chain reaction (PCR) at the 1987 International AIDS Conference, I had hoped we might someday use PCR to quantify the amount of virus in the bloodstream. While working in George's lab, we had focused on several other techniques to quantitate the amount of virus (so-called p24 antigen), but we'd only achieved crude estimates of the amount of virus in the bloodstream; and the p24 antigen values were often negative in patients without symptoms of advanced infection.

At the 1987 AIDS conference, we'd been told PCR could not be used to quantitate the amount of virus in the bloodstream because the PCR technology was so sensitive that even slight variations in the multiple rounds of dilutions in the test processes might lead to wild overestimation or underestimation of the amount of virus present. On the phone, Jeff explained that an approach he and Mike Piatak developed had solved this problem. I sketched his solution with a pencil on the only writing surface available, a paper towel.

"Do you think you have some specimens that you could send us that could help us see if our approach actually works?" Jeff asked. Of course we did. I promised I'd send them by overnight mail for delivery the next morning. After we hung up, I almost sprinted down the hallway to the repository. Since I knew our patients so well, I knew which specimens were drawn from people in specific stages of infection, and which were so-called controls from people not infected with HIV. I created an intentional range of specimens, noted what I was sending, packed the specimens in dry ice, and shipped them overnight to Jeff's California facility.

On July 2 around 10:00 a.m., Jeff called to say he was going to send me a fax with the results. This time I skipped the paper towels and grabbed a piece of graph paper on which I listed the specimen categories—negative, acute seroconversion syndrome, asymptomatic, AIDS-related complex, and AIDS—along a logarithm scale where I could plot the results from zero copies of the virus up to 10 million copies per milliliter. Then I stood by the fax machine, my anticipation building until the machine's bell rang and the pages spilled out. I sped back to my desk with the pages, noted each result with a dot on my graph—and when I was done, what I saw took my breath away.

The patients who were not infected with HIV had no signal whatsoever. Those with acute seroconversion, like WEAU, had well over 1 million copies per milliliter. Those with advanced AIDS had somewhere between 100,000 and 1 million. But those with asymptomatic infection—who would have been completely undetectable in our tests with p24 antigen or plasma (bloodstream) virus culture—every single one of them had *detectable virus*, ranging from 1,000 copies to well over 100,000 copies per milliliter. The test was showing us what we'd never been able to find before.

We've all heard sudden realizations or inspirations called "eureka moments." Supposedly, they were so named because ancient Greek mathematician Archimedes was so excited about an insight he got while drawing a bath that he ran into the street naked, shouting the Ancient Greek forerunner of the word eureka, which translated to, "I have found it!" I've been fortunate enough to be part of a few discoveries that I'd count as eureka moments. The first was being in George and Beatrice's lab and seeing the profusion of bands on the Southern Blot test that showed the quasi-species nature of the AIDS virus. The second was this moment: Glimpsing the potential of quantitative PCR (QC-PCR) in measuring viral load, and thus in transforming HIV/AIDS treatment. And all because of Jeff Lifson's and Mike Piatak's groundbreaking work with the 1917 Clinic's blood samples.

The first lesson from this new test is that we'd misunderstood how the virus worked. Previously, when we couldn't detect p24 antigen or plasma virus in tissue culture when people were doing clinically well, we had assumed there was a latency period during which the body was able to shut viral replication down. *Wrong.* It never went away; we just couldn't see it with the testing methods we had then.

Second, it demonstrated that viral replication occurs 24/7, around the clock, in somebody who is infected. This could well explain why patients' immune systems weaken over time under the onslaught of persistent, ongoing virus replication. I likened it to the effect of waves hitting rocks on a shore. At first there is not much impact, but after years of relentless battering of the waves, the rocks inevitably erode—just as the immune system does under the onslaught of persistent viral replication.

The ability to use QC-PCR was important for another reason: It could tell us almost immediately whether or not antiretroviral therapy was working. We no longer would lose precious weeks or months to see outcomes; we could measure viral load and know, practically immediately, whether a therapy was effective and, if so, how effective.

In almost every clinical trial of cancer and the early trials of AZT and other antiviral agents, *clinical endpoints* were the primary metric used to determine whether or not a drug worked. In the case of AZT, the original study took patients who were fairly sick and asked the question: How much death was prevented? Chiefly because the patients were so sick, that answer often came within six months. Either the patient got worse and died or, when AZT was able to show benefit, it took six months of study with the old modes of assessing before we could tell a real difference.

With the use of QC-PCR, we could tell whether a given regimen was working in a fraction of the previous time. And within six to twenty-four weeks, we could tell if the regimen had achieved the objective of getting the virus to so-called undetectable levels, where replication was so suppressed that the virus could no longer be seen in the plasma. It was absolutely game changing.

We published the QC-PCR findings in *Science* in March 1993. The timing of this discovery could not have been more fortuitous. We now could measure very accurately the amount of virus in the bloodstream and directly relate it to the antiviral *activity* of the drugs—just at the time when the drug companies were working on a new crop of antiretroviral agents that would be more potent, as well as better tolerated. Once these companies heard that we had validated the notion of a QC-PCR technology, they would flock to Birmingham so we could test their new drugs in relatively small numbers of patients, to assess whether and to what degree the drug had activity against the virus.

Wherever a possible HIV drug breakthrough was mentioned, the press was sure to follow. Thursday morning, February 18, 1993, the *New York Times* published an article by reporter Lawrence Altman under the headline "Drug Mixture Halts HIV in Lab, Doctors Say in a Cautious Report." The article said that when a Massachusetts General Hospital medical student named Yung-Kang Chow combined three anti-HIV drugs in a test tube, "the combination of drugs has blocked the virus from growing and from spreading to other cells." It also said Chow and colleagues "noted that the test-tube strategy apparently prevented infection of healthy cells and successfully treated HIV in cells that had been infected."

The NIH found the discovery so promising, the article said, that it planned to test Chow's approach right away in HIV patients across the nation. Chow's experiments had combined the commercially available drugs AZT and DDI with one of two experimental HIV drugs, the article said. But in the upcoming national trials, the AZT and DDI would be given in combination with just one experimental drug, nevirapine—a slightly less potent pharmaceutical twin of our own L–697,661.

The article quoted Dr. Martin S. Hirsch, Massachusetts General's director of AIDS research, Chow's supervisor, and a colleague I had long known and admired. As in any drug trials in humans, the potential existed for unfavorable interactions, Marty Hirsch told the reporter. But, he added, "No immediate adverse effects were seen at the University of Alabama in Birmingham where doctors have just started giving the combination to four patients in experiments . . ."

With that single hat-tip from Marty in the *Times*, the national media descended on Birmingham like paratroopers dropped into a war zone. CBS, CNN, NBC, and ABC producers called me in rapid sequence. "Can we come talk to you?" "We need to talk to one of the patients, can you make that happen?" "No, we need a patient of our own, we can't use a patient who has talked to one of the other networks."

I had ample experience with our local news folks, but the national news folks were a different breed. Like birds of prey, they swooped in aggressively and wanted exclusivity at all times. Starting Thursday and continuing through Friday, I was consumed with media interviews—in the lab, in the clinic, running from building to building. Several patients in the study had talked to media from local news outlets before, but this was very different: On a national news segment, folks they went to high school with, family members they hadn't seen in a while, former coworkers in different cities would all see them and know their HIV status. Needless to say, most were not keen to volunteer. But a few stalwarts were, including Alan Woelhart, a study participant whose story would end up on the *CBS Sunday Morning* news show.

Late Friday, when I got a call from NBC, I was confused: Hadn't I just given an NBC reporter an interview? But this was a producer from NBC's *TODAY Show*. The way she peppered me with questions, I felt like I was auditioning. Apparently she was satisfied with my ability to describe the triple-drug therapy in a comprehensible way, because she invited me to be on the show the following Monday morning in New York City.

Problem: I had to be in Washington, D.C., that day for one of the major AIDS Clinical Trials Unit meetings. No problem, the producer said, "We'll shoot you remote from our Washington bureau. We will send a car to your hotel at 5:30 a.m. Don't wear a striped shirt. We aren't sure yet if Katie (Couric) or Bryant (Gumbel, then the show's two hosts) will do the interview. We'll call you over the weekend to finalize details, okay?" The producer wound up calling three more times, including the night before the appearance, that time to mention that "Tony Fauci will be interviewed as well during your segment."

All I could think was: *I am going to be interviewed via live remote on the* TODAY Show *from Washington sitting next to an NIH rock star, Anthony*

Fauci, the consummate professional when it comes to national TV interviews.
Articulate, precise, polished, with an almost unique knack for taking complex scientific concepts and presenting them in a way that Bubba in Middle
America can understand. Maybe they will ask Tony all the questions and I
can be his prop.

———

When I got to the NBC car at 5:25 a.m. in the dark streets of Washington,
somehow I expected Tony Fauci to be in it. Then I remembered, he lives
here; he can find his own way to the studio. I met with Tony in the "green
room" waiting area after we had both had makeup applied (including, I
hoped, enough powder to keep the shine down if nerves and lights made
me sweat). Tony asked how the study was going, and we talked about the
potential we both saw in this three-drug approach.

An associate producer came and got Tony. I had thought we would be
interviewed together, but in a way, I was relieved that I'd be on my own. A
few minutes later, I was escorted to a room that looked like a library, seated
in front of a camera, and fitted with a microphone and earpiece. Through
the earpiece, the producer advised me, "Oh, by the way, Bryant wanted to
do the interview." I had hoped for the seemingly friendlier Katie. I asked
the producer if he had any tips. "Well, Bryant typically doesn't stay with the
script, so just try to stay with him." I thought an unprintable oath—but into
the mic I said, "Okay, no problem." Gulp. I wondered if I would sprout a
Nixon-esque sweat on my upper lip.

Bryant interviewed Tony first, and as usual, Tony was brilliant. Their
conversation covered the basics of what triple-drug therapy was about, creating a perfect setup for me. Commercial break. "Okay, Dr. Saag, we're back
in fifteen seconds. Ready?" And then, Bryant was live: "We're here with Dr.
Michael Saag of the University of Alabama at Birmingham . . ."

Bryant was incisive and insightful with his questions. I kept my answers
short and to the point. Before I knew it, we were done! Painless. Right when
we went to break, Bryant came on my earpiece and said, "The local stations
will be going to local news and weather, but we keep broadcasting to the
Armed Forces Network. Can you stick around another five minutes?"

"Sure," I said, and we continued our conversation where we left off, like we were old friends. I felt like a comic doing his first gig on *The Tonight Show* and getting that ultimate sign of approval from Johnny Carson, being asked over to the host's treasured couch after I'd delivered my shtick.

If dealing with the media sometimes seemed like managing a circus, it was also strategically critical to our patients and our research. The more publically we were seen as leaders in drug development and treatment, the greater our chance to get more clinical trials, more grants, more support for our work, including our drug research. That meant more treatment options for patients and more hope.

For more than two years, we'd thought we were close to turning the tide and having something that would slow the virus. But close didn't save a single life. My UAB colleague Jim Raper remembers it: "Everybody was sick and so many were dying. The grief was just unimaginable, every day. In that surreal situation, it felt like serendipity, or divine intervention, that I had the chance to be working at UAB with investigators like George Shaw and Beatrice Hahn and Mike Saag, where every day might bring a breakthrough. When I look back, it's so sad to think what could have happened if Steve just had been able to hold on a few more years . . ."

But Jim's partner Steve could not hold on. He had been on AZT, until that stopped working for him. And on DDI, until that stopped working, too. Jim had assumed that the great insurance coverage Steve had as a teacher would provide him with needed care—"but in Alabama, gay people were 'just queers' and had no kind of protection," Jim recalls now, his gentle voice edged with bitterness. "The insurance case manager was always trying to cut some kind of a deal with me to avoid providing Steve a caregiver. I loved being with Steve even when he was sick, so when I could, I'd stay at home and provide the care he needed. We saved the insurance company lots of money."

Steve died in July 1993. He'd been trying to reach his forty-fourth birthday. He got close.

Along with the lingering grief, Jim—a gifted, creative, generous healthcare provider—admits that there's lingering anger. "When he died, I had to ask for time off from work; I didn't have any bereavement leave coming because officially, Steve was nothing to me," Jim says. "The starkness of that is still hurtful. It puts a fire in your belly for doing the right thing, so maybe other people won't have to suffer like that in the future." A few years ago, I shared Jim's satisfaction when UAB instituted domestic partner benefits for same-sex couples, including family, medical, and bereavement leave.

———

By early 1993, Emilio Emini's efforts to find a protease inhibitor had born fruit. A lead candidate compound that was very potent at inhibiting the HIV protease gene product was ready for testing! Based on successful efforts with L–697,661, Emilio called me and asked, "Are you ready to go another round?" I said, "Absolutely."

Emilio flew to Birmingham to meet with George Shaw and me and plan the trial for the compound, originally called L–524 but ultimately known as indinavir. Since this drug was complicated and even perilous to produce (more on that later), only a limited amount would be available, so we made this study only for eight patients, one of whom was "Ben."

A gay man living in Atlanta and working in real estate, Ben had the rugged good looks—dirty blond hair, penetrating blue eyes—of a Robert Redford, only taller. Friends in Atlanta's AIDS Treatment Initiatives group told Ben that the 1917 Clinic was undertaking a study of a brand-new drug against HIV, and in July 1993, Ben was the first patient enrolled. Before he started the medicine, Ben had a CD4 count of seven and his p24 antigen was very high, over 1,000 pg/ml. Within days of starting the medicine, Ben reported how much better he already felt. By the end of the second week on the drug, all of Ben's numbers had improved dramatically.

But early on a Saturday morning, Ben called me at home and said the whites of his eyes had turned yellow. I gulped. "How yellow?" I asked, as calmly as I could. "They're pretty yellow." He was describing jaundice, evidence that the drug was probably affecting his liver. In other drug studies, acute liver failure had resulted in death. Sounding more composed than I felt, I asked Ben to meet me at the clinic.

When I saw Ben, his eyes were a light canary color, but otherwise he looked as healthy as I had seen him in some time. He said he felt great and, when I examined him, I found no sign that his liver was enlarged or even tender, or any other evidence of abnormality. I drew some blood, turned on the television as a distraction while he waited, and carried the blood to the laboratory for the quickest possible processing.

Sitting with Ben while I waited for the lab's call, thirty minutes seemed like forever. "Do I have anything to worry about?" Ben asked me. And with a straight face, I answered, "Nah, this is all a precaution. Since you are one of the first people to ever receive the drug, I just want to make extra sure that we monitor this very closely." Inside I was thinking, *I hope this medicine didn't just kill his liver.* I had six other patients lined up to take it.

In the world of drug development, liver toxicity is one of the most feared outcomes. The liver is responsible for metabolizing many of the toxins we encounter, and to the human body, drugs are just one more common toxin the liver's designed to manage. How the liver handles the drug has a lot to do with how long the drug remains in the bloodstream, how frequently the drug is dosed, and what maximum dose can be safely given, especially over time. In a study the previous April, a few patients had been given the drug over the course of one day to see how it was absorbed and how fast the liver cleared it from the bloodstream. But no one had taken the drug for multiple days in a row before Ben, who was now two and a half weeks into his treatment.

Liver toxicity can take many forms. The most dreaded is total liver failure, where the liver cells are killed and unless a transplant happens, the patient is sure to die. In the summer of 1993, there was no way that an HIV patient would receive a liver transplant. One common sign of liver failure is elevation of the bilirubin, which causes jaundice. The other telltale sign is a spike in the bloodstream of some enzymes the liver produces. If Ben's lab work showed that he had elevated liver enzymes as well as jaundice, that was a sure sign of liver cell injury and big trouble.

When the phone rang from the lab, I felt like running to it. But I answered it calmly, wrote down the blood test numbers—and then heaved a sigh of relief because Ben's liver enzymes were not just normal, they were better than they had been. Though his bilirubin was up (for reasons we later recognized as being a signature but benign side effect of the drug), it was a type of bilirubin that didn't signal liver injury. I called Emilio and explained what had transpired. After discussing it at length, Emilio and I agreed that since Ben was responding so well to the indinavir, we would pause it for three weeks and then, absent other complications, restart it. Ben agreed.

Our decision proved to be a good one. Four weeks after resuming treatment, Ben's bilirubin had risen only a little bit, his liver enzymes remained normal—and the virus in his bloodstream, as measured by p24 antigen, had plunged from more than 1,000 pg/ml to undetectable. This response, the biggest I had ever seen to any single agent, indicated this drug was working extremely well. Ben said he felt "like a new man," as good as he had in more than two and a half years.

About two months into Ben's treatment, George Shaw and I sat on one end of a conference call. On the other end were Emilio Emini and Ed Scolnick, Merck's global vice president for research and development. This was my first encounter with Ed, but I'd been told that many people who worked under him feared him and considered him a bit of a curmudgeon, gruff, opinionated, perhaps self-confident to a fault.

I told Ben's story in full, including his latest numbers: virus undetectable by p24 antigen, and CD4 risen from seven to more than 130. "My God," Ed exclaimed, "we've cured him!" Startled, George and I looked at each other incredulously. I mouthed to George, "Did he say what I think he just said?" After some awkward silence on the conference line, I got up the courage to say, "I hope he is cured, but I'm not sure I would count on that."

While we all were excited about Ben's success, several new challenges emerged that none of us had previously considered. Now that we knew that we had at least one drug that worked so well against HIV, how would we decide who would get it next? In the case of indinavir, this problem was compounded by the fact that it took twenty-three steps in chemical synthesis to make this particular protease inhibitor. While sufficient quantities could be made in modest-sized laboratories for the six to eight patients that we would treat in Birmingham in addition to Ben, how could Merck make enough drug to take care of the tens of thousands of people who would be clamoring for the drug over the next year, once they heard of the success that Ben had had?

For almost every drug that ultimately gets developed, the scale-up of drug production is a challenge for chemical engineers. But the twenty-three-step chemical synthesis required to produce indinavir was three to four times more steps than for most drugs—and because one of the steps was particularly volatile, it could blow up whatever plant was producing the drug if not managed properly. To Ed Scolnick and Merck's credit, they immediately poured vast resources into building a plant for the production of this drug at incredible speed. But even with the most optimistic estimates, they were at least nine to twelve months away from having large quantities of drug that met good manufacturing practices.

Recognizing this challenge, George and I agreed that at least for the time being, we would keep the success of Ben's treatment to ourselves. Once we could be confident that Merck would be able to produce the drug in sufficient quantities to be able to meet more of the need, we could break our silence.

George and I had gotten permission from Emilio to send small samples of Ben's blood to Jeff Lifson and Mike Piatak in Redwood City so that they could perform the QC-PCR test. Ben's PCR value prior to treatment was well over one million copies of virus per milliliter—but four weeks into treatment, just after the time Ben showed up with jaundice, his QC-PCR value had dropped below 1,000 copies, about the limit of the assay's detection capacity at that point. This degree of suppression of virus had never before been achieved and was truly breathtaking.

The good news didn't last. In early November, Jeff's test results showed the virus in Ben's blood was starting to rise again. George and I called Emilio, and he confirmed our conclusion: Albeit slowly, Ben's virus was becoming resistant to the drug that was saving his life. Emilio's response was precisely what I knew it would be: "I hate this virus!"

Notwithstanding Ben's developing resistance, he and the other participants in our indinavir monotherapy trial were still benefitting tremendously from taking the drug. But because it was in short supply and we lacked knowledge regarding its potential lasting benefit, we elected not to broadcast our findings. It was a brutally hard decision. Dozens of patients in our clinic and scores of patients I knew from Atlanta were in dire need of something, anything, that could bridge them to the next new drug, the next new finding. On each call with Emilio I would ask, "When is our next study?" "How soon could I get my other patients on this drug?" Looking at days on the calendar, I didn't have to wait long, but seeing patients in the clinic, the wait for the next study was agonizingly slow.

Marty Delaney, Tom Blount, and their fellow activists knew that there were limited slots in clinical studies and that only a few US cities had sites that hosted trials. They pushed pharmaceutical companies to expand their compassionate use programs as widely and quickly as drug production would allow and the FDA to accelerate approval of new drugs. To create more even access, Marty spearheaded a creative solution, the Parallel Track. While companies continued development of promising new agents through their traditional Phase II and III clinical studies, they would also create a centralized access program that would allow any clinician in practice to sign up for the program and have the drug delivered to his or her clinic for distribution to patients in the most need of access to the drug immediately. But these were institutional solutions, and institutions seldom move quickly.

Tom needed a solution now—or sooner, or yesterday—because his beloved, Jim Straley, was wasting away before his eyes. Jim was like so many other patients at this time: Their disease would almost surely have killed them by the late 1980s, but they were saved by AZT. Then the benefits of AZT became exhausted and they moved on to the next wave of newly released drugs—DDI, DDC, D4T—but the incremental benefit of these drugs when used after AZT failure was small. Hoffman-La Roche was the first to market with an approved protease inhibitor, saquinavir, but it was so poorly absorbed from the gut that very little drug made it into the circulation. Better, more potent drugs were needed. And for Jim and many others, there was no time to waste.

Tom and other activists made it their business to know which companies had what drugs in which stages of development, and which providers and trials had the most promising ones. They were relentless in seeking ways to get more drugs sooner for the use of the most desperately ill. This was Tom's quest on a humanitarian level to help anyone with HIV, and on an excruciatingly personal level to help Jim. In June 1994, when Jim's numbers disqualified him for inclusion in a study of L–524/indinavir, Tom pleaded for an exception to get Jim the drug. I could not support his plea in a conversation with Merck officials. In response, Tom faxed me a four-page letter full of agony, anger, and reproach.

"Only once has Jim been able to qualify for a clinical trial, and now, apparently, he never will have that chance again," Tom wrote. "Even as inclusion criteria were relaxed, he was always a few T-cells too short . . . His only hope has been that someone in the medical field would become interested in salvaging his life, his only available avenue is compassionate use, and the most feasible tool is L–524 . . . All we were asking for was twelve days' use of this drug, and no matter how rare it is, I can't believe that Jim's life has such little value to everyone but me. As long as there is a single dose of L524 that is not critically needed for research (and we both know they are there), I believe that the decision to not allow at least some compassionate use is completely immoral . . . The really sad thing, personally, about this development is that I truly believe Jim's life could have been saved by L–524."

———

Tom admits that he never expected to hear from me again after the "neck-wringing" (his words) that he gave me in that letter. And he did sound surprised when I telephoned him to thank him for his insight and candor. I think we each knew the other was trying to act ethically and with good intentions. I never begrudged Tom his view, and I was in awe of his determination. He literally worked every angle to try to get L–524 for Jim and others. He worked his connections on the Merck citizens' advisory board. He supported an underground effort to manufacture the drug privately. Tom's father even joined the effort, pleading Tom's case in a personal note to a friend of his who happened to be Merck's chairman.

"In late 1994 when I was chasing that drug, I think there were thirty-two or thirty-three humans taking it in clinical trials around the country, and through my work I knew thirty of them," Tom recalls. "I got people to give me a pill or two, to sneak it out of the trial, so that by the end of the year I had a thirty-day supply of L–524."

Then, early in January 1995, Tom phoned me to say Jim was on his deathbed. Tom did not say how he got a thirty-day supply of L–524 and

I did not ask—but he wanted a doctor's opinion on whether he should go ahead and start Jim on the drug, knowing that he might not be able to get any more. I told him, "Tom, do it." Even though starting a drug Jim could not continue might have built resistance to further treatment, in Tom's position, I would have done the same thing. On January 11, Tom gave Jim his first dose of L–524, then caught a 7:00 a.m. flight to New Jersey to talk to Merck officials about increasing access to the drug.

In a meeting that included Paul Reider, head of production at Merck, Tom pleaded for a compassionate use program that would provide L–524 immediately to patients who might not live until its FDA approval. Here's how Tom remembers it:

> Paul argued that Merck's plants could barely produce enough drug to supply the patients in clinical trials, and could not spare any for other patients. We had intelligence that said Merck did have L524 to spare, perhaps enough for 450 people. I was thinking of Jim and others at death's door, and I was weeping with rage. I had to leave the meeting to catch a 3:30 p.m. flight, to get home to give Jim his second dose of L524. But as I walked out the door, I turned and pointed at Paul and shouted, "We are talking about maybe 450 people, a fully-loaded 747 jet—and it's going down and you have the possibility to prevent that! Those lives are on you."

Tom made it back to Atlanta to give Jim his 6:00 p.m. medication. The next day, as Tom recalls it, "Jim sprang out of bed for the first time in months. And Paul Reider called to tell me that he and other Merck officials had been deeply affected by what I said, and they were determined to get the drug out to more people. In a couple of months, they did." Tom didn't know until later why his 747 metaphor had hit so hard at Merck. It was because Dr. Irving Sigal—the Merck chemist who was most responsible for the discovery of L–524—had been on Pan Am Flight 103 on December 21, 1988, when a bomb destroyed the plane over Lockerbie, Scotland, killing all on board.

After first seeing dramatic benefit from L–524, Jim developed resistance to it. Tom sought other remedies, but Jim was so depleted that nothing helped for long. Jim Straley was forty-two when he died on August 20, 1995. Ask Tom how long they were together, and he will tell you. They had "eighteen years, thirty days, and twelve hours."

———

When George and I were writing the paper on L–697,661 on Beatrice's grandmother's "good luck table," we made a glancing reference to how rapidly the AIDS virus must replicate. But it was not until we started looking carefully at the drop in HIV RNA, or viral load, in Ben's case that we finally asked the pointed question: "Just how rapid is rapid?"

To help us fashion an answer, we recruited Martin Nowak. A young Vienna-born mathematician who—George met at a professional meeting, Martin could create mathematical formulas to describe almost anything, from the seasonal patterns of bird migrations to the performance of professional bicyclists. We agreed he was the perfect person to work with us on modeling the virus's behavior during Ben's use of indinavir.

After several months of work together, George, Martin, Emilio, and I were able to describe an almost mind-boggling process of dynamic replication. George and I hadn't known the half of it—this viral replication wasn't just rapid, it was *incredibly* rapid. And relentless—the virus never stopped replicating. Other viral infections, such as influenza, produce up to 1 million copies per day. With HIV, between 1 billion and 10 billion viruses were produced in any given day, every day from the time a person was first infected until the time he or she succumbed. The virus would infect a cell somewhere in the body, typically in lymphoid tissue such as the spleen, a lymph node, or the gut, and convert that cell into a virus factory. In the day or less that each infected cell lived, the cell would produce several thousand viral particles, and then the virus would kill it just as another susceptible cell became infected to take its place.

Once, the central mystery of HIV had been why patients progressed from an asymptomatic state to illness and then death, a process that takes on average 12–15 years. But when we saw these numbers, I was more amazed that patients lived as long as they did under such an onslaught. Another eureka moment! It is a real tribute to the resiliency of the human body that such a challenge can be managed by the patient for so long without showing signs of infection or disease. When we give antiretroviral therapy, we block the ability of the virus to infect neighboring cells. Then when the cells producing virus die off, usually within a day, they are not replaced with a newly infected cell, and the amount of virus produced in the body is reduced exponentially. So as rapidly as the virus had been produced, it also could be seen to decline very rapidly in the bloodstream, by the QC-PCR assay.

Medical science works best when discoveries like these are shared freely and promptly, for others to refine and build upon. Such findings often are disseminated via national and international scientific conferences where investigators submit condensed abstracts of their work that are reviewed by peers in the field and judged to be of sufficient quality to warrant presentation. The scientific abstracts considered of greatest interest typically are showcased as oral presentations at the meeting, usually in front of large audiences. When not presented orally, the other accepted abstracts are presented at poster sessions, where the investigators summarize their data and conclusions on five-by-seven-foot posters, scores of which are displayed like billboards in the conference hall. Investigators stand by their posters at designated times during the conference, presenting repeatedly to whoever stops by and wants to hear the story of their work.

In October 1994, I was invited to present an oral abstract at the meeting of a leading ID organization, the Interscience Conference on Antimicrobial Agents and Chemotherapy (ICAAC). George, Martin, Emilio, and I had submitted an abstract on the viral responses to regimens using nevirapine combined with two or three other drugs, the so-called "triple-drug cocktails" that had gotten us so much media attention the previous year. While the results of our study did indeed show a benefit of triple-drug therapy over dual therapy, we had a different story to tell.

In addition to modeling the viral dynamics of the indinavir patients, we also had modeled some of the patients on triple-drug therapy and had seen the same story of 1 billion to 10 billion viruses produced per day, life span of an infected cell of approximately one day, and rapid decline of viral load in just weeks, or even days, of therapy. This was the story we wanted to tell.

Our triple-drug therapy trial was slated as an oral abstract, in the same session where Dr. David Ho was scheduled to tell the story of ritonavir, a protease inhibitor similar to indinavir but with substantially more side effects, especially nausea, stomach upset, and diarrhea. David and his team at Los Angeles's Cedars-Sinai Medical Center had been performing similar modeling exercises, except instead of working with Martin Nowak, he was working with a mathematical modeler at Los Alamos, Alan Perelson. Astonishingly, they had precisely the same findings we did regarding the dynamics and they too wanted to highlight their findings in the upcoming session at ICAAC.

For me, this was a *deja vu* moment. Four years earlier, at the 1990 International AIDS Conference in San Francisco, George and I had submitted an abstract describing the quantitation of virus from several patients (including WEAU) who presented early with acute HIV infection, using serial culture techniques and comparing the results from this technique to other quantitative measures such as p24 antigen. This study was the precursor to the study we eventually did with Jeff Lifson and Mike Piatak using QC-PCR, where we ultimately saw extremely high levels of virus, on the order of 1–10 million copies per milliliter among those with acute infection. I had my poster printed and ready to be hung in the conference hall the following morning.

Sunday evening around 8:00 I was in my hotel room and had just picked up my meeting materials, including my badge to get into the sessions and the abstract book. I hadn't gotten very far through the abstract book when I stumbled across an abstract from the Cedars-Sinai group describing *virtually the same findings* we were presenting in our abstract! Almost identical. I called George.

The lead author on the abstract was Eric Daar, a fellow then working in the lab of David Ho. (Eric has since gone on to become a leader in the HIV field in his own right and is now the division director of ID at Cedars). David Ho grew up in Los Angeles and had done his training in ID at Massachusetts General Hospital working in the lab of Marty Hirsch. He returned to Los Angeles where he started his own lab and was working on HIV pathogenesis. He had completed a prior study of quantitating HIV by culture techniques in the spinal fluid and later a study of HIV in the bloodstream using culture techniques. I remember that study in particular because it mirrored precisely what George, Beatrice, and I had been doing in the lab—but David published his findings first, scooping our findings in the literature. We ultimately got our study published, but we clearly were "seconding" David's study.

As I stared at the abstract in the book that Sunday night, I thought, "Damn, we got scooped again by David Ho!" George calmed me down, telling me to go to the conference hall in the morning, track down Eric Daar to see where they were in terms of publication deadlines, and get back to him.

———

As soon as the doors opened at the convention hall, I raced to Eric's poster showing data that mirrored ours almost point by point. As I was looking it over, Eric came by. I introduced myself and shared our data with him. He was intrigued. I asked where they were in the publication cycle and he said they were getting ready to write it up. I suggested, "Maybe we could submit back-to-back in the same journal?" "Fine with me," he said, "but it's really up to David." I asked George to call David. We worked on the papers simultaneously and published them back-to-back in the *New England Journal of Medicine*.

For scientists, the issue of competition is tricky. Like athletes in a team sport, our first allegiance needs to be to the team, and in a sense, David Ho and I and our colleagues were all on one team fighting HIV/AIDS. But in another sense, science isn't a team career: Scientists are individuals when it comes to being offered professorships, endowed chairs, equipped and staffed laboratories, salaries, and benefit packages. In this instance, the team had won. It felt good.

Standing outside the large auditorium at the ICAAC meeting in Orlando, I visited with David Ho. I mentioned how similar this was to our prior experience and wondered out loud if we might try publishing our findings once again back-to-back. He thought that was a good idea, but he was more focused on how we would coordinate our talks coming up in the next hour. We agreed that he would present his approach to modeling viral dynamics, with a focus on the methodology. Since my talk was initially based on the clinical findings from the triple-drug therapy trial, I focused my talk on the clinical meaning of the viral dynamics findings—that there was no virologic latency but instead a constant assault, eroding the immune system's reserves until there was nothing left to fight off opportunistic diseases. This viral churning also burned a lot of energy and caused a great deal of inflammation that, over time, reduced appetite and led to wasting.

To me, these data were urgent proof that the virus needed to be treated early and aggressively. David concurred. Over the weeks following the ICAAC meeting, David's group and our group pulled our manuscripts together and submitted them to *Nature*, where they were published back-to-back.

———

Earlier in 1994, a message I had received from David Ho had made me feel that we really *were* on the same team, in a much more personal way. He knew I was on the West Coast for an IAS-USA continuing medical education meeting and wondered if, while there, I could go by and see a patient who was struggling, on whose case he had consulted. I said, "Sure," and gave my hotel address to the car service that was to ferry me to the patient.

At the appointed hour, I went to meet the car and found a gleaming, full-sized limo. I don't remember the chitchat with the driver; I was taking in the view as we drove along palm-tree-lined boulevards, past successively ritzier mansions. At our destination, the driver pulled the limo up to the doors of an elegant Spanish-hacienda-style home, ushered me out of the car, and told me to ring the intercom. When I did, a woman's voice greeted me: "Dr. Saag, come on in, the door's open. Come up the stairs and turn right, I'm at the end of the hall."

It felt kind of eerie to walk into the exquisite, high-ceilinged house and see no one. Then I saw the scattering of toys in the living room and my tension eased: I was just a doctor, making a house call to a sick mom. I headed up the grand staircase.

Elizabeth Glaser was standing at the end of the hall in a pink velour robe, a frailer version of the outspoken advocate I had seen behind podiums and on television. After quick hellos, she described her concern: "I have this horrible pain, in my back and down my legs, and I can hardly walk." My fear immediately was cytomegalovirus, an infection that can be dormant and harmless in healthy individuals but that can cause shooting pain, muscle weakness, and other problems in people with compromised immune systems. I examined Mrs. Glaser and told her what I thought the problem might be. I told her I would like to start her on two medications that would help until I could talk to her doctor (Dr. Michael Gottlieb) about confirming my tentative diagnosis with a spinal tap. She thanked me and asked if I could find my way out. I returned to the front door, where the driver was waiting.

In 1981 when Elizabeth Glaser was giving birth to her first child with her husband, actor Paul Michael Glaser, she hemorrhaged and required a blood transfusion. Four years later, she learned that she had contracted HIV from the transfusion and that she had passed it to her daughter, Ariel, through breast milk and her second child, Jake, in utero. In 1988, Ariel died. On July 14, 1992, in New York City, Elizabeth gave a speech to the Democratic National Convention in which she vented her outrage at "leaders who say they care but do nothing." In her speech, I heard the cry of anyone who ever has faced devastating illness and felt ignored or ill-treated:

> I am in a race with the clock. This is not about being a Republican or an Independent or a Democrat. It's about the future for each and every one of us. I started out just a mom, fighting for the life of her child. But along the way, I learned how unfair America can be today. Not just for people who have HIV but for many, many people. Poor people. Gay people. People of color. Children. A strange spokesperson for such a group, a well-to-do white woman. But I learned my lesson the hard way and I know that America has lost her path and is at risk of losing her soul. America, wake up! We are all in a struggle between life and death.
>
> I understand the sense of frustration and despair in our country because I know firsthand about shouting for help

and getting no answer ... When you cry for help and no one listens, you start to lose your hope. I began to lose faith in America. I felt my country was letting me down, and it was. This is not the America I was raised to be proud of. I was raised to believe that others' problems were my problems as well. But when I tell most people about HIV in hopes that they will help and care, I see the look in their eyes. "It's not my problem," they're thinking. Well, it's everyone's problem ...

I believe in America, but not with a leadership of selfish- ness and greed where the wealthy get health care and insur- ance and the poor don't ... We need health care for all.

I knew when I saw Mrs. Glaser that there was little that I, or any physician, could do. She died a few months later, but her valiance lives on in the work of the Elizabeth Glaser Pediatric AIDS Foundation—and in her son, Jake, now in his late twenties.

———

The *Nature* articles on which my UAB colleagues and David Ho's crew col- laborated were published back-to-back in the January 1995 issue—another team win! And in August 1995, David hammered home the point in an editorial in the *New England Journal of Medicine*, headlined "Time to Hit HIV, Early and Hard."

Publication of the viral dynamics paper was perhaps the most meaningful scientific experience I have ever been a part of, not because I was a researcher but because I am a physician. I wasn't senior author or first author, indicat- ing I wasn't the first prime mover of the project. But I was part of the team, contributing the clinical meaning of the findings to the discussions and the paper. These findings, to me, indicated we had an angle on the virus for the first time. We could beat it—or at least we could *manage* it. I had something that could give my patients what most they craved: time.

The viral dynamics story took our understanding to a new level. We now had a clear view of *how* the virus caused sickness and what we could do to retard and hopefully reverse its progression. Stop the replication, stop the disease. It was that simple and that profound.

The inhibition of replication had to be complete and persistent, 24/7, day in and day out, fifty-two weeks a year, every year for the rest of the patient's life. It would take a combination of drugs, the so-called cocktail—and once successful drug cocktails were discovered, they had to be taken *every day, all the time.* Failure to do this would lead to drug resistance and return of the disease process, picking up from the time the drugs stopped. That ultimately would take the patient back to the point where he or she was prior to initiation of the cocktail and back on the doomed path to sickness, AIDS, and death.

And the viral dynamics discovery had an added bonus: For the first time we could see a clear path to a cure of HIV. More than 99 percent of cells producing virus naturally die off almost immediately, and with treatment they are not replaced by newly infected cells.

A very small fraction of infected cells, however, don't die. They persist as chronically infected cells, not actively producing virus but still harboring the virus in the host's DNA, ready for reactivation at some distant point in the future. The scientists' favorite guess is that the reason they persist is precisely because they are not actively producing virus and therefore aren't killed by any of the proposed mechanisms outlined above.

Were it not for this reservoir of longer-lived, chronically infected cells, the antiretroviral cocktail would lead to cure in everyone because the other infected cells die and are not replaced. An apparent example of this was the headline-making report at the 2013 Conference on Retroviruses and Opportunities Infections (CROI) describing a Mississippi case in which an infant was HIV-positive at birth, was started on aggressive antiretroviral therapy within hours of birth, and was later found to be free of the virus—essentially, cured. In this case, the infant's virus did not have sufficient time to establish the latent reservoir before treatment began. So when the replication was stopped, the infected cells died and were not replaced. Since no latent cells were present that could carry the infection forward, the child was cured. Further proof of principle!

Because most patients, unlike that infant, will not start treatment before the reservoir is established, the question becomes: How long do the chronically infected cells live? The answer to this question tells us how long we have to wait until patients are cured.

Initial estimates provided by Martin Nowak in our group and Alan Perelson in David Ho's group suggested that the half-life of the cells was between fourteen and thirty days. This meant that during that time frame, roughly half of the cells would die. So if we waited enough half-lives, the last remaining cells would die off, resulting in cure. In this model, it is much like uranium: How many radioactive half-lives would we wait until, say, we would let our kids play near Japan's Fukushima I nuclear power plant after the 2011 partial meltdown there? With the cell half-lives that our modelers had devised, it would take three or four years for the latent reservoir to disappear, at which point the patient would be cured. This was real news—and while it took a while for the news to sink in, there was ultimate recognition of the finding in the public media when David Ho was named *TIME* magazine's "Man of the Year" in 1996.

Then, a not-so-funny thing happened on the way to the cure. With more study and reevaluation, it became clear that the cells actually lived on average for thirty to forty *months*, not days. When that number is plugged into the "uranium equation," it turned out that it would take more than seventy years (!) of full suppression of the virus for all the cells to die off and result in a cure.

Elimination of the latent cell reservoir through more extreme measures, such as ablative bone marrow transplant, has since been shown to lead to cure in a few patients in the last several years. That confirms the theoretical model as proposed by the Ho group and our group in 1995, and it was something I would explore a few years later for a patient of mine, Cyndie Culpeper. But it was (and for the foreseeable future, would be) an extreme solution that might help a few.

Translating findings from a model to a person—in this case, our patients—matters. Discussions of models, replication inhibition, mathematical abstractions, academic papers, and authorship all speak to the world of science; these things matter too. But when the conferences end and we get off the airplane near home, those of us who were lauded by colleagues for our papers came back feeling less than triumphant. Dealing with the relentlessness of HIV always took us back to people who had entrusted their lives to our care. In our brief absence, new symptoms had surfaced for one patient and another had taken a nosedive. In a very real sense, this work wasn't about David Ho or Mike Saag or some unknown research assistant. It was about Steve or Brian—or Ben.

In mid-March 1996, in what was then the fastest drug approval in FDA history, the agency approved the drug first known as compound L–524, then as indinavir, and commercially as Crixivan. By then, Ben had been on the drug for more than two and a half years, and we had intensified his regimen with AZT and 3TC, a new drug similar to AZT but with fewer side effects. Ben clearly was ahead of his time, because that combination—indinavir, AZT, and 3TC—would become the "triple-drug cocktail" that marked the beginning of the Highly Active Antiretroviral Therapy (HAART) era.

Ben's virus never stopped battering away at the main drug in his regimen. When the virus finally figured out indinavir, we tried other antiretroviral combinations, but to no avail. Ben died from advanced AIDS in spring 1998. By bravely volunteering for the L–524 trial in summer 1993, Ben had bought himself nearly five years of life. How many years his generosity, humor, and courage added to the lives of others with HIV we will never know, but if we added them all we'd be talking about centuries. He lived for others, and died among the epidemic's unsung heroes.

Chapter 10

CYNDIE

I t's hard to explain why Cyndie Culpeper's case loomed so large for me. It wasn't just that she was accomplished and funny and kind; I've had many patients who were all those things. It may have been because she was a kindred spirit—trained in medicine, a singer, a Jewish searcher.

Certainly it was partly a matter of timing: Cyndie arrived at the clinic right when the remarkable new medications did. After years of despair and frustration, my colleagues and I could offer more than palliative care and hand-holding—we could finally hope to significantly restore health and prolong life. If I had been writing a movie, I couldn't have scripted it better: Enter the life-saving drugs, and right behind, bring in the patient with so much to live for.

Cynthia Ann Culpeper was born in San Francisco in the early 1960s. At age fourteen, as a Catholic high school student assigned a project on Judaism, she visited a Conservative congregation one Friday evening and was captivated by the Shabbat service.

Ostensibly to complete her school project, Cyndie interviewed the rabbi that night, then returned repeatedly with more questions for him. She resolved to convert to Judaism, which she did once she reached adulthood. I've heard but never confirmed the story that a nun from Cyndie's high school once told the rabbi with whom Cyndie was studying, "I know she'll never make a good Catholic, so make a good Jew out of her."

Out of college with a nursing degree, Cyndie worked as a surgical nurse at San Francisco General Hospital. When she felt her faith leading her elsewhere, she enrolled in the Jewish Theological Seminary in New York City. At first, Cyndie planned to become the cantor who sings and chants the prayers at temple services. Ultimately, she pursued studies to be ordained a rabbi. But she still sang at every opportunity, including joining her mother, Mary, and a friend of theirs, Karen Schanche, at annual sing-alongs of Handel's great oratorio, *Messiah*.

During seminary breaks, Cyndie traveled back and forth from New York to San Francisco, working her way through rabbinical school by taking nursing shifts at SFGH. In early 1994, on duty as a surgical scrub nurse, she jabbed her hand while cleaning a pan of bloody instruments.

"She was really scared about it," Karen recalls now. Karen was one of the first people Cyndie called because Karen was an expert. A social worker and psychotherapist, Karen was among the San Francisco healthcare providers who founded what became the San Francisco AIDS Foundation. She had collaborated with Paul Volberding and other SFGH heroes of mine, and had worked with infected people since the days when the virus was known as GRID.

After Cyndie's injury, she was given two AIDS tests at intervals, as was hospital policy for such incidents. When both tests, the latter in August 1994, were negative, Cyndie moved on with her life: "She knew she was exposed but not infected and did not let this exposure stop her from pursuing her rabbinical training and work," Karen recalls. After Cyndie was ordained in May 1995, she was chosen to lead a synagogue in Montgomery, becoming the first female pulpit rabbi in Alabama.

In September 1995, Cyndie was preparing to celebrate her first High Holy Days as a rabbi when she noticed some hoarseness in her voice. After seeing a Montgomery doctor, Cyndie called Karen, who remembers the conversation this way:

"Cyndie asked me, 'Karen, what does having thrush mean?' And I said, 'It means you should get an HIV test.' I put her in touch with Ruth Greenblatt, MD, and her Women's Care Clinic at UCSF, and she came to San Francisco to the clinic to be tested. When she got the results she called me and said, 'I have a T-cell count of three.' She had bypassed HIV and gone right to full-blown AIDS."

Somebody in Paul Volberding's office gave my name and the number of the 1917 Clinic to Karen, who gave it to Cyndie. I already knew the basics of Cyndie's story when I walked into the clinic exam room and first set eyes on her: a thin woman of average height, wearing a blue clerical hat over her short-cropped hair. She looked terrified and incredibly vulnerable.

"Hi, I'm Mike Saag," I said. "Could you stand up?" When she did, I hugged her. She burst into tears, explaining between sobs, "No one has hugged me since I got my diagnosis." And so began my saga with Cyndie Culpeper.

I held her as she cried for a while, and it seemed like a healing cry. I waited to give her what I considered good news, better news than I had been able to give patients for years. "There's a lot we can do," I reassured her. "All these new drugs are coming and we can get access to them now." I drew several tubes of Cyndie's blood, sent her home with medicines to prevent *pneumocystis* pneumonia, and hightailed it to George and Beatrice's lab.

When a sample of blood containing AIDS virus is placed in a lab dish in a tissue culture, it typically takes two to four days to grow, then ultimately consumes the culture cells within a week to ten days. The virus in Cyndie's blood was the most aggressive any of us ever had seen: It tore through the tissue culture in less than two days. We were up against CUCY, one of the most aggressive strains of the AIDS virus, and we would need to throw everything at it that we could as quickly as possible.

I contacted pharmaceutical companies Merck and Glaxo and got compassionate use drugs for Cyndie per a research protocol: indinavir, the new protease inhibitor from Merck that we had first tested with Ben in 1993, and lamivudine (3TC), a new drug about to be released in the United States, which was to be used in combination with AZT (zidovudine). After a few weeks on triple-drug therapy, Cyndie was responding nicely—well enough to heartily sing the Friday evening Shabbat prayers with her congregation.

Then came new hurdles. Cyndie sought my counsel about sharing her status: Whom should she tell, and when, and how? Some friends, fearing she would be ostracized, had urged her to keep the diagnosis a secret. But she could not live with that.

Karen told me later that by the time Cyndie visited her around Thanksgiving 1995, "her sense of vulnerability had turned into an incredible strength, a resilience. She had moved from fear about the disease and about how long she had to live to concern about everyone else. She was thinking of her congregation, and she didn't want them to feel afraid or obliged." For three days, Karen and Mary worked with Cyndie on a statement in which she would tell her congregants that she had AIDS. Cyndie brought her planned statement to 1917 Clinic's chaplain, Malcolm Marler, who offered both suggestions and support for Cyndie's plan to go public.

Mary Culpeper remembers these days in vivid detail. "On December 1, 1995—World AIDS Day—I went to Friday night services with Cyndie at her congregation. She and I wore red ribbons, and people in the congregation were asking us what the ribbons were. I was thinking, 'Oh my gosh, she's going to go public in a month and we don't know how people will react; she could be tarred and feathered.' We really were living on pins and needles for that final month."

Cyndie came back to Birmingham in December. She told me she had pretty much decided to go public with her congregation but she still had some lingering concerns: "What if they don't accept this? What if they reject me?"

I told her I thought that was highly unlikely, and my bet was that their response would be precisely the opposite. I believed they would accept her unconditionally. Why I believed this so strongly, even in retrospect, I'm not sure; intuition, perhaps, or hope. I likened her disclosure to her congregation as being very similar to a patient coming out to his or her parents about HIV status, sexual orientation, or both. Living with the secret was so much harder day-to-day; maintaining the silence drove a wedge into the relationships.

Perhaps I felt confident encouraging Cyndie to go public because of my experience. Out of all of the gay men I'd encouraged over time to reveal their status to their parents, I only had one situation where it didn't go well. And I knew Jewish people and their traditional, even visceral support of the oppressed, having been oppressed for so long themselves.

Cyndie's coming out process began in the first days of 1996. As Mary recalls it, "During the first week of January, Cyndie told the president of the congregation that she was not renewing her contract for the coming year and would explain at a meeting with the congregation on Sunday, January 7. In the morning before the meeting, she asked the congregation president to come to the house and she told him why she was not renewing. And he got on the phone and called everyone in the congregation and told them to drop everything, no matter what they were doing, to come to the meeting."

More than 150 congregation members assembled to hear their rabbi clear her throat, take a deep breath, and tell the truth she had so carefully prepared to tell in ways they could understand and accept. In part, she said this:

> Yesterday we finished reading the Book of Genesis, the stories of the beginnings of our people. And now we begin the Book of Exodus; its chapters are filled with the drama of national redemption and revelation . . . But despite these parallels, this will be a very unique address today. It is a revelation of a different sort . . .
>
> Since the beginning of my appointment here at Agudath Israel, I think most of you know that I have tried to stay out of any special spotlight. I did not want to be known as the first female Conservative pulpit rabbi in the entire state of Alabama; I did not want to be known as the rabbi who converted to Judaism. I just wanted to be known as "Rabbi" . . .
>
> There is however now another title I must wear, however reluctantly; one which for the past three months I tried to imagine could not possibly be true, and one about which I can no longer be silent. I am a rabbi who has Acquired Immune Deficiency Syndrome—AIDS.
>
> So why am I telling you this today, or even opting to tell you at all? I suppose on one level it is an emotional catharsis for me. In the past six months, some of you have privately confided in me as your rabbi what you were going through: your day-to-day struggles, or your own health issues. Whether I may have had a practical solution for you was not the point; simply talking about matters to the right person is in itself therapeutic.

. . . And now you are letting me confide in you. I am telling
you this because you are my family, and I hope to feel the support from you that a family gives, and today I need you to be
rabbi for me . . .

As an operating room nurse, I was privileged to witness
countless times how intricately our human bodies are fashioned, acutely aware of the subtle delicate balance and sym-
biosis existing between the flora and fauna within and on our
bodies. It scares me that my body no longer retains that balance—something [that] healthy people never have to think
about, but now I do a lot.

And yes, it scares me that now, God forbid, you may treat
me and relate to me differently. I wonder, will you flinch when
I drink from the water fountain, or from the Kiddush cup? Will
you invite me over for dinner, but serve me on paper plates, or
politely decline an invitation to my home? Will you discourage
your children from coming near me, or stop the exchange of
Shabbat Shalom cheek kisses and hugs that we have shared on
Friday nights? . . .

Please, please, please tell me regarding all of those fears, "No,
rabbi, you're wrong. We know that AIDS is not transmitted by
casual contact. We know we can't get AIDS from the air, or a
sneeze, or a kiss or a hug. We know we need not sterilize or run
our dishes and cutlery fifteen times through a dishwasher after
you have used them. We know we need not fear getting this
disease from you because it is spread only by limited, defined
bodily fluids."

A good number of my friends across the country tried to
talk me out of telling you all of this today. "You risk nothing
by being silent, Cyndie, but risk a lot if you are public," some
would say . . . But I knew for me this was the right thing to
do, because not only is this disease condition a part of who
I am now, talking about it is also a part of my Jewish value
system . . .

I thank you for allowing me to break my silence today with you, hard though it may have been, and no doubt will be at times still to come, for both you and me. May we, as a caring community, together break many walls of silence together over this most serious issue, toward *tikkun olam*, repairing the world and ridding the world of AIDS.

Cyndie had arranged for a social worker to be at the meeting to answer any questions. But as she told me in an email the next day, that proved unnecessary. When she finished her address, the congregation surged forward and crowded around her, adults standing in line for a chance to hug their rabbi, and children wrapping themselves around her legs.

"Yesterday was GREAT!" her email said. "I don't think I've ever been so nervous in front of a group (tho I've spoken to greater numbers before, this was to my 'family'). Afterwards I got 150 hugs and about 150 whispers of 'We want you to stay' . . . People came over to my house afterwards per my invitation (I had food in advance—how Jewish!!!)"

When a reporter later asked Cyndie about her decision to reveal her status, she said, "This is Torah. Torah is teaching, and that teaching is best shown by how we choose to live publicly, not by the silence we may maintain privately."

The Friday following Cyndie's speech, her mother Mary says, the congregation had a basket of red ribbons at the service for members to wear. And over time, the congregation raised funds to help with Cyndie's care. The congregation's response "was more curative than any drug she could have gotten at that moment," Karen says now. "After that, Cyndie decided to become not just 'the rabbi who has AIDS' but the rabbi who was an AIDS advocate, and she was fearless."

For about a year, Cyndie led her congregation in Montgomery and traveled every eight weeks to the 1917 Clinic, a three-hour roundtrip. But just when we had the virus on the run, one of the three drugs in her cocktail, indinavir, caused her to develop a kidney stone. That forced us to take her off that medication and put her on another one that worked about the same on her virus but had some wicked side effects. The drug, ritonavir, was available as both a liquid and as a liquid inside of a capsule. Having been told it caused a lot of gastrointestinal upset, I once took the liquid form, just to see what it was like, and was sick for two days with diarrhea. The drug made Cyndie so nauseated that once, on the highway on her way to a clinic visit with me in Birmingham, she drove past a delivery truck for Little Debbie™ baked goods, and the sight of the smiling little girl's snack on the side of the truck was too much for her. She pulled over and threw up on the roadside.

As if the nausea and diarrhea were not bad enough, the capsule would melt away in the stomach soon after ingestion, and the foul-tasting liquid would "repeat" (reflux) back into the patient's mouth, leaving a taste my patients likened to cherry-flavored motor oil. The capsule had to be refrigerated and taken twice daily. Cyndie complained that after taking it long enough, she would become nauseated every time she simply opened the refrigerator door, like Pavlov's dog—except instead of salivating, she would feel like barfing.

And so began the dance we did with so many patients: Try a new medication . . . wait to gauge the benefits and side effects . . . see the patient slipping more than improving . . . drop that medication and try the next. Cyndie endured the treatment changes with the proverbial patience of Job, a biblical figure to whom she could relate. But with the various drugs came all the problems common to those who suffer AIDS: severe, energy-draining anemia; painful kidney stones; neuropathy; inability to pay the cost of drugs her insurance wouldn't cover; more kidney stones; headaches and intractable nausea; immobilizing diarrhea. And yet somehow, she never lost her sense of humor—she loved it when I prescribed matzo, the unleavened bread eaten during Passover, to combat her diarrhea.

The entire 1917 Clinic staff had a natural soft spot for Cyndie. We'd all known others with charm and grace, although Cyndie's personality and courage stood out. But I think the fact that she'd contracted AIDS while doing our work, going through the same routines we go through every day, put her in a special category. New drugs brought new hope. Even more than we realized at the time, we were pinning that hope on her to be the patient with the dream outcome: Get on the right medications, get the virus under control, live happily ever after.

Eventually, the combined rigor of being a full-time rabbi, dealing with a significant illness, and traveling to the 1917 Clinic both for scheduled treatments and unscheduled problems became too much. Cyndie resigned her pulpit and moved to Birmingham, determined to pursue treatment as aggressively as the virus was pursuing her.

Because my wife's family had generations-deep roots in Birmingham's Jewish community, Amy and I had a unique vantage from which to watch Cyndie's reception there. Cyndie went right to work as an unofficial assistant rabbi at a Conservative synagogue, Temple Beth-El, and as a teacher at a Jewish day school. A gifted, natural teacher who always made time to talk to people about faith and life, she endeared herself to virtually everyone she met. She settled into the community with her precious companion, a golden-retriever-mix pup she adopted from the animal shelter and immediately named Annie Lucy—Annie because she was an orphan and Lucy (as in Lucille Ball) because she was a mischievous redhead.

Cyndie's mother, Mary, continued to live in their native California but visited Cyndie often in Birmingham and was one of the "patient moms" with whom I became especially close. "Mother Mary," as I came to call her, cherished every one of her daughter's sermons, whether she was sitting in the audience listening or reading the copy Cyndie would always send her. Mary particularly loved a series of sermons called "Life's Lessons from the Leash," Cyndie's reflections on how both she and Annie Lucy chafed at the restraints they faced.

"From a puppy's perspective, movement is life, and life is worth exploring and experiencing to its fullest," Cyndie wrote. "It's almost as if she thinks this is a last-time occurrence and therefore she's going to make the most of it . . . She resents the leash—she's ruined three so far!—because it prevents her from engaging the world at her preferred more rapid pace.

"Ironically, HIV/AIDS can also pull at each of us with the same choke-chain force, reminding us of how precious life is; calling us to experience every moment to its fullest," Cyndie wrote. "It can be scary. It can sometimes feel that some of our life experiences may indeed be last-time experiences . . .

"Both my puppy and I have our leashes in life, whether we like it or not," Cyndie's sermon concluded. "Nevertheless, Annie Lucy and I have both come to accept the limitations placed on us while still experiencing the world, and life, with a rich, spirited perspective."

It was 1996 when Rabbi Cyndie Culpeper showed her congregation what AIDS looks like: her. By then, I'd been treating others with her disease for more than a decade. I'd taken on not just their illness but their lives, their dreams, their loved ones and fears. I'd eaten Ed's food, mourned the loss of Jamie's baby, mounted Kevin's Crimson Tide hat on my office wall, and imagined Michael, free of pain, spinning and twirling in a place without ventilators. I could recall Andy's pungent smell and hear David's pilot voice explaining that Jesus would be found at the 1917 Clinic. When Jacob died, I wept openly in front of students; when Brian died, I treasured the art-work he'd left behind. I knew why Tom Blount counted not Jim's age but the number of hours they had spent together. And I'd lost every one of them: Ed, Jamie, Kevin, Michael, Andy, David, Jacob, Brian, Jim, and hundreds more. No matter how much magical thinking I brought to each one, it was never enough. Each of them was special, and I never saved any of them. Not one.

Looking back, I know that I allowed myself the secret indulgence of loving Cyndie Culpeper without reservation because she required no magical thinking. When Cyndie arrived, science had produced tools I didn't have before. Here, I knew, was one who would be saved. No magic needed. *L'chaim!*

Chapter 11

"BECAUSE IT HURTS"

I f you ask people in HIV/AIDS medicine to name the year that we turned the corner on the epidemic, many would say 1996.

For me, the medical landscape in 1996 shifted as the American social and political landscape had in 1968: There were so many momentous and emotionally charged events that, at times, it was hard to find the meaning within the tumult.

In 1968, things happened that once would have seemed unfathomable. First Dr. King and then Senator Kennedy were felled by assassins. Years of impoverishment shaped the Poor People's March on Washington, D.C. Fury over America's actions in Vietnam tore through the tear gas and bloodied police batons at Chicago's Democratic National Convention—and television delivered all of it to our living rooms.

In 1996, leading researchers were achieving results with antiretroviral medications that were once beyond imagining: driving the virus to undetectable levels in patients' systems and keeping it there, as nearly as we could tell, indefinitely. To an extent, I and others involved in clinical trials could say we had seen this coming for some time through our process of weeding out flawed drugs and protocols and refining promising ones. As it typically does, knowledge in the lab was running a year or two ahead of knowledge that could be applied—in this case, applied in HIV/AIDS clinics and broader patient populations.

Because we had an edge on the knowledge, I now realize, we also had an edge on optimism. We could feel reasonably hopeful because we could *see* that proverbial light at the end of the tunnel. But the patients and activists were in a place where they couldn't yet see it. They were still dying and cursing the dark. And so they took also to cursing the research establishment—suspecting us, blaming us, attacking us—because we talked about prolonging life but they didn't see it happening.

For me, 1996 was a dizzying year of internal conflict. I knew lives could be saved that would certainly have been lost. I knew it. And this knowledge did nothing to prepare me for the reality that, after investing my life in HIV/AIDS research care, I was seen by many as enemy more than ally.

———

If you've ever visited the Vietnam Veterans Memorial in Washington, D.C., you remember walking along the polished black granite walls sunk into the earth in a *V* shape. Where you enter, the wall is eight inches high. As the sidewalk next to it descends, the height of the wall increases until, at the walk's lowest point, the wall towers above you, ten-foot-high slabs inscribed with the names of the lost.

To me, that landscape looks a lot like how the fight against HIV felt. For years we were in the throes of the epidemic, descending deeper and deeper—until, almost suddenly, we could turn 90 degrees and for the first time see the beginnings of a way out, a way forward.

That turning point, for me, had come in January 1995. That's when I honestly felt we could begin to reclassify HIV/AIDS—that what had been a certain death sentence was becoming a chronic, manageable condition.

What did I see coalescing in early 1995 that led me to that conclusion? I saw progress on all fronts thanks to the collaborations of the pharmaceutical industry, academia, patients, activists, media, and key players in the federal government—Congress, NIH, CDC, FDA, and the Health Resources and Services Administration (HRSA), the agency charged with improving access to healthcare services for the uninsured and medically vulnerable.

The NIH provided strategic leadership through investment in basic science and clinical trials via their intramural programs and grants to individual investigators at academic medical centers and research institutes. The CDC provided continual monitoring of the epidemic and investment in tracking behavioral factors of transmission. The FDA helped by relaxing its previously rigid requirements for clinical outcomes ("body counts") in HIV drug development, and the HRSA helped through its management of the Ryan White programs. Congress also played a key role in keeping the funding streams flowing despite occasional crises.

(Notice anyone missing from this list of federal players? When I credit those who hastened the transition of HIV from a death sentence to a chronic condition, notably absent are the 40th, 41st, and 42nd presidents of the United States. Ronald Reagan did nearly nothing during his eight years, when AIDS exploded onto the scene, thus giving the virus an enormous head start, despite his close personal and professional relationships with members of the heavily affected entertainment community. George H. W. Bush did close to nothing despite his claims that his administration practiced "compassionate conservatism." Bill Clinton, during his two terms in office, was perhaps the biggest disappointment to me. I say that not because he did nothing, but because he voiced commitment to healthcare reform, science, education, and gay rights and yet never embraced HIV as a cause until he left office—meaning that he could talk about it but had no responsibility for it.)

Who *did* help bring about the turning point in the epidemic? The pharmaceutical industry contributed nonstop efforts to create newer, more potent, better tolerated, and more user-friendly drugs. Academia contributed creative, highly motivated, and collaborative investigators. The media contributed its generally sympathetic voice and persistence, a determination to keep the story alive even if the public was ready to dismiss it as "old news." And the plague gave us patient after patient who offered to try any drug, suffer any indignity, bear any pain—if only their sacrifice might mean a better, longer, more meaningful life for others. I had a clinic full of people who willingly participated in clinical and basic science studies, though many were spending their last ounces of strength in the process.

But great credit also is due to the activists for their *lack* of patience. They kept everyone's feet to the fire—industry, government, all of us—with their public insistence that "not enough is being done." Their actions fueled progress, even when their words were hurtful to those of us trying our best. To many activists, our best was simply not good enough. And it wasn't. Every time I lost a patient to the disease, I knew my best had not been good enough.

By the late 1980s and early 1990s, differences had sharpened among AIDS activists about what their goals were and how best to achieve them. In January 1992, activists Mark Harrington and Gregg Gonsalves left ACT UP to create the Treatment Action Group (TAG), a nonprofit organization focused on accelerating treatment research. They were hardly uncritical of the NIH, the pharmaceutical industry, and the academic community, but they took a different tack: They sat at the table with the establishment players, promoting institutional change from the inside while ACT UP continued to goad from the outside. TAG offered detailed analyses of how research and treatment could be improved. As Marty Delaney and Project Inform were doing, they injected urgency into the discussions and provided patient perspectives.

Meanwhile, direct-action AIDS advocacy was alive and well, and ACT UP founder Larry Kramer was its most prominent public face. His rhetoric was as stark as his group's logo: the words "Silence = Death" under a pink triangle, the mark the Nazi Third Reich had placed on gays targeted for extermination.

Larry never hesitated to pursue his goals by employing what he considered the most powerful human motivator: fear. He wanted ACT UP's words and actions to inspire fear in the scientists, the NIH, the White House, the pharmaceutical companies—anyone who might make things happen more quickly in HIV/AIDS medicine. He ridiculed high-profile investigators in public, often humiliating them in front of large audiences. Marty Hirsch at Massachusetts General Hospital was a favorite target because starting in the mid-1980s, he led the NIH's AIDS Clinical Trials group, a multi-million-dollar network of academic treatment centers that collectively designed and carried out large clinical studies of new therapies.

I tried to set aside my feelings as an investigator and look at the situation dispassionately, but I still came to the same conclusion: ACT UP was acting out against the wrong people. The accusation that Marty Hirsch was "doing nothing" was a baseless assault; he was pouring himself relentlessly into his work. So were other leading MD-researchers in the field. John Phair of Northwestern University, Margaret Fischl at the University of Miami, and Larry Corey at the University of Washington were precisely the people who were making things happen. Tony Fauci of NIH pounded the pavement of Washington, D.C., and the doors of Congress to seek more funding to support HIV/AIDS research, and he was extremely effective. Of all the people the activists could attack, why them? Why us?

It is easier to understand why in retrospect than it was at the time. But not all activists are created equal. Some patients and activists genuinely believed they were being lied to about the science, that they purposefully were being given poisonous drugs or denied helpful ones. Some had embraced the work of Peter Duesberg, a University of California–Berkeley biologist who claimed that AIDS-related diseases were caused not by a virus but by the use of recreational drugs and even the use of AZT. Some activists—such as members of ACT UP San Francisco, a rogue offshoot of the mother organization—contended that HIV does not cause AIDS and that the use of antiviral HIV drugs only served to poison patients. They argued, therefore, that the pharmaceutical industry pushed "deadly drugs" just to make money and that existing drug therapies weakened rather than strengthened the body's immune system and its ability to fight HIV.

Others who protested may simply have felt compelled to take some action, *any* action, in the face of all the death. My friend and patient David, the former fighter pilot, had explained this to me years before.

When Birmingham AIDS activists were marching on the 1917 Clinic demanding an experimental medication that we couldn't provide, I had groused to David that they were ingrates—they were attacking the people who were trying to heal them. I can still hear his astute answer: "It's not about you, Mike . . . It's the white coat they're marching on. It's The Establishment, which you represent, like it or not."

––––––

By January 1996, the good news I'd seen coming was ready for prime time. The venue was the annual meeting of the Conference on Retroviruses and

Opportunistic Infections (CROI). The International AIDS Conference had become something of a political convention where political correctness and inclusiveness had trumped science and scientific presentations. CROI was created to focus on the most significant clinical science in the field. It had quickly become THE meeting at which to present new data. My Merck collaborator Emilio Emini was attending to present findings on triple-drug therapy, including data from the UAB study in which my patient Ben had first swallowed indinavir.

After Ben and others responded well to indinavir in small studies, Merck had scaled up production and was in the process of completing two so-called pivotal trials. The FDA and other regulatory bodies used these critical studies to weigh approval of new drugs, typically by comparing them to standard, approved treatments. In this case, Emilio was reporting on a large number of patients randomized to receive either AZT + 3TC or AZT + 3TC + indinavir.

The main floor of the ballroom at the Washington Sheraton Hotel was standing room only, so I made my way up to the balcony to watch the presentation. Emilio's delivery was brilliant and his message was simple: The three-drug combination blew away the two-drug combo, no contest. Triple-drug therapy worked and unquestionably was the way forward. As I looked around the ballroom during his talk, the audience was listening intently. After Emilio, an investigator who worked with David Ho presented data from Abbott Laboratories' protease inhibitor ritonavir. When combined with AZT + 3TC, it yielded results similar to our outcomes with indinavir in triple-drug therapy.

By the end of the session it was clear: The future had arrived. Presented before a large international audience, all could see the power of the triple-drug cocktail. It was easy to extrapolate the impact: Treat everyone with one of the three-drug regimens and they would live happily ever after. Mission Accomplished!

While the drug trials were underway, advocacy groups such as Marty Delaney's Project Inform had been tracking trial results in real time. Seeing the promising outcomes from our indinavir trial, they began pushing Merck for immediate access to the drug. The company and the FDA balked, saying that the drug was too new and its safety unproven; for all they knew, the drug could *kill people*. To Tom and Marty, this was flatly ludicrous. Since the virus already was killing people, could a drug do any worse? And maybe, just maybe, it would save lives. The advocates put on a full-court press for accelerated approval of the drug for commercial use.

Hounded by Tom, Marty, and others, the FDA had approved both indinavir and ritonavir for use in HIV-infected patients by March 1996. The European regulatory agency, the EMEA, followed suit soon thereafter. Triple-drug cocktails were now available to patients who previously could have gotten them only within a clinical trial or through a compassionate use program. The entire process—from the "first-in-human" studies with Ben in the summer of 1993 to the FDA approval—took less than three years, compared to the five to seven years that such approvals ordinarily take. The FDA deserves credit for adopting policies to fast-track drug approvals. But in my opinion, the lion's share of the credit for hastening the approval goes to the impassioned, relentless activists.

After the January CROI meeting, and even after the March drug approvals, I didn't hear the kind of buzz that I had anticipated after such game-changing developments. It's possible the findings were so stunning, like a reprieve for someone on death row, that it took time for them to sink in. For whatever reason, the conversation about new HIV therapies was pretty muted for about ninety days, April through June. Then, in July, the 11th International AIDS Conference opened in Vancouver, British Columbia, and all hell broke loose.

In the natural world, it's called a "feeding frenzy" when wolves or sharks descend on a quarry with mindless, ravenous abandon. In the information age, I've seen a similar sort of frenzy in pursuit of headline news. A Twitter mob formed online in the wake of the 2013 Boston Marathon bombing, naming as suspects people who were totally innocent. As the Vancouver conference neared, journalists arrived in droves to cover the triple-drug therapy breakthrough. They came armed with preconceptions and superlatives, while the scientists and activists and drug companies came armed with their own, often deeply personal angles on the story. The emotion of the time fairly crackled in news reports. *POZ* magazine reported:

By the International AIDS Conference in July, the elation had
reached such a frenzied pitch that longtime AZT investigator
Dr. Paul Volberding was ambushed by a camera-and-micro-
phone-wielding throng while checking into his Vancouver
hotel. "Would you characterize the tone of this meeting as
'euphoric'?" one reporter asked—even before the convention
had officially started. Volberding demurred.

Amid the rush to declare victory, responsible scientists tried to strike a balance that reflected reality: We had new tools to prolong lives but we had
no cure.

On July 10, reporter Elizabeth Farnsworth of the *PBS NewsHour* interviewed two distinguished conference participants: Dr. Helene Gayle, the
CDC's director of HIV prevention, and Dr. Roy "Trip" Gulick, a clinician
and researcher at the New York University School of Medicine and a valued
colleague of mine. In this exchange, Trip reflected the cautious optimism
many of us felt.

> FARNSWORTH: So, Dr. Gulick, is it too early to say that
> AIDS is no longer an incurable, inevitably fatal disease?
>
> GULICK: Well, I think that what we've shown is using com-
> binations of drugs which can actually lower the virus to very
> low or undetectable levels for periods as long as months, that
> what we're really saying is that that's an important first step
> toward making HIV a chronic, treatable illness. I think it
> would be misleading to say that we have the answer. Certainly
> I would not use the word cure to describe these therapies, but
> we're making a positive step in the long-term treatment of
> this disease.

While PBS was interviewing Trip Gulick, I was preparing to be on a
panel discussing the new antiretroviral therapies. The panel was organized by my old friend Donna Jacobsen, president and executive director
of the International AIDS Society-USA. My panel mates were top-notch

researchers and clinicians including Margaret Fischl, Paul Volberding, and Doug Richman, whose laboratory was among the first to identify HIV drug resistance. Because we were going to address the clinical basics of using these new drugs—when to start therapy, what to start with, when to change therapy and what to change to—the symposium drew a big, curious crowd. Doug was at the podium, partway through his presentation on primary infection, when the doors of the venue were slammed open and the circus began.

I've seen videotapes of the event, but they don't really capture the scene as I felt it, chaotic and alarming and ridiculous all at once. Twenty young men from the rogue ACT UP San Francisco group burst into the ballroom, shouting unintelligibly. They ran down the aisles, mounted the stage, and slung containers of red liquid so it sprayed across us panelists. They doused us with fake blood, they later said, to make their point that if the researchers themselves were infected with the AIDS virus, that might spur more urgency and progress in fighting it.

Some of us sat there startled; others retreated from the dais as the protesters charged. They jumped on the dais, raised their arms in power salutes, and their shouts became rhythmic chants: "Toxic chemotherapy! Ban AZT! Toxic chemotherapy! Ban AZT!"

The conference center security personnel, showing a restraint I've long associated with Canadians, didn't apply any muscle. But they did step in to position themselves between us and the demonstrators, who variously shouted at us, grabbed for our microphones, knocked papers and water off the dais, and pumped their fists in the air. Our audience of colleagues began its own roaring chant toward the unwanted protesters: "Get out! Get out! Get out!"

As a panel of MDs, we knew immediately that we hadn't been showered with actual blood. Upon further inspection, we concluded it was probably beet juice. Margaret was among the worst hit, vegetable gore splashed on her eyeglass frames, her cheek, her blouse. I remember mentally cursing these clowns for ruining one of my favorite jackets, the one I had worn to my son Andy's bar mitzvah. Somebody passed us a couple of tablecloths and we tried to mop up the area and ourselves.

After a few minutes, apparently satisfied that they had made their point, the protesters walked off stage with a security escort to a chorus of boos and shouts of "Shame!" A representative of ACT UP's New York chapter came to the podium to apologize. He said the protesters were members of ACT UP San Francisco, the rogue band that had split from the official group, "and we disown them. We never disrupt information, ever." Years later, Donna Jacobsen still was struck by "how very different this was from any other 'activist' activity. Rather than a demonstration or protest about the lack of progress, it was an attack on the dissemination of information. It was just unconscionable."

A meeting organizer appeared with enough white *VANCOUVER 1996* conference T-shirts for all the panelists. We took off the most soiled of our clothes, put the T-shirts on, and went back to our seats at the dais. I'll always remember Doug Richman retaking the podium, straightening the microphone, and delivering the deadpan line, "Now, where was I before I was so rudely interrupted?" I still have my printed program from the symposium with its juice-stained cover.

I also still have something I received a few days after that symposium. It's an email from Billy Pick, an HIV-positive man then working for the AIDS office of the San Francisco Department of Public Health. Billy wrote to both me and Margaret Fischl, saying that he had recognized our faces in news photos of the "blood"-splattered Vancouver panel "and decided to write. I want to express my outrage and sorrow that you had to be the targets for such unwarranted and misguided actions. I want you to know that the people who did this do not represent the HIV community in San Francisco . . .

"I wanted to thank the both of you for your commitment to people with AIDS because I don't know if anyone else has or will," Billy's email continued. "It takes a tremendous amount of patience and character to deal with the pain and the anger that many of us in the community feel sometimes. It also takes a lot of courage to stand up to systematic abuse and terrorist tactics. I would ask that you continue to do so, not just because we need your scientific expertise but because I really believe that both of you care about finding a cure for those of us with this disease."

As long as I was serving people like Billy—and I am, to this day—I could put up with all the hecklers and the beet-juice bombardments. (And thanks to an emergency dry-cleaning run by the resourceful Donna, my favorite jacket wasn't ruined after all.)

The incident in Vancouver deserves not only to be remembered or criticized, but understood. It'd be easy to dismiss the protesters in Vancouver as crazy, their tactics as childish and counterproductive, their charges as ignorant nonsense, and their claims that HIV does not cause AIDS as bizarre. More representative are the other activists, like Larry Kramer, ACT UP New York, Marty Delaney, and Tom Blount. Their rage at The System was real and completely on target. Many times since then, I have heard other health-care consumers—and not just HIV patients—express frustration and outrage. They can't get the care they need. They can't get the care they see others get. They don't understand either their health problems or their health coverage. They can't get a straight answer from a doctor, or even a call returned. They can't afford care a loved one needs. Or they paid for the care, the loved one died, and the crushing debt lives on.

If I knew all this in vague, intellectual terms in the late 1990s, I know it now in the most intimate and personal of terms. Hour after hour in the 1917 Clinic, as elsewhere, the opportunity to care for people is thwarted by The System. Within the past seven days I have lost my patience, delivered rants, and felt the frustration of being denied the opportunity to treat and care for patients—felt it so keenly that I nearly wept. Perhaps now more than ever, I've begun to understand the origin of the activists' action. It wasn't so much about logic; it was about having nothing left to lose. More than anything, it was about grief.

There was plenty of progress against HIV in 1996, significant achievements and milestones. In 1996, the number of new AIDS cases diagnosed in the United States declined for the first time since the epidemic began. In 1996, UNAIDS (the Joint United Nations Programme on HIV/AIDS) was established to promote global efforts against the disease, and the International AIDS Vaccine Initiative was formed. In 1996, the FDA approved key consumer tools for HIV detection, including the first HIV home testing and collection kit. Starting in 1996, AIDS no longer was the leading cause of death for all Americans ages 25–44.

Optimist that I am, I could make the glass-half-full argument about 1996 and probably about every year since. I could say that when there's been so much improvement, it's ungrateful to dwell on what has not improved. But if we don't look hard at the deficiencies, we'll never force The System to come to terms with them. And we must.

I remember learning early in my medical training that surgery is, no matter what else you say about it, messy. It's just a messy, sloppy, unappetizing process. So is much of medicine, frankly. We deal with human waste as well as human intake; we spend our days examining smelly sores and draining wounds. One of the reasons we use such incredibly Latinate terminology for simple procedures—colonic disimpaction, hemipelvectomy, radical debridement—may be to mask the unpleasant realities.

When most of us think of research, we think of sparkling laboratories where impossibly clean women and men wearing spotless white coats perform sterile procedures. When we think of advances in medical science, we think of heavily vetted journal articles and highly technical conference presentations delivered in a language and style that would cure the average insomniac. And all of this is, to some extent, true.

It's also true that research is sometimes a messy process, despite our best efforts to clean it up. Research findings morph into journal papers and conference presentations, but they also make their way into the clinic where we're out of bullets to treat Michael, and he's going to die unless we have something new. Medicine doesn't treat findings or reports; it treats Ben and Andy and Cyndie, and therein lies the source of its messiness. And research dealing with human suffering does not hover over the affected population and drop papers from the air. It, too, finds its way in front of glaring cameras and skeptical reporters and people who have suffered, are sick, are dying.

As ironic as it sometimes seems to me, the same phenomenon that drove protests led for over a decade by ACT UP and Larry Kramer—a public outcry, a scream for change, a patient-based revolution—might be needed today to address America's failing healthcare system.

So long as "healthcare policy" is removed from those who suffer and die, so long as "healthcare financing" is measured in the bottom-line billions instead of Uncle Ted's copay or Mom's need for a home nurse, so long as the debate is conducted by those who are both well and well insured—we are going to continue spiraling downward with ever-declining outcomes and ever-increasing costs.

Turning the tide on this is going to take something stronger than beet juice. It may take a critical mass of Americans speaking out against the status quo.

Once after my old friend and "nemesis" Larry Kramer had chewed out someone at the top of his lungs, he was asked why he so frequently was heard screaming. His answer was absolutely convincing: "Because it hurts."

Chapter 12

ONE STEP UP, TWO STEPS BACK

I have never quite forgiven the editors of a distinguished medical journal (which shall remain nameless) for clipping my literary wings in an invited editorial I submitted in 1994 about HIV medications. I was writing after our great hopes for AZT had been dashed, when the drug many thought might be The One had in fact begun to fail in patient after patient. The opening of the article I submitted—both an apt and an elegant opening, I thought—went something like this:

> For many clinicians providing care for patients infected with the human immunodeficiency virus (HIV), their mood with regard to the use of antiretroviral therapy reflects the opening of Samuel Beckett's play *Waiting for Godot*, where Estragon declares, "Nothing to be done." To which Vladimir responds, "I'm beginning to come around to that opinion."

The editors rewrote it. I argued. I lost.

Upon reflection, though, I suppose they had a point. Instead of Beckett, I should have been quoting The Boss.

I'm a diehard Bruce Springsteen fan, and particularly fond of his 1987 album, *Tunnel of Love*. The songs he wrote, as his first marriage went south, are full of ambivalence and heartache. One of his lyrics perfectly describes how the fight against HIV felt to me in the mid to late 1990s:

Same old story, same old act
One step up and two steps back

The new drugs we could combine in the triple-drug cocktail of highly active antiretroviral therapy (HAART) were life-saving, miraculous—except when they weren't. They were not doing everything we needed. Or they were too much, too strong. Resistance was breaking through triple-drug barriers we had considered impermeable. Drug side effects were unpredictable and baffling, threatening the people we were trying to heal.

This state of affairs proved unbearable for some of the most fragile, most frustrated members of the HIV community. From where I sat, I could see real progress—one step up—even when the drugs still weren't quite right. But for some patients and activists, if the drugs weren't 100 percent right, *everything* was wrong. It was hard to hear their dissatisfaction, their impatience, their complaints. On my worst days, the feeling of being unappreciated hardened into a stark image: In my mind, and my self-pity, I saw myself holding out a golden cup to someone dying of thirst, only to be told . . . well, the Beatrice Hahn version of "screw you."

I knew only one way to proceed: Continue to focus our research on whatever held the most promise *for the patients*. Give each new therapy our best shot. If it didn't pan out, try to learn what we could from the setback and move ahead. If we just kept at it, I believed, we'd eventually crack the codes and demolish the roadblocks.

That belief didn't even strike me as magical thinking. It just seemed like a logical progression, given our experiences and breakthroughs so far. And once we had the means to keep HIV-positive people alive and healthy, I also believed the US healthcare system would be ready and eager to help deliver that salvation.

There is a line between hopeful, magical thinking and hopeless naïveté. Unfortunately, I don't always recognize it. Even when I trip over it.

From the outset at the 1917 Clinic, we had tried to conduct as many pharmaceutical company drug trials and research projects as humanly possible so we could enroll every patient who qualified and wanted in. Investigators in the United States must follow exacting federal regulations when conducting research that involves human subjects. Among other things, the regulations forbid the use of coercion of any form to encourage or entice a patient to participate in a study. And that was an issue in our work, because many HIV-positive people were so desperate that they would grab at any possible lifeline. We had to be careful that offering the new therapies to patients was not viewed as coercive but rather as presenting an alternative to existing therapy.

I think most MD-researchers in the field were in much the same position that I was. We knew the drugs weren't likely to be perfect at that point and probably would not be for some time. But perhaps we masked the truth a little with patients, wanting to inspire hope; or maybe we had false hopes ourselves.

The narrative we laid out for patients typically went like this: You have a terminal disease. The drugs we currently have available to you by prescription generally work for twelve to eighteen months and then fail, and are associated with a fair number of toxicities. Toxicities are not good. Neither is doing nothing.

If you have health insurance, your copays for these medications may be as high as 20 percent; that adds up quickly when medications cost $600 to $1,000 a month. And if you are one of the poor schmucks who has a paying job but *no* health insurance, you are totally screwed because even if your income is modest, you probably make too much money to be eligible for low-cost or free medications through the compassionate use programs run by pharmaceutical companies or through ADAPs, the AIDS Drugs Assistance Programs run by states with Ryan White money.

Your other choice—assuming you are eligible based on your health status, as most of our patients were—is to join a clinical trial. In the study, you gain access to the up-and-coming medicines before they are released, though there is a risk they could have some unknown toxicities that could seriously harm (read: kill) you. The medicines, lab tests, and all activities associated with the study are provided free of charge to you. And for every visit, we will give you a stipend to cover the costs of transportation and/or participation.

(For example: If the patient took part in a pharmacokinetic study, one where he stayed at the clinic for 8–12 hours for frequent blood draws to see how his body metabolized or eliminated the drug, we paid a stipend to cover his time, usually up to $100 a day.)

An extra perk of volunteering for the studies was that patients were assigned to a nurse dedicated to the study they were on. These RNs became a personal nurse for each patient in the study. They scheduled appointments at times that worked best for the participants, called them with lab results pro-actively, took their calls outside of office hours, and got them into the clinic immediately whenever a problem arose. They essentially served each study patient as what the medical field is now calling a "healthcare navigator"—a knowledgeable, reassuring person to guide them through the complexities of treatment.

I'm confident we provided outstanding care to all patients in the clinic. But study patients were followed at more frequent intervals, enabling us to more carefully track their response to treatment and the potential side effects and toxicities. I always told patients enrolling in studies that "every patient at the 1917 Clinic is special, but study patients are extra special." As participants, they took medications that they knew might or might not help them, but that they also knew might advance medical science by building our knowledge of new treatments. Should the drugs in their study work well, their participation would help assure more rapid drug approval, and thereby, more universal access to medications for everyone.

I don't think there were many patients who volunteered for studies solely out of altruism. However, I do think that serving others definitely made many of them feel really good about what they were doing, and it made me feel good too. With the launch of every study, I would look into the faces of some new recruits and longtime patients like Pearly James, who'd been with us through regimen after regimen. With every new therapy, I felt more hope that we could keep those patients around—that I might still be seeing those faces years into the future, smiling and lined with age.

Because UAB had both heavy enrollment of patients into clinical trials and very early access to new drugs via those trials (many of them in the earliest Phase I or Phase II testing), we were in the catbird seat in terms of seeing how drugs worked or failed. This meant we, compared with others in the HIV medicine community, often had earlier findings and different feelings about emerging treatments. For example: In 1993, many mainstream HIV providers were despairing as AZT's initial success in patients turned to failure—but while they grappled with that disturbing realization, we who were doing research on emerging drugs were beginning to see the dramatic successes of newer therapies. Conversely, by the 1996 Vancouver meeting, when euphoria about triple-drug regimens was sweeping over providers, patients, and the public, we in the vanguard were getting a sobering view of the underbelly of the beast: regimen failure.

Regimen failure took different forms. Sometimes it showed itself as emerging toxicities, such as the relentless diarrhea and frequent nausea Cyndie Culpeper experienced. And some of the toxicities were particularly insidious, such as those experienced by "Clarence," a patient we admitted to the hospital in fall 1997.

With his ready smile and football-player build, Clarence made me think of "The Big Man," saxophonist Clarence Clemons from Springsteen's E Street Band. Our patient Clarence lived in rural Alabama, in the "Black Belt" region that is so named not because the majority of the population is black (although it is) but because of its dark, rich soil. Though many good physicians practice in Alabama's Black Belt, there weren't ID specialists or HIV experts there in the mid-1990s.

Although Clarence had done fairly well on AZT alone for several years, when he came to us his viral load was over 100,000. We started him on a cocktail, AZT/3TC/indinavir, all of which were now available commercially. Within a few weeks, Clarence's viral load had dropped to undetectable levels, and he was enjoying improved health. But he also was tiring of the 140-mile trek to and from Birmingham every three months. So he chose to be followed primarily by his hometown family physician, who would partner with us on his HIV care. That seemed like a reasonable approach, and for a year and a half, the cocktail kept Clarence's virus undetectable. He seemed to be stable and out of the woods.

We hadn't seen Clarence in Birmingham for about four months when we heard from his local hospital: Clarence had been admitted with abdominal

pain, weakness, and unexplained shortness of breath. He was transferred to
UAB, and when I saw him in the ICU, he was ill and weak and moaning
incoherently. The medical records from the referring hospital showed they
had provided good care and had worked through all of the usual suspects of
possible diseases: pneumonia, pancreatitis, biliary obstruction, pulmonary
embolus. But one line of notations on Clarence's chart alarmed me: the
blood chemistries. The slow, downward creep of his bicarbonate indicated a
buildup of acid in Clarence's bloodstream.

That phenomenon most commonly occurs when diabetics show up in
ketoacidosis, or diabetic shock. But Clarence was not diabetic and his blood
sugars were normal. A quick calculation showed that his anion gap—an
indicator of unmeasured acids in the blood—was over twenty-three, more
than twice what would be considered normal. What was causing this?

Thumbing through Clarence's medical records, I found the report on a
liver ultrasound that had ruled out gall stones but confirmed his liver had a
consistency of fat. My heart sank. The condition known as fatty liver, when
severe enough, leads to the liver being unable to process acids normally produced by the body, especially lactic acid. And fatty liver was a known, albeit
infrequent, consequence of long-term use of AZT (and some other drugs
including DDI and D4T).

Humans experience a transient buildup of lactic acid when we exercise
intensely. That's why we breathe hard after a 100-yard dash; lactate builds
up and stimulates the lungs to blow off the excess acid, which would be
poisonous if it remained. I asked the lab for a measure of the lactic acid level
in Clarence's blood, knowing what it was likely to show. When the results
came back, the only surprise was how high the level was—a value of 12.5,
the highest level I had ever seen, and one I previously had thought was
incompatible with life. The acid was poisoning all of the cells of Clarence's
body to the point where they were not working.

We tried everything we could over the next twenty-four hours to get
Clarence's acid level under control, but it was too late. AZT had killed his
liver; less than two days after his transfer to UAB, Clarence was dead. What
killed him was heartbreakingly clear and, at that point, utterly beyond our
control. What killed him was the simple fact that the new drugs were new.

We were still learning about their long-term side effects and how to best manage them.

Typically, for all drugs in development, the candidate drug is evaluated in 1,000 to 3,000 patients during clinical trials that generally last no more than two years. This is deemed enough time for regulatory agencies to get the data they need to approve the drug for widespread use. But until many more patients take a new drug for longer time periods than clinical trials afford, there is no way to know if the drug has unapparent, longer-term side effects. We providers knew, and we told our patients, that some drug ("side") effects might not develop or be recognized until the drug had been used *for years* by large numbers of patients. Patients like Clarence.

Clarence's case demonstrated the critical need to remain vigilant about already-approved drugs, to keep studying them over time. Time was the currency activists did not want us to spend, and the gift we could give our patients. Lacking the benefit of time, Clarence paid with his life.

The case of another patient, "Tommy," proved a different but related point: that even when we thought we knew what was optimal timing for HIV therapies, we had a lot to learn.

A jovial man with sandy blonde hair and an appealing drawl, Tommy was simple in his approach to life but not a simpleton. He hunted and fished. He rooted for the Auburn Tigers football team and often wore their team colors, blue and orange. Tommy wouldn't mind me calling him a classic "good ol' boy." But he was petrified that someone might call him gay, because where he grew up in rural Alabama, to be gay was a crime against nature, an act of treason against God, and a one-way ticket out of town.

Tommy was good at keeping things from his family and friends. When he heard that a former sexual partner of his had been diagnosed HIV-positive, he went out of state to get tested for fear he would be "found out" in Alabama's medical system. When Tommy got positive test results, he moved to Birmingham so he wouldn't have to reveal his diagnosis or his sexual orientation to his family, whom he believed would disown him if they knew.

In 1994 when Tommy came to UAB for care, we were running a study comparing patients' responses to two regimens: a two-drug combo, or that two-drug combo plus nevirapine, the first so-called "non-nucleoside" inhibitor of HIV. We started Tommy on the triple-drug cocktail and saw his health improving during the first four weeks. When he reported fatigue and malaise during the sixth week, I brought him in for an exam but found nothing amiss and sent him home.

A few days later Tommy felt worse, so I examined him again. Finding a slight tenderness over his liver, I ordered some liver enzyme tests. When they returned slightly elevated, I ordered a liver ultrasound and a few other tests, stopped his medications, and scheduled him to come back two days later. I wasn't too concerned at this point; after all, my longtime patient Ben had had some apparent liver trouble in the first couple of weeks on indinavir but went on to do very well.

When Tommy returned two days later, he was much worse. We admitted him to the hospital and though he was terrified, he let us contact his family.

The conversation I had with Tommy's parents in the hospital lounge was one of the most difficult I had ever had, but not for the reason Tommy had feared. I told them their son was very sick. I told them their son had HIV (and though I said nothing about how he got it, it was clear that they made accurate assumptions). Then I told them their son had a serious liver problem that we were struggling to understand.

In that moment, Tommy's parents were very upset—but only because their son was gravely ill, not for any other reason. In that moment, they focused on just two things: They loved their boy and they wanted him to get better. When the crisis forced a choice between their concerns—homosexuality and HIV on one side, their flesh and blood on the other—they chose in favor of their son instantly and wholeheartedly.

So many of my patients over the years have dreaded telling their relatives about their sexuality, their HIV, or both. But almost without exception in those difficult conversations, I've seen relatives come through as Tommy's parents did. Their child was very sick. They were going to stick by him until he got well.

But he never did.

We reported Tommy's death to the sponsor of the study, the multinational drug company Boehringer-Ingelheim Pharmaceuticals Inc., which at that point had no reports of similar events. Well after Tommy was laid to rest in his hometown, we were still looking at his charts, at the drug study protocols and literature, and racking our brains: What had we missed? The liver biopsy showed no evidence of infection, just liver damage consistent with a drug effect.

To the drug company's credit, it stayed on the case. Over time, among the toxicity reports that US providers filed with the company and the FDA, several cases surfaced that sounded similar to Tommy's. Ultimately, similar deaths were reported during a nevirapine study of patients thousands of miles away, in Africa. Boehringer-Ingelheim investigated each report thoroughly and discovered a pattern: The rare liver failures seemed to happen only in those patients who started treatment with nevirapine when their CD4 counts were above very specific thresholds.

Most of the patients in UAB nevirapine studies in the early to mid-1990s—including Jim Straley and Ben—had advanced disease when they started on the drug. That was not the case with Tommy. He had been diagnosed early, when his CD4 count was 490, and wanted to start treatment right away. We all believed that was a wise approach that would enhance his chances of survival. But Tommy died because we didn't know—couldn't know, so early in the drug's use—that giving nevirapine to patients with higher CD4 counts could have a tragic result.

In 2000, four years after the drug was originally approved for use by the FDA, Boehringer-Ingelheim wrote a "Dear Doctor" letter directing that nevirapine be used in HIV-positive patients whose CD4 count was less than 400 cells/*ul* for men and less than 250 cells/*ul* for women. In its package insert, the drug began carrying a so-called "black box" warning, alerting consumers and healthcare providers about the drug's risks for higher-CD4-count patients. It took four years after the drug's approval to fully understand and describe this rare complication of therapy that occurs in less than 1 percent of people taking the drug, and only in those with higher CD4 counts. Such is the nature of rare side effects of new drugs.

At the height of the HIV/AIDS epidemic, new HIV infections in sub-Saharan Africa were running about 2.6 million a year. By 2010, new HIV infections in sub-Saharan Africa had dropped by more than 26 percent, according to data from UNAIDS (the Joint United Nations Programme on HIV/AIDS). The number of new infections in infants was reduced dramatically by preventing transmission of HIV from mother to child during pregnancy and at birth by treating the HIV-infected mom prior to delivery. Throughout sub-Saharan Africa, nevirapine is one of the drugs most frequently used to prevent that transmission. Today, women with higher CD4 counts are not placed on nevirapine but rather some other effective agent. That's progress based on knowledge. And that knowledge was bought at the price of lives, Tommy's and others'.

I still feel guilty about Tommy. Could I have known this prior to putting him on study and at risk? Was my zeal to prove the effectiveness of the avalanche of new drugs and new knowledge so intense that I inadvertently pushed him over the edge? Could I have recognized the symptoms sooner, even by a day, and stopped the drug in time to prevent his liver from being destroyed?

Pondering these questions is humbling. I will never know the answers. But what I do know is this: Tommy was a hero. He joined the study as a soldier in the fight against HIV. He hoped to save himself but also to improve the prospects of those who would follow. A son like that would make any parent proud.

Cases like Clarence's and Tommy's were a sobering reminder that while these new drugs were a tremendous leap forward, they were not a solution. They had warts and limitations, some of which we knew, some of which we would discover. Yes, triple-drug therapy had revolutionized the approach to HIV patient care. Combine that with our increasingly sophisticated understanding of HIV pathogenesis (how the virus causes disease), and we had a solid plan of attack to get the virus under control. But we were up against the Houdini of the disease world. We could strap it into a straitjacket, seal it in an airtight container, drop it fifty feet deep in the Hudson River—and watch helplessly as it still got away from us.

Of all the virus's tricks and evasions, there was one that alarmed me most of all, though it didn't surprise me. Researchers Brendan Larder, Graham Darby, and Doug Richman first described the phenomena in a 1989 *Science* magazine article when they said longer-term use of AZT had led to the emergence of virus with "reduced susceptibility." That phrase, of course was a euphemism for the dreaded word *resistance.*

In the field of infectious disease, the concept of resistance has been around since the first use of antibacterial therapy almost a century ago. The concept is simple: If a drug is used that kills all the bugs or suppresses replication completely, there is no chance for resistance. But if some bugs survive or the suppression of replication is only partial, then the organisms that grow in the presence of the drug will mutate into a form that is no longer susceptible to the drug.

This is what happened to HIV when treated with AZT monotherapy. When it first was used, AZT clearly had antiviral activity and suppressed viral replication to a good degree by itself. So the patient's viral load was reduced and CD4 counts rose, as did overall well-being. That obvious clinical improvement was seen in the early studies and led to the approval of AZT by the FDA in 1987. What was not seen at that point was that residual replication of HIV continued, churning in the background.

Over the next twelve to eighteen months, while the patient continued on AZT, the ongoing replication led to the slow emergence of viruses with reduced susceptibility to AZT. As these viruses emerged, they became the predominant virus replicating in the body. With further time, these viruses developed additional mutations in a stepwise fashion, until the predominant virus in the body was almost completely resistant to AZT, rendering the drug useless. Simply put: At this point, the virus is laughing at the drug.

If the patient continues on therapy with that drug to which the virus is no longer susceptible, what's ahead? Continued decline caused by relentless replication of HIV, this time by a virus that is resistant to the original drug. Initially, some had thought, or hoped, that the resistant viruses were somehow less virulent (destructive) than their wild-type (nonresistant) counterpart. But in most cases, unfortunately, the emerging resistant viruses are just as harmful as their progenitor wild-type parents.

What's more, the resistant HIV is a textbook example of Charles Darwin's "survival of the fittest." The ongoing replication at very high rates, under the environmental pressure of antiviral drugs, spurs the virus to mutate into new variants that are even more "fit" to thrive in the antiviral therapy environment. Then those variants emerge as the new population of viruses that cause disease.

To top it all off, this Darwinian triumph of adaptation—a process that takes centuries or millennia among humans, animals, and most plants— occurs in just months, even weeks, for HIV because it replicates so quickly. It takes a century for five generations of human beings to come into existence; it takes days to produce five generations of HIV.

My colleagues and I had our work cut out for us. We were studying and fighting drug toxicities while studying and fighting drug resistance and while trying to mitigate the effects of it all on our frightened, stigmatized patients and increasingly weary colleagues. I was pumped to do battle in the lab against the virus; that was important work, the search for knowledge. But increasingly, I was wasting time and energy on a lot of other tasks that had less to do with pioneering science than with propping up failing systems.

Why did we contract for more and more clinical drug trials and research projects, working to the point of exhaustion? Primarily, of course, because without the pharma companies' newest drugs, our patients were on a sure path to the grave. But there were other reasons. In addition to giving us new medications, the companies paid us for administering the trials. And while the government claimed its "social safety net" protected the neediest Americans, no agency or system covered many of our patients' needs—payment for other drugs they could not afford, transportation to appointments, help from nurses and social workers to fill out forms and slice through red tape. So that's where we ended up spending our clinical trial checks. We were paying for things that The System absolutely knew people needed to keep body and soul together. But The System left it to us to find a way to provide these things with absolutely no reimbursement. All the uncompensated goods, services, and advocacy for our patients—because if we didn't do it, who would?—led me to write this bitter declaration:

> The safety net that catches patients as they fall through the cracks of our diseased healthcare delivery system is made up solely of the fabric of healthcare workers who give a damn.

———

Every drug trial and research project we took on demanded fixed amounts of my time and attention: grant writing, negotiating, building relationships with pharmaceutical company contacts to secure the project. First I was short on knowledge to save lives; soon I was short on time. My days and nights were being lavished on the minutiae of project administration, from setting the schedules of study participants and staff to assuring compliance with regulatory requirements and human subjects rules, plus monitoring the finances to make sure we didn't run too far in the red, then writing up project findings, shepherding them through editing and publication, writing textbook chapters, giving lectures on the latest findings from our studies— all while continuing to tend the pharma relationships to keep the research grants coming.

At first, I liked the metaphor of the sky bridge between my UAB lab and the hospital where I saw patients: that easy stroll between bench and bedside, research and patient care. But as time went on, that transit got harder and more complicated. I started feeling like my friend the former US Congress member who left office because the time spent fundraising and campaigning so outweighed the time spent making law and serving constituents. Many days, I spent most of my time leveraging my credentials and UAB's reputation to get projects and funding—and then I spent whatever time was left being a researcher and a doctor, not to mention my four other roles: teacher and faculty member, husband and father.

I've always been decent at deductive reasoning. I'm pretty good at scanning my surroundings and identifying factors that produce a given circumstance. But it took me a while to put together the answer to this question: Since we had solved the big scientific questions about treating HIV, why wasn't the process of providing treatment getting easier?

Here's the answer I came up with, one that I found maddening. My life in HIV medicine was getting harder not because we didn't have the science; increasingly, we did. Life was getting harder and more complicated because The System wasn't our friend. My job no longer revolved around trying to beat the virus. Now, I was trying to beat the virus and The System. By jury-rigging and improvising to fix problems that The System dumped on us. By using pharma money to underwrite treatment-related costs that The System couldn't be bothered to cover—among them, paying for extra staff to circumvent the barriers to care the The System erected. By designing academic projects to retain the staff to care for the patients that The System left to fend for themselves.

When we in HIV medicine started winning the fight against the virus, it was a source of great satisfaction and pride for me. But as it became clear that we had another fight on our hands—to get the US healthcare system to actually serve the patients we were saving—satisfaction gave way to frustration. For the first time in my life, I felt like I was being optimistic out of necessity. If I didn't force myself to look on the bright side, I might not want to open my eyes at all. I needed help. I needed hope. I called Jim Raper.

After Jim's partner Steve died in 1993, Jim soldiered on, teaching at UAB's school of nursing and completing his doctorate in nursing. The next year, our colleague Mark Mulligan got an NIH grant to open an AIDS vaccine program at UAB. Mark needed someone who could set it up from scratch and then run it like a pro—so of course he offered the job to Jim, who accepted. That put Jim in offices in the same building as the 1917 Clinic, just down the hall from my office. It was great to run into him more often and easy for us to plan meet-ups at the gym (although the disadvantage of working out with Jim is that his discipline and hustle puts me and others to shame).

Jim was working out at the YMCA in 1996 when he met Scott, a loan officer at a large bank in town. A year later, they were in a committed relationship and bought a house together (where they still live).

By the time Jim was two years into running the vaccine program, I was at a crossroads as director of the 1917 Clinic. With the continuing rise of patient volume I felt increasingly overwhelmed trying to do everything myself: leading the clinic, generating the research dollars, and doing the research. The clinic clearly needed reorganizing to meet the evolving challenges but I didn't know where to begin.

My cousin Mary Fisher took pity on me, and as a present she gave me a one-hour consultation with A. James Heynen, an organizational expert and writer with whom she had worked for years. Early in 1995, Jim Heynen sat down with me, listened and asked questions, and then demonstrated why Mary so valued his counsel. He described the clinic's weaknesses, then listed the clinic's goals, and mapped out how we could eliminate the former and reach the latter.

Following Jim's plan would leave the clinic with leadership vacancies that I had no immediate way to fill. Still, I knew his re-org plan was the right one, so I plowed ahead as usual with no Plan B. I was hoping some magic would happen and the perfect person would walk into my office to help me reshape the clinic.

Even magic needs a shove now and then. I phoned Jim Raper and invited him to drop by.

I asked Jim if he would consider leaving the vaccine unit and becoming the administrator of the 1917 clinic. I gave him my best sales pitch: all the reasons the job would be a great step for him and he'd be a great fit for the job. Jim wears a hipper version of the round, black glasses frames popularized by Harry Potter, and behind those glasses his eyes can be hard to read. He said he had to think about my offer and would let me know.

Several days later, Jim arrived in my office to give me his decision. I distinctly remember listening to his wind-up and thinking, *Just get to YES.* He was talking about being loyal to Mark and the vaccine unit, being fair to all concerned. I maintained a cool exterior but in my head I was shouting, *DAMMIT, just say YES!* Finally, after Jim had given his earnest and thoughtful explanation, he looked me in the eye and delivered the verdict: "I feel passionate about this opportunity to make a difference, Mike. I think I should do it."

Jim may not have actually uttered the word *YES.* But whatever he said, that moment marked a huge turning point for the 1917 Clinic. Within days—literally, days—Jim's character and stamina earned him the admiration of clinic staff and patients. He was demanding but fair, and he ran the operation on the motto of his former mentor, heart surgeon Dr. John W. Kirklin: "If you're not helping me, you're not helping me."

I like morphing the quote further to say, "If you're not helping me, you're hurting me."

Jim expected everyone to work hard, and those who didn't were invited to leave. His approach was a godsend and quite a departure from my own: I had tended to tolerate those who weren't carrying their weight, hoping they would someday get better. I realize now that I'd not only kept incompetence in the organization but demoralized workers who were busting a gut both to do their work and the work of the slackers. Unlike me, Jim held out no hope that those folks would magically reform. "People change—but not much," he would tell me as he cleaned out more of the deadwood.

Jim's commitment and competence freed me, as clinic director, to hand off responsibilities and share authority without a second thought. More than once, I've described Jim Raper as the thread that ties the whole clinic enterprise together. The better the 1917 Clinic was run, the better it could serve our patients. For some of the most desperate patients, clinic staffers were the closest thing they had to family, and clinic services were all that stood between them and utter despair, or worse.

When Jenny started frequenting the clinic in the late 1990s, she was still in her twenties but already had lived a tough life. Things started well for the Tuscaloosa native, who excelled in high school and went to business college on a scholarship. She earned her certification in office administration, and by early 1991 she was on a career path she loved as a paralegal with a venerable Tuscaloosa law firm. About that time, Jenny started a relationship with Johnny, a truck mechanic. They married in August 1992. As Jenny tells their story,

> We had been married for a little over a year when we began to notice that Johnny was losing weight and was having trouble swallowing food. A trip to the ER in October 1993 revealed that he had thrush. He was told that a blood test would be needed immediately to determine whether he had leukemia or AIDS. Two weeks later, the doctor called us back in and announced that Johnny did indeed have full blown AIDS and his T-cell count was a mere 15. I was advised to be tested immediately, and two weeks later I was told that I, too, had the HIV virus, but my T-cell count was in the 800s.
>
> We lived in a small town and Johnny became the topic of conversation at the shop where he worked on diesel trucks. Working for a lawyer, I made a few phone calls regarding the workplace harassment he was experiencing. Johnny ended up being sent home with full pay and benefits while he became sicker and sicker. His eyes became worse. We had to have special walking shoes made to mold to his feet. Ultimately he

was confined to a wheelchair, and he began to show signs of dementia.

On March 30, 1995, Johnny's home nurse called me at work to tell me he wasn't acting normal. I knew at that moment it was his time and called all of the family. While lying in my lap, Johnny was able to speak to everyone and say his good-byes. Then he looked up at me, told me I was his angel, took a deep breath and died. I buried him with insurance money from his job, purchased my mausoleum space beside his, and prepared for my battle.

Through bad breaks and bad choices, Jenny's life became harder. With a guy she thought was the next love of her life, she began abusing alcohol and cocaine. They were planning to marry until she caught him cheating on her, ended the relationship, and checked into rehab. Deeply depressed, she vowed to make a new start. She moved to Birmingham in early 1997, got a job at a law firm—and became a 1917 Clinic patient.

"I had escaped the familiar faces in Tuscaloosa, only to come to Birmingham and find more men to take advantage and more drugs around every corner," Jenny told me. The clinic staff did everything we could to help her stay on an upward path. The nurses' regular monitoring kept her HIV counts and meds where they needed to be. Support from her social worker extended the lifelines of counseling for depression and addiction. During her clinic appointments, I spent extra time in conversation with her, encouraging her to stay clean and take her meds regularly. For several years, "things were very rough," she admits. But a few months into the new millennium, she was working steadily as a paralegal and seeing "the kindest man, someone who understands my health situation."

Jenny's story reminds me that life doesn't assure any of us a permanent hold on anything—not on employment or love, not on prosperity or peace of mind, and certainly not on good health. Every day could just as easily bring something to knock us down as to bear us up. Jenny had learned to roll with that, she once told me, because "the bright side is that I have the 1917 Clinic. You have always been there for me and I know you always will be."

With Jim Raper as administrator, I knew the 1917 Clinic was in good hands when I was out of town. That made it easier to indulge my desire to visit other fronts in the war on HIV/AIDS. In 1998 I made my first trip to Africa under the supervision of two superb tour guides, Susan Allen and Sten Vermund.

An MD who is part rebel and part Indiana Jones, Susan Allen began running AIDS research projects in Rwanda in 1986. After the 1994 genocide in that country, she relocated her work to Zambia. Sten Vermund, tall and bearded, is a pediatrician and infectious disease epidemiologist who worked at the AIDS division of the NIH. We recruited Sten to UAB in 1993 to lead the division of geographic medicine in the School of Medicine and as director of the department of epidemiology in the School of Public Health. Susan was one of Sten's first recruits. By the time Susan joined the UAB faculty in 1994, Sten had worked extensively with the NIH's AIDS International Training and Research Program (AITRP), a project that brings medical personnel from around the globe to train at US facilities. Among the AITRP scholars that Sten brought to UAB were two physicians from Lusaka, Dr. Moses Sinkala and Dr. Isaac Zulu. Both were smart and gifted; Moses was shrewd, aggressive, and ambitious, while Isaac was soft-spoken, big-hearted, and humble.

In January 1998, Sten, George Shaw, Eric Hunter, Mark Mulligan, and I flew with other UAB colleagues to Lusaka for a five-day working visit hosted by Susan.

Our group stayed just outside the city at Lilayi Lodge, where the lodgings were traditional thatched-roof huts fashioned from handmade bricks, and the grounds were a game park full of herbivorous wildlife. Every morning a group of us (including my hut-mate, George) would go for a run during which we'd see giraffes, impala, and zebras who would briefly run up next to us and then break away, leaving us in their dust. Every evening, we'd return to the lodge for a gourmet dinner (featuring some of our erstwhile running buddies—the impala stew was delicious).

Our days were spent exploring the realities of HIV/AIDS in Africa, a phenomenon that was both very like and very unlike the disease I knew in Alabama. On subsequent trips to Africa, I would make whole movies about what I saw, including a 2004 documentary, *The Plague that Thunders*, which was screened publicly in Birmingham. But from my first trip, though I shot some footage, the most poignant scenes and stories I brought home were recorded mostly in my memory.

At UTH, the University Teaching Hospital of Lusaka, Dr. Isaac Zulu led our delegation on a tour followed by rounds with the hospital's ward team. The emergency room was an impressive operation, dealing with roughly 250 new patients per eight-hour shift. At the end of each shift, "disposition" was required—that is, the patient either had to be admitted to the hospital or sent home. If the illness was judged not severe enough for hospitalization, the patient was sent home. If the illness was deemed severe but the hospital lacked the drugs or tools to treat it, the patient was sent home. Of any 250 presenting patients, most were sent home.

For patients admitted to UTH, the wards were large rooms typically crowded with about forty beds. When there were more patients than beds, as there often were, the staff would place a thin foam pad (think yoga mat) in the floor space between two beds, cover it with a sheet, and assign it to a patient. If the patient on the floor needed an IV, it would be hung from a nearby bedpost. As a last resort, patients would serve as human IV stands, holding their IV solution bags themselves.

When patients were admitted, the relatives who accompanied them to UTH would set up camp, literally, at the hospital. UTH had no American-style hospital kitchen preparing food for patients. Families cooked all meals for their hospitalized relatives on cooking fires in their makeshift encampments around the hospital grounds.

As our group walked among the beds on rounds, Isaac, the attending physician, asked the ward team members to describe each patient's case. I heard all the familiar diagnoses—"malaria," "pneumonia," "tuberculosis," "lung cancer"—and one I did not recognize: "R-V-D." I leaned over and whispered to one of the medical students: "What is R-V-D?" As if surprised that I did not know, she whispered back: "Retroviral disease."

In a ward where more than half the inpatients had HIV or AIDS, those acronyms were not said aloud. TB was TB. Cancer was cancer. But in this hospital, in a country and a region where HIV/AIDS was overwhelmingly the greatest threat to life, it was referenced only in code. R-V-D.

In one corner of the ward, I saw a man holding up his own chest X-ray as if reading it. Though I was across the room, I could clearly see the physical signs: The man had TB. He was surrounded by other patients within a few feet of his bed. If they did not get the TB bug, it was only because the ward's many windows were open, admitting a cleansing breeze. As for holding his own X-ray: Why not? After all, he purchased it. Any UTH patient needing an X-ray was required to pay for it up front, typically one or two US dollars. Those without cash simply went without an X-ray.

Our group arrived at the bedside of a patient with pneumonia. Inviting me to share my expertise with his medical trainees, Isaac asked what I thought the likely organisms were and what I would treat the patient with. After listing a range of pathogens and bacteria, I recommended a two-drug regimen of pretty powerful antibiotics that I thought would be effective against those bugs. Isaac smiled at me before he spoke, shaking his head ruefully: "We don't have those drugs here."

I nodded, thought a moment, and recommended two others. Isaac smiled and again shook his head no.

"Okay then," I asked, "what is on your formulary?" Isaac recited the list, a relative handful of common drugs that was essentially the hospital's entire arsenal: "Penicillin, ampicillin, amphotericin, prednisone, some malaria drugs, TB drugs, and sulfa."

Hmm. "All right then," I said, "I would use ampicillin and sulfa."

Isaac smiled, more broadly this time: "That's what the patient is on."

"Good!" I said, grinning back. We went on to the next case.

As I watched Isaac lead the rest of the rounds, one word sounded in my head: *remarkable*. Trained in Great Britain and in the United States, Isaac was a doctor's doctor, as talented as any of the medical "stars" I had met around the world. He could easily have found work in another country where conditions were easier and pay was better. So could many of the nurses, technicians, and other doctors at UTH. But Isaac and the others chose to stay in Zambia—to stay where they were needed—despite the deficiencies of the system and the personal and professional sacrifices they had to make.

Some of us can only be who we are in a specific setting. Jackie Robinson could only have been Jackie Robinson in Brooklyn, in baseball, in 1947. I suspect there are parts of Mike Saag that can only be Mike Saag in some clinical setting, any year. I know for sure, after seeing him there, that Isaac could only be Isaac in Zambia. He didn't want prestige or money or ease of life. He wanted to be a healer and he wanted to be home.

———

In addition to our time at UTH, my UAB colleagues and I visited several hospices, heartbreaking places jammed with late-stage AIDS patients of all ages. We also held meetings with officials of the Ministry of Health to discuss establishing a collaborative project in Lusaka. Those efforts bore fruit in 1999 with the founding of the Centre for Infectious Disease Research in Zambia (CIDRZ), a nongovernmental organization working in partnership with the Zambian government and UAB.

In much the same way that UAB personnel combined research and clinical care at the 1917 Clinic, CIDRZ personnel would provide HIV prevention and treatment services to Zambians at clinics around Lusaka, while also conducting clinical trials and other biomedical research. CIDRZ's founding staff, besides Sten, included Drs. Jeffrey and Elizabeth Stringer, a young husband and wife, both OB-GYNs; Robert Goldenberg, a mentor of the Stringers who had tremendous experience in obstetrics research; and Moses Sinkala, who directed operations in the Lusaka district. By focusing on preventing mother-to-child transmission of the virus and rapidly getting HIV-positive people (especially pregnant women) on antiretroviral, CIDRZ had a swift and dramatic impact in Zambia. It continues to do groundbreaking work there today.

When I went on the 1998 trip, I thought I would be taking lessons from the 1917 Clinic to enlighten healthcare providers in Zambia. But as I realized on that visit and every visit since, there is much that America can learn from the developing world about healthcare. Despite the tremendous lack of resources in such settings, the community members come together to care for one another. The practitioners sacrifice more luxurious opportunities to provide service for the neighbors they grew up with. The Ministry of Health, the nation's chief government health agency, works with the university to maximize the services of the University Teaching Hospital. Patients' families commit to fill the gaps in services by providing meals and supportive care to their loved ones in the hospital, and the friends and neighbors care for the family members left behind in the villages while loved ones are caring for those in the hospital. They are all in it together, working for the common good.

In the America of yesteryear, physicians and other healthcare workers didn't have the drugs or technology or megaintensive care units that we have today. But what they did have was community—the Norman Rockwell doctor kindly "listening to the heartbeat" of a girl's doll or checking a boy's temperature, the night nurse sitting with a hospitalized patient so he will not die alone. The doctor, in that bygone era, might have been paid with a chicken instead of a few dollars, or he might not have been paid at all. But she did her best to foster healing among her neighbors, and everyone pulled together to help her do her job. With all of our technology and medical marvels, we seem to have lost our sense of health as part of the commonweal, the welfare shared in common by inhabitants of a neighborhood, a region, a nation, a planet.

We don't pull together for a common good. Rather, we seem to be pulling apart. Physicians vs. Insurance Companies vs. Hospitals vs. Politicians vs. Bureaucrats. Each stakeholder fights for a share, like pigs at a trough. The systems that operate in the name of health rake in more and more money, but instead of spreading wellness and peace of mind, the money foments moneygrubbing and drives wedges between onetime collaborators, fragmenting whatever community existed in the past.

Yes, I remain an optimist. My optimism tells me we can repair this shattered "system of care." If I did not believe, I do not know who I would be. I cannot be Jackie Robinson or Isaac Zulu. Neither can I be a pessimist. Therefore, The System that is failing will be reformed through the ordinary agents of truthfulness, common sense, courage, and human dignity. And, if necessary, magic.

Chapter 13

THE PROMISED LAND

he last event reported in the Torah is the death of Moses. The people he led out of Egypt had been ungrateful and disobedient to God, we are told, so God let the Israelites wander in the desert for forty years until a new generation could enter the Promised Land. Before Moses's death, according to the book of Deuteronomy in the Torah portion I invoked at my bar mitzvah, he tells the Israelites, "Go in and take possession of the land the Lord swore he would give to your fathers—to Abraham, Isaac and Jacob—and to their descendants after them."

In the summer of 1999, the descendants entering the Promised Land (for a nine-day tour) included Amy, Andy, Harry, and Julie Saag, and me.

None of us had visited Israel before. So when the Birmingham Jewish Federation decided to sponsor a family trip during the year in which Harry would have his bar mitzvah, we were excited to join. Amy and her Federation friend Ann Mollengarden spent most of a year working on plans for the tour, which would include a joint ceremony for the delegation's bar and bat mitzvah youths.

I've always been a cultural Jew more than a deeply religious one. I love the threads of Jewish traditions woven through the generations of my family. I'm proud that Jews in the United States historically have been advocates for social justice and champions of the downtrodden.

But I'm not a fan of institutional, organized religion. I've seen too many "believers" who are frauds, praising God while muttering, "Those queers with AIDS are getting what they deserve." Or those who sit by idly while poor people have no access to care or, worse, accuse them of being freeloaders on the system. I have no patience for people with a holier-than-thou attitude—the folks for whom Jesus created the rebuke, "You hypocrite! First remove the beam from your own eye, and then you will see clearly enough to remove the speck from your brother's eye."

In short, I welcomed the Israel trip as a social and cultural experience more than a religious pilgrimage. It would be a time to see sights and make movies, time to be with family and friends—including Cyndie Culpeper, the only rabbi along on the trip. Cyndie had gone to Israel before, though not since her disease had become more complicated to manage. I think it was reassuring for her to know her doctor would be along on the trip. For the rest of us, visiting the Holy Land with Cyndie was like having an interfaith interpreter: Since she was raised Catholic before converting to Judaism, she could talk to us as knowledgeably about the Stations of the Cross and other sites of Christian significance as about the destruction of the First Temple.

Our first day in Israel was a Friday, seen through the haze of jet lag. Straight from the airport, we went to a woodsy spot outside Tel Aviv to perform a ritual upheld by generations of Jewish tourists: planting a tree for Israel. Next was the Galilean countryside, where the youngsters in the group rode donkeys. Marci, a nine-year-old girl in our group, fell off her steed, causing what I was pretty sure was a fracture in a bone in her upper arm.

As a result, my first Shabbat morning in Israel was spent being a doctor: accompanying Marci to the hospital, staying with her through the exam by the orthopedist. His diagnosis was, "Yes, it's broken, nothing to be done but put her in a sling," which is precisely the proper treatment for an aligned midshaft fracture of the humerus.

As geeky as this sounds, I didn't mind visiting a hospital on my vacation. Just four years before, Israel had overhauled its healthcare system and instituted a national health insurance program. I was curious to know if it was working—and by all appearances, the answer was a resounding yes.

Today, more than a dozen years later, the Israeli healthcare system has been cited as a model of success by, among others, the 2012 Republican presidential candidate Mitt Romney. After presiding over sweeping "Romney-care" health system reforms when he was governor of Massachusetts, Romney ran against President Barack Obama by denouncing "Obamacare" as, among other things, too much government intervention in healthcare. But in July 2012, speaking at a fundraising breakfast in Jerusalem, Romney praised the Israeli healthcare system, especially its cost-effectiveness.

"Do you realize what health care spending is as a percentage of the GDP (gross domestic product) in Israel? Eight percent," Romney said, according to the *Washington Post*. "You spend eight percent of GDP on health care. You're a pretty healthy nation. We spend 18 percent of our GDP on health care, 10 percentage points more . . . We have to find ways, not just to provide health care to more people, but to find ways to fund and manage our health care costs."

I agree with Mitt's last sentence, so I'm happy to tell him—and any other politicians and policymakers who will listen—how the Israelis have accomplished this.

In a paper published in September 2011 in the journal *Health Affairs*, authors Jack Zwanziger and Shuli Brammli-Greenberg report that since Israel reformed its healthcare system in 1995, "in contrast to many other developed nations, it has . . . experienced relatively low rates of growth in health spending, even as health outcomes have continued to improve." The authors say this has occurred because the Israeli government "exerts direct operational control" over about 40 percent of healthcare expenditures in a variety of ways, including caps on hospital revenue and some other costs.

In the reformed system, the government pays the entire premium for insurance coverage that citizens and permanent residents buy from one of four competing nonprofit health plans. What the government pays the plans varies depending on the person's age and whether they have especially costly diseases to manage, including kidney failure, hemophilia, and AIDS. Funds for the plans come mostly from general and payroll tax revenues, with a small percentage from copays. The national insurance plan does not cover every medical service, so to get coverage for, say, dental and vision care, consumers can buy supplemental policies—which roughly four out of five Israelis do.

In this system, the cost control essentially is up to the health insurance plan, which must figure out how to cover its enrollees with the money the government has provided. So far, Zwanziger and Brammli-Greenberg report, "the system has performed well." In a 2009 survey, 90 percent of respondents said they were satisfied or very satisfied with their health plans.

In their paper, Zwanziger and Brammli-Greenberg conclude, "The governments of all industrialized countries face the same intractable problems: how to provide services for an aging population without letting the increased use and cost of the healthcare system overwhelm other financial needs. Israel's experience in dealing with this problem through the use of considerable government leverage over the healthcare system provides a useful case study."

America's political leaders could learn from other nations' efforts to reform their healthcare systems. But to do that, our leaders will have to get beyond this "OpponentCare" name-calling mentality. They'll have to rise above being swayed by the big-money interests who favor the status quo precisely because it makes them big-money interests. And even if it risks offending some of their most cherished constituencies, elected "leaders" will have to demand that all stakeholders in the US healthcare system play their part in making it both more patient-centered and more cost-effective.

———

Once we got Marci and her broken arm out of the hospital and back to the tour group, the adventures in Israel continued. One of Harry's most memorable moments is also one of mine. The Arbel Cliffs tower more than 1,200 feet above the Sea of Galilee, and the view is breathtaking. But the descent is hair-raising, one of those Outward Bound, "builds character" hikes. You traverse the cliff face by keeping your feet on ten-inch-deep rock ledges and your hands on a series of thick metal staples driven into the rock.

Some in our party chose not to try it and were taken by bus to the bottom of the cliffs. Most of our family (except nine-year-old Julie) was going to try it, but Harry was looking, frankly, squeamish. Midway down the cliff trail, hovering 800 feet above the bottom, our trail guide asked him, "What's the matter, Harry, are you afraid of heights?" To which Harry replied, "No, I'm afraid of edges." It was a good example of something I've always loved about my kids, and that's the way they express themselves—each different, and yet each with an element of wry, Switow-Saag humor.

In my memory, the trip is a series of snapshots (or video clips) like that. The ceremonial, braided candles casting light on worshippers' faces as we gathered for the traditional Havdalah service (led by Rabbi Culpeper) marking the end of Shabbat. The amazing view over the Old City of Jerusalem from Mount Scopus, the most impressive of the seven hills on which the city is built. The starkly beautiful architecture and incredibly moving exhibits of the Yad Vashem Holocaust Memorial Museum. I found myself marveling at all that had happened in this small slice of the planet over 3,000 years, just breathing it in and trying to process it.

On the day we rode Jeeps up the Golan Heights, my thoughts were more mundane: How will Cyndie make it? I knew one of her antiretroviral medications caused vicious diarrhea, and I could not imagine how anybody could hold it together on a long, bouncing journey up those slopes. She was a strong-willed, self-sufficient kind of person, so she rarely mentioned issues like this to those around her. As soon as the Jeeps rolled to a stop at the crest of the heights, she hopped out and speed-walked toward the restrooms. But nothing ever was said (except to her doctor) about how difficult that ride had been.

On day five of our trip, while others went touring, I was again at an Israeli hospital. This time, I was there to meet with someone who I hoped might help me cure Cyndie, and then others, of HIV. Dr. Shimon Slavin was an Israeli physician who had pioneered bone marrow and stem cell transplantation in his country. He was working on curing cancers with nonmyeloablative transplants, sometimes called "minitransplants," in which chemotherapy was used to wipe out some of the bone marrow and then the patient was infused with healthy donor blood cells that rebuilt the blood system and also attacked the cancer. Slavin and I discussed how the same principle might be applied to Cyndie's HIV. Here's how it would work:

Chemotherapy would be given to Cyndie to reduce the number of immune system cells in her body to create space for new cells to take up residence. The amount of chemo used for this is much less than what is given to those undergoing a traditional myeloablative transplant (where *all* of the patient's cells are eliminated). First, Cyndie would be "conditioned" with lower-dose chemotherapy, and donor lymphocytes obtained from a genetically matched donor (preferably a sibling) would be transfused into her at frequent intervals over many weeks to months. Over time, Cyndie's cells would slowly be replaced by the donor cells until there would be 100 percent donor cells and no more of her own HIV-infected cells remaining. If this could all be done under the "cover" of anti-HIV therapy, the newly infused donor cells would not be infected with HIV, and when they completely replaced Cyndie's cells (including any containing latent HIV), she would be cured.

Ideally in this procedure, the donor is a sibling of the opposite sex who otherwise is a perfect match. In this way it is easy to track what proportion of the donor cells have taken over the patient's cells simply by looking to see how many cells contain the XX or the XY sex chromosome. In Cyndie's case, her brother Cliff was deemed a perfect match. Dr. Slavin proposed using the procedure to attempt to cure Cyndie of HIV.

When this first was broached, Cyndie was all for trying it. After we returned to Birmingham, her congregants and other friends even put together a transplant fund to help underwrite it. But because we were managing Cyndie's HIV pretty well with more-proven approaches, I could not justify the risk involved in such a new procedure. And when I sought guidance on this approach from experts at NIH, they gave me lots of reasons not to do it.

In essence, we were trapped in a catch-22. If patients were well controlled on ARV therapy and had a good chance to live a long life, it would be ethically untenable to do a non-myeloablative transplant because it would put them in harm's way; they could easily develop graft-versus-host disease (where the donor cells attack the patient's normal cells in the gut, skin, liver, etc.) or a terrible opportunistic infection from the chemo. Conversely, a patient with very advanced AIDS and poorly controlled viremia would be a terrible candidate because the transplant procedure could kill them—and even if it didn't, the inability to suppress HIV would lead to immediate infection of the donor cells on infusion, thereby defeating the chance for cure. So as disappointing as it was to do so, we set this option aside for Cyndie.

After my consultation with Dr. Slavin, I rejoined the tour group at the one site in Jerusalem on almost every visitor's itinerary: the Western Wall. This towering retaining wall, built by Herod around 20 BC, is what remained after the Romans destroyed the sacred Second Temple and most of Jerusalem in 70 AD. For centuries since, Jews have returned to the wall to lament the temple's destruction, so it came to be called the Wailing Wall. It's now a site where people of all faiths come to pray, some writing prayers on scraps of paper and tucking them into the cracks between the ancient yellowish-white stones. Out of respect, men who approach the wall are asked to cover their heads.

As I approached the wall, I was wearing my kipa and no doubt looking every inch the tourist. I had become separated from our group and had drifted into the subterranean area to the left-hand side of the wall when I felt a hand on my shoulder. I turned to see a Hasidic rabbi, recognizable by his traditional black coat and hat and his long beard and curling sideburn locks.

"So, where are you from?" he asked.

"Alabama," I said. "The United States."

"Do you have any children?"

"Yes, three."

"I should say a prayer for you," he offered. Not sure what I'd done to inspire that, I asked him: "What do you mean?"

"Well," he said, "you're here; you should have a rabbi pray for you. You give me a few shekels and I'll bless your family."

I was tempted to let fly that expletive that Beatrice favored in the lab. But, mindful of where I was, I made a civil, if terse response. "I don't need you to pray for me," I told him. "I can pray for myself."

Cocking an eyebrow, the rabbi challenged me: "But your prayer won't be heard by God."

To which I replied, "Neither will yours."

———

I most certainly didn't need a panhandling rabbi to pray for me. Not that I do much praying myself; I tend to fill my days with research and treatment and care, public education and patient advocacy and family support and a thousand other things. I'm always short on time; maybe I'm also short on faith. I definitely marveled at the depth of Cyndie's faith—her conviction that her prayers were heard and that whatever happened in her life, it was in God's hands.

A dear friend of mine, a former seminarian, has described my approach to religion this way: "You may never have been a religious guy, Mike, but you've always been a spiritual one." I tend to agree with his assessment. It certainly felt true on the Israel trip, especially during one solitary walk through Jerusalem.

———

It's about 5:00 a.m. on a Saturday, the last day before we would fly home. The sun is not yet up when I leave the Sheraton Plaza Hotel, just me and my camera. I wind through empty streets, kicking up the dust of history, and magical thinking grips me. I feel like some force is guiding me as I climb stone steps to rooftops, in search of the perfect shot.

I look to my right, where the sun is just breaking the horizon. There's the Church of the Holy Sepulchre, one of Christianity's holiest sites, built on the hill where history says Jesus was crucified and entombed. It's so close that I almost feel like I could throw a football and hit its gray-domed roof. I look about sixty degrees to my left and see the Western Wall, a site that Jews have consecrated over centuries of prayers and pilgrimages; the Temple Mount, a site held sacred by Muslims as well as Christians and Jews; and the Dome of the Rock, the golden-domed temple Muslims built on the spot from which they believe Mohammed began his ascent to Heaven (the same spot as the altar of the First and Second Temple of the Jews).

I pause to take it all in. I think to myself: "What is *with* this place?!" I mean, here I am, surrounded by awe-inspiring monuments to the three great religions of the Western world, all within a stone's throw of one another. Standing where I'm standing, wouldn't most people have some sort of transcendent experience? Shouldn't I be feeling some sort of spiritual presence, maybe receiving a divine revelation? And yet the thoughts filling my head are at least unorthodox and possibly heretical.

I am thinking: *It could all be made up.* The dogmas of organized religions, the notion of earning your way to heaven—it could all be a fiction devised to make people behave in this life for fear of punishment in the next.

If someone had been with me on that rooftop, I'm not sure I would have shared those thoughts aloud. Although I'm not a traditional believer, I'm not a militant unbeliever either.

What I do believe—and what I felt profoundly on the Israel trip—is this: We each are given one life. Our task in this life is to be the best we can be, not just for ourselves but for other people, our neighborhood, our nation, our planet. We can speculate about an afterlife, or we can just get on with it and make the most of our situation right now. Instead of arguing about heaven or hell, your version or mine, wouldn't it be better if we were just good to each other in *this* world?

Who knows if it's a Jewish belief, a Saag/Switow/Weil belief, a magical belief, or all of the above? But in my family, we believe that as long as we're remembered, we live on. It's only if we're forgotten that we ever really cease to exist. On the Israel trip, my son Harry and his siblings were barely starting the journey that will build their lives into legacies. Cyndie, as she well knew, could have been nearing her journey's end. Amy and I, the clinic staff, the many patients now living with HIV—none of us has any idea how much longer we might have. But when we act with love and integrity, when we strive to benefit our community more than ourselves, then we build good and memorable lives. This, I think, is immortality.

So get on with it, I think to myself, and I climb down from the rooftop.

Chapter 14

WOULDA-COULDA-SHOULDA

hen I begin to list what's wrong with the US healthcare system, almost every item on the list fits a single category: things we *could* do and *should* do but *don't* do. Time after time, we possess the science, the resources, and the know-how to improve healthcare for Americans—but cannot seem to find the resolve or momentum to change.

Those of us who once could do very little for HIV/AIDS patients are keenly aware of how much we can do now. We're like people who survived the Great Depression to live in a time of prosperity: We never forget how it felt to have nothing, and this memory colors how we value what we have now. And we're not alone: Healthcare professionals dealing with a vast array of mental and physical ailments have more knowledge, more therapies, and more ability to heal than even a decade ago. Given this reality, it strikes me as inexcusable—a tragedy, really—that we fail to implement healthcare solutions that are within our reach.

Songwriter, children's author, cartoonist, and poet Shel Silverstein has a name for such regretted missed opportunities: "woulda-coulda-shouldas."

In the US healthcare system today, the woulda-coulda-shoulda atmosphere has become paralyzing. Each stakeholder argues for what *should* be done, making a high-flying case for its own self-interest. Each faction insists that something dire absolutely *would* befall the nation if their opponent's approach wins out. So it's a standoff and nothing gets done. Meanwhile, the politicking is so intense, and the smoke-and-mirrors so blinding, that the populace loses sight of what actually *could* be achieved if everyone pulled together: We could have appropriate, accessible, cost-effective healthcare across the board.

It's certainly not just institutions that fall prey to woulda-coulda-shouldas. Individuals do too. Like me, chiding myself that I *could have* saved Clarence and Tommy if I had understood their liver issues sooner. Or like many HIV-positive patients who know they *should* take their medications, and who said they *would* take their medications, except . . . well, it's complicated. Glenn Treisman can help me explain. He's a psychiatrist who works with HIV/AIDS patients, a no-bull kind of guy, and a good friend.

While the HAART drugs we got in the late 1990s were effective against the virus, they often required dosing two or three times a day with multiple tablets. Not surprisingly, medications of that number and strength were associated with some wicked side effects. But the biology dictated that the drugs had to be taken precisely, consistently, every day, lest the missed doses allow the virus to replicate with some drug still present—a recipe for developing resistance.

When patients took the medicines every day, a significant majority—by 2004, perhaps three-fourths of them—achieved such suppression of the virus that it was undetectable in their bloodstream. Once patients get to that state, it's almost as if they don't have HIV anymore. As I would say to them, "It's like you rounded up all the virus in your body and locked it in jail. Although it's still there, it's not in a place that can hurt you. But if you stop taking the drugs, JAIL BREAK! The virus will come roaring through and put you back on the path to AIDS."

For all the sermons our patients heard about resistance, the presence of so many side effects led to folks skipping doses. When they needed a break from the nausea, the loose stools, and the abdominal pain, one missed dose led to relief—and that relief often outweighed their guilt at skipping the meds. After a while, the dose-skipping that had started as a desperate impulse became, for many patients, a habit, and one they were reluctant to confess to their providers—people like Glenn Treisman.

During more than two decades with the AIDS Psychiatry Service at Johns Hopkins Hospital in Baltimore, Glenn has gained great insights into HIV-positive patients' behaviors. On the matter of skipping medication doses, he tells this story.

A physician and good friend of mine at Hopkins's Moore Clinic for HIV Care, Dr. Joel Gallant, asked Glenn to talk to a patient who was an enigma. The patient claimed to never miss a dose of medicine, yet his viral load remained high. Joel would ask him on every visit, "Are you missing *any* doses of medicine?" "No," replied the patient, "not a single dose." Joel checked a drug resistance assay and found that the virus from the patient was wild-type virus, meaning there was no resistance present. Now Joel was totally stumped: The drugs *should be working*, he thought.

At Joel's request, Glenn followed up, asking the same questions. Again the patient stated he had not missed a single dose. Glenn asked the patient when he had taken his most recent dose and the patient answered, "Earlier this morning." So Glenn ordered a blood sample drawn, knowing that just a few hours after the drug was taken, it should be readily detectable in the patient's blood.

The blood level results—no drug detected in the patient's bloodstream—proved unequivocally that the patient had *not* taken the medicine as he had claimed. Glenn brought the patient back in and confronted him: "You told Dr. Gallant over and over that you had been taking your medicines every day without missing a dose, but the drug level indicates you haven't taken your medicines at all. Why did you tell Dr. Gallant you were taking them?"

The patient looked up at Glenn, shrugged, and said sympathetically, "Because it seemed so important to him."

Mary Fisher and Cyndie Culpeper each struggled through several HAART regimens in the first years we had the new medications. At one time or another, each experienced almost every side effect the drugs had to offer: headaches, skin rash, fever, nausea, vomiting, diarrhea, and neuropathy (numbness and/or pain) in their feet and legs. And periodically, each pleaded with me to approve of them taking a "drug holiday," going off the medications for a while.

I can still hear Mary pressing me about it: "Mike, do I *really* need to take these medicines? I am doing so well. What would happen if I stopped?" To such questions from both Mary and Cyndie, my answer was the same: "The *reason* you are doing so well is *because* of the medicines you are taking—it's *not* a good idea for you to stop." But ultimately, a doctor (even when he's a cousin or a friend) must respect a patient's choices.

In late 1999, after more than eight years battling the virus, Mary decided the medications' side effects were unbearable and stopped taking them. She felt better almost immediately, more able to care for her sons and keep up her speaking schedule. But she had given the virus an opening, which it took. In June 2001, Mary described her experience in an incredibly moving speech to a conference of AIDS doctors. The speech was titled "Passing Communities," and in it she declared, "Community is still the driving need for us, for all of us—physicians and patients, researchers and reporters. Our only real hope is what Martin Luther King used to call 'the beloved community.'" I was in the audience, fighting back tears as she spoke.

> With Michael's consent I went off most AIDS drugs more than a year ago. Then came the tests that said, in effect, that my body had gone into AIDS free-fall. Numbers we wanted to be low were skyrocketing and numbers we wanted to be high were tumbling. Michael wanted me back on drugs instantly. And I resisted. We talked about length of life. Then we talked about quality of life. And somehow we stumbled into the reality that Michael wants to keep me alive for ten more years because he's convinced that, by then, he'll hold a cure.
>
> Three months ago in Birmingham, I was incredibly ill. Michael kept shifting the combination therapies to see if he could find one that I could survive. We both hung in there until Michael heard me say that I didn't think I wanted to do this for another ten years . . . that I wasn't going to do this for another year, let alone ten . . .
>
> Michael has no clinical response to my hopelessness. At those moments he always resorts to the same thing. He says "I love you, and I do not want to lose you." He uses the language not of the university lab but of the beloved community—and we start again, together, to find a glimmer of light.

In 2002, to Mary's great relief and mine, we found a drug regimen that worked for her. With her success a matter of record, Mary's experience gave me hope the next year when I went through much the same thing with Cyndie.

Cyndie had dropped her medications before. In December 1996, she told me in an email, "I'm following Nancy Reagan's advice to 'say no to drugs.' I quit all of them. Can't take the side effects anymore." But her health grew increasingly precarious, and in January 1998, when she developed *pneumocystis* pneumonia, she agreed to get back on drugs. By 2003, Cyndie had settled into a three-drug regimen she could tolerate, and it was keeping her numbers where we wanted them. I was very pleased; Cyndie, not so much.

Cyndie may have lacked energy, but she never lacked gratitude. Cyndie was grateful that being on medication enabled her to teach young students at the Birmingham Jewish Day School, attend Shabbat services regularly, take her dog Annie Lucy for long walks, and travel. Cyndie *loved* to travel. After every trip, it became her standing joke to bring me a "barf bag" from the airplane (a little dig at me, I think, for prescribing such nauseating meds). She made a point of trying different airlines so she could scope out the different colors and styles of barf bags on each airline. Over the years, she enabled me to assemble an impressive collection.

Though the therapy was successful and occasionally she could joke about it, Cyndie was serious about wanting off the medications, which she called "the poison." I wasn't sure if there were some troublesome side effects she didn't tell me about, if she was just tired of taking medicine every day—or if taking it reminded her too often about her HIV status. For whatever reason, she just wanted to stop taking her medicines once in a while. In late 2003, Cyndie notified me she was again taking a brief "drug holiday."

On a Wednesday morning in January 2004, I received an urgent phone call from nurse Carol Linn at the 1917 Clinic. She said that Cyndie had been vomiting and was "very sick," and that I needed to come immediately. When I got to the exam room, Cyndie was feverish and balled up in a fetal position, moaning. Asked what was wrong, she barely could croak out, "My *kishkes*" (Yiddish for intestines).

Cyndie's abdomen was rigid and exquisitely painful, not just when touched but with any movement. As a former nurse, she was prepared for what I told her: This was an "acute abdomen," most likely from a ruptured stomach, intestine, or appendix—and a surgical emergency. We called an ambulance to take Cyndie from the clinic to the UAB emergency room, and I met her there.

After X-rays confirmed the diagnosis, Cyndie was taken to the operating room where surgeons discovered a perforated cecum, the pouch at the beginning of the colon. An ulcer more than five and a half inches across had eroded through Cyndie's colonic wall, leaking bowel contents into her abdominal cavity.

Surgeons successfully removed the diseased bowel and patched her up; she spent several weeks in the surgical intensive care unit, and then in a step-down unit. When she felt well enough to talk, I explained to Cyndie that in AIDS patients, such ulcers commonly are caused by a cytomegalovirus or a mycobacterium avium complex infection (as in Brian's and Michael's cases). But her pathology report revealed neither of these causes; the cause of the ulcer in her bowel wall was unknown. So in all honesty, I couldn't tell her that stopping her ARV medicines led to the development of the ulcer. Even so, the episode convinced Cyndie to go back on her medicines and to stay on them.

Mary had started treatment with a higher CD4 count than Cyndie's, and her virus in the test tube was *much* less aggressive than Cyndie's virus. Nonetheless, I didn't think either of them could afford the "drug holidays" they both craved, and I struggled to understand why they'd take the risk.

Glenn Treisman used his psychiatric expertise to lend me some perspective. As he reminded me, most of us will agree to try medicines we believe will do something good for us. But if the medicine makes us feel awful, after a while most will make a choice—to skip doses, or to continue despite our misery. The former choice is what Glenn calls "feeling oriented" and the latter "thinking or consequence oriented." He explains:

> Think of personality as a bell-shaped curve: on one extreme of the curve are those folks who are thinking, or consequence, oriented, and on the other extreme are those who are

feeling oriented. A classic consequence-oriented person is your accountant. They don't want to miss a single penny on the ledger, it drives them crazy. On the feeling-oriented end of the spectrum, think of Madonna or Brittany Spears or most folks in the performing arts, who act chiefly on emotion. Most of us are, by definition, somewhere in between. A good illustration is when we are in school and have a test tomorrow. Most of us don't feel like studying, but the prospect of failure is so unacceptable that we study anyway. The thinking-driven student will stay up all night studying. The feeling-driven person will say, "Screw it, I don't feel like studying, so I won't. Maybe I'll pass anyway!"

Glenn tells another story from his practice that helped me understand just how foreign the consequence-oriented approach can be to a feeling-oriented person. The story was about a patient whose cocaine addiction had once led him to tangle with, and get shot by, his drug dealer.

As Glenn tells it, the patient arrived requesting Valium, explaining, "I have been very nervous lately because I have been buying cocaine from the guy who shot me."

Glenn asked, "Why do you buy cocaine from a guy who shot you?"

The patient replied, "Because he has cocaine."

Perplexed, Glenn replied, "Look, I love prime rib, but if I went to the best prime rib restaurant in Baltimore and the maître d' SHOT me, I wouldn't go there anymore."

Without hesitating the patient retorted, "You know what, doc, with an attitude like that, you'd be missing out on some good meat!"

Glenn's conclusion: "The patient was not stupid; he processes data differently than I do." Feeling oriented versus consequence oriented.

Rounding out the profile, Glenn explained that feeling-oriented individuals also tend to be focused on the "now" more than the future and to be motivated more by a hunger for rewards than by an aversion to consequences. This paradigm has helped me better understand how to approach the care of patients. But I can also see a broader use for it. I think we should consider which aspects of US healthcare policy generally are feeling driven, which are thinking driven, and whether the balance needs adjusting.

As I've told medical students who see me weep at losing a patient, I believe that conscientious healthcare providers are emotionally invested in their work—to an extent, feeling driven. And I believe that a world-class healthcare system must be run with heart as well as with reason.

That said, I also am a researcher, a lab rat who believes good data guides us in achieving good patient outcomes. I believe we should insist that healthcare interventions be judged by the quality of their outcomes. I believe those outcomes should be evaluated in a thoughtful way, through a process that is scientific, comprehensive, and objective. And I believe we should prioritize interventions that do pass—and drop interventions that don't pass—three important tests of their outcomes:

- How well they serve the patient,
- How well they utilize provider skills and resources, and
- Whether they deliver sufficient bang for the buck.

This approach is basically what we've come to call "best practices"—taking measures of performance and then using them to devise procedures and standards that foster excellence. In the healthcare realm, it's an approach that gets more lip service than serious implementation. I suspect that's because if performance were rigorously measured, we'd find too many spots where the current system is neither health-effective nor cost-effective.

As I worked on this book, I sought out Glenn because he's smart, compassionate, and doesn't mince words. I asked him the central question: If the United States doesn't have "the best healthcare system in the world," why not? What needs to change to bring us closer to that goal? Even a portion of his longer, more thoughtful response points to the key problem:

> If you're an upper-middle-class person and you need a hip replacement, we're the best health care system in the world. If you're a guy on the assembly line in Detroit and you're diagnosed with bladder cancer, we're the best health care system in

the world. But if you're talking about the most bang for the buck, or the fairest system, or a system that does the best job of distributing resources, we suck.

The U.S. health care system is in terrible trouble and needs fixing. It is extremely idiosyncratic: If you don't know the doctor and the doctor doesn't know you, you might get great care or terrible care, there's no way to predict. In the private systems of what's called "managed care" medicine, the way they manage care is to deliver less of it and then they get to keep the money.

As the system operates now, the only way people can make a profit is by not providing care, by cutting corners on what they deliver. And that kind of system is doomed to fail, just as the auto industry and the steel industry failed when they took the same approach.

If Glenn could script the overhaul of the US healthcare system, he'd make it a government-run, single-payer system structured like those in Canada and England. In a system like that, he says, "the needs of the many could be met. The doctors and administrators of a clinic would get X dollars for that clinic and would decide how to spend it to cover caring for all their patients. If a patient needed some arcane kind of treatment, it would not be available to everybody at that clinic, but people would have the latitude to access additional care either by paying for extra insurance or by paying out of pocket.

"Critics of this approach say, 'Oh no, that's a two-tiered health system, you can't do that!' But right now in the United States we have a two-tiered, even a five-tiered system," Glenn contends, because patients with more money and/or insurance can access almost any kind of care, and patients without money and/or insurance struggle to get even basic care.

Glenn figures that he spends about a third of his hours in the clinic "yelling at insurance companies who say they won't pay for this or that. They're trying to figure out, *Can we get away with screwing this person so we can keep the money?* Generally, I can get payment for almost any patient if I argue with the insurance companies enough—but it wastes my time. I'm penalized because I'm trying to get my patients good care."

Glenn doesn't get paid to advocate. So when he spends one third of his time advocating for his patients against a system in which people are paid to avoid approving pay for care of others, all that time is totally uncompensated. Like countless caring healthcare providers, he advocates because it is the right thing to do—because he cares.

If all the Good Samaritan healthcare providers stop contributing the unpaid services that are holding this dysfunctional system together, we'd see more chaos and collapse. So far, those of us who care continue to submit, knowingly, to abuse by the system. We let ourselves be used to fill the voids created by cut-corner policies and practices that generate tremendous profit for institutions and their shareholders. We do it because to stop would be to turn our backs on the patients. But to have to continue on this way . . . to quote my forefathers, "It's a *shanda!*" A crying shame.

Glenn sees his psychiatric profiles at play in the decline of the US health-care system. "The people who used to run the system were doctors who were future-oriented, thinking-oriented people," he says. "Today, the people who administer US healthcare are business people and they are *now* oriented, feeling oriented. The more you let big-business people run it, the more you get a healthcare system that says, 'Look, we can't make any money on X, so let's not do it.'"

And then we're back where we started—faced with what we *could* do and maybe *should* do, but *don't* do.

———

As our therapeutic options for fighting HIV grew, we could save more patients than I dared to imagine back in the 1980s. But even when we could beat back the virus, there were AIDS-related fights we could not win. Elliott's was one.

Before Elliott got sick, he was an award-winning roller skater who prided himself on wearing outrageous costumes (kind of Evel Knievel-meets-Elvis). An Alabama native who studied at the University of Alabama in Tuscaloosa, Elliott was also an activist for what he believed in. His mother, Jean, tells of the Sunday morning her husband, Bill, "came in reading the front page story in the *Birmingham News*, saying, 'Oh my gosh, Elliott is suing the University of Alabama!' It seems Elliott and his gay friends were in one of the joints along the strip in Tuscaloosa when they started to be harassed by some rednecks. The gays were asked to leave and the troublemakers stayed. The next day found Elliott in the office of the president of the university, requesting that gays be given the same recognition as other groups on campus. That request went nowhere until he sued the university"—and after the university approved the establishment of an LGBT alliance, Elliott was a founding member and its first president.

Elliott was just twenty-six years old when he first visited the 1917 Clinic within months after it opened. At that point he had fairly advanced HIV infection and was placed in an AZT study. From then on, Elliott proceeded to participate in almost every study we initiated at the clinic. He played the guinea pig with DDI, saquinavir, ritonavir, L–697,661—and probably others that I'm forgetting. He was dauntless. And to help others coming to the clinic, he organized and chaired a patient advisory board that provided information, counsel, and encouragement.

By 1996 Elliott was on a steady three-drug regimen (AZT/3TC/indinavir) that was keeping his HIV in check. But throughout most of the 1990s, he was fighting related illnesses, and those battles were taking their toll. He suffered one GI problem after another. The rectal cancer diagnosed in 1998 required chemotherapy and radiation that left him with enteritis (inflammation of the bowel). That made Elliott wary of going out lest he be unable to make it to the bathroom when needed, and that drastic restriction of his activities weighed heavily on him.

In summer 1999, Elliott was winning the battle against HIV: His viral load was consistently below 50 copies/ml and his CD4 count was 107. Then in August, he developed abdominal pain more severe than anything he had experienced, and we admitted him to the hospital. An X-ray revealed that there was "free air" in his abdomen, meaning his intestines had perforated somewhere. I consulted UAB surgeons who agreed Elliott needed an emergency operation.

With the surgical team standing by, I explained to Elliott what we needed to do. He answered me through teeth clenched in pain, and there was no mistaking the words or his conviction. "No more, Dr. Saag. I've had enough."

My immediate reaction was to argue: "Elliott, no! This is *fixable!* We can get you through this. Your virus is totally undetectable, you're controlling HIV—you've WON!" But from the look in his eyes, I knew the truth: He was done. So I held my tongue. In the past, he would have regarded this emergency as just one more battle to fight. Now, even in the grips of agonizing pain, he saw it as relief. Deliverance.

For several seconds, we sat in silence, searching each other's eyes. Then I said, "I'll be right back," and went to give the surgeons Elliott's decision.

The surgical resident said something offhanded like, "He's probably right, he might not make it through surgery. We'll sign off. Call us back if you need us." Though I'm sure the words were well intended, I wanted to scream at the resident, "You don't know who you're talking about—this guy has fought through worse than this and made it!" But instead I thanked the resident and waved him on, so I could be alone to compose myself.

Giving up, when he had a condition we could remedy—that's what I felt Elliott was doing, and it devastated me. How many other patients of mine would have given anything to be in that situation? Brian, Jacob, Jim, Ed, and so many more. We kept HIV from taking this guy's life, and now he was giving it over. How could Elliott do this?

It took a few minutes before I realized that what I really meant was: How could Elliott do this *to me*? This wasn't my professionalism talking. It was my grief, my sense of avoidable loss, my pain from watching all those other patients die of things they couldn't avoid and I couldn't fix.

Elliott *had* been through a lot, physically and emotionally. He had weathered too many illnesses. Felt too much pain. Lost too many friends. Suffered too much survivor guilt. The ruptured intestine had given him an out, and he was taking it with dignity and grace. Who was I to get in the way?

We started Elliott on opioids to dull the pain. His family gathered immediately: His parents Jean and Bill, sweet, loving people who had embraced Elliott unconditionally from the very beginning. His devoted older sister Pat, who to this day sends me birthday greetings via Facebook. I told them of Elliott's condition and asked them to visit with him for a bit. When I returned ten minutes later, I spoke to Elliott for his family to hear. I told him his condition required an operation that he might not survive, but that it was much likelier that he *would* survive it and have a complete recovery from the episode.

Elliott smiled as he quietly confirmed his choice. "Thank you, Dr. Saag. Thank you. You've been great from day one, and I love you for everything you've done for me and my family. But my mind is made up. I'm ready to go. My family understands. I hope you do as well."

I sat on the hospital bed with Elliott and gave him a big hug, then embraced his relatives as we all wiped away tears. "Visit with your family as long as you'd like," I told Elliott, "and then we'll increase your pain medicine to make sure you are not suffering." He told me again that he loved me. I told him I loved him, too. And I waved good-bye.

Jean later told me that her son's last words were quintessential Elliott, concerned about others and touched with good humor. "Momma, will you be all right?" he asked. "Please don't cry and look like Tammy Faye Bakker . . ."

Of the many patients' funerals I have attended, Elliott's was one of the few where I gave a eulogy. I spoke of all Elliott had been through and all he had accomplished. I said that from day one until his last breath, Elliott did things his way. And I said that he was, in every sense, a winner. A champion, in roller-skating and in life.

———

About a decade into the HAART era, though there still were problems with the drugs, we had learned another critically important thing they could do. Once the medications suppressed a person's HIV to undetectable levels in the blood, that person was highly unlikely to transmit the virus during sex, pregnancy, or childbirth. Indeed, such transmissions are so rare today they are considered "reportable." We have less conclusive research data on whether people with "undetectable" HIV can spread the virus by sharing needles (transmission via the bloodstream). But we have almost 100 percent certainty that suppressing the virus to undetectable levels prevents sexual transmission and transmission from mother to child.

This was an enormous achievement. Before the medicines, there was a 25–30 percent chance of a baby acquiring HIV during pregnancy or during labor and delivery. Now, if we get women into prenatal care, identify those who are HIV-positive prior to the third trimester, and put them on medications that suppress viral replication to the point of undetectable virus in the bloodstream, there is *no* transmission to the baby. Just as for any HIV-positive person on medications that suppress the virus to undetectable levels, the likelihood of transmitting the virus to others via sexual activity approaches *zero* (perhaps not absolutely zero, but close to it).

Now, consider this: If we could identify *all* people infected with HIV, get *all* of them into care and on treatment, and have *all* of them achieve undetectable levels of virus in the bloodstream, three really good things *could* happen: People with HIV would live a near-normal lifespan, they would be spared illness caused by HIV—*and* they would be very unlikely to transmit the virus to other people. Theoretically, we could stop the epidemic.

There's that word again: *could*. Because there's a catch.

The drugs work best when started before the patient has more advanced disease. The mortality rate increases dramatically when therapy is started at lower CD4 counts than when it is started at higher levels. In our clinic, among those who start therapy with CD4 counts less than 50 cells/*ul*, mortality is 50 percent at eight years. Among those who start at counts greater than 200/*ul*, the mortality at eight years is less than 10 percent.

So for better outcomes, we need to get folks into care earlier—but the problem, is, most don't show up for care until their CD4 count is less than 250 cells/*ul*. There is one group, however, that consistently presents with CD4 counts greater than 450 cells/*ul*. Who are they?

Pregnant women.

Why? Because since the late 1990s we have recommended routine testing of *all* pregnant women for HIV. (This is done through so-called "opt-out" testing, meaning the mom is offered the test as part of routine practice, but may opt out of having the test done. Very few moms refuse the test.) Once identified, a woman is referred for HIV care and started on treatment to prevent transmission of HIV to her baby and prevent progression of her own disease, an unquestioned a win-win situation.

I'm certain that if tomorrow I magically invented a conclusive "cancer test," people would be lined up for miles to find out if they had cancer so they could be treated early and have a chance for long-term, meaningful survival. But for years we've had an HIV test—conclusive, noninvasive, inexpensive—that can tell people if they have the virus so they can be treated early and have the opportunity to live a near-normal life span. We don't see any miles-long lines; we don't see any lines at all.

Why would people rush to be tested for cancer but avoid being tested for HIV? You already know the one-word answer: stigma.

As my cousin Mary Fisher, who's had HIV for decades and was diagnosed with breast cancer months before she finished her 2012 book *messenger*, wrote: "If you have cancer in America, you look for a great doctor. If you have AIDS, you look for a place to hide." That, as Mary rightly observes, is because "we've infused American AIDS with so much shame that women and men at risk are too afraid to be tested; they'd rather die than know. And once you *are* diagnosed positive, you head for silence, not support."

For all the education campaigns and consciousness-raising during the past thirty years, HIV-positive people still face ostracism and condemnation. They are told they have HIV because they did something wrong, aberrant, unclean; that their disease is God's will or God's curse. This hateful treatment at the hands of their "community" makes them feel shame, and the shame keeps them from going to "that clinic" to get tested, lest someone see them. Add to the mix an unhealthy dose of denial, plus ignorance of how treatable HIV is if caught early, and you have a perfect storm of testing avoidance.

Since 2006, the CDC has recommended routine HIV testing for all individuals between the ages of sixteen and sixty-four. I don't know how or why they came up with those ages, though it's a good start. If it were up to me, I'd say that *all* patients followed in primary care settings should be tested for HIV. Those identified as HIV-positive should be referred immediately for care in an HIV treatment center.

We *could* do this—today, in all fifty states effectively—and yet we *don't* do this. To me, this is the new tragedy of AIDS, a tragedy of missed opportunities.

As a result, patients show up in our emergency rooms with symptomatic HIV. Often they have had encounters with the health system in the months preceding their ER visit and no one ever considered the possibility of HIV. The patient "didn't look like" they had HIV, or "had no risk factors." The provider was in too much of a hurry to consider the possibility of HIV. So

Amy and me (circa 2012)

Amy, "The Big E," and Julie in Louisville in Big E's kitchen (2012)

Andy and Brittany (2012)

Harry in Zambia as a high school senior, shooting the movie The Plague that Thunders *(2004)*

Beatrice Hahn and George Shaw (1986; photo courtesy of UAB Media Relations)

Shaw/Hahn lab group, 1986: back row, from left to right: me, Lilly Kong, George Shaw, Paul McNeely; seated, Beatrice Hahn and Maria Taylor (photo courtesy of UAB Media Relations)

A sign of what we were/are up against. A church in Birmingham whose billboard says it all. The stigma against people with HIV was heavily linked to gay lifestyles. Many churches and church communities struggled with this topic, making many HIV-infected patients feel unwelcome in their churches. (Photo courtesy of Rev. Chris Hamlin, 1917 Clinic.)

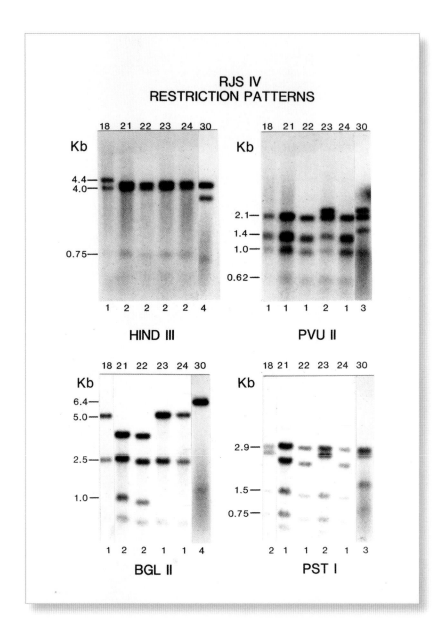

Southern Blot from patient "RJS." Note the different patterns of bands within each of the restriction enzymes used (e.g., panel for HIND III, PVU II, and so forth). Each unique pattern per blot is indicated by the small numbers at the bottom of each lane (1, 2, 3, or 4). Taken together, the number of unique patterns indicated that multiple co-existing viruses were present, each genetically distinct yet highly related (the so-called "quasi-species" nature of HIV).

Without fanfare, UAB opening clinic for AIDS patients

By **John Mangels**
News health/science writer

It's called the 1917 Clinic, and even the name, in a subtle way, is intended to help its patients cope with their deadly disease.

The spare 1960s-style brick and glass building in the midtown district could have been called the AIDS Clinic. But the medical personnel figured that acquired immune deficiency syndrome still carries a hefty social stigma that anyone walking into a building with the word "AIDS" on it would automatically be branded with it.

The 1917 Clinic (named for its street address) will open its doors Thursday with no fanfare, but with the significance of being the first facility in Birmingham to deal specifically with the medical, educational and social problems of AIDS.

Clipping from the January 28, 1988, Birmingham News announcing the opening of the 1917 Clinic

Andy, me, and Harry (left to right) on a deep-sea fishing trip just off the coast of Destin, Florida (1992)

"Michael." This photo was taken in New York City while Michael was dancing for the Joffrey Ballet (circa 1982; photo a gift to me from Michael; unknown photographer).

"Kevin's" hat, given to me approximately six weeks before he died, on display in my office (photo courtesy of Brittany Saag)

Photo of an airplane flying in the clouds, given to me by "David"

Serial Christmas drawings given to me by "Brian," from 1989, 1990, and 1991. Brian died in the fall of 1992. Each of these pictures were drawn by Brian after he had become blind owing to his severe case of cryptococcal meningitis. These drawings still hang in the CFAR office and 1917 Clinic.

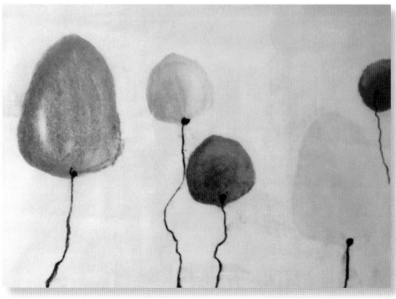

My primary mentors at UAB: Glenn Cobbs, Bill Dismukes, and Claude Bennett. They made all of the magic happen! (Photos courtesy of UAB archives, University of Alabama at Birmingham.)

Glenn Cobbs

Bill Dismukes

Claude Bennett

Jim Raper, director of the 1917 Clinic, on one of our many trips together to Capitol Hill

Paul Volberding, a close friend who helped guide the establishment of the 1917 Clinic

Merle Sande: always larger than life (photo courtesy of Tom Quinn)

Marty Delaney and Tom Blount together in Hawaii, just months before Marty passed away (photo courtesy of Tom Blount)

Donna Jacobsen, executive director of the International Antiviral Society-USA (IAS-USA), and Glenn Treisman, a close friend and advisor, in Vienna, Austria, at the International AIDS Meeting (2010)

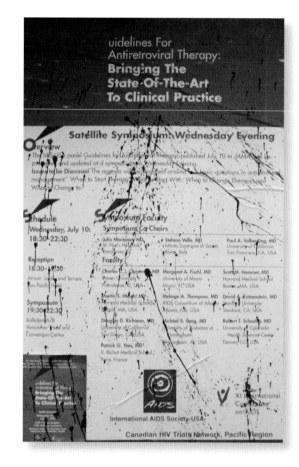

Poster from the 1996 IAS-USA guidelines panel symposium that was interrupted by misguided protesters, who threw beet juice on all of the panelists, claiming that antiretroviral therapy would shorten lives and kill people. They could not have been more wrong! (photo courtesy of Brittany Saag)

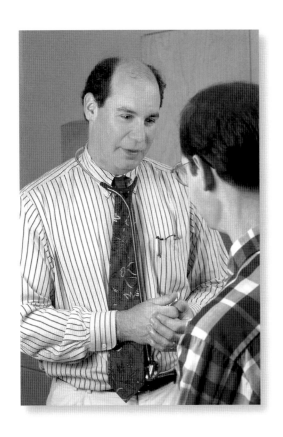

Exam room photo of me with "Alan" during one of his visits while he was participating in a clinical research study (circa 1995; photo courtesy of UAB Media Relations)

Picture drawn by "Alan" in tribute to Mary Fisher. The picture hangs in an exam room in the 1917 Clinic.

Cyndie Culpeper communing with a wolf (2004; photo courtesy of Cliff and Mary Culpeper, Cyndie's brother and mother)

Cyndie at the Sea of Galilee on one of her many trips to Israel (photo courtesy of Cliff and Mary Culpeper)

James Willig and me in Chicago holding the award we received for Excellence in Information Integrity in 2007 by the Information Integrity Coalition (photographer unknown)

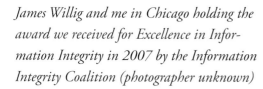

Michael Mugavero and me at a pub in Prague (2009)

Julie Saag and me during homecoming halftime ceremony during her senior year

My dad, Eddie Saag (a.k.a. "Pops," "Big Fred," "Fast Eddie"), and me (circa 2004)

Fire at the 1917 Clinic, February 2013. The burning building (just to the left of the large tree) is just adjacent to the clinic building. Fire trucks are on the scene and the trees in the foreground have burning branches.

Jim Raper talking to a reporter as the fire is being brought under control. Fortunately, the clinic only suffered some smoke and water damage.

Pulpit of the Baptist Church of the Covenant, where the 1917 Clinic held a memorial service. Behind the pulpit are rows of seats that I imagined were filled with the spirit of those who are no longer with us.

Mary Fisher celebrating her sixty-fifth birthday at the twenty-fifth anniversary celebration of the clinic: "Birthdays are our Business!"

Celebrating successful therapy with one of my patients, 2013. Winning! (Photo courtesy of UAB Media Relations.)

their diagnosis is delayed until they present with *pneumocystis* pneumonia, cryptococcal meningitis, or another of the telltale diseases of advanced HIV. And in those cases, even with all our miraculous new drugs, we all too frequently cannot save them.

This is a failure we could prevent, or at least mitigate, with two relatively simple actions.

The first would be to educate the public about the advances in managing HIV disease. We need to replace the old notion of HIV as a death sentence with the new medical reality: If people with HIV are treated early and appropriately, they can live a near-normal life span. Driving home this message will go a long way toward reducing the stigma that makes people fear disclosing their HIV status or even confirming it.

And that brings us to the second action we must take: aggressively implementing the policy of testing *everyone* for HIV, regardless of perceived risk. In this way, we would begin to make the test no more stigmatizing than other checks many people get during regular physical exams. And when we identify those who are positive before they experience advanced disease, they can reap the full benefits of modern therapy.

Gone are the days when we imagined the at-risk population could be circumscribed, as in the "4-H Syndrome" (for homosexuals, hemophiliacs, heroin users, and Haitians) of the early 1980s. Now that we know the virus crosses lines of age, gender, race, class, religion, sexual orientation, and more, how could we expect physicians to determine a given patient's risk of HIV infection and thus who should or shouldn't be tested? I often say that anyone who is sexually active, or even *thinks about* being sexually active, should be tested routinely for HIV. The testing is easy, quick, and accurate. Rapid oral tests can be administered in physicians' offices and a result is available in twenty minutes.

This one-two punch, routine testing followed by linkage to care, is one of our best chances as a society to stop HIV transmission and, ultimately, eradicate the virus. If we're interested in savings lives, here's a way to do it. If we're interested in saving money, here's a way to do it.

In the United States today, it's estimated that about 20–25 percent of people who are HIV-positive do not know it. Sadly, because they're not on

medications that would suppress the virus to nontransmissible levels, this
20–25 percent is responsible for more than 55 percent of the new HIV
infections spread each year. By not knowing their status, they're losing time
getting into treatment that could save their lives—and they unwittingly pull
others down with them. If we identified those folks earlier, got them into
care, and initiated treatment, imagine how much benefit they and we could
realize.

Could.

———

In the beginning, there was AZT. A few years later we got DDC and DDI—
but that didn't mean we had three approaches to treatment; it meant we had
six when we used different drug combinations. And then once we had four
drugs in play, we had as many as twenty-four combinations . . . and on and
on, expanding exponentially. By the time we perceived triple-drug combinations as the best way to go, we had at least eight drugs we could administer
by threes, creating hundreds of potentially therapeutic combinations with
more on the way.

To track options and selected treatments, we needed a medical records
system a little more robust than the database I had launched in 1988 on my
home computer.

We were enrolling more and more people in care at the 1917 Clinic
and in trials—and just for their care and treatment, there was so much we
needed to track. Every one of them presented with a unique combination
of factors, many of which had an impact on whether their HIV regimens
were effective. There were medical issues: not just AIDS-related conditions
but non-AIDS-related conditions ranging from diabetes and food allergies
to drug and alcohol dependence. There were mental and emotional factors:
depression, anxiety, family and marital upheaval, all of which could interfere
with steady adherence to medical regimens and clinic visits. And there were
social and economic factors—patients who drifted in and out of homeless-
ness and joblessness, on and off insurance—that complicated treatment. To
provide the most coherent, farsighted care, we needed to keep our arms
around all those variables.

From the founding of the 1917 Clinic, we intended to use our database and repository to conduct research and then apply our findings to treatment. By the late 1990s, we saw just how dramatically we could scale up this process—how gathering high-quality data over a large range of patients would give us a remarkable, even unprecedented, capacity for research. And it was research that could inform best practices not just of care but of healthcare policy, a benefit that I hadn't even imagined in 1987 when I dreamed up the clinic.

First, though, we needed the right tool. I could see it whole, in my mind, and it was a grand vision: a dream-machine system to collect, store, and draw findings from large amounts of patient and scientific data. A few electronic systems existed for that purpose, but the few built for research scientists weren't user-friendly for care providers, and the many built for care providers focused on billing and appointments and weren't adequate for researchers. The right tool for both jobs would have to be custom designed and custom built.

A streak of luck (or magic) brought me just the right people to make that happen—one of whom was Flohoney Switow's daughter. Especially since I had been involved in Mary Fisher's care, her parents, Marjorie Switow Fisher and Max Fisher, had been interested in my work at UAB. Max was a brilliant entrepreneur who had grown a tiny oil reprocessing business into the largest independent oil company in the Midwest. He was a regular on the *Fortune* magazine list of the world's wealthy, a Republican Party power player, and, with Marjorie, a great benefactor of Detroit, the state of Israel, and other causes.

In March 1999, I went to Max and Marjorie's winter home in Palm Beach, Florida, to seek support for a project to develop an electronic medical records system from scratch. I was perhaps four minutes into my spiel when Max interrupted me to ask, "How old are you?" Taken aback by the abrupt question, I responded, "Forty-three." "Hmmm. Young man," replied the ninety-one-year-old. I realized Max was already several steps ahead of me: Assuming that it would be successful, he wanted to be sure I had enough career time to convert this to a business. To him and Marjorie, this was the best gift they could give to me. As the conversation continued, it was clear both Max and Marjorie understood what this project could achieve; they "got it."

In 1999, the Fisher Foundation made the initial grant to develop the UAB Electronic Medical Records (EMR) Database Project. I've never forgotten my great-uncle Sam declaring that only SOBs thrived in business, and I still didn't think I was an SOB. But if Max Fisher thought I had enough business smarts to lead this new product development project, I was not going to argue.

We immediately began building an EMR from scratch. We started with a systems analysis to assess the origin of every data element we needed to include in the EMR, who entered the information, who used it, and in what form. The analysis took more than two and a half years to complete—but it was worth the time because with the groundwork laid by the systems analysis, the programming was much easier and much faster.

In August 2004, we launched an EMR system that was groundbreaking. Patient information could be entered simply, in formats personal enough for doctors' use yet uniform enough for research analysis. If a clinician tried to order a medication that might interact with a patient's other prescriptions, an alert popped up on the EMR screen. And perhaps most importantly, the providers loved working with it.

That year, the team got a new member: Dr. James Willig. Because he brought both a medical degree and computer expertise from his native Dominican Republic, he could understand the features physicians and researchers needed in the EMR, then help our technologists build them. One of the first questions James asked me was a stunner: "How do you know data in the EMR are accurate?"

Incredulous, I answered, "Because they are entered directly by the providers—no middle man. The data are coming directly from the medical encounter."

James listened, thought for a moment, and asked, "Do you mind if I do an experiment?"

Over the next six months, James dug into the data that had been entered in the EMR. He carefully compared the information that the providers had entered in two places. The first was the problem list and medication profile, the data fields that were discrete and analyzable, the essence of what we use for research. The second was the free text comments at the end of the encounter note—in essence, what the provider was truly thinking at the time of the encounter. His results were shocking: In fields where medication data was recorded, accuracy was only 73 percent. In the problem list fields that concerned diagnosis, accuracy was only 53 percent.

What James obviously had suspected was borne out: Our EMR had a serious accuracy gap. We played the findings back to the providers and their performance improved in entering data. But James's point was made: We needed to continuously reconcile the provider's intent with the discrete, analyzable data elements in the EMR. Under James's leadership, the quality-control software was backed up by a medical team that reviewed every piece of EMR data within seventy-two hours after it was entered, flagging discrepancies, correcting errors—a 100-percent, 24 /7 data reconciling process that produced one of the most error-free bodies of HIV/AIDS patient data in the world.

In 2007, UAB was notified that our EMR had earned an Excellence in Information Integrity Award, an international honor for achievement in information technology. Out of seventy nominees in the not-for-profit category worldwide, we won first place—an honor that James and I were proud to accept at the award ceremony in Chicago.

In medical school, James had imagined a career of hands-on patient care. With the EMR, a much bigger world opened up in front of him. He described it to me in an equation, x^{yz}, exponentially expanding. "Say x is the amount of patients we can care for directly at UAB. When we publish research findings from the EMR, you expand the impact by y, all the scientists and physicians who can do their jobs better because of that knowledge. Then you increase that to the z power, all the patients around the world whose care will be improved because of what has been learned and shared." And the gains would keep redoubling, as we incorporated EMR users' feedback to make the system work even better.

At which point, we welcomed "Mugs." Mugs is the affectionate nickname of our beloved team member Dr. Michael Mugavero, who's played a key research role for both the 1917 Clinic and the UAB CFAR. A Long Island native, Mugs came to UAB as an internal medicine resident, fresh out of Vanderbilt University Medical School and inspired by his work at a Nashville AIDS clinic. He later joined the UAB faculty, where he found that the research gains made possible by the EMR were "dramatic." While other institutions might spend months doing studies with older and incomplete information, the EMR gave UAB researchers what Mugs called "100-percent quality-controlled, real-time data" as fresh as the weekly computer run. That capacity vaulted us ahead in developing scientific knowledge and in publishing what we learned in the world's top medical journals.

The strengths of the EMR helped Mugs—who went on to be leader of the UAB 1917 Clinic Cohort, director of the UAB CFAR Clinical Core, and ultimately codirector of the CFAR overall—win a five-year NIH grant to study HIV/AIDS care access issues. The EMR helped UAB secure a lead position among eight US universities merging their AIDS research data in a $2.45 million NIH project called CFAR Network of Integrated Clinical Systems. And with EMR data, we documented how the consistent use of ARV drugs dramatically reduced healthcare expenditures by keeping HIV patients healthier overall—findings that were published in an ID journal and shared on NPR's *All Things Considered* program where I was interviewed by host Michelle Norris.

In 1999 we wanted the EMR system because it would advance patient care and research capacity. In the years since then, EMRs and related tools—known collectively as Health Information Technology (HIT)—have been identified as a key element in curbing healthcare costs. A research report by the nonprofit Rand Corporation concluded that "Properly implemented and widely adopted, [HIT] would save money and significantly improve healthcare quality. Annual savings from efficiency alone could be $77 billion or more. Health and safety benefits could double the savings while reducing illness and prolonging life." The Rand report projected that the savings from HIT would be vastly greater than the costs: "Implementation would cost around $8 billion per year, assuming adoption by 90 percent of hospitals and doctors' offices over 15 years." Since Rand produced those estimates in 2005, the cost of implementation undoubtedly has increased, but I'm sure the savings we could reap have increased even more.

There's no silver-bullet solution to all of what's broken in the US healthcare system. But I know, based on my own experiences, that HIT has enormous potential for improvements in quality and cost-efficiency in healthcare.

With just our relatively small system at UAB, we were able to guide treatment and enhance quality of care significantly, in real time. With knowledge developed from our data, we became much more proficient at saving lives *and* saving money. And if an EMR system could handle a hydra-headed monster of a disease like HIV/AIDS, it certainly could prove useful in other medical fields.

As usual, Max and Marjorie Fisher knew a good idea when they saw it.

————

I traveled to Zambia again in 2001, the year that Drs. Jeff and Elizabeth Stringer and their two young children moved there full time to lead the Centre for Infectious Disease Research in Zambia (CIDRZ). As a nongovernmental organization working in partnership with the Zambian government and UAB, CIDRZ set up research facilities in government-sponsored clinics that delivered primary care. By colocating, CIDRZ practitioners could swiftly adapt treatment based on what their research revealed, helping immediately to stem the HIV epidemic that infected an estimated one in six Zambians.

Jeff and Elizabeth, both gynecologists, focused intensely on developing therapies for prevention of mother-to-child HIV transmission (PMTCT for short). Their challenge was to find PMTCT approaches that were feasible and affordable even in such a resource-poor setting. And our ongoing challenge back at UAB was to help them roll up as much additional funding as possible so their work could continue and expand.

I distinctly remember a conversation with the Stringers in fall 2003. Elizabeth was eight months pregnant with their third child, and they had returned to the United States for the birth. Jeff said they had heard of a possible new source of funding, but he would need UAB's help to position CIDRZ to compete for it. "It's this thing called PEPFAR," Jeff said—an odd-sounding acronym that at that moment meant little to me. But since then, of course, PEPFAR—the US President's Emergency Plan for AIDS Relief—has become one of the best-known and most widely hailed global health initiatives ever.

Zambia was named one of PEPFAR's first fifteen "focus countries," and CIDRZ was one of the early grantees. In March 2004 I went to Lusaka with several UAB 1917 Clinic staff, including Jim Raper, to help CIDRZ set up its PEPFAR-funded programs. At our first organizational meeting after arriving, I remember thinking about what I knew of federally funded programs and cutting to the chase. As I opened our meeting I said, "It's great that the US government is giving this amount of money to support treatment here in Zambia. But in two or three years, Congress is going to call us in and ask us, 'What did you do with all that money?' We need to be able to respond with data, not emotion. We need to know precisely how many patients have been treated and what their outcomes were."

Echoing what we had done Alabama with the 1917 Clinic, we set up the CIDRZ PEPFAR-funded treatment program to enroll patients as rapidly as possible and to serve them as comprehensively as possible. Alongside the treatment facilities, we set up labs and computers so the staff could study and document every patient outcome, logging results both for CIDRZ research and for accountability to its funder, the US government.

If the PEPFAR start-up wasn't exciting enough, this trip had another bonus: My son Harry, then eighteen and a high school senior, took time off school to go on the trip with me. The principal of Harry's high school, Dicky Barlow, had agreed that Harry could do a special project on AIDS in Africa. I suggested that the project's "term paper" be a documentary video, and Principal Barlow agreed, on the condition that Harry would show the documentary to the entire school at an assembly upon our return. I said, "No problem."

Because this was Harry's first visit to Africa, and his first experience of HIV/AIDS in the developing world, he saw everything with fresh eyes. Here's how he would later recall it:

> I knew the basics about Africa and had watched documentaries, but there is no movie or picture that can do justice to what it really is like when you're there. Nothing could have prepared me for the way the people live—which is, obviously, how people live in a large part of the world but so different from how we live in the United States.

The other thing that struck me was how different the AIDS epidemic was in Zambia and in the United States, like night and day. By 2004, HIV had become more of a controlled phenomenon in the United States—but in Africa, it might as well have been 1980 in terms of the lack of control, the unmitigated spread, and the death rate.

I've always thought my dad had a lot of foresight. In Africa, it was amazing to watch him and his colleagues basically build out an entire HIV care machine—to identify how to allocate funds, how to build alliances with the government and other groups, how to set things up from the pharmacy side to the doctor side to the lab side, and how to get people into care.

While in Zambia, Harry and I shot twenty-seven hours of video. When we got back to Alabama, we spent hours editing it into a twenty-four-minute production he could show at the high school. On the border between Zambia and Zimbabwe, we had photographed the breathtaking Victoria Falls. In Swahili it is called *Mosi-ao-Tunya*—"The Smoke that Thunders"—because the waterfalls create smoke-like clouds of mist and a thundering roar that's heard for miles. Playing off that name, we gave the documentary the title *AIDS in Africa: The Plague that Thunders*.

After Harry showed the video to the school assembly, there was a short discussion period. Harry answered his classmates' questions about the experience—and then I asked the final question. "Since we got back, all of the parents have asked me, 'Did this trip change Harry at all?' Well, did it?" I asked.

Without hesitation, Harry said, "Yes, it did." And then turning to the audience, his peers, he continued: "We think we have problems here. We don't get the car we want. We don't get the date we want to the prom, or get into our first choice of college. Now I know, *we* don't have problems. *They* do." The audience responded with a standing ovation.

With support from PEPFAR, UAB, and others, CIDRZ began to turn the tide of HIV/AIDS in Zambia. Its antiretroviral therapy (ART) program enrolled more than 53,000 children and adults in long-term HIV/AIDS care by the end of 2006, treating 33,000 in the first twenty-four months. A Centers for Disease Control and Prevention official hailed CIDRZ's ART program as number one among those PEPFAR funded. And CIDRZ's PMTCT program expanded to serve hundreds of thousands of women and infants at dozens of sites across Zambia.

As CIDRZ's reach grew, Lusaka's mortality rate dropped, falling by more than half in just a few years. When I returned to the United States from a 2008 trip to Zambia, I was delighted to tell Harry of my conversation with Medicine, the improbably named gentleman employed as a driver for CIDRZ.

As he was driving me across town late one morning, I said, "Medicine, I know you are proud to work for CIDRZ and you can see how the programs are helping, but does the average person on the street see a difference?"

His response was instant: "Oh, yes. Just look at us."

I didn't understand: "What do you mean, Medicine?"

"Look at us! Right now. We are moving. No traffic jams."

"I don't get it, Medicine. What was the cause of the traffic jams?"

"Funerals."

No gridlock; no delays. No more coming to a halt so a funeral procession—or two, or three, or a dozen—could pass through the city to the cemetery. Before, the daily deaths from AIDS resulted in all those funerals and all those traffic jams. Now, traffic moved freely. And the people of Lusaka could see the difference—a visible victory of the health system in Zambia over the thundering plague.

I've been hard on presidents. But the PEPFAR program that President George W. Bush initiated was rightly hailed as "a lifeline" in a congressionally mandated Institute of Medicine (IOM) evaluation released in early 2013. As I write this, PEPFAR has funneled more than $44 billion to more than 100 countries. The IOM report says that PEPFAR "has achieved—and in some cases surpassed—its initial ambitious aims. These efforts have saved and improved the lives of millions of people around the world."

From the beginning, PEPFAR required countries to have created a national AIDS strategy in order to be eligible for those US aid dollars. Makes sense, right? And yet, the United States itself did not devise such a strategy

until some six years after the launch of PEPFAR—and two years after President Bush left the White House.

The good news is, when the Obama administration unveiled the
National AIDS Strategy in 2010, it set the right priorities. It emphasized
universal testing, linking newly diagnosed people to care, and then retaining
them in care.

It's great that US leaders have gone to bat against HIV with PEPFAR—
but while looking to Biafra, they sometimes lost sight of Birmingham. And
it's fine for presidents to unveil strategies and lawmakers to make speeches
and think tanks to release reports. But when AIDS was ravaging Lusaka a
decade ago, what cleared the funeral traffic jams was testing, care, and treatment, offered as quickly and broadly as humanly possible. Just that simple.

I don't mean to sound ungrateful. I mean no disrespect when I say this.
But when it comes to mounting a response to HIV/AIDS at home as well
as abroad, and it when it comes to dealing with the health of our people as
well as of our economy, it's painfully clear: America really *could* do vastly,
vastly better.

Could.

Chapter 15

THERE ARE NO WORDS

E lliott Jones was the first case in which I wasn't ready to give up on life-prolonging interventions, but the patient was. The second case came a few months later, in summer 2005. Cyndie.

She had been unable to hold food down for more than a year. Every time she tried to eat, she was overcome by abdominal pain and vomiting. Placing a feeding tube in her stomach didn't help. Running the feeding tube directly into her jejunum, the middle part of the small intestine, worked better. But she still needed some supplementary feeding, which was delivered through an IV PICC line. One of the complications of long-term IV feeding is bloodstream infections, particularly yeast infections or fungemia. That's what Cyndie developed in the summer of 2005.

Ordinarily, we would treat the infection with IV antifungal therapies, remove the line, and hope the fungemia would resolve. When I explained it to Cyndie, she was emphatic: "I don't want you to treat me for this, Mike. I'm ready to go."

I could not argue. She had been miserable during the last year, between the constant infusions and the frequent bouts of abdominal pain. Despite a litany of tests and visits to the GI specialists, we were stumped. We didn't know how to relieve her suffering.

Cyndie called her mother, and Mother Mary flew in from San Francisco, followed shortly by her brother Cliff. Then came a parade of people who loved

Cyndie. Some came to cling to her, some to love her, some to say good-bye. One of the visitors was Lynn, a friend of Cyndie's since kindergarten; even though she was slipping away, Cyndie brightened visibly at Lynn's arrival.

Among the visitors was Cyndie's fellow clergy, clinic chaplain Malcolm Marler. He still remembers:

> I walked into the hospital room to find my friend in the bed too tired and weak to respond with words. All of her life energy was focused on providing each breath and heartbeat for her body. Her mother was weary from sitting next to her daughter's hospital bed for too long and from grieving the last 10 years knowing her only daughter would someday die from AIDS. That time was now very near.
>
> My friend's mom said, "Hi, Malcolm, please sit here beside the bed. I'll move into the lounge chair." Within a couple of minutes, she was asleep.
>
> I spoke softly to my friend, "Are you tired?" I think she nodded yes. It wasn't time for conversations like we had in the past as one clergy colleague to another. It wasn't time to talk about the similarities and differences of our faith backgrounds that were always so rich and instructive for me.
>
> Instead, it was time to be present. Time to just be. I sat down and leaned over the bedrail to hold her right hand that rested on her chest. She put her left hand on top of mine. I closed my eyes and silently thanked God for a person who has made such a difference in so many persons' lives. I thanked God for the difference she has made in my life in particular.
>
> Dr. Saag first introduced us in the clinic in 1995. She asked me to read the sermon she was going to give soon to her congregation. It included telling her congregation that she was HIV-positive and that she would humbly appreciate their prayers and support. She would teach them that it is okay to be cared for by others.
>
> She was understandably frightened and yet also resolute in this sermon that this was the right thing to do. "It's my duty

to educate them about this disease," knowing that it could also mean the end of her employment. She gained strength from the experience and became a powerful spokesperson in so many ways. Thankfully, in the days following, most of the congregation gave her the support she (and they) needed.

As I sat beside her bedside, her portable CD player was close to her ear as songs from her faith played softly. It was such a sacred time. I stayed for thirty minutes or so, listening to the music, reminiscing, and stroking my friend's hand.

There were no words to make it all better. Her life lived has already spoken volumes.

When I look back at the speech Malcolm mentioned, in which Cyndie told her synagogue that she had HIV, I am struck by two passages. One is the sentence that I know is Mother Mary's favorite: "I got AIDS while caring for those in need—and I still care." The other is Cyndie's statement about what she hoped would be the future of her disease:

> Hopefully, in my lifetime, AIDS will be a thing of the past— what people used to die from in the latter part of the twenti- eth century. I have no intention of giving up myself. I am on medication now that is not even FDA approved, and I live by the words of my doctor up in Birmingham, where I have been going once, sometimes twice a week. He reports that this has been a record year for new drugs to combat AIDS; that we're getting to the point where AIDS may soon be a chronic medical condition like diabetes or high blood pressure, which with proper treatment and medication need not diminish one's quality nor quantity of life. I live every day according to those words, and the words of [Deuteronomy], "Choose life." They're all I have to go on.

In retrospect, I don't recall being as prophetic as Cyndie said. But what she described did come to pass.

In the database I started when the 1917 Clinic opened in January 1988, each patient is assigned a code, a combination of letters and numbers. A four-digit number in each code indicates when the patient came to us; for example, the patient assigned 0124 was the 124th patient the clinic enrolled. Not surprisingly, most of the patients with the lower-number codes died years ago. I wept hardest at the deaths of 0006, 0039, and 0136. I have kept in touch with the mother of 0018 and the widow of 0084. I continue to marvel at the resilience of our longest-term survivors, 0061 and 0123.

The years passed, the drugs got better, and the code numbers went up. At roughly the same point in the mid-1990s, we got our 2,000th patient and a windfall of new ARVs. I felt lucky and confident. Finally, we had the tools to keep most of these newer patients alive and in good health.

Most, but not all. Not the patient that the database knew as 2236 and that I knew as singer, rabbi, friend, Cyndie.

The infection in Cyndie's bloodstream spread to her heart, causing fungal endocarditis. The treatment of choice for this condition is open heart surgery with valve replacement. For Cyndie, there would be no surgery.

The final time I saw her, she was awake but weak. She smiled at me, squeezed my hand, and mouthed the words, "Thank you." I couldn't speak. I smiled back, tears welling in my eyes, and squeezed her hand gently. I leaned over, with my tears dripping on to her gown, and gave her a kiss good-bye. I turned and gave Mother Mary a long, heartfelt hug. We both knew the end was near. We simply nodded to each other, and I turned and left the room.

On August 29, 2005, around 9:00 a.m., Rabbi Cynthia Ann Culpeper lost her long, defiant fight.

In the early days of AIDS when our patients died, we autopsied as many as gave permission, hoping to better understand the virus. We did autopsies even when the pathologists were scared witless that they might be exposed to infection. We did them in an autopsy suite that, over time, had so much safety equipment added that you could have handled anthrax in there. As Cyndie's friend, her autopsy was not something I wanted to attend. But as her doctor, I needed to be there. I hoped I might discover why we couldn't feed her for more than a year. And as always, I hoped I might learn something from one death to help prevent another.

Standing in the autopsy suite was a surreal experience. My friend Cyndie had let me know her "heart," her fears and feelings. Now my patient Cyndie was on the autopsy table and the pathologist was showing me the inside of her heart: there, on the aortic valve, a flowering of infection, just as we had suspected.

With the examination of Cyndie's intestines, the mystery of her last year was solved. Almost certainly as a consequence of the ruptured colon and peritonitis she had suffered in January 2004, Cyndie's intestines were encased in scar tissue. No wonder she could not eat without abdominal pain and vomiting: The scar tissue inhibited the normal peristalsis, the wavelike contractions of muscle that push food through the digestive tract. No surgery or intervention could have fixed this problem. Cyndie would have suffered from the inability to eat, the pain, and the vomiting for the rest of her life. It was as if she somehow knew this when she decided against treatment.

By authorizing the autopsy, Cyndie allowed her provider team finally to understand the condition that had marred her last months. Even in death, Cyndie was still teaching.

I was honored that the Culpeper family asked me to serve as a pallbearer at Cyndie's funeral. Even during the mourning, though, my role as her doctor tugged at me. As we carried her simple casket to its grave, my mind kept straying back to images of her at the autopsy. Frankly, that was horrible.

But after the burial came the event that Cyndie had requested, a gathering of those she loved and who loved her. Jewish tradition encourages a *seudat havra'ah,* a private "meal of healing" served to family after the return from the cemetery to signify that life goes on. Cyndie's gathering, though, was a bigger, noisier affair hosted by her relatives and synagogue at Temple Beth El. There were Cyndie's favorite foods prepared by friends' hands, and wine for rounds of toasts.

We cried and laughed together as we told each other our best Cyndie stories. Recalling how bravely Cyndie would conceal or laugh off pain, I told of the email she sent me with the subject line "SCREAMING KID-NEYS"—how, before describing the painful kidney stone condition caused by her medication, she joked that Screaming Kidneys would be a great name for a rock band. Person after person shared memories of Cyndie laughing, dancing, and singing, teaching and counseling her congregants, blessing the newborns, and sitting shiva for the departed.

In the Jewish faith that Cyndie so passionately embraced, the observance of shiva may end with a reading from Isaiah. "No more will your sun set," it begins—a fitting benediction for someone who brought light to all who knew her.

> *No more will your sun set,*
> *nor your moon be darkened,*
> *for God will be an eternal light for you,*
> *and your days of mourning shall end.*
> —Isaiah 60:20

Chapter 16

TURNING SUCCESS INTO FAILURE

All by myself, with no one to tell me anything different, I'll never grow up. I like this about myself, a lot, even if I don't want my university president or august audiences to know. In my head, I'm fourteen years old, innocent in my thinking, exuberant and hopeful.

Or if not fourteen years old, then eighteen years old at most, like the college freshmen in a play I started writing when I was at Tulane. Called *House of Doors*, it was a terribly earnest play and a deep one. I won't spoil the ending for you, in case I become a published playwright in retirement. But in Act One, the students are running excitedly through a huge, magical house, opening the doors to dozens and dozens of rooms.

The scene's fairly transparent message is that options are limitless; everything is possible. I wrote it this way because that's how I want life to be. The tragic reality that everything is *not* possible is something that I rail against, to this day. Resisting such reality is my way of fighting cynicism—which is, after all, only frustrated idealism.

I admit that my idealism has taken some hard knocks during my career in AIDS medicine. It seemed like an honorable part that we scientists were playing, discovering new ways to tame disease. I expected that if we did our part, the other players in this enterprise—politicians, regulators, insurers—surely would do their part, building on our discoveries to expand and improve healthcare.

Such great expectations. But, in many ways, so little progress.

In the 1980s, we had one overriding question: How do we stop the dying? In the 1990s, we had an answer: antiretrovirals. Decades later, we still have the damned question: *How do we stop the dying?* We succeeded at the science, and we brought the science to medicine, but it wasn't enough—because nobody has succeeded at fixing the system that embraces both science and medicine. (Were it not for the Ryan White program—a Band-Aid, not a systemic fix—more than 60 percent of the patients with HIV would go without treatment.) I appreciate ironic plot twists as much as the next guy, but this one is getting old: snatching defeat from the jaws of victory, transforming success into failure.

Does anybody really believe that in America, home to some of the most gifted and inventive thinkers on the planet, we can solve healthcare's medical mysteries but not its procedural or economic ones? I'm not buying it.

If Beatrice Hahn could clone and sequence the newly discovered AIDS virus, then *somebody* can clone the most patient-friendly, cost-effective approaches to healthcare delivery and propagate them nationwide. If the 1917 Clinic's EMR data could prove that early, comprehensive treatment dramatically reduces healthcare costs, then *somebody* can adapt and apply that approach to illnesses and patient populations nationwide.

Simplifying the system for patients, reining in costs, improving provider performance, moderating the influence of the pharmaceutical and insurance industries—every one of these objectives can be achieved. But only if we all step out of our separate fiefdoms and our precious profit centers and work collaboratively.

It's time for all parties in this debate to account for what they bring, or fail to bring, to this flawed system. Because people keep falling through the cracks in it, and try as we might, we don't pull them all out alive.

———

Accessing healthcare in America today is so complicated that at one time or another, almost every one of us will need an advocate, a knowledgeable guide, to get through aspects of it. Why is this situation allowed to persist? Either the system should be made navigable for everyone who has to use it—or those at the top should admit that they don't want it to be. They like it as it is, even if their favorite theme is, "It's too complicated for us to change."

If every patient, including the most vulnerable, can't move through America's healthcare system without expert assistance, then that's what must be provided. A whole new category of personnel must be built into the system expressly to explain its arcane aspects and help consumers navigate them. These navigators will be valuable to any patient but absolutely indispensable for patients who are disadvantaged by infirmity, age, or lack of education. And in the coming years, we'll need ever more of them as the aging baby boomer population experiences more chronic illness and as healthcare becomes more technologically advanced, specialized, and fragmented.

Patient care is fragmented in major ways. Individual aspects of a patient's health are regarded one at a time instead of as a continuum, a whole. Then aspects of a patient's care are parceled out among many different providers. The further we move into the twenty-first century, the less we are likely to find a provider who thinks longitudinally about a patient's whole story. Increasingly, providers look at chiefly (or only) whatever complaint the patient showed up with *today*, trying to make that go away *today*. In many cases, we do this because we lack the time, resources, and perspective to address a complaint within the context of everything going on with the patient.

Perhaps the best—and most scary—example of how we're cementing this fragmented approach is found in the training of physicians today. When I went through training, all patients who came into the hospital on my day "on call" were admitted by me. I followed them every day; when it was time for them to go home, I discharged them. I was their doctor. To accomplish this continuum of care I had to work 90 to 100 hours per week, but I did.

Nowadays, owing to fairly radical changes in house staff (medical resident) duty hours, a physician in training cannot stay in the hospital more than fourteen consecutive hours, must have eight hours between shifts, and cannot work more than six days without a day off per week. On the surface this sounds both reasonable and humane. For the medical resident, it is.

But when these rules are implemented, it's common—even the norm—for a newly admitted patient to be worked up by one doctor, handed off to another the next morning, to still another in the late afternoon, and covered overnight by yet another. It is uncommon for the same person who admitted the patient to discharge them home. No one knows the patient as a person; each of us know their immediate need and our immediate response.

My son Harry, who as I write is a first-year resident at NYU Medical Center, went through his first seven weeks of training without following a single patient from admission through discharge and without either handing off the patients' daily care to someone else or picking the patient up from a colleague who admitted them first.

This story is not unique to NYU. Rather, *every* training program is experiencing the same phenomena. One month recently when I was attending physician on the medical service at UAB, 68 percent of the patients admitted to my service were initially admitted by *someone not on my team.* This means that a night-float resident did the initial workup and handed off the patient to someone on my team the next morning.

The reason for restricting duty hours is to minimize fatigue, with an eye toward minimizing errors made by tired residents. But my question is: How many errors are generated now owing to handoffs? In terms of the provider, I fear that the quality of care can't help but be affected by a lack of continuity and familiarity with a patient's case, not to mention the alarm from the patient and family's perspective of not having a clue who their primary doctor really is.

Do you know what the most common question is among patients in the hospital today?

"Who is my doctor?"

The sad reality is that this is a symptom of our health delivery system careening into fragmentation and chaos. Providers are more and more becoming shift workers who check in at 0700 and check out at 1700 hours. This may work for nonprimary care services like the emergency room, pathology, or radiology—but it endorses discontinuity and lack of ownership of the patient's full experience by the primary provider. We are teaching our new doctors how to hand off, not how to hold on. And these are the providers who will be taking care of me as I get older. Not a comforting thought.

A related problem, according to Shannon Brownlee, is that "Our medical workforce is upside down."

Long one of the most respected US journalists covering healthcare and medicine, Brownlee now heads the health policy program at the nonpartisan New America Foundation. In a 2012 article in *The Atlantic* magazine, Brownlee noted that, "Most developed countries have many more primary care docs than specialists. In the United States, it's the reverse, with nearly two specialists per primary care physician. Not coincidentally, those other countries' populations are also healthier than ours, and they stay that way while spending less on medical care. There's no reason to keep paying academic medicine to produce more specialists than we need, while millions of Americans don't have a regular primary care doctor."

The proliferation of specialties and subspecialties further raises the risk of fragmentation. By increasingly staffing the system with specialists who work either in just one aspect of medicine or in one medical service location, we insure that a patient's care will be delivered by a greater number of practitioners, none of whom are expected to know all the patient's medical needs or full medical history.

I'm a specialist who works with hundreds of first-rate specialists every year, so it's not specialization per se that I'm questioning. It's the movement toward crossbreeding medical specialization with a sort of factory model. It reminds me of what occurred in the US auto industry. In the early days of auto production, cars were made one at a time by teams of craftsmen who had a bumper-to-bumper understanding of the finished product. Then in 1913 came the assembly line. From then on, many workers would have fleeting contact with each car. They became knowledgeable about parts, not cars. The factory model does the same for patient care: Caregivers know charts, not patients. It *might* make it faster or more efficient for institutions, but it absolutely makes it less personal and less coherent for patients.

The fastest-growing medical specialty in the United States is hospital medicine—that is, the training of so-called "hospitalists" to provide general medical care to patients while they are in the hospital. Increasingly, a primary care physician (PCP) will refer a patient to a hospital medicine practice when the patient is admitted. The practice's hospitalists will care for the patient throughout the stay, ostensibly in consultation with the patient's PCP and other specialists. Then upon release, the patient is returned to the care of his or her own PCP and specialists.

Early in the 1990s, the use of hospitalists was touted as a way to increase care quality by having providers with inpatient expertise working full time in the hospital. But it also was promoted as a way to decrease healthcare costs, and that may have been its most seductive trait.

According to the original concept, the hospitalist was to be part concierge, part advocate, part ringmaster. He or she was to know all the ins and outs of the hospital, including staff strengths, then create the right teams to surround and care for each patient. But as it has worked out in most US facilities, hospitalists rarely have time to organize or deliver such coherent care in concert with the PCPs or specialists on whose behalf they are seeing the patients. So the hospitalist, too, becomes more a shift worker than a continuity-of-care provider—just one more character in an ever-changing cast of practitioners who, under those circumstances, cannot possibly follow individual patients and circumstances comprehensively.

In many cases, soon after hospitalists were put in place, their role was redefined, whether or not they wished it (and whether or not this was openly stated). Hospitalists came to operate almost as part of the business office; it fell to them to try to make each patient at least a revenue-neutral creature and, better, a profit center. One of my colleagues tells of a large Midwestern hospital where the first task of the hospitalist when he or she came in for a shift was to find out which expensive pieces of medical machinery and which high-dollar-billing staff members were not fully allocated for the coming six to ten hours. If they established that some resources would not be in constant use—i.e., not making money for the hospital every minute of every hour of every day—then they were encouraged to look for patients who might fill the open spots in those dance cards.

Most of the time when patients get tests, treatments, or care that's unnecessary, duplicative, or excessive, it's because their many providers haven't communicated enough with each other to head off such foul-ups. The delivery of unnecessary healthcare services is part of the reason the United States has higher healthcare spending but a less healthy population than other countries, according to healthcare expert Brownlee, author of the book *Overtreated: Why Too Much Medicine Is Making Us Sicker and Poorer.*

"The way to fight waste is by reorganizing the way doctors and nurses and hospitals provide care," Brownlee said in a 2008 *Reader's Digest* article. "There are models out there of high-quality, low-cost care, and they include some of the most trusted names in medicine: the Mayo Clinic, Kaiser, and Intermountain Healthcare. These programs have a primary provider coordinate all the care. They understand that twenty-first-century medicine is a team sport. They also put a premium on analyzing the best available evidence and then ensuring that their doctors follow it." The savings from this kind of reform would be significant, according to Brownlee: "Cutting out even half of the unnecessary health care in this country would be enough to cover every citizen who is now uninsured."

I would never say that hospitalists are bad doctors. They go through the same kind of training as other MDs and are fully committed to providing their best service while in the hospital. Nor would I argue that having 24/7 hospital-based doctors is, on its face, a bad idea.

But if the use of hospitalists initially was seen as a way to enhance patient welfare, over time I believe it has become a way chiefly to enhance financial margins. That is probably the chief reason that hospital medicine practices have grown so rapidly and why so many hospitals foot the bill to entice hospitalists to work in their system. In 2003, hospitalists were in only 29 percent of hospitals, but by 2009 they were in 58 percent of all hospitals and in 89 percent of hospitals with 200+ beds, according to their professional organization, the Society of Hospital Medicine.

Put another way: If you spend a few days in a good-sized hospital anywhere in America today, there's a very good chance that "your doctor" will be someone (or a series of someones) that you've never laid eyes on before. This doesn't increase anyone's chances—yours, the doctor's, or the hospital's—for patient-centered medicine with great outcomes. And by great outcomes, I mean patients getting consistent (nonhandoff), appropriate, cost-effective care, staying only as long as necessary, and not needing readmission because they were sent home prematurely.

———

Perhaps a majority of physicians feel frustrated by the healthcare system today. A good number find enough satisfaction because of the personal wealth it brings them. They focus less on whether they get joy out of the work day to day and more on how much money they can make. I like material things, too, but I've always fought the notion that the acquisition of things is the purpose of my career.

It would help if the US health system assured not just fairness in access and coverage for patients, but fairness in reimbursement for providers. I don't see any reason a cardiovascular surgeon gets paid ten times more than an internist. They're all equally replaceable; if one were to die, you'd find another. And in what Brownlee rightly calls the "team sport" of modern medicine, it could be argued that PCPs—family practitioners, internists, pediatricians, OB/GYNs, nurse practitioners—are the most valuable players in the system.

If I were czar and could magically transform the financing of US healthcare, I would pay the same number of "tickets" to a surgeon as to an internist. Why? Because today a patient (or insurer) pays $4,000 an hour for a twenty-minute cataract procedure, but $180 for a consultation with an infectious disease provider when they're in intensive care with a life-threatening infection. How did we get so out of balance?

Not reimbursing fairly for work done means that some healthcare providers are abused by The System and that others are unfairly rewarded.

Say you're my patient and you need something from me for which I can't bill anyone—a letter to bolster your insurance claim, or a "prior authorization" request so you can get a medicine you need. I think it's important to your health and it's my professional, moral duty as your doctor, so I'm going to do what needs doing. Unpaid. And while I know prior authorizations do save money in any system, we need to find another way to do it properly, fairly.

Currently, The System *banks on* my behavior, and I mean this literally. Insurers and hospital leaders count on providers doing what's necessary to meet patients' needs even if they don't get reimbursed. Every single day, The System earns interest on the dollars it is *not* paying for those providers' services. It makes profits on our backs by not paying us for what we do to keep our patients whole. Our good will is the safety net that catches folks as they fall through the cracks of our diseased healthcare delivery system. And each time we do "the right thing" to serve the patient, we are bailing out The System. It's abusive. And we not only put up with it; we enable it.

Even if healthcare providers feel shafted by those who hold power over us—in government, academia, corporate medicine, the insurance industry—most of us try to do right by our patients. To borrow a lyric from soul legend Curtis Mayfield, we just "keep on keepin' on," no matter what. It's a point of professional honor, moral certainty, and probably self-respect.

I know that's what Laura Secord does. Laura is a free-spirited child of the '60s who attended college in Berkeley, California, when it was the hippie movement epicenter. She's an exceptional poet who loves the color purple; her house is painted purple, and every day she wears something purple, which sets off her flowing, curly blonde hair. Laura is a very spiritual person, in touch with what she calls the "mojo" of the universe—and so she writes and performs under the name Mojo Mama.

Laura's generosity and warmth make her a great nurse practitioner. At the 1917 Clinic, she works with me on Wednesday afternoons; she sees patients as their primary provider, then I meet with the patients after Laura checks them out to me. Laura has been a guardian angel to some of our longtime patients, like Jenny.

Remember Jenny, whom I introduced a few chapters back? That "kind man" that she met in 2000 became her husband, and for a while it looked like both her HIV and her personal life were under control. But that didn't last. She got back into substance abuse. She lost a home to foreclosure, and she and her husband were fighting.

Jenny is a "dichotomous" patient: She's either on or off. When she is on, she takes her medicines regularly, shows up for her appointments, smiles easily, excels at her job, and is genuinely happy. When she is off, she takes medicines when she remembers, misses appointments, is tearful, may get fired from work, and is mostly unhappy. On the personality spectrum that my psychiatrist friend Glenn Treisman described, Jenny is at the feeling-driven, live-for-today end.

When I've rounded with Glenn in his clinic at Johns Hopkins, I've heard him tell patients like Jenny, "You know, when we were born God gave us certain attributes, including our feelings. When you were born, you got a 'double scoop' of feelings!" Patients are delighted that Glenn "gets" this about them, so they're willing to hear what he says next:

"Because of your 'extra scoop,' when you feel good, you feel extra good. But when you feel bad, you feel extra bad, and it is harder for you to tolerate feeling bad than most other folks. So here's how it plays out: Picture yourself on a bus on a narrow road winding along on a high mountainside. Who do you want driving the bus? You or your feelings? If you are driving, you can take the curves and navigate your way down the mountainside. But if your feelings are driving the bus, they are going to drive you and the bus off the cliff."

When Jenny is driving the bus, she is fabulous, in control, very functional. But when her feelings take over the bus, she begins drinking, becomes less responsible, and ends up going off the proverbial cliff. In summer 2010, Jenny and her husband divorced; a few months later, she was fired from her job. And that, says Jenny, "is where it *all* went downhill. I couldn't afford COBRA [the short-term extension of insurance coverage that employees can buy after a job loss]. I wasn't married so I couldn't get on a spouse's coverage; I was too old to be under my parents' insurance and too 'well-off' to be on Medicaid. I had no income, no health insurance, and no savings. So I worked whatever temp job was offered and borrowed from parents and friends. I went to shelters for meals, I got on food stamps, I prayed . . . and I stayed reliant on the 1917 Clinic."

As providers, Laura and I can tell immediately who's driving Jenny's bus. In bad times, Laura will get Jenny's urgent calls. "I'm in trouble, I've run out of medicines." "My boss is about to fire me because I've missed too much work." "I got into a fight with my boyfriend." Laura returns all calls promptly, including Jenny's, often after hours. Laura doesn't get paid extra to make the calls, or fill out paperwork to get patients the medicines they need.

Even when Jenny had insurance, gaining access to medicines she needed wasn't easy. We could get the antiretroviral medicines as they were covered by her insurance. But several of her other medications were "nonpreferred," which means the insurance company did not negotiate the low price with the company that made the drug we wanted; rather, their deal is with another company that makes a similar product. In some cases, the drugs are similar enough that we can simply prescribe the insurance company program's drug. But in other cases, we determine that the nonpreferred or "nonformulary" drug is a much better choice for a given patient—and this leads to trouble.

In such cases, the 1917 Clinic has to have one of our providers help the patient apply for a prior authorization (PA) to use the nonformulary drug. This process is not only disruptive and anxiety-producing for the patient, it is costly to our clinic and our staff. To figure out that a drug is nonformulary, determine whether the formulary drug will work instead and, if not, find out where to file the PA request, actually complete the paperwork, and then track and manage the outcome is a grueling, lengthy process. It's also totally uncompensated.

We became so frustrated with these experiences that Jim Raper took on a project of tracking the time he spent filling out PAs and analyzing the cost to the clinic. We published the findings in a paper in the journal *Clinical Infectious Diseases* in 2010. After examining two years' worth of PAs, Jim determined that going through the process for a PA cost us on average about $42 per prescription in terms of his time filling out the forms—and that's without considering the dollar value of the time if he had been able to spend it doing other things, like seeing more patients.

Our journal paper concluded, "Although evidence supports that PA reduces third-party expenditures, it significantly delays medication accessibility for patients and imposes high costs that negatively impact operating margins for health care providers." In short: PAs save insurers money—success for them!—but cost the clinics time and money and slow our patients' access to essential meds, unquestionably a failure for our patients.

Early in 2012, Jenny emailed me this:

> I'm just a simple girl with no unrealistic dreams. I just want
> to work hard, be healthy, be able to keep my townhome and
> my used 2007 Ford Edge and live a long time with my four-
> year-old cat named Charley, who is the love of my life. I hope
> 2012 is better, but for now, I'm scared, even terrified, of losing
> everything I have (up to and including my life). I turned 41
> last December, and I just hope that since half my life is over
> that before I leave this world, I wake up just one day—just
> one—and can say, "Today, I'm happy."

A year later, in early 2013, Jenny sent an email recapping another tough
year. The law firm would not put her on full-time status with benefits, and
she could not afford the $500 a month that private insurance cost. She was
"in the wrong crowd" again, with drugs and drink. She was in debt to the
IRS, had filed for bankruptcy, and her bid to refinance her townhome was
denied on Christmas Eve. "I prayed for a fresh start" Jenny wrote—and on
Christmas Day, she got a phone call: "A friend of mine who recently moved
to Pennsylvania to work called me and asked if I wanted to start over and
move in with her.

"I packed, drove 18 hours straight with a U-Haul, and arrived at her
house at 10:00 p.m. on New Year's Eve. It was the bravest thing I ever did
voluntarily . . . I will miss you all dearly and hope that one day I will see you
again, but I know it will probably be a long time. I will keep you updated
with my status because I feel like we are all family. Sorry to have not had
time to say good-bye in person . . ."

Jenny has enrolled at her local AIDS clinic and is seeing a new ID doctor there. We have forwarded her 1917 Clinic records. Her new doctor has
written letters to help her qualify for aid and disability there, her email said:
"Also, if any of you could write letters for me about my issues over the year,
I may need them . . ."

Nobody compensates Laura or me—or Jenny's new providers—for the
time we spend on letters, calls, and emails, trying to keep patients from

going off the cliff. Sometimes their problems are their own demons. Sometimes the problems are caused by forces beyond their control, or even by the devilish complexities of The System that's ostensibly there to help them.

I've hung on to these emails as a reminder of the importance of listening to patients like Jenny. The controlling institutions in US healthcare today have concluded that it's not important—at least not important enough to be compensated. We do it anyway because these people matter and, if we can, we're going to improve their odds of success. Just that simple.

———

In Monty Python's Spamalot, one of my favorite Broadway musicals, there's a song called "All for One." The last two lines, *Slightly less for people we don't like / And a little bit more for me,* too often summarize how the American people think about each other. It's really a sad commentary. For a while after the videotaped police beating of Rodney King sparked the 1991 Los Angeles riots, people earnestly quoted King's plaintive line, "People, I just want to say, can we all get along?" But lately I've heard it quoted cynically, as a punch line in situations where people have no intention of trying to compromise or seek consensus.

It's a question worth asking another way: Why *can't* we get along? What is it that's keeping us from seeking the common good on something as integral to life as achieving and sustaining good health? Why are we getting in each other's way so much? I see the energy expended by people working their asses off trying to do the right thing for other people—the healthcare workers who are just jury-rigging or patching together solutions so people don't fall through the cracks of a fractured system. But they're all working independently; nobody is pulling it all together.

We need to rally around a common vision and work together for the betterment of healthcare. We need to behave as if we're in an honest-to-god medical neighborhood, where we all can feel comfortable, where we nurture each other. I don't have the magical formula to make that come to pass—but I know that demonizing those who don't think like me, or dismissing others' opinions out of hand, won't get us anywhere.

We have the tools available to cure many ailments and manage many that we can't yet cure—but we can't use the tools because The System has cut off our hands. As currently structured, it expects the healthcare providers to be shock absorbers who provide whatever's needed, whether compensated or not. The System expects providers to do this until we're stretched to our limits and beyond, to the point of burnout.

Before, in the darkest days of the AIDS epidemic, the burnout among my colleagues came from watching so many people die. Now the burnout is because we're watching The System consciously, intentionally fail—abdicating responsibility and trusting that providers will make up for The System's failures. By acting as an indentured servant to the health insurance companies, I am keeping them profitable—and, therefore, motivated to keep The System (not) working as it is.

Worse, I know I'm actually better off than a lot of the really overburdened, heroic providers toiling in America today. As so often happens in my life, I got lucky. I came into the field before things got this desperate. I have contacts. I have contracts. I have some professional standing earned by years and years in these trenches. So I'm protected—or can protect myself, and maybe my team—from some of the worst effects of belt-tightening or imposition of irrational rules.

Other healthcare professionals almost certainly share my insights, frustration, and rage. But many don't have the same job security, so they can't freely express what they are facing and feeling. Some of the most valiant providers I know—who put sweat, tears, time, and their own cash into keeping patients alive—can't afford to be seen criticizing The System, the insurance industry, the government, or other entities with control over their livelihoods. I can.

———

The crazy currents of life can carry a person from digging postholes in Kentucky to making movies in Paris. Perhaps it's timing that determines fate, as when a new doctor works his first shift hours after a deadly "mystery disease" is first reported. A common enemy can turn strangers into allies, as research teams worldwide log countless lab hours, cheering each breakthrough and cursing each setback. In the history of AIDS, the tide began to turn as one researcher's eureka moment built on that of another. Finally, we had it in our hands to halt the virus's advance and salvage so many lives.

Riding the whirlwind of an epidemic left little time to be what I also was: a husband, a father, a son. While I was conducting research and tending to patients, who was tending the home fires? Amy Weil Saag. Day after day, she was the tireless, primary parent while I, working or traveling, was secondary. I owe her for this, big time. I also owe her for believing—and for assuring our children—that while I love my work a lot, I love my family more.

I've made many movies featuring Amy, Andy, Harry, and Julie, some of which they've allowed me to show in public. I could easily write an entire book about each of them, but for various reasons—from being shy to being overscheduled—I doubt any of them would sit still for it. I asked to interview each of them for this book, and promised them final say-so over passages that concerned them.

When Amy became pregnant in 1982, we each felt the typical parent-to-be mixture of elation and panic. Things seemed fine until the sixth month when, while we were on a vacation cruise, we lost the pregnancy. Amy was heartsick, guilt-ridden (without reason), and left wondering if we would ever have children. Though I tried to summon some professional detachment, I was hurting, for Amy and myself.

That would be our only pregnancy that didn't end in joy. In 1983, Andrew Weil Saag was born, a "buster" from the day he was born, yet kind, sensitive, and always insightful beyond his years. Three years later, we gave him a brother, Harry Switow Saag, named after Papaharry, a name he has more than justified in spirit and smarts. And five years after that—fulfilling both Amy's and my hope to have a daughter as well as sons—came Julie Diane Saag, the fair princess with a mountain's worth of common sense and heart.

Now that the kids are grown, I see the impact Amy has had. They all share a trait bred into generations of Weils and Saags: a desire to give back to the community. In Judaism, it's called *tikkun olam*, "repairing the world." Beyond that, each of the kids is quite different from the others, even in terms of the second trait we consider a family birthright: a highly active sense of humor.

Andy says one of his earliest memories, from when he was about two, was of roughhousing with me, as we often did. I was holding him by the arms, swinging him boisterously through my legs and into the air. It was great fun until his right shoulder dislocated, and we had to take him to the emergency room to get it manipulated (painfully) back into the socket. Today, Andy charitably says that episode "kind of epitomizes life in our family: a combination of fun times and goofiness juxtaposed with seriousness when necessary." For my part, I'll always remember feeling stricken that I had hurt him, and a little embarrassed to face the ER staff as a Doctor Dad who didn't know better than to play that boisterously and didn't know how to fix the problem once it materialized.

Andy was a football star in high school, a pursuit I memorialized during his senior year in *Under the Helmet,* a "week in the life" movie of his team as it prepared and played a rival squad. Andy started college as a premed major "for no good reason other than the fact that my dad was a doctor," he says now. A few brutal organic chemistry classes changed his mind; he ended up majoring in psychology, and later earned both a law and an MBA degree. He's a real estate and consumer finance attorney at a fine Birmingham law firm. His wife, Brittany Benamy Saag, is a part-time internet marketing executive and a part-time nanny. She married Andy in 2010 despite his eccentric family; we love and thank her for that.

Julie and Harry say Andy is "the leader" of the three kids. They also say Andy is the "parents' favorite." Like most parents, Amy and I don't feel we have favorites. Andy has not been deposed on this question.

Harry is the middle child, a position that's shaped his perspective on the rest of the family. "I often felt like I got the short end of the stick," he says, and responded by "being too hard on my sister and nagging my brother too much. I was the overachiever, always trying to best myself, and probably more stubborn than either my brother or sister. The stubborn overachiever who didn't know when to shut his mouth."

Harry does have strong opinions and is not afraid to voice them. I wouldn't quarrel with most of his appraisals; I second what he says about his mom, and am grateful for what he says about me. In Harry's view, "My mom is a rock. She has been the one holding down the fort, putting up with my dad's extremely busy schedule, and understanding that he had to be that busy because of the work he was doing. I think my mom's cooperation and understanding has allowed my dad to be as successful as he has been. As for my dad, all three of us have said that he's a good father but a great friend, with the right level of hands-off approach to let us be our own people."

I recapped Harry's high school football career in a movie titled *Under the Helmet, Redux* (because nobody else appreciated the title I wanted to use, *Under the Jockstrap*). Harry explored lots of career options, with summer jobs at a law firm and on Capitol Hill as well as at the 1917 Clinic. Then, as he puts it, "I decided to hedge my bets and go into premed. I think part of my choice was seeing how much my dad enjoyed his job, seeing the energy there." Harry became a first-year House Officer (resident) at New York University after completing his medical degree at UAB. He's interested in many areas of medicine, but he likely will find some way to merge his interests in patient care with his strong affinity for healthcare financing and policy work.

I traveled so much when the kids were young that, to explain it at their level, Amy would sometimes point to airplanes flying overhead and tell them I might be on board. One day when Julie was a toddler and the two were outdoors, Julie spotted a plane, waved her tiny hand at it and said, "Hi, Daddy!" As Amy recalls it now, "On the one hand it was funny, but it also was telling."

Despite all my absences, I had no trouble staying close to my sons because we enjoyed a lot of the same sports and activities. But I didn't relate as easily to Julie. Despite having two older sisters, I was pretty clueless about Girl Things. Both Julie and the boys tell me that she figured this out early, and decided that to find common ground with me, she had only one recourse. Since I couldn't get to her, she got to me. And she still does.

"I know songs from all the big Broadway musicals, I can recite parts of many Broadway plays, and I basically memorized all the *Austin Powers* movies," Julie says now. "That was my way to get my dad's attention and for him to connect with me, through his love of music, theater, and movies. There's this long, elaborate song from *Ragtime*, I've been able to do the whole thing by heart since I was about eight years old—and he laughs every time."

When Julie says, "I guess I can 'thank' my dad for my sense of humor," you can hear the quotation marks around the word *thank* as if she toyed with saying *blame*. "Where my brothers are more sarcastic and clever, I have more of the goofiness my dad has and the silliness," she says. "Though I don't have that to the extreme my dad has, because he can be *too much*."

In my defense, I say "*too much*" is a matter of perspective. Julie says she can give plenty of examples—like when I was escorting her onto the Mountain Brook High School football field to be crowned homecoming queen.

"All the other dads escorting the homecoming court were in nice suits, looking like they were going to a wedding," she recalls. "My dad walked me onto the field and he had on a sport coat and he was wearing a fricking baseball cap—and he tosses it in the air in front of everybody in the stands, to get people to laugh.

"But then, at my bat mitzvah, I was expecting him to give a goofy speech—he was quoting the Disney movie *Aladdin*, saying 'Beeee yourself' where the genie turns into a bee—and he started to cry in front of the entire congregation. I was just dumbfounded."

When Julie was considering career paths, she says she looked for "something exciting like my dad did every day, and something meaningful like my mom did as a teacher." Today Julie is a special-needs teacher at a suburban Atlanta school, working with students who have physical and developmental disabilities. "We do the silliest, goofiest things—I never go a day without laughing," she says. "Where some people might think it's intimidating or difficult to work with special-needs kids, I see it as a positive; they really make the job fun."

If unbridled optimism were an inherited trait, I'd like to claim Julie got it from me. I do know that we reinforce that spirit in each other. "My dad would rather be happy than sad," Julie says. I'd say the same about her. She's the one I've put in charge of getting the inscription I want carved on my gravestone—a lyric, of course, from the musical *Spring Awakening*: "I Don't Do Sadness."

Behind all of this is the unspoken reason I wasn't broken during the worst passages of my career. It isn't optimism. It's that, at the end of every day, there was Amy and our family.

I joke that if I awoke to find my home on fire and I had only moments to escape, I'd wake my wife . . . so she could help carry out the films I've made. Amy is such a good sport that she wasn't offended the first time I told this joke (or the scores of times since). But she also knows the truth behind my foolishness. Amy is my better half in every sense of that phrase. Calmer, kinder, steadier than I am; more resourceful, more patient, more unselfish. She is cheering section, sounding board, and wailing wall; tonic, refuge, and anchor. And she's smart.

Amy is a phenomenal mother who calls raising our children "the best job I've ever had and ever will have." She is an accomplished community leader who has headed almost every Jewish organization in Birmingham, and who volunteers out of gratitude for all she has received in life. I could pretend Amy has been too busy and fulfilled in this work to notice my many absences all these years, but that's not true. It's more that she has made a considered choice about what she calls "Michael's journey" in HIV/AIDS medicine.

"I've never questioned if Michael is the right person for me, or questioned us as a couple," Amy says. "It's more like, can I handle what I call 'married single life'? You look around and see other people doing just typical things with their husbands, taking walks, going to movies, going out to dinner. And with Michael, we do those things but they're rarities, they're planned activities that we have to work at doing. We have friends who joke that the secret to our thirty-six years of marriage is that we've only been around each other for twenty of them, because of how much Michael is away.

"I realized once Michael started this journey that he was basically devoted to it. Not to the exclusion of a family—he wanted it all, he wanted to have the family while still fulfilling what he felt was his purpose on this earth. So I had to make a decision early on as to how I was going to handle it. I could slip into that mentality of, 'Woe is me, I don't have my life partner doing things with me,' and let that tear the family apart. Or I could be the cheerleader and be supportive. I had to reach a place with myself where I said,

'This maybe isn't the way I envisioned my married life, but this is the way it's going to be because he has to fulfill this purpose.'"

How can I account for Amy, what she's given to our children, to me, to my patients and my research and my dreams? Maybe magic. Maybe grace.

Chapter 17

POLITICS AND BIRTHDAYS

One of the most liberating honors of my life was announced in summer 2007, in a four-paragraph UAB press release. "Thomas A. Blount has graciously and generously provided the funding for the Jim Straley Endowed Chair in AIDS Research," the release began. "And Michael S. Saag, MD, has been named the first holder of the new chair."

An endowed chair gives its holder a lasting source of support beyond the academic salary—support, for example, for additional research projects. Especially these days when grant funding is so scarce, an endowment is a huge asset. What made it even more valuable, to me, was the way Tom Blount dedicated the chair: "I get a very good feeling from making this gift in memory of my life partner and in honor of Dr. Mike Saag, one of the true heroes of the HIV epidemic," Tom said in the press statement.

In reality, it is Tom and Jim who were heroic in their dogged pursuit of new HIV treatments and their fierce devotion to each other. I gratefully accepted the appointment to the Straley Chair, and I have pledged always to use it to push the frontier of HIV/AIDS therapeutics in tribute to them both.

If I feel pretty secure professionally thanks to the allies, tenure, and credentials I've acquired over the years, an endowed chair affords another level of security and independence, a buffer of sorts between me and that pervasive, often corrosive force: politics. On any given day, the politics of grantsmanship may pit my NIH connections against those of friends in the competition for federal funding. The politics of the Old Docs Network may influence who gets invited to present a paper, publish in a journal, or fill out a golf foursome. The political dance with the pharmaceutical industry may require doctors to get close enough to contribute but not so close as to be co-opted.

The politics of academia may elevate one UAB official and topple another: In my three decades here, I've worked for six presidents and four deans in the School of Medicine. And the university also gets involved in local politics in Birmingham, whether it's top UAB officials courting city support for campus projects or the 1917 Clinic just trying to get the abandoned building next door torn down.

So, politics can intrude on all aspects of life, and to an extent I'm resigned to that. But for sheer magnitude and destructiveness, nothing else approaches the politics surrounding US healthcare. I can ignore the politically motivated shenanigans that are merely irritating or an insult to Americans' intelligence. But the politicization of serious healthcare issues has taken an enormous, morally intolerable toll on my colleagues and our patients.

In 2012, the *New England Journal of Medicine* marked its 200th anniversary by publishing several special reports. One that caught my eye was by Jonathan Oberlander, PhD, a professor of social medicine and health policy and management at the University of North Carolina–Chapel Hill, and an expert on the politics of healthcare reform and cost control. The report was titled "Unfinished Journey—A Century of Health Care Reform in the United States."*

Oberlander observed that it was a century ago, 1915, when reform-minded Americans put forth "the first major proposal for national health insurance in the United States," and that "Americans are still debating health care reform, the perils of 'socialized medicine,' and the tensions between individual liberty and government aid." While the debate has raged, he says, "Americans have been singularly unsuccessful in restraining health care spending."

---

* Oberlander, Jonathan. "Unfinished Journey—A Century of Health Care Reform," *New England Journal of Medicine*, August 16, 2012, Perspective.

I'm convinced that Oberlander has it right:

> The United States has moved through fads at a dizzying pace in
> recent decades—from managed to consumer-driven to account-
> able care—but they have thus far failed to produce reliable cost
> control. Rising health care costs are an issue throughout the
> industrialized world, though other countries manage to spend
> much less while insuring their entire populations. Still, les-
> sons from international experience are largely ignored by U.S.
> policymakers and analysts intent on fashioning a "uniquely
> American solution." The United States has not adopted the
> cost-containment policies that work in other countries: global
> budgeting, system-wide fee schedules and payment rules, mon-
> opsony purchasing, and supply-side controls on expensive tech-
> nologies. Instead, America continues to abide high prices and
> the staggering administrative costs imposed by our byzantine
> insurance system.
>
> U.S. health policy is a story of progress, with substantial
> gains in health insurance coverage over the past century, cul-
> minating in the (Affordable Care Act's) enactment. But U.S.
> health policy has also been an abject failure, having produced
> an inequitable, inefficient system that is the most expensive
> in the world and that leaves 20 percent of the nonelderly
> population uninsured . . .

Here's where Oberlander gets to what I consider the bottom line—how the
system's failures affect patients:

> Too many Americans who fall ill are forced to worry about
> how to pay their medical bills and the threat of medical bank-
> ruptcy, rather than focusing on getting well or coping with
> maladies that won't improve. Too many Americans cannot
> obtain decent, affordable insurance because they have preexist-
> ing conditions, lack the financial resources, or work for a small

business. Too many Americans with permanent disabilities must wait too long before Medicare covers them. Too many Americans who are eligible for Medicaid and CHIP (the Children's Health Insurance Program) fall between the cracks. Too many insured Americans are only one illness away from discovering they have inadequate coverage that leaves them with overwhelming bills. Too many Americans have to fight their insurance companies to obtain covered benefits.

That these and other indignities have persisted so long is an indictment of U.S. health policy and its moral quality. If there is one thing we should learn from the experiences of other countries that have universal coverage, it is that it doesn't have to be this way. None of these problems are natural or inevitable—they are all the result of policy choices that the United States has made.

I do not quarrel with Oberlander's use of the term "policy choices." But let's break it down and consider the words separately.

Policy. In the United States, healthcare policy is an amalgam of rulings, regulations, and laws shaped by interest groups, market forces, and all three branches of government. And the amalgamation process has been repeatedly, horribly distorted by special interests' manipulations and money—what I call "politics" for short.

Choices. Oberlander blames the many problems in US healthcare on "choices that the United States has made." But I say The System's in crisis because the important choices—such as how people get care and what they pay for it—have *not* been made by "the United States" in any real and representative way. The important choices get made by the tiny fraction of Americans who are "leaders" (political or corporate), under pressure from the somewhat larger fraction of Americans who are powerful (monied lobbies and special interests). And the truly important choices appear to be made with shocking disregard for the needs of the vast majority of Americans, both healthcare consumers and the providers who serve them.

If "we, the people" do not drive these choices, what does? Mostly political expediency, the profit motive, and in my view, a lack of the integrity and courage that we expect from leaders.

The Center for Responsive Politics is an independent research group that tracks money in US politics. For the period from 1998 to 2012, the center reports that healthcare industries and organizations spent nearly $5.36 billion lobbying Congress. To put that in perspective, that's more than triple the spending in the same period by a sector known for lobbying largess: defense interests (which spent $1.53 billion). Close to half of the total—$2.55 billion—came from the pharmaceutical and medical devices industries.

We all owe a lot to the pharmaceutical companies. They've pioneered, refined, and manufactured the medications that keep patients and loved ones alive. In HIV/AIDS medicine, at first I had no useful drugs to give my patients. Later, I'd have to prescribe literally handfuls of pills for them to take every day on a strict and intrusive schedule. Today, the newest drugs are very well tolerated and can be given as a single daily pill containing all three or four of the active drugs. One pill, once a day. And companies are now working on formulations that could allow a medication to be taken once a week or perhaps once every three months. I cannot say enough good about these achievements.

But the scorecard on the industry casually known as "pharma" is decidedly mixed. The industry's lobby on Capitol Hill is so formidable that neither law nor regulation has done much to affect how it does business. Specifically, it has stifled competition in two concerning ways. First, through the Medicare Part D legislation—mostly written by lobbyists—it prohibits the government, as a payer, from negotiating for lower drug prices. Second, it established systems to buy out generic companies' products so as to limit or eliminate generic drugs as competition for its brand-name products after the patent life of the brand drug has expired. This practice is now under review at the US Supreme Court. Both practices hurt consumers and force providers to use certain companies' products—whether they're the best choice or not—in ways I find unethical.

In the twenty-first century, my old pharma friend Howie Reiss's approach—selling a disease as a means of creating market share for a new drug product—has been applied with dramatic results to other conditions such as erectile dysfunction and restless leg syndrome. Neither of these dis-orders was a public concern until new drugs were created to treat it. And by the time these drugs came of age, a new pernicious marketing tool had come into fashion: Direct to Consumer (DTC) advertising. Instead of pitching to the providers, this approach pitches the disease directly to prospective patients. The guy with erectile dysfunction may not have thought of it as a treatable "disorder" until he saw the ads on TV for Cialis, but soon, he's heading to his provider to ask for the treatment. (Judging simply by the number of times I have seen that man and woman holding hands between two bathtubs perched on the top of a hillside, I guess the DTC approach is working quite well.)

In the HIV world, more companies bringing more drugs to market means more competition, so the companies have to do more to secure and maintain market share. From 1996 on, as the HAART era emerged, more companies got into HIV and more products entered the marketplace. This was great for patients and treaters—more options, better options—but it sent drug companies scrambling to figure out how sustain sales. They reached out to Howie Reiss's firm and others like it to help them plan a market strategy through CME, the continuing medical education sessions that physicians and other healthcare providers attend to keep their knowledge current.

CME sessions often were scheduled as "satellite meetings" associated with major scientific conferences that many providers would be attending. The satellite meetings would be scheduled to bracket the conference ses-sions—in the evening with dinner after the last conference session of the day, or in the early morning with breakfast before the conference began. The meals would be accompanied by three or four twenty-minute lectures given by Key Opinion Leaders (KOLs). Attendees would flock to the satellites for the free food and the chance to hear the latest information synthesized into digestible points they could take back to their practice. And they may or may not have grasped how carefully that information had been groomed to further the marketing objectives of the funding company.

There was one event in particular that sealed my understanding of the process. A few years ago, my esteemed colleague Paul Volberding and I were two of the four presenters during a satellite meeting at the Interscience

Conference on Antimicrobial Agents and Chemotherapy, an important annual event in ID circles. A drug company covered the costs of the satellite meeting, including paying the commercial CME firm that organized the session on the topic "Adherence to Treatment."

The CME firm had asked me to serve as chair of the meeting, a role I took seriously. As the firm was planning the meeting, I made suggestions for session topics and presenters. Once all presenters were chosen, I reviewed their slides to make sure there was balance in the presentations. And at a pre-conference meeting with presenters, I emphasized the importance of two things: avoiding even the appearance of bias toward the funding company, and staying on time. To me, any presenter who talks longer than his or her allotted time is essentially making the statement, "My talk is more important than everyone else who follows me!"

Going into the meeting, I felt good about the balance of the program and its content. And I couldn't help reflecting on how far we had come: The company funding the meeting was just about to release the first single-tablet, three-drugs-in-one-pill formulation of a HAART regimen. One pill, once a day!

Paul was the meeting's first speaker. His presentation was first-rate but running a little long, so, mindful of finishing on time, Paul closed his talk prior to showing the last two slides in his presentation. The lights came up and Paul left the podium to hearty applause. From my position near the table where the conference organizers sat, I could see them huddling and speaking in urgent whispers. The next thing I knew, one of the organizers had run up to Paul and, after they exchanged a few words, Paul returned to the podium and the hall lights went back down.

Paul leaned toward the microphone and said, "I have been told to finish my talk." He then showed his presentation's last two slides—one of which showed a patient's hands outstretched, a handful of pills in one palm and a single tablet in the other.

Paul, being a good speaker, did not want to run long. The CME firm, however, didn't care about that. They knew if they did not fulfill the mission of its funder, they would no longer get any business from this company. Their job, in their view, was to be sure that the key slide—contrasting a handful of pills with the funding company's single pill—would be put before the audience, in hopes that it would indelibly impress the marketing message, "one pill = better adherence." I'm sure many providers did get that message, but I came away with another one: That no matter how much I tried to assure balance and impartiality in the meeting, I was not in control.

That was the last satellite meeting in which I participated.

With the creation of the IAS-USA, providers in infectious disease medicine were spared CME concerns. By eliminating pharma influence on content at IAS-USA CME events, we were free to choose the information we felt was most important and the speakers we deemed well versed and unbiased. We've used that freedom to explore innovative ways to educate, such as web-based programs. I consider it a quiet but important victory.

Then there are "advisory board" meetings in choice locations for KOLs, with all expenses paid and sometimes a fee for consultation services.

In my view, there are two types of ad boards: those who truly seek input from the KOLs for scientific direction and assessment of the marketplace, and those whose mission is to influence the thinking and opinions of the KOLs. The former type of meeting I appreciate. They enable us to think through what the patients need, what the providers need, and what the scientific community needs. It can be a brainstorming session where everything is on the table, and it often leads to creation of new products that clearly advance the field.

I abhor ad board "Indoctrination Meetings." When they are done well, the participants can hardly tell they are being "pitched," which makes them all the more insidious. When they are not done well, I feel like I need to take a shower afterwards. Such indoctrination meetings aim to influence KOLs to think the way the company wants them to think so that when the KOLs present data in public, they are "on message" with the drug company's marketing objectives.

Pharma companies are not evil. They do what they are supposed to do: create new drugs and, once created, sell as many of them as they possibly can. That is their job, their mission, both for themselves and their shareholders—and along the way they create breakthrough products that change people's lives. Generally speaking, they do their job very well. The communications firms that help the drug companies pitch their message are not evil either. They're doing their job, managing the message of the KOLs and the satellite meetings. And the KOLs are not evil. They are simply trying to communicate what they feel is important. But like the combination of three safe chemicals which, when mixed, yields an explosively dangerous product, if pharma and marketing and experts are inappropriately aligned, the result is dangerous and, in my view, wrong.

Some claims at "reforming" the relationship between pharma and physicians are comical, or would be if no one took them seriously. Just as restaurants used to give branded books of matches or as car companies give key rings bearing their logo, pharma may give providers pens, note pads, umbrellas, and other minor gifts. A few years ago, Republican Senator Charles Grassley of Iowa began a crusade against such practices. He found a direct line between pencils given to providers and Medicare's rush toward bankruptcy. The senator convened hearings, called for FDA investigations, and tried to shame providers who'd accept gifts. Ultimately this led the Association of American Medical Colleges, the organization that oversees physician education and medical schools, to adopt new policies that prohibited providers who were faculty from taking *any* gift from pharma.

As UAB considered implementation of this policy, I conducted a small study. For years I'd invited drug company representatives to purchase lunch and bring it to our Friday noon HIV clinic conference that all providers may attend. In return, I allowed the pharma reps to make a short presentation regarding their company or their product(s) as the meeting started. Most often, the reps' whole speech was, "Glad to be here, enjoy your lunch." My study involved sending a short survey to the clinic staff asking (1) if they had attended any of the lunch meetings over the previous four weeks; (2) if so, did they recall the name of the company that provided lunch for the meeting(s) they attended; and (3) could they please name at least one drug that company sold.

Less than a third of the attendees could remember the name of the company providing lunch for any of the meetings—and among those who did remember, less than half of them could name a single drug that company sold.

Brand-name drugs are prescribed with great frequency, mostly because the newer drugs (for which there aren't yet generics) are often better. This is certainly true in the world of HIV, where older drugs such as DDI, DDC, D4T, and AZT are less well tolerated than newer drugs such as tenofovir. Brand names are generally more expensive than generics. But generic drugs are often hard to come by or in short supply. There are shortages of simple drugs like penicillin, doxycycline, and intravenous acyclovir. These drugs are easy to make, yet from the supply you'd think that someone was paying generic companies *not to make* these drugs so that providers have no choice but to prescribe the more expensive drugs.

Consider also the case of colchicine, a plant-based drug used for decades to treat gout that had long been available as a generic drug at a cost of pennies per tablet. A company conducted a study that "proved" colchicine works for gout (surprise!), and the company is then granted patent protection for the drug. This leads to a monopoly for the sale of colchicine such that the cost for a thirty-day supply increases from less than $8/month to more than $100/month. Senator Grassley didn't notice.

I have no problem with a law the Senator cosponsored, the Physician Payments Sunshine Act, which as of 2013 requires that drug and medical device manufacturers' payments to physicians be published on a federal website. But while Mr. Grassley has attacked providers for accepting trivial gifts like pens, he and his senatorial campaign accepted hundreds of thousands of dollars from pharma as Mr. Grassley worked to pass the Medicare Part D prescription drug benefit or to fight the passage of the Affordable Care Act. Between 2006 and 2012, four of the top ten interest sectors contributing to Mr. Grassley were health products, professionals, and services—and they gave more than $1 million of the nearly $6.2 million Mr. Grassley took in, according to MapLight, a nonpartisan research group that explores money's influence in politics

Senator Grassley's actions would be insulting if they were not so laughable. I couldn't care less about the pharma tchotchkes that Grassley wants withheld. I'm much more concerned about how Mr. Grassley and his friends accept millions of lobbyist dollars while depriving my patients and colleagues of needed healthcare resources.

"As chairman of the finance committee, Mr. Grassley championed the legislation that created a prescription-drug benefit under Medicare," the so-called Medicare Part D benefit, as editor-in-chief Jacob Weisberg reported on Slate.com. A provision in the legislation actually *prohibits* the government from negotiating lower prices from pharma; the government must pay retail for the drugs, which obviously means lots more cash for drug companies than if the prices could be negotiated down. Small wonder that by the time it passed, Part D's estimated cost had been revised up from $395 billion to $534 billion over ten years—a price tag Medicare's chief actuary later told Congress he was warned not to release if he wanted to keep his job.

As correspondent Steve Kroft reported on CBS's *60 Minutes*, at least a half dozen former senators and Congress members "registered as lobbyists for the drug industry and worked on the prescription drug bill." US Rep. John Dingell, a Democrat from Michigan, told Kroft that "when the bill passed, there were better than 1,000 pharmaceutical lobbyists working on this." A couple of months after the bill passed, a representative who'd championed it, Louisiana Republican Billy Tauzin, "accepted a $2-million-a-year job as president of PhRMA—Pharmaceutical Research and Manufacturers of America," Kroft reported. And in the months after the vote, Kroft reported, "at least fifteen congressional staffers, congressmen, and federal officials left to go to work for the pharmaceutical industry, whose profits were increased by several billion dollars."

To my knowledge, none of these activities are illegal. Senator Grassley and his friends have kept America safe from notepads and umbrellas. But the senator's self-righteous concern about special interests' contacts with physicians appears not to extend to his own reelection campaign and political action committees.

When elected "leaders" approve the Medicare Part D benefit, a major tax cut, two long and expensive wars, and then use the resulting federal deficit to justify cutting spending in NIH research—something is wrong with this picture.

———

While lawmakers tinker at the margins of the crisis, the cost of America's healthcare is on its way to $3 trillion. Since 1960, healthcare spending has climbed so steeply that it increased almost five times as much as the nation's gross domestic product did.

These and other statistics jumped off the page at me in March 2013 in a remarkable issue of *TIME* magazine dedicated to US healthcare.* The cover story was a 24,000-word investigative piece by journalist Steven Brill headlined "Bitter Pill: Why Medical Bills Are Killing Us." Brill spent seven months examining bills from hospitals, physicians, pharmaceutical companies, and other participants in the US healthcare system, in an effort to understand where all the money goes.

Just how much money? Brill cited studies showing that the United States spends more on healthcare than the next 10 biggest spending nations combined—among them, Germany, the United Kingdom, Canada, and Australia. To put other national expenditures in perspective, he noted that the $60 billion that was spent cleaning up after 2012's Hurricane Sandy is roughly what America spends on healthcare *in an average week.*

Brill's examination of bills showed staggering discrepancies among the amounts that patients are asked to pay for the same items and services—and no apparent medical reason for those differences. He described how a hospital's internal price list, called a chargemaster, may dramatically mark up items or services—charging patients $1.50 for a single tablet of acetaminophen, for example, or $157 for a CBC (complete blood count) test for which Medicare might pay only $11. Why does this occur? Because it can. That is, because sick patients are hardly in a position to bargain when they're told their health depends on them getting a medication or treatment, whatever the price.

The conclusion to Brill's report is sobering. Under the current system, he contends, "we've enriched the labs, drug companies, medical device makers, hospital administrators and purveyors of CT scans, MRIs, canes and wheelchairs. Meanwhile, we've squeezed the doctors who don't ... game a system that is so gameable. And of course, we've squeezed everyone outside the system who gets stuck with the bills."

The man has a way with words.

So does Dr. Milton Weinstein, a professor of health policy and

---

* Brill, Steven. "Bitter Pill: Why Medical Bills Are Killing Us," *TIME*, March 4, 2013.

management at the Harvard School of Public Health and also a professor of medicine at the Harvard Medical School.

Professor Weinstein is an expert on assessing cost-effectiveness in health-care. With computer simulation models and other analytical methods he developed, he evaluates the value of spending on healthcare practices—that is, how much cost produces how much health benefit. When I asked him to describe an exemplary healthcare system that does right by patients, payers, and providers, here's what he envisioned:

> First of all, in that system, the interventions that are not effec-tive are not implemented. Now that's easy to say but the prob-lem is, we don't know which interventions are effective and which are not. There may be incomplete evidence; a lot of things get done in medicine for which there's not a random-ized, clinical trial, and that is understandable because we don't have the time or resources to do randomized trials of every-thing. So that's a fairly weak statement, to say we shouldn't be doing things we know aren't improving health. But . . . health care decisions have to be made without the kind of ideal evi-dence we might like to have.
>
> Once you identify those interventions that are either harmful or clearly not beneficial, then you start looking at cost-effectiveness and value for money, taking into account that the benefits and costs of most health care interventions are uncertain.
>
> What would an ideal, well-functioning health system look like? A well-functioning system would basically be investing in interventions that are more cost-effective than the interven-tions they're not investing in. Or turning that around, they wouldn't be doing things that are basically more expensive ways of providing the same health improvements for which there are less expensive ways of providing.
>
> For example, let's consider how the health care system is investing in end-stage treatments. In AIDS, they're not

investing broadly enough in getting people on treatment, which has a very high value for the money. But they are doing things that have a low value for the money spent, such as low-value laboratory tests.

Another example: We spend a lot of money on end-stage cancer treatment. There are compelling reasons that we do that, but at the same time we don't spend a lot of money—or perhaps enough money—on cancer prevention. Only about half of the people in the United States over age 50 have ever had any kind of colorectal screening, and that's a very cost-effective thing to do whether it's a fecal occult blood test or a colonoscopy. So we don't do enough of that but we spend a lot of money on end-stage treatment when people get cancer.

It's hard to say, "If someone is dying of cancer, should we spend the money for a drug that could increase their survival for two more weeks?" Maybe we should spend $100,000 for those two more weeks; we tend to do that in this country. But we don't go out of our way to do things upstream that might prevent more deaths, extend life and improve quality of life more than those end-stage treatments.

So the way to improve the system if you don't want to spend more money is to scale back on the interventions that are costing a lot per unit of health bought, and put the money into interventions that could buy more health. By doing that, you'd be spending the same amount of money and getting more health improvement for the money.

Thanks to data Professor Weinstein and his colleagues have developed, we can know in detail which healthcare interventions are most cost-efficient. But having this knowledge is one thing, and changing America's system to act on it is another.

Countries with single-payer, national healthcare programs can standardize cost-efficient approaches throughout the system. But as Professor Weinstein observes, "We're not going to have a single-payer system any time soon.

In this country, we're kind of wedded to the idea of the 'free market' even though many health economists would tell you that markets don't work very well in health care."

If we're going to evaluate the effectiveness of services, we should start by understanding the metrics used in US healthcare today. On the receipt from your latest medical appointment, your provider checked one or more boxes on lists of possible diagnoses, each followed by a string of numerals. Those so-called ICD codes are the numerical identifiers assigned to each diagnosis under the International Statistical Classification of Diseases system overseen by the World Health Organization.

If your illness requires hospitalization, those ICD codes will be used to help assign a diagnosis-related group, or DRG. A computer program looks at your age and gender, the procedures you'll need, your primary diagnosis, and other significant conditions (or "comorbidities"), and it classifies you into one of about 500 DRGs. Because each patient in a given DRG is clinically similar, each should (at least theoretically) use roughly the same amount of hospital resources. So the DRG establishes a standard reimbursement rate, what the hospital should be paid for the care of that patient. Medicare started using DRGs in the early 1980s as a way to slow the increase in hospital spending; since then, most major insurers have adopted the system.

Right now, physicians for hospitals have DRGs and a payment schedule based on *cost*, not based on *benefit*. What if we modified these payment schedules so that instead of making money on services that Professor Weinstein's research has shown to be cost-*ineffective*, providers would get paid more for doing things that are cost-*effective*? Interventions that represent the best value for patients in medical *and* monetary terms? Medicare could do this right away if there was the will to do it—but there's no will, because the cost-ineffective treatments are profitable for those hiring lobbyists. As in the case of using DRGs, if Medicare did it, then a lot of the private insurers might do it, too. It's not a sweeping solution, but it's a start. And it embodies the two goals that must be our top priorities: bringing down costs while putting patients first.

I've seen firsthand what it looks like when care genuinely is centered on the patient. In the early years of the AIDS epidemic, in the midst of horrendous loss and pain, professionals and untrained but committed people created their own care community, and what they built was—and in some instances still is—magnificent. That's why I've often said that though I don't want to have HIV, I'd love to be cared for in an HIV clinic. Many of these clinics created and still maintain the very definition of a caring, collaborative, communal-spirited healthcare system. It wasn't just about the management of one disease by a few paid but disinterested professionals. It was about figuring out what everyone needed—patients, loved ones, practitioners—and what everyone could contribute, to the point of self-sacrifice. At least in the Ryan White clinics, and at least for a while, there was a genuine feeling of medical community, of neighbors pulling together to seek wellness for all.

Wellness. It was a curiosity in the late 1970s when a few medical visionaries used the word to define health as more than just the avoidance or absence of sickness. But then, according to the *New York Times*, "Carping over *wellness* faded away in the '90s as the term gained a foothold in everyday use." By now, the word may have been so co-opted by marketers that we could forget its true value, which is significant. Genuine wellness means total well-being, not just physical but mental and social and spiritual, a state grounded in maximizing potential as much as minimizing illness.

Wellness, in my opinion, is best (perhaps only) achieved and maintained in the context of community, the collective. My asthmatic neighbor can't be well if the local factory pollutes our air. My school district's children can't learn if they're hungry for lack of nutritious food or can't see the whiteboard because they need eyeglasses they can't afford. If we all are to strive for wellness, everybody can't be shooting everybody else, somebody has to help me with my kids when I'm sick—you get the idea. The ultimate goal of the healthcare we actually want is to foster wellness for individuals in community.

In the United States today, neighborhoods of any sort are pretty scarce. Sure, people live in geographical proximity and come together periodically around common interests, creeds, or tasks. But only in some of those settings is there a real "neighborhood spirit," where a cohesive, intentionally interdependent group of people look out for one another and promote a common good. The trick is to include everyone, including those who are not like me. When we think of a neighborhood that encompasses differences—where the "we" is not just "everyone like me"—we're on our way to imagining an intentionally interdependent group.

So we'd have to lay a lot of groundwork to encourage community-minded healthcare and medical neighborhoods. And the greatest barriers, in my opinion, are the people who really just don't believe in community. Lately, many of them carry the banner of the Tea Party; in times past, they may have marched with the Moral Majority, the Ku Klux Klan, the isolationists, or sundry other "me-first" groups. If my child is dying and you believe in community, you and our community will help me with my burdens, including my child's medical bills. You'll likely do this through a shared contribution often called "tax." If you do not believe in community and my child is dying, you ask, "Why should *you* get any of *my* (tax) money to keep *your* child alive?"

That's not the pay-it-forward philosophy that was handed down from the Switows and Saags and Weils to Amy and me, and that we strove to pass on to our children. It is not the ethic that my friend Jim Heynen was raised with by his Calvinist dad, who often told him, "God gave us money as a loan, and we repay him by giving it to others." It's not the kind of healthcare that I want to practice. It's not the kind of healthcare that I want delivered to anyone I know—or anyone I don't know, for that matter.

And it's certainly not the best healthcare we can offer in a nation this prosperous, entrepreneurial, and magnanimous.

———

I hate it when my idealistic bubble is burst, when the great things I imagine just can't be realized. Basically, I hate it when I don't have control over things, which happens a lot.

Most of all, I hate it when evil wins. That's what HIV/AIDS is, an evil thing that hurts innocent people. Like my old research buddy Emilio Emini said, "I hate this virus!" Thus, I love it when we triumph over the virus, and I hate when we lose.

I also fear loss. I fear losing whatever has meaning to me, things I've worked hard for, things that I love and consider irreplaceable.

After my family, among the things I most fear losing are cherished colleagues and patients. The damned virus—and I use that term with theological precision—has robbed me of more patients and colleagues than I can count. But I've also lost patients and colleagues to the screwed-up US healthcare system—patients who slipped through the cracks and colleagues who burned out trying to save them. At some terrifying moments, both the virus and The System have conspired to make me question the reality of hope. I cannot even contemplate life without hope.

About a decade ago, I thought I was going to lose Jim Raper. To explore options beyond banking, Jim's partner Scott had decided to go to law school at night. "If he does that, we'll never see each other," Jim told me. So to preserve his time with Scott, Jim enrolled in law school, too. He got a law degree at night while working full time during the day; he never missed a day of work, and I never even saw him studying while on the job. He not only passed his classes, he passed the state bar in 2003 on the first attempt.

In the back of my mind, I'm thinking, *Oy, when he gets this law degree, he's going to have such an amazing resume that he's going to leave the clinic.* But he really did go to law school to be with Scott, and he really wasn't looking to leave. Thank God.

In April 2007, when Jim became the director of the 1917 Clinic, he became the only nonphysician director of a clinic at UAB (a distinction he still holds as I write). A few months after Jim became the clinic's director, the American Academy of Nurse Practitioners named him a fellow, making him the first nurse practitioner in Alabama to receive the honor. That year he also received the Academy's State Award for Excellence for Alabama.

In 2009, Jim was inducted into the Alabama Nursing Hall of Fame. In 2012, five years after he took the helm of the 1917 Clinic, the journal *Science* profiled it as one of ten outstanding sites in the nation for HIV clinical care and research.

Now that Jim has acquired a wall full of honors, I subject him to kidding that, unlike much of my humor, is actually based in fact.

"Jim," I tell him, "you've got more initials *after* your name than you have letters *in* your name!" With all those degrees, fellowships, and certifications, it's the truth, even if you spell out his whole name. You do the math: James Luther Raper, JD, MSN, DSN, FIDSA, FAANP, CRNP.

Here's a person who is incredibly competent and knowledgeable about HIV/AIDS, at least as good as, if not better than, half the physician providers I know. But because he's a nurse practitioner, his title creates a ceiling, especially in Alabama. Of course, there are entire counties in Alabama that go without care because there's no physician practicing there—but a nurse practitioner who could ably fill that void is not allowed to have his or her own practice.

That's one more kind of wall that needs to be broken down if we're to fulfill the potential of US healthcare. The whole concept of a medical home and a medical neighborhood is based on teams of people collaborating. It's a horizontal org chart, not a vertical one, a chart where there is no more hierarchy than absolutely necessary. It's a commitment to delivering health not via a factory model but a family model, one where people come to know and genuinely care about each other.

By now, as Jim has observed, "Mike and I know each other so well that we don't even have to tell entire jokes, just the punch lines." Jim is brutally honest with me when necessary; he is also generous and encouraging. When I heard that he had said of me, "Mike works as hard as I do," I thought there could be no finer compliment. And then he proved me wrong (and choked me up) by going that one better: "Mike works like my grandpa worked, and my dad."

I don't know what I would have done all these years without Jim Raper. I am proud that he regards me as a mentor. I value him enormously as a colleague, a workout partner, and a friend. I love that he calls himself "the unofficial uncle" because my family includes him in so many of our special days, from our kids' bar and bat mitzvahs to Andy's wedding. Jim and Scott are family.

I regard many of my 1917 Clinic patients as family, too, even when I scarcely see them because they're off leading healthier lives. Since my longtime patient Jenny relocated to Pennsylvania, I still hear from her by email. I still try to give her good advice based on how well I know her—for example, encouraging her fragile resolve to stay clean and sober, and telling her which versions of her medications are the smallest (she hates swallowing big pills).

I still keep in touch with numerous clinic veterans—people like Alan, who participated in at least five different drug trials over two decades but is now on a solid regimen and doing very well at age fifty-three. Alan lost so many friends in the worst days of the epidemic that he stopped going to funerals after his fiftieth. But when he comes to the 1917 Clinic, Alan still sees a few stalwarts from the drug trial days, including Pearly James.

In drug trials, only code names can be used. Pearly James is the code name selected by one participant in loving homage to his late father—whose given name was Pearly George Raper.

Pearly James runs the clinic under his other name with so many letters behind it: Jim Raper.

Jim learned he was HIV-positive in 1989, but he has never gone public with his status until now.

"I keep asking myself, how I can make a difference?" How often have I heard Jim Raper say this to me—dozens? Hundreds? Thousands? When he knew I was writing a book, and why, he offered to break his silence.

Although in 1982 no one knew for sure how acute HIV infection presented, "I think I remember when I first got infected," Jim says now.

"I was in the army, I had been to New Orleans, and about a month after I got back to Huntsville I was so sick with fever, rash, sore throat, and abdominal pain they admitted me to the army hospital. They couldn't figure out what I had; they thought it was a strep infection. But the strep tests were negative, and then I got better." A year later, Jim was in a relationship with Steve, a music teacher who lived in Birmingham, and relocated to be with him.

In the mid-1980s, before an HIV test was available, Steve began to get sick. Because a former lover of Steve's had died of AIDS, "we realized what probably was happening," Jim says. "But I hadn't gotten sick." In 1989, still in the army reserves, Jim ran into an officer friend while on reserve duty "and I told her that my partner was getting sick. By then, the HIV test was available, and my friend said, 'Everybody in the military will have to get tested soon. You should get tested while you're here.' I was really scared. She drew my blood and sent it through anonymously, and it was positive. I came home and told Steve, 'I'm positive and you've got to get tested, too.' And of course he was positive."

We were conducting a study at UAB comparing AZT and DDI as mono-therapy and in combination. Steve enrolled. So did "Pearly James." When Steve talked about the horrendous taste of the DDI tablets, Jim knew what he meant because Jim was taking them too; he had been randomized to the arm of the study that would take DDI for six months, then add AZT. As Jim recalls it, "I went on the AZT and was intolerant to it. My hematocrit [red blood cell count] dropped so low that they wanted to give me a blood transfusion, but I refused." So weak he struggled to walk from UAB's park-ing deck to his office, Jim came to work nonetheless. He and I got to know each other well during this time when we were allies on so many levels: col-leagues at the clinic, friends in the break room, researcher and subject in the drug study.

We substituted stavudine (D4T) for the AZT in Jim's regimen, and the intolerance symptoms vanished. "I took that combination for years, my CD4 counts remained in the 600s and 700s, and I didn't have any more problems," Jim recalls. The reprieve from his own illness was well timed, because it enabled Jim to care for Steve until Steve's death in July 1993.

Though Jim never said so, I felt like he took on a formal period of griev-ing, as in the old southern tradition of mourning a departed spouse for a year and a day. Jim worked his long hours at UAB, completed his doctoral degree, and exercised at the gym. But it wasn't until 1996 that he reclaimed his personal life after meeting Scott, a bank loan officer, while working out at the YMCA. "It was difficult sharing the secret," Jim says of revealing his status to Scott. "He took it really well . . ."

By 1997, Jim was administrator of the 1917 Clinic, and he and Scott were in a committed relationship. They had bought a house together with a living room large enough for the enormous number of grandfather clocks Scott collects and a garden out back for Jim to till. Pearly James didn't par-ticipate in clinical trials after 1994. Jim kept a close eye on how various drug regimens were affecting his health and other patients'. By making careful adjustments, he warded off side effects such as elevated liver enzymes and peripheral wasting, and his virus remained undetectable.

Jim now takes his HAART cocktail as one pill once a day and another pill twice a day, which gives him virtually no side effects. Scott continues to get tested annually, but because Jim's undetectable and they practice safe sex, "it's never been an issue," Jim says. Scott and Jim recently returned from a cruise vacation where they met Louis and Sebastian, life partners celebrating thirty-one years together. When Jim spoke of the couple, it was clear how much he wants what they have, love in longevity. With only fifteen more years until that milestone, I think he's a shoo-in to achieve it.

"You take advantage of the cards you're dealt," Jim says of his approach to life. "I don't know how long I'll be able to do this, but I love what I do. I work ninety-plus hours a week, and I still get up every morning and wag my tail to work. When I get there, I see patients whose lives are good and full—and they're taking advantage of the opportunities given to them, just like I've done."

So I rail and curse about the politics and the screwed-up system while I take a cue from Jim and find satisfaction in how we've played the cards we've been dealt. I love the ways, small and large, my clinic team has made things better for patients, and how we've shifted the balance away from nothing but loss, suffering, and death and increasingly toward life and health.

When we first started saying that the 1917 Clinic's slogan was "Birthdays are our business," it had a fingers-crossed, whistling-through-the-graveyard feel to it. Now, we say it like we mean it. When we get a patient through to a big number—whether that's a birthday or a CD4 count—we make a fuss. We celebrated Jim's fifty-sixth a few months ago with a song and some cake. We plan to do it again, often.

In spring 2013, we marked two milestones I sometimes doubted I'd see: my distant-cousin Mary's sixty-fifth birthday and the "silver anniversary" of the 1917 Clinic.

For Mary, we baked a cake with enough candles to bring out Birmingham's fire brigade.

For those we've loved and lost, we had a memorial service where we sang and prayed, hugged and wept.

And for Pearly James and all he represents, we printed a banner to remember the joyous occasion:

Chapter 18

DAD

To describe my mother, I only dare use words she's applied to herself. Elaine Koppel Saag is a perfectionist. She is "always honest," "rarely wrong," and has a clear definition of what is "right." Nothing is too good for her family. If you buy something, you buy "the best"—no off brands or overstock merchandise, and buying retail means it's better. When you throw a party, it is a bash folks will talk about for years. When you give a gift, it is something fine and memorable.

Her reputation for demanding excellence and exerting control earned my mother the affectionate nickname The Big E. She wears it proudly, in life and on the BIG E vanity license plate on her car.

The Big E was a feistier, more assertive version of June Cleaver from television's *Leave It to Beaver*, the classic stay-at-home mom of the 1950s. She was known for her chopped liver and her cheesecake, which rivaled the famed version from New York City's Carnegie Deli. She played some golf and frequently won the nine-hole ladies' championship at the Standard Country Club. She served as president of the Sisterhood women's group at our temple while retaining her status as a social more than a strongly religious Jew. Through sixty years of marriage, she and my father complemented each other like a well-rehearsed vaudeville team: Eddie was the free-wheeling, fun-loving rascal, Elaine the anchor and enforcer.

Mom has a cackling laugh and a sharp, sarcastic tongue. From my youth, she labeled me "a smartass." Once I got my medical degree, I was "The *Fercockta* Doctor" (Yiddish for screwed up), in contrast to my cousin Dr. Ken Saag, a rheumatologist whom she dubbed "The Good Doctor." I recognize the labels as terms of endearment just as much as when she calls me "My Michael," a nickname so persistent that even her friends call me that. When Amy and I left Louisville after medical school to go to Birmingham, The Big E sat on her porch and cried, whispering to my dad, "They're not coming back." Mothers know.

Mom has taken obvious pride in seeing her children launch into the world and raise families of their own, me in Birmingham and my sisters in Louisville. Firstborn Terry, the overachiever, became a speech pathologist; her husband Gary is a dentist. Barbara, the onetime rebel, became an educator; her husband Greg went into the family lighting business. As Terry has said of the siblings, "You look at the three of us and *oh boy*, are we all different!" I believe Barbara would second that (and note wryly that it's one of the few things on which she and Terry agree). I'm still the baby, the get-along guy, the one the others probably indulge too much. My sisters say they see a lot of our parents' good traits in me, and I say the same about them—we didn't turn out so badly. And we gave The Big E and "Pops" a total of seven grandchildren.

When our clan gathers for holidays in Louisville, the evenings overflow with great food and drink, ribald humor, and old songs. My mother, now in her mideighties, may ignore a detail from present-day information but recalls stories from the past in exquisite detail.

Since October 11, 2008, there's an emptiness at the center of all this joy. It's the place where Pops should sit. If we hold Mom extra tight, it's because we fear the moment her place will be empty as well. Amid the chaotic and happy clamor of a family gathering, when we think of Pops's last days we know what we all wish for: the peaceful passing, the "good death."

From his youth, Eddie Saag was a vibrant man, fit and athletic. He entered the US Army at age eighteen and sailed through basic training. When it came time for his platoon to be sent overseas, he somehow wrangled a promotion to corporal so he could be in charge of training new recruits. That meant he had to be in superior shape and outperform them at the obstacle courses, fitness, and endurance tests. But that was fine with Dad, who already was living by the philosophy he later would preach to his kids: *Never give up. No matter what the circumstance, don't be a quitter.*

The first time I remember my father talking about aging, I was eight years old. He was complaining to another relative that his Uncle Sam, his mother Lela's brother, was "not growing old gracefully." Because Sam couldn't do everything he once could do, he was becoming angry and bitter, Dad said. "Such a *shanda* [shame]." As with many grown-up conversations on which I eavesdropped, I didn't comprehend everything. But I could tell Dad felt Sam was wasting time lamenting the inevitable. I now realize I was listening in on Dad's philosophy of life: Embrace what we have, make the most of it until there is nothing left to embrace.

To celebrate my graduation from medical school in 1981, The Big E insisted on throwing a party that was grand even by her standards. She moved the furniture to make room for a crowd, put out enormous buffets of food, and invited everyone she felt had contributed in any way to my MD degree. That meant key professors and mentors from the University of Louisville such as Jeff Callan (head of dermatology), family, friends, and fellow students including three—Eddie Tillett, Barry Klein, and David Robie—who were my classmates both in medical school and at Mrs. Chance's Nursery School. It was a great celebration, a great afternoon.

When the party was over and everyone had left, my father took me back to the bedroom and closed the door. He told me how proud he was of me, and how this accomplishment was a shining example of sticking with what you start. Then he said, "Michael, one day I'm going to need a favor from you. One day I'm going to become a GOMER."

That term was one Dad had picked up from me when I was reading *The House of God*, a satirical novel about medical internship written by "Samuel Shem, MD" (the pen name for psychiatrist-writer Stephen Bergman). In the fictional hospital in the book, GOMER was the staff's acronym for Get Out of My Emergency Room, a label they applied to aged or incurably sick individuals who had lost the essence of meaningful life yet were still alive.

My dad's father, David Saag, died at age eighty, and after my dad reached that milestone himself, he used to joke, "I made a deal with God that if I could live to eighty, I'd be a happy man. At seventy-nine, I renegotiated!" However, my dad also had watched as his aging mother, Lela, lost her hearing, most of her sight, and many of her friends. By the time Lela died at age ninety-eight, she was lonely and miserable. When Dad used the term GOMER, I knew what it meant to him: a person who had reached that place where life doesn't seem worth living anymore, where the suffering is too great and extending life only prolongs that pain.

"I don't know when that time is going to come," Dad said to me, "but I'll know when I see it. And then I'm going to turn to you and I'm going to need your help."

I nodded, I hugged him, and I said, "Pops, I don't think that will be any time soon." We left the room and never again spoke about it. The covenant had been made.

I have now seen the age Dad was when our first child, Andy, was born. For some reason, he seemed a lot older than I feel now. Yet even as he aged, he was still vibrant, still a foundation and an inspiration for everyone in our family.

When I asked Terry and Barbara for their reflections, Barbara recalled,

> Dad always seemed able to pull out the silver lining in a situation. He had a sensitivity to other people, a soft spot for people in trouble, and a way of finding the best in people, even in the worst times.

Added Terry:

> He always had a joke or humorous quip to tell. Whenever he stopped joking, that was our signal he was not feeling well or was in pain; but he never, ever complained.

Dad's health began to decline in his seventies. Erosion of cartilage in his knees left him with a pronounced limp. Arthritis caused him pain in virtually every joint, especially his wrists and back, and necessitated first one hip replacement and then a second. By the late 1990s, the part of the artificial hip joint that was embedded in the marrow of his right thigh bone had become loose and was painfully "pistoning" (moving up and down) inside the bone every time he took a step.

I brought Dad to UAB for an evaluation by Dr. John Cuckler, an orthopedic surgeon who specializes in hip "redos." In an X-ray of Dad's right hip that also showed the thigh bone, the femur, a sharp-eyed radiologist noted a circular, less-opaque area that was consistent with a type of blood cancer called myeloma. When Dr. Cuckler operated, he put in a new hip that worked well for the rest of Dad's life; he also scooped out the suspicious area of the femur, sent it to pathology, and replaced it with a bone graft. Examination of the material confirmed that Dad had myeloma.

Multiple myeloma is a blood cancer in which certain cells of the immune system, the ones responsible for producing infection-fighting antibodies, clonally expand and grow uncontrollably. These cells can set up a nest inside bone or other tissues and destroy the area around them. Not much can be done about this condition, which often leads to "freak" fractures in which the weakened bone snaps during mild activity such as picking up a bucket or pulling a car door closed.

On one level, my dad was lucky. The lesion in his femur was the only one in his body. After its removal and the bone graft, he never had another problem with his bones, in part because of an osteoporosis medication that he took in monthly intravenous infusions for the rest of his life. But he still had the myeloma, which has another pernicious effect. The tumor cells that circulate in the blood and live in the bone marrow secrete antibody protein fragments that get deposited in tissues throughout the body, including the liver, heart, muscle, and brain. This condition, called amyloidosis, began to wear away at my dad in much the way I had seen HIV wear away at my patients. As the years passed, his heart couldn't pump as strongly as in the past, his gut didn't absorb nutrients as well, his lungs became a bit more stiff, and his thinking slowed "just a titch," as southerners say.

Barbara:

> When they found the myeloma in his leg, I think Dad took it

as a heads-up that he wasn't going to be around forever, and he began making plans. He had built the house where we grew up, and while Mom sometimes would say, "Let's go to a condo," Dad never wanted to move. But then three or four years before he died, he's the one who decides to sell the house and move. He wanted to get her settled while he could.

He was also plagued with pulmonary artery hypertension. Think of it as high blood pressure of the artery that leads from the heart to the lungs. When the blood pressure increases in the pulmonary artery, it causes a sort of traffic jam of blood trying to leave the heart and get into the lungs. This backs up the blood flow into the liver and the lower extremities, causing accumulated fluid to bloat Dad's legs and occasionally ooze out into his socks.

Between the amyloid weakening his heart and the pulmonary artery hypertension affecting blood flow, Dad was feeling all of his eighty-three years at his birthday in September 2007. He was having significant short-ness of breath and trouble getting around, and he needed more and more help from his children—typically, Terry during the week, Barbara on the weekends, and me on the phone with his providers as needed. Like so many "sandwich generation" adults, my sisters were the heroes, tending to their own kids and careers while also being on-site caregivers to our parents.

> Terry: We siblings joked that, as opposed to all the dysfunc-
> tional families you hear about, we were a "functional family" in
> helping Mom and Dad. Each of us had a natural role and knew
> what our role was. It worked out very well. And Dad was a very
> easy person to take care of. He was just always super-apprecia-
> tive of whatever was done for him by anybody. As his decline
> continued, there was dignity after dignity that was taken away
> from him, and each time you could see it just killed him to
> have to give up whatever it was, whether it was going from a
> cane to a walker, or having to use oxygen and carry it around
> with him. But once he got over the initial shock of any of that,
> he would start making jokes about it. [He called his cane "cane

yehi ratzon," a pun on the phrase recited at Yom Kippur, ken
yehi ratzon, which means "May it be God's will."]

In a survey of adults over fifty conducted by the nonpartisan healthcare
advocacy group Campaign for Better Care (CBC), three out of four participants said they wished their doctors communicated and shared information with each other more effectively. When that doesn't happen, the CBC
survey found, patients and family members struggle to close the information gaps. Both my sisters played this role for my parents. They attended
medical appointments, took notes, asked questions, and intervened whenever necessary to help my parents manage the baffling, frustrating aspects of
the healthcare system—including insurance. Terry, especially, became Dad's
"healthcare navigator."

For the thirty years that Dad owned and ran AM Electric (the lighting
company he bought with proceeds from the sale of the drive-in theaters),
he had health insurance through Blue Cross Blue Shield of Kentucky. Like
most people who are insured through their employer, the company paid the
majority of Dad's health insurance cost, and he paid the rest. After retirement, his insurance became Medicare plus a supplemental policy he bought
from Anthem BCBS of Kentucky.

There are dozens, perhaps hundreds of Medicare supplemental policies,
each with its own costs, benefits, limits, and nuances. Customers are either
at the mercy of an agent or on their own in trying to determine which varia-
tion is best for them. It is difficult if not impossible for even the most competent consumer to fully understand all the features of these programs and
select the product that is best for them—in part because of the complexities
of the programs, but also because no one is quite sure what their healthcare
status is going to be one, two, or three years from the time they purchase the
insurance when illnesses emerge, sometimes catastrophic ones.

So we learned. In spring 2008, when we tried to get Dad on a new drug to
treat his pulmonary artery hypertension, the pharmacist apologetically told
him that his insurance didn't cover the drug. From then on, every month for
the rest of his life, it seemed like Dad's battles were as much with flaws of the
healthcare system as with his body.

In my dad's case, things were complicated by the passage of the Medicare Part D program. I know the popular spin on Part D was that it would be a godsend, ensuring drug coverage for the elderly and other Medicare beneficiaries. The reality is that the 2003 law creating Part D was essentially designed by lobbyists and "friends" of the pharmaceutical industry to ensure payment for products that they manufacture. Here's a simple summary of the bill from ProPublica:

> As ideas for the prescription drug benefit were being debated, several proposals were introduced that would have allowed the government to negotiate for lower drug prices, as it does for the drugs it buys for Medicaid and for the Department of Veterans Affairs. But after intense lobbying by pharmaceutical companies and strong-arm tactics by House leaders, the final bill instead specifically barred the government from negotiating lower drug prices. It also banned importation of cheaper drugs from Canada and gave drug companies stronger protections against their generic competitors.

So, Medicare was left to pay top dollar for all medications. And under the philosophy that delivering essential medications is a "business" and should operate as a "free-market" enterprise, the consumers (read: the elderly) were left to *choose* which of the forty or fifty Medicare Part D plans would best fit their needs. I tried to help my mom and dad make this choice by going to a website, plugging in the medications that they were taking, and seeing which Part D supplemental program would cover those medications at the lowest premium cost.

Like countless other Americans who help elderly parents and friends with this task, I did my best to enable my parents to cover their needs and not bust their budget. But also like countless others, I couldn't anticipate that Dad would develop new conditions that required more drug spending and that he'd land in "the doughnut hole," The System's cutesy name for the Part D coverage gap where seniors must pay all their drug bills until they hit the out-of-pocket threshold where coverage resumes.

I also couldn't anticipate that Dad would require a drug not included in the Part D plan we chose, and thus we would have to go through a mind-boggling process to seek special authorizations and approvals—or else find a way to pay for it himself. Paying out of pocket for the supposed new "wonder drug" for pulmonary artery hypertension would cost Dad around $7,200 per month. (Yes, $7,200 per month!) I called the company to inquire about a compassionate use program, which they had, but even on his fixed income, Dad didn't meet the program's financial qualifications. At that point, his options seemed clear: Either go without the medicine and let the pulmonary artery hypertension take its course, or dig into the nest egg he had built for sixty years to support his retirement and my mom after he was gone.

Dad was all for option #1; he had no interest in draining their savings to add months to his life. Then Terry, to her credit, found another way. Though Dad was an honorably discharged veteran with two Purple Hearts, he had not gone to the Veterans Administration hospital for care because he had private insurance most of his life, then Medicare. But Terry approached the VA to see if Dad could get the medication covered there.

> In early May, we went to the Louisville VA Medical Center to get Dad evaluated for this drug. I remember Dad was in horrible shape that day; he was really short of breath and could hardly get to the hospital. The doctor examined him and talked to us about getting the drug, but he said, "My gosh, that is the least of his problems right now!" He said that because Dad's heart wasn't pumping efficiently, the space around Dad's lungs was filled with fluid and he was getting very little oxygen. So Dad ended up in the hospital to have the fluid drained. And that helped for a while.
>
> At the end of May, I went with Dad and Mom to another appointment. The doctor turned to Dad and said, "I think you need to get your affairs in order, there's nothing more we can do for you." Mom had tears streaming down her face. But Dad said, "That's okay, I've had a wonderful life, I have

no regrets." He asked how long the doctor thought he had and the doctor said, maybe three months. At that point, we wondered if getting the new drug was worth the aggravation, but Michael said it might improve Dad's quality of life.

In late June, thanks to Terry and the VA, Dad finally began receiving the new drug. Perhaps we had started it too late, or perhaps the drug wasn't potent enough to treat the degree of pulmonary artery hypertension that he had. For whatever reason, the costly drug we'd battled to get simply didn't seem to be helping him. In July, Terry took him back to the VA hospital for a checkup and, "as opposed to the physician who had recommended that Dad take this new drug, we saw another doctor who said it was completely inappropriate and not necessary," she recalls. "After all the aggravation of trying to get it and anguishing about the cost of it, Dad had to sit through that."

Within weeks, the wonder drug would be dropped. By now, Dad was on steroids to deal with the constant, pervasive pain of the arthritis in his back and extremities. It was a struggle for him to get up from a sitting position or to get his clothes on. His skin was thinning. Because even the slightest bump against a surface or a doorway could cause him to bleed profusely, Mom started carrying bandages with her everywhere they went. There were repeated trips to the hospital to drain the fluid around his lungs and treat sepsis (bloodstream infections). Terry recalls one episode in August:

> Mom called and when I got to their house, Dad was sitting in a chair shaking, having trouble breathing, and shivering—he was septic, and it was really hard to look at. We were in the ER for the longest time and there he was with his arthritis, lying on that uncomfortable bed. He was being examined by one of the staff physicians, the so-called "hospitalists," and it seems like any time you mention anything, they run a test.
>
> I'll never forgive myself for this, but I made an offhand comment that Dad's toes looked a little blue. So what did

they do? They ordered a test, a venous doppler to check his circulation—a test he had had not that long before! To do the test, they had to take him down to the bowels of the hospital, and they left him there in a cubicle with a curtain closed around him. He was waiting so long that he needed to go to the bathroom, but there was no one there to help him—so he had to start screaming, "Help, help!" From then on, whenever he went for tests in the hospital, one of us went with him.

Just before Labor Day that year, 2008, I went to Louisville with my video camera. I knew why I brought it. Dad knew why I brought it. But all I said was, "Hey, Dad, let me interview you here for a little bit," and all he said was, "Fine." I clipped a microphone to his shirt and set up the camera on a portable TV table in the living room. We sat facing each other, him in the black leather swivel rocker known as "Pops's Chair." For more than three hours, we talked.

I asked Dad to sing the old songs, including the outrageous, lewd ones that we had sung around Papaharry's piano: "Dan Dan the Lavatory Man," "Uncle Bud," "Grandma's in the Cellar." I reminisced with him about family stories, like the time he got a Shelbyville, Indiana, restaurant to serve me beer with my fried chicken—at age twelve.

I had him recount his experiences in France during the war and especially after the war, when US soldiers were left for a year or two longer in the European theater because there wasn't an easy way to get them back home. During that time, Dad had gone to film school and had made a scrapbook of his experiences, something I had never before seen. As the video camera hummed softly, Dad flipped the pages of the scrapbook and described every picture. He did not need to say what we both understood—that we might not turn these pages together again.

Though I visited Louisville as often as I could as Dad's health declined, most of the time it fell to Barbara and Terry to guide him through the minefields of the healthcare system. Terry says that most of the people involved in Dad's medical care "were compassionate and wonderful," and I believe her.

But the care was delivered despite the obstacles we place between caregivers and patients. A typical primary care physician who sees Medicare patients must coordinate care for those patients with 229 other physicians who work in 117 different practices, according to the *Annals of Internal Medicine* (2009). And in the current system, doctors generally aren't reimbursed for their time making those contacts—so their efforts to practice collaborative, coordinated patient care while paying staff and other expenses mean they lose money with every call.

My sisters are smart, determined women who fiercely protect those they love, and they monitored Dad's care intensively. But for all the providers' good intentions and for all my sisters' diligence and advocacy, Dad still suffered from medical missteps that were unfortunate and, given The System, inevitable.

Early in September, when Dad again needed fluid drained from around his lungs, Barbara was at the hospital to be his watchdog.

> Dad was there to get the lung procedure, that was it—but they were still trying to do all these other tests. I had told the hospital that his skin came off when anything was stuck to it and I literally posted signs all over the room—"NO TAPE!" "DO NOT PUT TAPE ON THIS PATIENT!"—but at some point in the night, someone put tape on his skin. So the next day, I talked to the hospitalist, and he's like, "I'm so sorry." And the next minute, some lady comes in to do an electrocardiogram for which they have to stick on the electrodes—and I said, "NO, you are NOT going to do that to him! I will sign off, I will take responsibility if he has a heart attack, but there is to be NO tape on this man!" And after that, one thing we all decided is that Dad would not go back to the hospital again no matter what. And he didn't.

To manage his growing list of ailments, Dad was taking lots of medications. That's not unusual for people his age: According to a study by the Centers for Disease Control and Prevention and the Merck Institute of Aging and

Health, the average seventy-five-year-old in America has three chronic conditions and takes five prescription drugs. Shortly after that final hospitalization, Dad had spent his way into the Part D "doughnut hole" where Medicare would not cover hundreds of dollars' worth of drugs that he had to have to stay alive. Terry again contacted the VA, which rode to the rescue and covered the medications that Medicare would not. Dad and Mom were so grateful that they had Terry deliver one of those "edible bouquet" fruit baskets to the VA staff. But for many seniors, the "doughnut hole" will remain a burden until 2020, when it is to be eliminated by Affordable Care Act reforms.

Dad turned eighty-four on September 21, 2008. When I came to Louisville to celebrate, I was struck by how much he had deteriorated physically since Labor Day. But in his heart, he still was "Big Fred," the free-wheeling, fun-loving rascal. And he still had a few birthday toasts in him, the saltier the better.

Barbara says I got out the shot glasses and Jack Daniels; I could have sworn she did. No matter. She, her husband, Greg, Dad, and I sat around the condo's dining room table. With Mom looking on, Dad proceeded, with good humor and a sort of backhanded forgiveness, to toast every single person in the US healthcare system who had done him wrong. "To the guys who left me on the gurney in the hospital basement: F—'em!" he said, and we clinked glasses, took a swig, and poured refills. "To the person who didn't listen when I told them 'No tape': F—'em!" Another clink, another swig, another pour. He named each injury and indignity, turned it into a joke, laughed harder than any of us—and concluded, "F—'em all!"

Late September and early October brought the Jewish High Holy Days, and some of the sweetest hours Terry and Barbara remember with Dad.

On Wednesday night, October 8, Mom was at the synagogue for the Kol Nidrei service that begins Yom Kippur. Terry stayed with Dad until Barbara could spell her, and then was heading to North Carolina for a brief visit to celebrate her grandson's birthday.

> Terry: The home healthcare workers had been called in because Dad could no longer walk to the bathroom, even with the

walker. For weeks before this, I had spent parts of most days with him and we had had these wonderful discussions. He had told me all these stories from his life, things I never knew had happened, things that made me laugh and things that made me admire him even more. I knew he wanted me to go visit my grandson, but as I was walking down the hall after saying good-bye to him, I was sobbing.

Barbara: I can't stand going to services, so I stayed with Dad on the holidays, and that was some of the most memorable time. Dad and Michael and I are all alike in that we have music in our heads all the time, and no idea where it comes from. So I would bring music to play for Dad. He liked show tunes and funny songs, so I would put on Alan Sherman and Smothers Brothers routines . . . songs from *My Fair Lady* . . . "I Did It My Way," and "What a Wonderful World."

I had been with Dad the Monday before Yom Kippur, returned to Birmingham during the week, and then came back to Louisville on Friday night. I found Dad in his bedroom, which had been made over with a hospital bed and bedside commode. We hugged and talked. Though the home health nurse would remain overnight, I told her I would stay in the room with him. I encouraged Mom to get some sleep on the pullout couch in the living room and urged Barbara to head home for a break. For a while, I squeezed into the hospital bed next to Dad, who rested his head on my shoulder. I remember thinking two things: that at the end, the child becomes the parent—and that this moment was too precious to last.

About 11:00 p.m., Dad said he had to go to the bathroom. I helped him sit up on the side of the bed and asked if he could stand, but he had no power in his legs at all. I put my arms under his armpits and lifted him enough that I could pivot him on his heels and half-drop him onto the bedside commode. After he had finished, I picked him up, but I couldn't lift him enough to place him back in bed, so we lunged forward and fell onto the bed together. Three hours later, about 2:00 a.m., he called out again. I helped him sit on the side of the bed and placed his arms around my neck.

His face was right next to my ear and in a raspy voice he whispered, "I gotta pish," so we repeated the awkward maneuver to get him on and off the commode. Lifting him repeatedly had sheared off patches of skin in his armpits, leaving large swaths of bright red, denuded skin, so when I lifted him the last time, he grimaced in pain. Seeing what pain I'd caused, but not wanting him to see me cry, I blinked back tears as I adjusted his sheet and blankets.

Dad reached up, grabbed my hand, looked me in the eye, and said two words: "It's time." I stared at him for a minute and asked, "Are you sure?" He said "Go get your mother." I went to the living room, woke my mother, and brought her into the bedroom.

Dad turned to Mom and said, "Elaine, this is it."

"What's it?" she replied.

"This is it," he repeated. "I need to go now."

My sisters and I had known The Big E was living in denial. She looked at Dad in disbelief and tried to argue: "You're not that sick. You're not going anywhere."

Dad's voice was firm: "It's the end, Elaine, I need to go." Mom bent her head down and they hugged. She was crying softly; Dad did not show much emotion. He simply knew it was time.

There was no medicine left to change the situation—nothing that would return strength to his legs or heal his skin, nothing that would relieve his shortness of breath or replace the sixty pounds he had lost. There were, however, medicines that could ease his pain. Up until this time, he never took any pain medicines. That's the medicine he wanted me to administer.

I called Terry in North Carolina and asked if she wanted me to wait until she got back to administer the pain medication. We knew that in his debilitated, weakened state, the medication would put him right to sleep and he would not likely reawaken. She said, "No, go ahead; he and I have already said good-bye." I called Barbara, who came over immediately, in time for Dad to deliver a parting joke. As Election Day was nearing, he said with a weak smile, "I think I'm going to send in an absentee ballot. But it's going to ask me where I'm relocating, and I'll have to say, I don't know . . ."

While Barbara loaded the cassette tape recorder with the music Dad loved, I put on a fentanyl patch, the prescription we had been given by his doctor, to deliver pain relief through Dad's fragile skin. As Barbara sang along to the show tunes, Dad briefly waved his hands in the air as if conducting an orchestra of angels. Then he drifted off to sleep and was peacefully sleeping when Terry and her husband, Gary, arrived about 11:00 a.m. Saturday. I couldn't tell for sure if he was having any pain, so I administered a little morphine under his tongue. As relatives moved quietly in and out of the bedroom throughout the afternoon, his breathing became slower. His breathing slowed to a stop near 7:00 p.m.

In Judaism the biggest mitzvah you can provide any other person is to bury them. It is considered the greatest good deed because it is the one favor you can do for someone else that they never can repay. In my Dad's case, we were able to perform a double mitzvah: to bury him, but also to help him die with dignity on his own terms, in his way, in his home and not in a hospital. It was little enough to repay him for all the gifts he gave us throughout our lives. But for me, it is the most meaningful gift I have ever given anyone in my life.

To this day, I have not looked at the videos I made of Dad. I'm not sure when I will.

Every year on Dad's birthday, I get an email from Barbara, the same request she sends to Terry and Gary, to Greg and Amy, and to all of Eddie's grandkids. "Sometime during the day," the email says, "I hope you will sing one of the Pops's songs." Everybody emails back to everybody else, naming the song they chose. And when we do this, we smile.

———

All his life, my father played by the rules, worked hard, and looked out for the people he loved. At the end, it was our privilege to look out for him.

But we're just one family in a pervasively screwed-up system. Who's watching out for all the other people, like you?

Chapter 19

CHAOS

ebruary 18, 2013, 7:53 p.m. When I clicked my cell phone to take the call from Jim Raper, the first words I heard were, "The house next door is on fire!" I'd not yet gotten out, "Oh no, Jim, are you and Scott okay?" when Jim continued: "I've been telling them for years, Mike. They wouldn't listen. And now it's in flames and the clinic is in jeopardy."

Then I got it: Jim wasn't at home. He was at the clinic. He was referring to the dilapidated, two-story wooden tinderbox building adjacent to the 1917 Clinic building. For more than ten years, Jim had pleaded with city officials to condemn the building so it could be torn down. No response. Repeatedly. He went to UAB officials who said there was nothing they could do. We joked that it proved healthcare wasn't the only screwed-up system in America.

"It's gonna burn down, Mike, and it will take the clinic with it. It's only a matter of time."

The building wasn't just adjacent to the 1917 Clinic building; it virtually abutted the clinic building, less than a foot of space between its rotting wood wall and the brick exterior of our clinic.

Dr. Bob Bourge had tried to help Jim get rid of this eyesore. A burly Cajun and UAB cardiologist, Bob was the vice chair for clinical services in the department of medicine. Hearing Jim's concerns, Bob poked around and learned that the building was owned by a local bank that had foreclosed on it years earlier. During several meetings and phone calls with the bank, Bob encouraged them to donate the building to UAB, which would tear it down at university expense to prevent a future catastrophe. Bob pitched the idea as a win-win: The bank would rid itself of a liability and get a tax deduction, the menacing building would be gone, and UAB would pave the area to add an additional twelve to fifteen parking spaces for 1917 Clinic patients. Somehow, the deal never materialized.

During the twenty-minute drive to the clinic, all I could think was, "Jim's prophecy came true." I envisioned the clinic engulfed in flames. I began a mental inventory. The clinical data was safe because it was stored off site. Many of the office contents could be replaced—the equipment, the computers, the furniture. But science depended on the 400,000-plus specimens in the repository, which I had begun to collect in 1986. I thought about the letters and keepsakes from patients and families. The artwork created by patients and donated to the clinic, including the chalk pictures Brian had drawn for me while he was blind. Gone. Irreplaceable. Senseless, preventable, foreseeable loss—all of it. No one had cared enough to do what had to be done. Including me.

As I drove up, the streets surrounding the clinic were blocked off. The air stank of smoke, and I could see it billowing into the night sky, illuminated by the orange flames below. I got out of the car and headed at a trot toward the building. When a policeman blocked my path, I told him, "I work here, I need to meet with the UAB officials on the scene," and he waved me through.

As I rounded the corner I saw Jim, staring at the scene in disbelief. Firefighters were on all sides of the burning building, pouring enormous amounts of water on it—and, to my great relief, an equal number of firefighters were on the roof of the clinic building, hosing it down to keep it from catching on fire. The clinic building was mostly unharmed. We had dodged the bullet.

When I went by Jim's office the next day to see how the cleanup of the clinic was going, he turned toward me with an anguished look.

"They found three bodies in the rubble, Mike."

Squatters had moved into the building. To escape the twenty-five-degree, wind-chilled night, they'd probably started a fire to keep warm, and it had gone out of control.

"These people are dead because we couldn't get the job done," he said. "They were seeking shelter they couldn't get elsewhere. And now they're gone."

Our nation's healthcare system is like the abandoned building that until recently stood next to our clinic.

In the 1950s, the building housed the office of a family physician, Dr. Rhett Barnes, who also lived in the house. I bet Dr. Barnes provided compassionate care to his patients. In the custom of the day, he probably accepted whatever payment his regular patients could provide—and if they couldn't pay, he'd see them anyway. That was the way physicians practiced in those not-so-long-ago simpler times. There was less they could do technically—fewer drugs, simple X-rays, no CAT scans or PET scans or monoclonal antibody therapeutics. But they were their community's healers, public servants who took pride in making house calls on stormy or freezing nights.

That bygone approach to healthcare has been abandoned as surely as the tinderbox Dr. Barnes left behind. In comparison with what once existed, the structure that remains is barely recognizable. We can see it is a building. But it is a building in serious disrepair, ready to burst into flames at any moment, taking with it all the unfortunates who seek shelter there. Is this "the finest in the world," the pride of America? Can we even say this is consistent with our political, moral, or religious principles?

In the days after the fire, the local newspaper identified the men who died. As county residents, they would have sought care at the county indigent hospital, Cooper Green Mercy Hospital. But two and a half weeks earlier—February 1, 2013—Cooper Green had closed. Among other displaced persons were all 800 HIV patients being seen at its outpatient clinic, all of whom were transferred en masse to the 1917 Clinic patient rolls. We absorbed them into our clinic as best we could, stretching staffing and resources that were near the breaking point already.

When asked about the fire, Birmingham's mayor was quoted as saying, "Condemning that building was on our short list in the short term."

I suppose lawmakers in Washington will say the same thing if asked about the nation's healthcare infrastructure when it goes up in smoke. Like the tinderbox next to our clinic, it's a disaster waiting to happen. When it does, who will we blame for the truth: No one had cared enough to do what had to be done, including us?

———

If you did a person-on-the-street survey and asked, "Who has the best healthcare in the world?" I suspect most Americans would say proudly, "the United States, of course!" The answer implies that we have our healthcare act together; that people can get the healthcare they need when they need it in a cost-efficient fashion.

Under just the right circumstances, the United States does provide the best healthcare has to offer—say, for certain cancer treatments, or the latest technology to fix clogged coronary arteries. Unfortunately, these are the exceptions to the rule—and the illustrations always cited by "leaders" who love the status quo.

But in aggregate and in truth, we are far from the best. To be best would imply a persistent, reliable pattern of best outcomes for the cost, and this nation is nowhere near this. In almost every category of objective outcomes, we have worse outcomes than found in other industrialized countries.

In 2011, the National Research Council (NRC) reported that life expectancy at age fifty had been increasing at a slower pace in the United States than in other countries. The obvious question was, Why?

To answer this question, the NIH commissioned a study by the NRC and the Institute of Medicine (IOM), branches of the National Academy of Science, an independent advisory body to the federal government. In 2013, the NRC/IOM study panel released a report whose title summarizes its findings: *U.S. Health in International Perspective: Shorter Lives, Poorer Health.*

Perhaps I should just leave it there. The title says it all. But it's amazing to see how the researchers arrived at their title.

"The United States spends much more money on health care than any other country. Yet Americans die sooner and experience more illness than residents in many other countries," said their report, and they listed "elements of the U.S. health disadvantage":

- Americans have shorter life expectancy than people in almost all other high-income countries.

- This disadvantage has been growing for the past three decades, especially among women.

- This disadvantage is pervasive—it affects all age groups up to the oldest ages and is observed for multiple diseases, biological and behavioral risk factors, and injuries.

- More specifically, when compared with the average of twenty-eight other high-income countries, the United States fares worse in nine health domains: adverse birth outcomes (e.g., low birth weight and infant mortality); injuries, accidents, and homicides; adolescent pregnancy and sexually transmitted infections; HIV and AIDS; drug-related mortality; obesity and diabetes; heart disease; chronic lung disease; and disability.

The study pointed to contributing problems such as "adverse social conditions" (read: poverty), then summarized findings in a two-sentence indictment: "The U.S. health system is highly fragmented, with weak public health and primary care components and a large uninsured population. Compared with people in other high-income countries, Americans are more likely to find care inaccessible or unaffordable and to report lapses in the quality and safety of ambulatory care."

Astoundingly, the report also noted that most Americans "do not realize that their expensive, world-class health care system—and the very large economy that supports it—has not enabled them to keep pace with the health gains achieved by people in other high-income countries."

If we are willing to sniff around the US healthcare system today, we can smell smoke. Victims are already being claimed. And crisis of massive, senseless, preventable, foreseeable loss is upon us. Someone needs to care enough to do what needs to be done. Including me.

After more than three decades serving and observing the US healthcare system, I see a burning need to tackle three big issues: Inequity, fragmentation, and information (or lack thereof).

Inequity

The quality and quantity of Americans' healthcare varies so dramatically, and dangerously, because of profound inequities in access to care—what I earlier described as differences in "tickets." What ticket we have when we enter care dictates who sees us, what they are able to do, and at what speed they can do it—and, ultimately and most importantly, with what results.

When we call for a medical appointment with a new provider, we almost always will be asked what insurance we have. When we get to the medical appointment, we need evidence that we've told the truth: our insurance card. The Ticket. Once the ticket has been reviewed, the inequity will begin: services are chosen based on the type of ticket we have.

When we have a good ticket, we are smugly entitled to the best the provider has to offer. When we have a new symptom, we don't think twice about calling the provider's office to request an appointment. Our provider performs preventative tests, sees us at regular intervals, and encourages healthy lifestyle changes. We gain comfort and security from having the ticket in our pocket. We have confidence that our access to care is assured and our health outcomes are among the best in the world, so . . . "Bless our hearts."

But if our ticket is for the "cheap seats," a low-cost insurance plan, we have much less certainty of care. We think we're *probably* covered should we experience a catastrophic illness or injury, but we know we have to pay out of pocket for most of our routine care. And when we're charged for the care provided, we don't get the deeply discounted rates the insurance plans pay; rather, we get bills for inflated, full-cost charges. God help us.

That's what happened to many of the 800 HIV-positive patients our clinic absorbed at the closing of the Cooper Green and its HIV outpatient clinic, the St. George's Clinic. In an agreement made in 2011 with the Ryan White program at the Health Resources and Services Administration (HRSA) and the St. George's leadership, the UAB 1917 Clinic agreed to provide care for those patients followed at St. George's should the day ever come when they had to close. When that day came in February 2013, the Ryan White Part C grant that covered patients at St. George's was transferred to us to help cover the cost of outpatient HIV care because it paid part of the salaries of nurses, nurse practitioners, and physicians at the 1917 Clinic.

But for services provided outside of our clinic by other clinics in the UAB system (e.g., urology, radiology, cardiology, and the like), the grant had to be used as a quasi-insurance policy that would pay for services delivered at the Medicare/government rate. In the first two months after 1917 Clinic assumed these patients' care, the non-Medicare-discounted charges for care they got at other clinics totaled $179,810, of which $38,755 was covered by the grant.

Where does this leave patients who do not have insurance that covers these other clinics' outpatient services—that is, patients with the "cheap seat" tickets, or no insurance at all? They are billed at the full rate, or in this case $179,810 in aggregate. Were it not for the Ryan White program, they would have had to pay out of pocket at the top dollar rate.

An unintended consequence of this inequity is the barrier it builds between the patient and the healthcare system.

"I have this new lump in my neck—but I don't want to see the doctor because I'd have to pay $250 just for the appointment, $550 for the lab tests, and more than $1,200 for the CT scan. I don't have that kind of money. I'll just wait a while; maybe the lump will go away." This means this patient's cancer diagnosis just got delayed by several weeks or months—time that providers might have used to save the patient's life, had he or she come in the day they found the lump.

As of 2011, about 48 million Americans were without health insurance, according to Census Bureau data. Between 2003 and 2010, the number of Americans who were underinsured—in other words, holding the "cheap seat" tickets—rose by 80 percent to some 29 million, according to data reported by the Commonwealth Fund. Having poor or no insurance discourages these Americans from seeking preventative and early medical

care—and that obviously affects the nation's overall health outcomes. Here's
how the NRC/IOM study report described it (italics mine):

> One explanation for the health disadvantage of the United
> States relative to other high-income countries might be defi-
> ciencies in health services. Although the United States is
> renowned for its leadership in biomedical research, its cutting-
> edge medical technology, and its hospitals and specialists,
> problems with ensuring Americans' access to the system and
> providing quality care have been a long-standing concern of
> policy makers and the public (Berwick et al., 2008; Brook,
> 2011b; Fineberg, 2012). Higher mortality rates from diseases,
> and even from transportation-related injuries and homicides,
> may be traceable in part to failings in the health care system.
> *The United States stands out from many other countries in not*
> *offering universal health insurance coverage.*

A related, unintended consequence of the United States' approach to healthcare delivery is the poor access to primary care services. It's the same point
author Shannon Brownlee made: While most industrialized nations have
many more primary care physicians (PCPs) than specialists, in the United
States we have nearly two specialists for every PCP, as well as millions of
patients who are without a regular PCP.

Lack of a well-staffed, high-functioning, first-line primary care system is
the main cause of what I consider the second big problem area in US healthcare today: fragmentation.

Fragmentation

Let's go back to our person-on-the-street survey and ask this question: "Do
you think preventative care is associated with better health outcomes?" I bet
almost everyone who knows the meaning of the word "preventative" would
answer yes. As Americans, we say that we value primary care and its providers; we love our pediatricians and respect our internists (whom I fondly

describe as "pediatricians for adults"). We appreciate the value of routine colonoscopies after age fifty, mammograms and Pap smears for women, and annual digital rectal exams to assess prostate cancer for men.

So we say we love our PCPs, our primary care physicians, but this statement rings hollow considering how we reward them. There are huge discrepancies in pay between primary care folks and specialists, particularly the specialists most associated with doing procedures (e.g., surgeons, radiologists, dermatologists). We reward for Doing, so all eight hours of, say, a surgeon's eight hours of surgery are billable. Very billable. But we don't reward for Not Doing, so when our much-loved PCP carefully evaluates all the possible data on our case and concludes that "watchful waiting" is the most prudent choice—after hours of deliberation, consultations with others, and an extended conversation with us—no payment results. If "follow the money" is the rule for making a career choice, head for a specialty practice.

This flow of money toward rewarding procedures skews the system in both obvious and subtle ways.

The obvious effect: Surgeons, radiologists, and dermatologists are paid substantially more per year than pediatricians, internists, and psychiatrists, often four to ten times more per year. As a result, a disproportionate number of graduating medical students choose the better-remunerated Doing specialties, which creates an overabundance of specialists and a shortage of PCPs across the country. As the NRC/IOM report puts it, "The United States has a relatively weak foundation for primary care and a shortage of family physicians."

The subtle effect: The overspecialization of medical practice gives rise to greater fragmentation of care. Specialists are very happy to perform their particular procedure and move on to the next case. They prefer not to engage too much in the broader details of a case or the long-term view of the patient they are asked to see. They need to know only enough to (1) determine whether the procedure is indicated, (2) prepare for the procedure in a way that heads off complications, and (3) conduct the procedure for the desired outcome as safely and effectively as possible. But no more than that.

To the patient, this proceduralist is just another provider who breezes in and breezes out of their care. After the procedure, Dr. Do-er reappears only on the patient's extensive bill as a name barely recognized, who may have performed a procedure the patient can't even remember having. The ultimate in piecemeal care.

The NRC/IOM report did not mince words about the harm done by this approach:

> In the United States, health care delivery (and financing) is deeply fragmented across thousands of health systems and payers and across government (e.g., Medicare and Medicaid) and the private sector, creating inefficiencies and coordination problems that may be less prevalent in countries with more centralized national health systems. As a result, U.S. patients do not always receive the care they need (and sometimes receive care they do not need): One study estimated that Americans receive only 50 percent of recommended health care services (McGlynn et al., 2003) . . . The difficulties Americans experience in accessing these services and receiving high-quality care . . . cannot be ignored as a potential contributor to the U.S. health disadvantage.

Thanks to the inequity and the fragmentation in the US healthcare system today, many patients lack an affordable, reliable way to get treatment. "Access to health care services, particularly in rural and frontier communities or disadvantaged urban centers, is often limited," says the NRC/IOM report. As a result, "Many Americans rely on emergency departments for acute, chronic, and even preventive care."

The use of emergency rooms for primary care is pervasive in the United States. But in terms of continuity of care and cost-efficiency, it is everything we do *not* want healthcare to be.

"Experts estimate that the cost of an (emergency room) visit for a non-urgent condition is two to five times greater than the cost of receiving care in a primary care setting for the same condition," says a research brief by the New England Healthcare Institute. The brief reports that emergency room "overuse is on the rise across all patient populations, irrespective of age or insurance coverage"—and that the use of ERs instead of an office or clinic for primary care "is responsible for $38 billion in wasteful spending each year."

Each time a patient accesses primary care in the ER, they are very likely to see a provider they never have seen before and never will see again. The ER provider is expected to focus solely on the primary complaint: "What brought you in to see us today?" Once that problem is addressed, the provider is done. All of us who've worked shifts in an emergency department know the unofficial slogan, "Treat 'em and street 'em."

I worked in the University Hospital emergency room as the attending physician throughout my chief residency and fellowship years at UAB. It was a nice way to make extra money. All by itself, it's an advanced course in stress. Our ER was busy. I moved from room to room like a hummingbird skitters from flower to flower, extracting the information I needed to address the primary complaint, ordering just enough tests to assure my diagnostic hunch was correct and that I wasn't missing something big. Then I prescribed a therapy or remedy that I hoped would resolve the current problem.

In "working up" these patients, I thought very little about their home circumstances, who their families were, or whether they were likely to take the medicines I prescribed. I tried as best I could to assure they could access the medicines, frequently contacting the social worker on call to get medicines that the patients had no apparent means to buy themselves. But once I signed the paperwork that discharged them from the ER, they disappeared from my consciousness. I moved on to the next patients. I certainly *hoped* they would keep the appointment I ordered to help assure follow-up as they left the ER, but I really had no way to see that they did. It wasn't my job. Even then, as a moonlighting ER physician, I was paid more than many primary care physicians. And ER docs today typically are paid more than outpatient internists and pediatricians.

From many nights in the ER, I recall one in particular. We were swamped from 7:00 p.m. until 1:00 a.m., when it got quiet. A half hour passed with no more new patients arriving; I actually got caught up on my paperwork, a very unusual circumstance. I headed for the call room to get whatever rest I could and was soundly asleep at 3:30 a.m. when I got the call: "Someone for you to see in room 7."

I got up, threw some water on my face, and staggered down the hallway to room 7. Waiting for me was a memorably sweet, reserved eighty-one-year-old African-American woman, her hair wrapped in a scarf. She was in a wheelchair with her right foot elevated, her shoe off, and her swollen knee visible at the hemline of her skirt.

I summoned what I hoped was a convincing smile and asked, "What brings you here to see us at this time of the morning?"

"My 'gouch' is acting up," she explained, pointing to the inflamed knee suffering from what is otherwise known as *gout*.

"How long have you had the 'gouch'?" I asked.

"Oh, honey, for years. I can't remember when I didn't have it!"

"Who follows you for this?"

"Dr. Heck, the rheumatism doctor."

"When are you supposed to see Dr. Heck again?"

"I had an appointment yesterday morning, but I didn't keep it."

"Why not?"

"My leg hurt too bad to go!"

So, I think to myself, *your "gouch" was acting up all day and into the night, you didn't see Dr. Heck, but you are now here in the emergency room to see me at 3:30 in the morning?* The question that passed my lips was much more civil: "Ma'am, why did you come in now as opposed to seeing Dr. Heck yesterday morning? I'm guessing your leg hurt as badly then as it does now."

"It did," she said brightly. "But by coming in this time of day, I didn't have to wait to see you!"

It took all of my professional training to keep from screaming.

This episode spotlights the third area where the US healthcare system falters, and it's the most multifaceted and complex of the three: information.

Information

Many of the most vexing problems in US healthcare today relate to information and communication, or lack of it. Among them:

- An antiquated approach to information. In the twenty-first century, "the best healthcare system in the world" *should* leverage technology to insure that the information it uses is accurate, current, comprehensible, and secure—and that that is true in every transaction among patients, providers, payers, and other system players. Updating America's approach to healthcare information would have wide-ranging implications; it would include everything from broadening the use of "health IT" tools to making medical and insurance communications straightforward enough for every patient to understand.

- An abundance of misinformation. Today, every American who goes online is surrounded by unvetted, questionable information on diseases, symptoms, and treatments. On every information platform, marketers encourage Americans to do and buy things that will fill up companies' coffers, whether or not they improve Americans' health. This misinformation overload makes it all the more important that the core institutions of US healthcare be honest brokers, delivering trustworthy, unbiased scientific data and analysis. To hold that ethical high ground, they must not be swayed—or even appear to be swayed—by entities that make money by influencing Americans' healthcare choices.

- A lack of factual knowledge and comprehension—healthcare illiteracy, if you will—on the part of patients. There's blame enough to go around on this issue: some for insurance and medical institutions, whose jargon and practices are confusing and intimidating; some for policymakers and politicians, who should challenge institutions to be more consumer-friendly; some for providers, academia, and community groups that currently provide precious little consumer/patient education; and, in the final analysis, some for healthcare consumers, who must do more to inform and advocate for themselves.

Realistically, in this media-saturated age, we aren't likely to eliminate medical misinformation. But if we help patients become smarter healthcare consumers, they can arm themselves against the propaganda. We're still a long way from universal implementation of electronic medical records and other health information technologies that could improve care and reduce costs. While we're waiting, patients' best defense is to become their own advocates—to educate themselves about their conditions, their providers, and the broader system in which they obtain care. And as we approach our senior years, we should be informing someone trustworthy and younger who can become our advocate and navigator.

Consider that system in the context of US economic history. The United States long has prided itself on certain traits of a free-market economy, such as limits on government interference and prices determined by competition more than by regulation. Fans of the free-market approach want it applied to the delivery of healthcare, but there's a fundamental flaw in their reasoning. The essential components of a market system—in which the equilibrium of supply and demand determines prices—are a seller who doesn't have to sell and a buyer who doesn't have to buy. In the case of healthcare, however, when the patient needs the service, he or she *has to buy!* When someone's sick, they don't have time to shop around for the best hospital or surgeon or ICU.

Here, let me be frank, at the risk of being insulting: Even if they did have time to shop, most patients in the United States would not have a clue how to go about judging the quality of healthcare services. Most patients don't know how to access the healthcare system to get the best possible outcomes—and they don't anticipate that if they don't access it properly, they may wind up both a lot sicker and a lot poorer. The System doesn't reward or incentivize patients for consuming services properly; it only punishes them for doing it improperly.

Most Americans don't know much about how our healthcare system works and know even less about how our health insurance system works. It's one thing not to know what your insurance plan will or won't cover; many of us don't know for sure until we go to use it. What I find more disturbing is that most Americans have no idea that the for-profit health insurance system, by its nature, is stacked against them.

Like any for-profit business, the health insurance company needs to make money for its shareholders. In the company's quest to roll up profit, the patients it must cover are a liability. The more the company has to pay for services—that is, buying health for policyholders—the less it can return to shareholders. So the for-profit company "succeeds" by paying dividends to shareholders, not by paying claims to patients. Are most US policyholders mindful of this when they buy health insurance? I think not.

When consumers fail to inform themselves about the entities that control their healthcare, they play into the hands of those who profit from their ignorance.

Taken together, the inconsistent and inequitable access to care, the fragmentation of healthcare delivery, and the relative ignorance of consumers produces more chaos than care. The confusion of the chaos works to the advantage of two groups: policymakers who use the chaos to obscure the truth and payers who use the chaos to increase their profits. The disarray in the system creates cover for political untruths and payer inefficiencies while enhancing reelection for officeholders and building profits for insurers. The more chaos there is, the more politicians can obfuscate and payers can profit. Meanwhile, the public pays for the inefficiencies, picking up bigger healthcare bills than the rest of the developed world while enduring worse overall health outcomes.

How do we pay for this extra cost of care for worse outcomes? Certainly we pay in dollars. Our health insurance premiums have skyrocketed: The average cost of a family health insurance plan nearly doubled from 2002 to 2012, from about $8,000 to more than $15,700, according to a Kaiser Family Foundation report.

We also pay for our inefficient healthcare system in terms of a loss of competitiveness of American businesses as they engage in the global marketplace. In Japan, Germany, Switzerland, and Israel, businesses pay for healthcare through higher taxes; but their expenditures in extra taxes pale in comparison to what our businesses pay in insurance premiums.

US businesses, on average, are paying between $8,000 and $15,000 per employee per year for health insurance coverage. This does not include the employee contribution to the premium payment, usually $2,500 to $5,000 per employee per year. And the premium costs keep escalating annually. To try to reduce costs, some businesses have cut workers from full time to part time so the company won't have to cover their health insurance costs; others simply eliminate the benefit. This led to further increases in the number of uninsured Americans over the last decade—and those increases helped fuel the passage of the Patient Protection and Affordable Care Act (ACA for short). We're feeding our own failing system with new failures.

The ACA requires small businesses to pick up insurance coverage for employees they didn't cover previously, and this poses challenges. But beyond some complaints from the small business sector, we seldom hear businesses objecting to how much they pay for insurance premiums. I often wonder: Would there be a different response if we didn't call these payments "premiums" but rather called them "taxes"? I'm guessing many businesses would rage against that. Yet for decades, just as with taxes, massive sums have been paid—the bulk of premiums by employers, and a share by employees—to these large entities supposedly acting in our interest. When we do that with government in paying our taxes, we at least have some measure of public accountability, open records, and transparency. But we know a great deal less about the disposition of the premiums insurance companies collect, the portions spent on customers or returned to shareholders. Why has there been so little outcry about this? Because "business as usual" is easy to conduct under the cover of chaos, and the Tea Party opposes "taxes," not "premiums."

Another population that pays dearly for the inefficiencies of our healthcare system is medical providers and their staffs. The insurance companies, in their effort to restrain expenditures, create hurdles for providers to access procedures (e.g., CT scans, MRIs, and the like) and for patients to access medications not on their insurance plan's preapproved list, or formulary. At the point of care, neither patients nor providers can easily know what's allowed, preapproved, or "preferred" on the plan a particular patient has. So first, this needs to be untangled. Then, to get approval for such procedures or medications, the providers and nursing staffs must submit forms seeking prior authorizations (PAs). As documented by the study Jim Raper conducted, completing a PA costs the clinic an average of thirty minutes of a nurse practitioner's time, or about $42 worth of uncompensated time. That is for *each prescription*—and in a month, we might go through dozens. Chaos on top of chaos.

The more barriers a payer creates, the more hoops providers need to go through to be paid, the less likely the payers are to make a payment to the provider. The resulting vast array of reimbursement forms, paperwork filings, and communication with multiple insurance plans is burying providers in costs for time and labor.

A study by Dante Morra, MD, and colleagues published in 2011 in the journal *Health Affairs* compared the costs of doing business for providers in the United States versus those in Ontario, Canada. Practices in Ontario spent $22,205 per physician per year interacting with Canada's healthcare system versus $82,975 per physician per year spent in the United States, nearly a fourfold difference in overhead costs. When the researchers broke down where the costs were generated, they found that nursing staffs in the United States spent 20.6 hours per physician per week interacting with health plans, compared to 2.5 hours per physician per week in Ontario: a staggering eightfold difference.

The study's conclusion: "The U.S. could save almost $27.6 billion in annual health spending if administrative costs were similar to those in Canada."

And these extra overhead costs disproportionately affect primary care providers, making it even less desirable for America's aspiring healers to enter that important field. For those committed physicians, nurse practitioners, nurses, and others who do choose to work in primary care, early burnout is common. And understandable.

So there is it, in detail: the inequity and fragmentation, the failures of information and communication that have given us this broken-down US healthcare system. If we don't demand positive change, and soon, the NRC/IOM report's title has told us what we can expect:

Shorter Lives, Poorer Health.

———

The ACA, or "Obamacare," was passed in response to these inequities. Originally, it was to have a public option that would, in essence, compete against other insurance companies in health exchanges within a health insurance marketplace. The idea was to create at least some degree of open market in which patients could choose a health insurance plan where at least one option wasn't driven by an overwhelming drive for profits or to keep a stock price high. Rather, they could choose a health plan that simply makes decisions about which services are medically necessary. For the poor and uninsured, the federal government would fund the expansion of Medicaid in each state to cover those who were at or below 133 percent of the federal poverty line. In a state like Alabama, where the current Medicaid plan covers only those who are at 20 percent of the federal poverty line, that is a lot of people. The feds would pay 100 percent of those additional costs for several years, reducing the amount of federal support slowly to 90 percent, but no less than that. It is a windfall for the states, and the poor.

But a funny (bad) thing happened on the way to passing Obamacare. The special interest lobbyists and the members of Congress who receive lots of their cash eliminated the public option because they said it was "unfair competition" to have the government compete against the private sector. Yet these same members of Congress espouse that the government can't do much of anything well, especially healthcare. So what was there to worry about? These same members of Congress have voted, futilely, to repeal Obamacare forty times, claiming that it will bankrupt the country. But not one of them acknowledges that keeping the status quo has already put us on a path to bankruptcy. We cannot afford to pay for the chaos and unchecked costs. Obamacare is not the "answer," but it is a critical first step toward gaining control of an out-of-control system. And the folks who are vehemently opposed to it have no solutions, just objections. The irony of all of this: The premise of Obamacare was originally proposed by the Heritage Foundation, a right-wing think tank, as a response to the Clinton's administration push for healthcare reform. These tenets were implemented in Massachusetts under Governor Mitt Romney's leadership, where by most every metric, it has been successful in assuring nearly full (97 percent) access to care of all citizens in the state while slowing the rise of healthcare costs dramatically, especially when compared to other states in the nation. A bad idea that won't work? C'mon. What we had pre-Obamacare is much, much worse. Why on earth would we want to return to that?

———

In fall 2009, my friend and 1917 Clinic chaplain Malcolm Marler was asked to become director of the UAB Department of Pastoral Care, which provides chaplain services for the university's medical system. Nobody could have been better suited to the job. Thank goodness this move kept Malcolm around so I still can catch the occasional lunch or workout date with him, and I still can lean on his wisdom.

I always try to read what Malcolm writes because it is, like him, insightful and useful and often inspiring. He'll start out recounting some everyday occurrence, and then, like magic, he's produced a full-fledged parable.

One of Malcolm's stories gives the best description I've ever heard for what patients really want to get out of healthcare. It also says a lot about why providers go into this work. It's a story from his first month at the 1917 Clinic, when he counseled his first HIV-positive patient.

> A clinic colleague said to me, "Malcolm, can you come talk to this patient, she just found out she's positive and she's really sobbing." I thought to myself, *What do they want me to do?* I walked into the room and sat down. The woman, whose name was Robin, kept crying. Then finally she looked up and said, "Who are you?" I said, "My name's Malcolm, I'm one of the chaplains here, I just heard you were having a hard time and thought I'd come in and be with you." We talked a little; I found out she was a Baptist, as I was raised. And then as she was talking she stopped midsentence and she said, "I want to know the answer to three questions. I want to know, Does God still love me? Will anybody ever love me again? And will anybody ever hug me again?"
>
> I said, "Stand up, Robin," and I walked over and hugged her. Generally there's a protocol when hugging someone you don't know well—ONE one thousand, TWO one thousand, THREE one thousand and then you break, you don't just keep hugging. But I pulled her close and hugged her and she just cried so hard on my shoulder. And I told her, "You can come here and get a hug any day, if you have an appointment or not." So that answered her third question.
>
> As for her first question, I told her, "Robin, because of your faith background, you know what grace means. It's forgiveness,

it's unmerited love given freely, just poured out. So there's not anything you can do that God will stop loving you. And as for other people loving you, I think there's going to be a way soon for us to introduce you to people who will love you." That was around the time we started creating the support teams matching people from area churches with HIV-positive patients. And we did link her up with a support team, people who became close friends with her and did incredible things like having a Christmas party in her home when she was too ill to get out.

Robin was the first person who taught me that everybody, deep down, wants to know the same things. It's true not only for people with HIV but for anybody with a significant health care issue. They want to know, is there something larger than me in all this, a God who will love me? Second, they want to know, who are the people around me who are going to love me and care for me during this time? And third, they want to know, does being ill mean I have to give up everything, including somebody just to hold me? Those are the universal issues that people with any illness deal with, at one time or another.

Malcolm has captured what brings most of us to the role of "provider": our desire to make a positive difference in the individuals and communities around us. That's really all there is. It doesn't cost anything for providers to listen, to care, and to heal through acts of kindness. The human touch is no less vital today than it was in the 1920s when doctors made house calls and had little to offer except hand-holding and comfort care, much like it was for me when I first started taking care of HIV patients in the 1980s.

Because the reality of why we came is clear and simple, our constant frustration and sometimes fury at a healthcare system that blocks healing and punishes patients (and us) is equally clear and simple.

In the case of HIV, can any of us imagine what it would have been like had the Ryan White CARE Act not come along when it did in 1990? When it was first passed, we had very little to offer HIV patients and their families.

Ryan White was designed to help patients access care so they could access AZT, a medication that would at least buy time—and when that failed, they could die with dignity.

As scientific advances exploded through the 1990s, the Ryan White program assured access to care and access to life-saving medications. Among HIV-positive patients in the United States, fully 40 percent are uninsured and another 20 percent are underinsured—so the Ryan White program made sure that *every* patient was taken care of. To those with no other way to access care, Ryan White has been an absolute lifeline. Gratitude abounds.

But it begs the question: Why did we have to create such a solution to get one group of patients care?

Isn't something wrong with our system if we had to "carve out" an exceptional program just to provide what's right and humane for patients and their families? And then, of course, we arrive at the larger question: What about all the other patients and families with other disorders who deserve Ryan White-caliber programs but for whom no such program exists?

The US healthcare system is an abandoned tinderwood building full of disadvantaged inhabitants seeking shelter from the cold and chaos. Healthcare should be a warming blanket, not a burning building.

It's the chaos that keeps us from listening when Jim Raper warns, "It's gonna burn."

The chaos keeps us from believing that it's our problem, our lives, our parents, and our children who will be sacrificed. It enables politicians to say outlandish things taught to them by lobbyists and pollsters. It keeps profits rolling and the poor coming through the doors of the ER.

Who can change The System? We can. But we need to stop yelling at each other and start listening to the facts. The facts are our friends. They show us where we are, how we got here, and how we can get out.

Chapter 20

IMAGINE

If you have AIDS, come see me. I know AIDS and the heroes who've won so many battles against it.

I could make a very long list of topics on which I'm *not* an expert. My wife, Amy, would probably have an even longer list, starting with childbirth. But, for starters, I'm not an expert on US or international politics or economics. I'm not an expert on the internal workings of the pharmaceutical and insurance industries. I'm not an expert on every political, economic, and corporate influence that has shaped US healthcare policy. What shocks me is how much time I've devoted to what is not my field of expertise.

I've backed into each of these fields. In league with my patients and colleagues, I one day found myself taken up by The System. We may not be experts on the entities that control US healthcare, but we are stakeholders in their decisions. We may not be experts on The System's inner workings, but we're painfully familiar with their consequences. And I think that makes us, if not experts, at least reliable witnesses.

I've seen how the US healthcare system confuses patients like Jenny and bankrupts patients like Brian and his partner Joe, how it frustrates genius providers like Jim Raper and drives other gifted healers completely out of the field. My family, my patients, and my colleagues have combined to give me urgency, sometimes to the point of rage.

Meanwhile, my expertise on healthcare reform lies mostly in knowing where it's most needed and why. That's the vantage from which I look for worthwhile programs we might emulate, new ideas we might try—and reasons for optimism and hope.

———

The US healthcare system can boast of some phenomenal successes in HIV/AIDS medicine and overall. These successes are vitally important for what they can teach us. They also are important because they encourage us to persevere when we hit disappointments and failures.

Patricia is a success story, pure and simple. When she came to the clinic in late 2011, she had advanced AIDS, HIV dementia, and a parasitic infection called toxoplasmosis. Though Patricia is about five foot five, she weighed only seventy pounds by the time her mother brought her in. When Jim Raper lifted her onto the exam table, she was curled in the fetal position and drooling on herself.

Today Patricia is alert and active, completely recovered from the dementia. She weighs 140 pounds and looks like a fashion model: gorgeous, smiling, and happy! She recovered because we got to her in time with a regimen of drugs we did not have to save so many others before her. Patricia's experience on these drugs will yield data we can use to make the next rounds of drugs even better and save more patients in the future.

It's easy to appreciate the kind of success we're having with Patricia. It's harder to know what to say about the success we had with my friend Granger.

I wish I had known Granger growing up. He was born in Alabama exactly six days before I was born in Louisville. Like me, he was a storyteller: While I was at Tulane making movies, he was at Florida State University writing, producing a slim book of short stories as his master's thesis.

Though he was a talented writer and teacher, Granger really made his name in another realm: antiques and interior design. People were enchanted by his style, his wicked sense of humor, and what one friend called his "Southern Gothic charm." If you asked me to describe him, I'd tell you he was one of the most angelic human beings I've ever met, incredibly sweet and kind.

In August 1999, Tom Blount called me. He said his close friend Granger had what sounded like *pneumocystis* pneumonia (PCP), and asked if I could see him. When Granger arrived at the clinic, he appeared to have not only PCP but a small Kaposi's sarcoma (KS) lesion in his throat. I admitted him to the hospital.

Granger told me he was shocked because he believed he had been careful in his love life. "I just never thought it would happen to me," I remember him saying. He was scared about how his father would take the news and convinced he didn't have long to live. I talked to him about how HIV was rapidly becoming a manageable condition and how, if we all played our cards right, he should live to be an old man.

We got Granger into care immediately. George Shaw, then the 1917 Clinic oncologist, quickly brought his KS under control. Granger bounced back from the PCP, and thanks to a new antiretroviral regimen he got through one of our drug trials, his HIV was rapidly brought down to undetectable levels. To Granger's surprise, his father took the news of his diagnosis well, and was very accepting and supportive. From then on, I saw the fighter in Granger, the man determined to live long and joyfully.

Granger and I hit it off right from the start, as much as I had with any patient. He was an immediately likeable guy, a tall, husky man with a winning smile and an infectious laugh. Once we got his viral load down, he enjoyed generally good health, thriving in the design world, running an antiques store, and enjoying getaways with his dog at his North Carolina cabin.

For years before I knew him, Granger had been a smoker. He quit when he got the HIV diagnosis, but he started again in 2004. He smoked off and on until he had a heart attack in 2009, when he swore off tobacco again. Then, early in 2011, Granger started experiencing what he called "funny sensations" in his chest. A chest CT scan revealed a large mass in his right lung that impinged his esophagus. Tests showed that of the two major types of lung cancer, small-cell and non-small-cell, Granger had the former—the more aggressive type in which cancer cells multiply rapidly and often have spread widely through the body before causing any symptoms.

Granger responded extremely well to the initial rounds of chemotherapy. The mass all but disappeared. When the chemo caused him to lose his dark brown hair, Granger's defiant reaction was to buy a cheeky blond wig. During one of his visits, we took "before and after" photos: blond Granger wearing the wig, and then bald Granger laughing at me trying it on.

Early in 2012, a surveillance MRI scan of Granger's head revealed multiple metastatic lesions throughout his brain. Radiation treatment and some more chemotherapy had virtually no effect. We had thrown everything we had at his cancer. We were hungry hunters who'd found our prey, and we were out of bullets.

In 1999 when I met him, Granger was determined to stay alive. In spring 2012, riddled with cancer, he was just as determined. I was the specialist for his HIV, not his cancer—but when he came back to the hospital in June with intractable nausea and vomiting, I knew I needed to be the one to tell him where he stood.

During that visit, I sat with Granger and had a wonderful conversation. He thanked me for all I had done, then said he wanted to make a confession. Though he'd rallied after his diagnosis and shown a brave, determined face to the world, Granger said, he continued to feel shame that he had HIV. Intellectually he knew he had done nothing wrong and was just a patient with a disease. But somehow, perhaps because of his proper southern upbringing, he still felt embarrassment. He had never told anyone this, he said.

I thanked Granger for confiding in me and reassured him that as opposed to doing anything wrong, he had done everything right. He got diagnosed a bit late, but as soon as he knew his status, he sought treatment, took his medicines well, and got control of the virus. Even though it was hard for him initially, he told his loved ones. That gave him precious years of an honest, supportive relationship with his father, who'd died in 2003, and many others.

We then moved on to the hardest topic: his impending death. Granger admitted he didn't know quite how to behave with loved ones. He had been downplaying his condition and trying not to talk about his terminal prognosis in hopes of sparing them pain. He was behaving as he always had, trying to take care of others.

I listened to my friend until I saw him reach into the hospital nightstand, pull out one of his washcloths, and hand it to me to wipe my tears.

When I could compose myself, I told Granger what I thought. He owed it to the ones he loved most to tell them the end was near. He should not soften the news but address it head on. He should reminisce and share stories, laugh and cry. He should speak openly of his coming death so he and his loved ones could grieve together—because very soon, his loved ones would have to grieve without him.

"But I was always told not to quit!" Granger said, his voice breaking.

"Granger, you're not quitting. We all know we're going to die. And when the time comes, if we can embrace our situation, we can make the most of it not only for ourselves but for those we love." At this point, tears were streaming down Granger's face. I handed back his washcloth and struggled to finish what I wanted to say.

"Get on the phone and tell people. Let them visit. Tell them you love them, and let them tell you. If you can do this, you will not only leave them memories of you; you'll help them, when their time comes, to have a model of how to go in peace. If you can do that, you'll be an angel to them."

By now, we were smiling. We shared a few "I love yous," a long hug, and I headed to the next patient.

A few days later, I visited Granger just before he went home for the last time. Before I could ask how he was doing he broke into a huge smile and said, "THANK YOU, thank you, thank you! Your advice to tell people the end was near was so liberating! I've had some of the best conversations with so many people. Sure, we cried a lot. But it was *so healing*, for both them and me."

I asked Granger if he'd let me include his story when I told mine, and he said he'd be honored. Then, because Granger had no illusions about what was coming, I made a request I could not make to other cherished patients: to take a final photograph. In the picture, the veins stand out on Granger's hollow temples and his cheeks are lined. But his eyes are shining and his smile is, as it ever was, angelic. It's a candid shot of soul mates, two members of the Band of Brothers who'd fought the war together and won. We knew what was coming, but we had tasted victory.

I loved Granger no less than any other longtime patients I've lost, but I've grieved him differently.

Even if there were such a thing as a perfect medical community, it still would know death. The victory for Granger was in cheating death of one more HIV/AIDS patient. He lived a dozen years longer than he expected and twice as long as many HIV patients before him. He didn't die of AIDS but of something ordinary—sadly, the number one cause of US cancer deaths. The evil virus had stalked Granger, but it could not run him down.

I loved Granger, and I miss him. He surely died too young, at age fifty-six, on June 22, 2012. But this mattered to Granger, and it matters to me: He didn't die of AIDS.

———

Reflecting on Patricia's and Granger's stories, I'm struck by the good things that have happened for our patients over the past twenty-five years. Scientific breakthroughs allowed us to rein in HIV/AIDS, and with the help of the Ryan White program, we've restored and maintained the health of hundreds of thousands of Americans.

It's worth remembering that the Ryan White program was designed by Congress specifically to close a gap. Congress *knew* that the majority of patients with HIV were poor, lacked health insurance, and generally were disenfranchised from the existing healthcare system. And members *knew* that unless something closed that gap between what the existing system provided and what the patients needed, a couple of things would happen: (1) infected people would die unnecessarily, and (2) infected people would spread the virus to others at a higher rate. I was appalled at how many law-makers dreaded the second consequence and appeared willing to accept the first.

But motivations aside, the Ryan White CARE Act was passed in 1990, and it has done its job *exceedingly* well. So much so that, as I noted earlier, a 2012 study of people followed at a Johns Hopkins University clinic could not demonstrate any differences in health outcomes (including mortality rates) between those with financial means and those with incomes below 100 percent of the federal poverty rate. This is remarkable because in almost every other disease state, poor patients in the United States have *much worse* outcomes in every category. Not so with HIV/AIDS, because Ryan White funding significantly closed that healthcare gap between the Haves and the Have Nots who have HIV.

Everyone within the sound of my voice (or sight of this book) knows my belief that in our broken healthcare delivery system, the "safety net" that keeps patients from falling through the cracks is made up solely of healthcare workers who give a damn. In the case of HIV patients, those tenacious workers were paid and equipped in large part through the Ryan White program. I shudder to think what would have become of those patients if Ryan White had not been created. And I lose sleep—particularly when it's budget reauthorization season on Capitol Hill—thinking about what would happen if Ryan White went away.

While this is my particular nightmare, here's what keeps other healthcare professionals awake at night: They have no Ryan White equivalent. They have no supplemental, gap-closing program for whatever disease has their attention as HIV/AIDS has mine. They have no dedicated source of additional funding to do for their disadvantaged patients what the current healthcare system fails to do.

Actually, no other country in the industrialized world has a Ryan White program. Why is that? Because they don't need it. Ouch.

All the patients with HIV in Japan, Switzerland, Australia, France, Italy, Canada, Spain, Sweden, Norway, Austria, Netherlands, Finland, Portugal, Germany, United Kingdom, and Denmark, have full access to care without a Ryan White-like program. That's because each of these countries has a system of universal healthcare that covers *all* of their citizens in a coherent, reliable fashion. And compared to the US system, those countries' systems deliver healthcare outcomes that are better by almost every measure and accomplished at about half the cost, according to the 2013 NRC/IOM report.

If you do not find the previous paragraph disgusting, try reading it again.

As I travel around the world to attend different meetings, I make a point to ask my physician colleagues as well as folks I meet on the street, "What do you think of your healthcare system?" Almost universally in the nations I listed above, both the providers and the citizens register approval, with responses ranging from "It's good" to "I love it." In the United States when

I ask the same question, I find almost no one expressing such satisfaction—and plenty of people saying they're afraid even to seek treatment because they can't afford it. I hear these contradictions: Our system is best, and I am terrified. Elsewhere in the developed world, I don't hear heartbreaking accounts of people declaring bankruptcy because of a medical bill. But in the US, two-thirds of all personal bankruptcies are associated with healthcare debt and three-fourths of these by people who have health insurance.

In spring 2013, a blog post by Ezra Klein of the *Washington Post* caught my eye with this bold headline: "21 graphs that show America's health-care prices are ludicrous." As Klein reported, "Every year, the International Federation of Health Plans—a global insurance trade association that includes more than 100 insurers in 25 countries—releases survey data showing the prices that insurers are actually paying for different drugs, devices, and medical services in different countries. And every year, the data is shocking."

Klein then unfurled a long swath of twenty-one bar graphs showing dramatically higher costs for frequently needed drugs and procedures in the United States than literally anywhere else in 2012. For most countries, each cost was listed as a fixed amount, while for the US it was listed as a range. This is necessary, Klein explained, because "In other countries, prices are set centrally and most everyone, no matter their region or insurance arrangement, pays pretty close to the same amount. In the United States, each insurer negotiates its own prices, and different insurers end up paying wildly different amounts." Then he let the graphs tell the story. Comparing the average and the highest costs in the United States with the next-closest nation in terms of cost:

- A routine physician's office visit would cost an average of $68 and up to $176 in the United States, compared to $38 in Chile.
- An appendectomy would cost an average of $8,156 and up to $29,426 in the United States, compared to $5,467 in Australia.
- An angioplasty would cost an average of $16,533 and up to $61,649 in the United States, compared to $14,366 in the United Kingdom.
- The medication Nexium, often prescribed for acid reflux, would

cost an average of $187 and up to $373 in the United States, compared to $72 in the Netherlands.

"This is the fundamental fact of American healthcare: We pay much, much more than other countries do for the exact same things," Klein concluded.

Despite all these cost and access issues I've described, many US leaders continue to call America's system the best in the world and claim we have nothing to learn from other nations' healthcare models. I find that mind-boggling—denial of the first order. If they actually believe this, they should be disqualified from leadership. In fact, if they don't believe it and say it anyway, they should also be disqualified.

For help in facing some hard truths about the future of healthcare, I turn again to my colleague Dr. Milton Weinstein, the Harvard School of Public Health cost-effectiveness expert.

In a 2001 essay he wrote for the *Journal of Medical Ethics*,* Professor Weinstein explored the unalterable reality that there is a limit on medical resources available for the use of Earth's inhabitants. His essay threaded together two intriguing earlier works: biologist Garrett Hardin's landmark 1968 article about resource allocation, "The Tragedy of the Commons," and a later *New England Journal of Medicine* article in which physician Howard Hiatt discussed healthcare resource allocation using Hardin's construct—a common pasture where, if herdsmen took no control over access, some animals ate their fill while others starved to death as the pasture was overgrazed and destroyed.

"Although Hardin's essay was written in the context of population growth, Hiatt saw its relevance to health care," Professor Weinstein wrote. "Physicians, each acting in the best interests of their own patients, collectively reach the limits of health care resources, with the result that access to care and quality of care are compromised.

> There is no obvious ethical solution to the problem of rationing
> the medical commons, because any solution involves compari-
> sons between the value of health services provided to different
> patients with different conditions. Nonetheless, the remedy

---

* Weinstein, Milton C. "Should physicians be gatekeepers of medical resources?," *Journal of Medical Ethics*, 2001, 27:268–274.

must lie in some form of collective action: physicians, like the herdsmen in Hardin's parable, can save the commons only by adhering to a set of mutually acceptable covenants which govern and limit their use of the shared resource.

If health care were "free," there would be no need to limit its use. Health care is not "free" because the use of resources (physician time, hospital beds, health care budgets) by some precludes the use of those resources by others. The overall result of failing to adopt covenants that lead to restrained use of resources by well-meaning physicians is unacceptable.

If a society mandates universal access to health care, and if all physicians provide their patients with the most beneficial treatments available, then the cost of health care will be unacceptably high to their patients, either as taxpayers, payers of insurance premiums, at the point of care, or in combination. The alternatives are compromises, either with the principle of universal access, or with the principle of unlimited care.

Professor Weinstein is right: Whether we like it or not, it is inevitable that healthcare will have to be rationed because no system can afford to give every patient every desired service at every point in care. Today in Europe, such rationing is done through careful assessments of outcomes versus costs, asking the question, "Are we getting the benefit we paid for?" In the United States, we now have a sort of haphazard, de facto rationing that allots services based on who can afford them; those who have money get plenty, those who lack money often go without. But every time we attempt a national conversation about practical, moral ways to ration care, some demagogue starts shouting about "big-government medicine," "playing God," or "death panels"—and the noise helps build the chaos so that fear prevents any reasoned discourse.

In his essay, Professor Weinstein envisions a system in which physicians help develop guidelines to allocate available resources according to the hierarchy of needs in their patient population, medical effectiveness, and cost-effectiveness. In such a system, he writes, physicians would operate "like parents taking care of their several children" in a big family—making "decisions about what clothing to buy for each, which ones to send to sports camp, which to send to college . . . in a caring, compassionate way." Having physicians help devise standards for rationing would allow them to "continue to exercise their roles as agents and advocates for patients," Professor Weinstein writes.

Reasonable? Of course. But to date, no key player in the US healthcare system has called for a serious, transparent, public discussion of rationing. We fear those who will scream more than we love the truth. It's a classic example of what Professor Weinstein calls "our country's avoidance of unpleasant truths" when it comes to the future of healthcare.

———

If we can't tackle the tough questions, how will we ever cure what ails the US healthcare system? I don't know.

Many ambitious attempts at healthcare reform have been floated in recent decades. The Patient Protection Affordable Care Act ("Obamacare") became the law of the land in 2010. Though it remains under steady attack by those who would repeal or defund it completely or in part, implementation of the law's provisions moved ahead. States and the federal government are gaining experience with the "insurance exchanges" the ACA requires. It's an element of The System that need not add to chaos, if we're willing to understand it.

One thoughtful explanation, drafted by an MD, appeared in a 2012 column in the international online newsweekly TheWeek.com and read, in part:

> Originally a Republican idea, the state insurance exchanges mandated under the Affordable Care Act (ACA) will offer a menu of private insurance plans to pick and choose from, all with a required set of minimum benefits, to those without employer-sponsored health insurance. These exchanges are expected to bring health insurance to an additional 16 million Americans. Unlike the Medicaid expansion, these Americans

will gain private insurance, and can choose the plan that's right for them.

The exchanges should facilitate competition among private insurers as they design new benefit packages and cut prices to stay ahead of the game. While I'm slow to favor a mandate, these exchanges will offer those who can benefit from insurance a broad array of tailored options and varying prices that should help them find it. Helping more Americans find and compare the private insurance they need and can afford should be an easy principle both political parties agree on.

The MD who wrote this? Dr. William H. Frist, who is not only a nationally known heart transplant surgeon, but also the former Republican Majority Leader of the US Senate. I've certainly questioned some of Bill Frist's actions, especially in 2005 in the Terri Schiavo case, where he tried to insert the will of the federal government into a personal health decision about withdrawing support from an individual in a persistent vegetative state. But I appreciate his stand on this issue. While many others in his party were demonizing the exchanges mandated by Obamacare, Frist was hailing them as "the solution. They represent the federalist ideal of states as 'laboratories for democracy' . . . 50 states each designing a model that is right for them . . . I love the diversity and the innovation."

Frist's bottom line: "With soaring health care costs one of, if not the most, dangerous threats to America's greatness, a new round of national health care experimentation is exactly what we need . . . I urge everyone—citizens, small businesses, health industry stakeholders, churches, large employers—to actively participate in shaping your exchange so that it reflects your state's values, economy, and common sense." Sounds supremely logical, doesn't it? Like everyone who resides in a neighborhood getting together to fashion a workable delivery system for something they all need.

I appreciate the intent of the exchanges and other provisions of the ACA. It's a necessary first step in longer-term healthcare reform, but it is only a first step because a fundamental problem remains. The problem isn't with this or that kind of insurance, but with the concept of making Americans' healthcare reliant on insurance at all.

Here's why I say that. Typically when Americans buy insurance, we do so hoping we never will have to use it. With most kinds of insurance, there's a high probability that we won't. How many of us ever will have to use our homeowner's insurance to rebuild our house after a fire? Our liability insurance to protect us against a lawsuit from a serious car accident? Our term life insurance because a family breadwinner died before accumulating enough wealth to support the young family left behind? You get the idea.

But here's where health insurance is different from those other types: There's no real question of *whether* any given American will use his or her health insurance; the only question is *when*. If we are lucky enough to have health insurance, we know we will use it. Period. We will use it throughout the year when someone in our family has an illness or complaint. We will use it each year to help cover expenses associated with a wellness visit (if we have a good plan). We will use it to pay for screening laboratory tests, mammography, or colonoscopy to pick up early cancer.

And in many cases, if we don't have health insurance, we won't seek care. The last time I was on service at University Hospital, seeing general medicine patients, I didn't even have to look at their charts to tell who had insurance and who didn't. I simply looked at how they presented, and asked the last time they saw a provider—and in 100 percent of the cases, the ones who had put off seeking care and had arrived in the worst condition were the ones who lacked insurance.

To maintain health, we need healthcare. To access healthcare, we need to cover its costs. To cover healthcare costs in the existing system, most of us have counted on insurance. And about 50 million Americans do not have insurance to count on.

What if there were another way? Imagine this: a comprehensive healthcare service system that is not reliant on individuals' insurance payments. We eliminate the concept of "fee-for-service" and instead have the system available for use on an as-needed basis. Ideally, such a system will be self-contained and vertically integrated, where the most expensive care (e.g., hospital care) shares cost expenditures with outpatient care and promotion of *wellness*, in the true sense of the word. The critical component of such a system is that all the financial resources will be placed in a central pool and distributed based on utilization.

The system's metrics will enable its providers to assess the medical effectiveness and cost-effectiveness of an intervention, to determine when it is likely to work or when it is futile. Providers will be in charge of establishing rules for expenditures and interventions: which drugs will be on formulary, what criteria are used for approval of an MRI or CT scan, and when is it appropriate to discharge a patient from an ICU bed owing to futility. Those systems that use their resources most judiciously, in the most cost-effective manner, will be able to provide more services to the patients who subscribe to their system.

In such a system, charges for participation will be based on a per-patient fee structure. They will be discounted for people with less means. They also will be discounted for people who engage in healthy lifestyles. The patient who smokes, is obese, or doesn't take medicines as directed would pay more. The patient who doesn't smoke, has a body mass index below 25 (nonobese), exercises regularly, take medicines as directed, and shows up for screening exams when indicated (annual physical, mammography, colonoscopy, etc.) would have annual payments discounted.

Is such a system realistic? Can it exist? Absolutely. Absolutely.

In the United States today, the Kaiser Permanente (KP) system is designed very much like this. KP owns (or has control over) its own hospitals, clinics, pharmacies, laboratories, and imaging facilities. Providers are employees of KP and are paid salaries. They are held to performance standards to assure cost-efficient delivery of healthcare based on quality metrics; those who perform well are rewarded, those who don't, aren't. The performance standards are determined with input and buy-in from the providers themselves. The providers also have input on the drugs selected for formulary; generic drugs are used as often as possible when appropriate, and formulary drugs' prices are negotiated with pharmaceutical manufacturers to assure best pricing.

KP patients, who are called "members," buy into the concept as well. As I write this, KP serves more than nine million members in nine states and the District of Columbia. These members understand they are part of a contained system with finite resources. And yet, they have access to all the best US healthcare has to offer: sophisticated cancer therapies, solid organ transplants, and bone marrow transplants. Use of emergency room services is reserved for true emergencies; urgent, drop-in visits for new illnesses are funneled back to KP outpatient clinics whenever possible.

The system has a single payer. This eliminates the need to keep track of which insurance plan each patient has or to fill out various plans' forms. It also eliminates uncertainty regarding which drugs are on formulary and which aren't. If some divergence from a treatment routine requires a prior authorization, it's handled within the KP system according to mutually agreed upon guidelines, and it's processed not by some foreign "them" but by a friendly "us."

KP is not a health insurance system; it is a comprehensive health system. KP provides healthcare and wellness services that compare very favorably to the offerings of most insurance plans, but without the down sides of those plans such as restrictions on benefits and uncertainties regarding coverage in times of need.

In short, KP works remarkably well. If you'll forgive a scientist this relatively unscientific statement: I can tell that KP works because it's about the only place I know in the United States where the primary care providers are happy! Any organization that satisfies PCPs—arguably the most overworked, underpaid, and essential players in medicine today—must be doing something right.

Another place where primary care providers are mostly happy is "at the VA"—the Veterans Affairs medical system established in 1930 by President Hoover. Before the VA was established, it was not uncommon for a soldier who was injured in battle to come home from war with a disabling condition, yet not be able to receive medical care after leaving the service. Creation of the VA system corrected that injustice.

After World War II, VA eligibility was expanded to include all honorably discharged veterans regardless of whether they had a service-connected disability (although those with service-connected disabilities are prioritized above those with non-service-connected illnesses). The availability of the VA for our nation's veterans helps make up for the gaps in access to care within the US healthcare system and provides a respite from the chaos there. My dad was an example of someone who had both Medicare and a supplemental Blue Cross policy—but when those other systems failed him in terms of obtaining a medication for pulmonary artery hypertension, the VA came through.

So the VA is a refuge for veterans, as Ryan White-funded programs are a refuge for HIV/AIDS patients. But they are needed primarily as work-arounds, to compensate for the failures of our existing healthcare system.

Instead of using programs like this as stopgaps, why not take what's working about them and make this the model for all healthcare delivery in America? Create a system with consistently applied rules of engagement that enable coordinated, cost-efficient care delivery of the kind that exists in the VA and KP and that are clearly why providers are happier there than in the wider system. Create the self-contained, vertically integrated, comprehensive systems that can coordinate services and purchases of expensive technologies and can establish centers of excellence for provision of expensive interventions such as transplants and open heart surgery. These operate in the VA and KP and eliminate much of the redundancy and excess costs that plague the wider system.

Bringing down costs remains a goal of former Senator Bill Frist, MD, as evidenced by his recent service on the National Commission on Physician Payment Reform, a study panel convened by the Society of General Internal Medicine. In a 2013 *New England Journal of Medicine* article*, Frist and fellow commission member Steve Schroeder, MD, presented the panel's enlightened recommendations to eliminate our archaic and costly fee-for-service model of healthcare delivery. Among their recommendations:

- Standalone fee-for-service payments to medical practices should be eliminated and new systems transitioned in over the next five years.

- Fixed payment models should be utilized in which each patient represents a predetermined cost paid to the practice that is managed by the system (see KP example above).

- As these new systems are adopted, fees for procedures should be frozen, while management-and-evaluation payments (read: primary care payments) should be increased.

---

* Schroeder, Steven A. and Frist, William. "Phasing out fee-for-service payment," *The New England Journal of Medicine*, May 23, 2013, 368:2029–2032.

- Focus of the new systems should be on quality and outcomes rather than on unit payment for service without regard to outcome(s).

- Small practices should collaborate with larger systems to improve efficiencies.

- Reforms should focus first on areas where the largest cost savings and improved outcomes can be achieved.

The commissioners' bottom line: The nation will not get a handle on its healthcare expenditures without changing the ways providers are paid and incentivized. The authors acknowledge that the transition away from fee-for-service will not happen quickly and that the transition will be painful, to put it mildly. But they believe that new models and systems of care delivery must be focused on rewarding those whose practices fill gaps and provide care to patient populations that have more complex diseases and that are otherwise underserved.

I applaud Dr. Frist and his fellow panelists. But I wonder what prevented him from proposing such sweeping reforms while he was one of the most powerful people in the US Senate? I suspect the answer is, at least in part, politics.

Elected leaders live in fear of rousing the ire of voting blocs that could swing the next election. Depending on what positions incumbent politicians take, well-heeled interest groups can spend barrels of money trying to defeat them—or pour that money into the incumbents' reelection efforts. Health-related groups gave more than a quarter of a billion dollars in the 2011–2012 federal election cycle, making them among the top contributors, according to Federal Election Commission data. Bill Frist might have felt the fundraising pressures less than some lawmakers: He's personally wealthy, and he entered the Senate in 1994 promising to leave after two terms, which he did. But any lawmaker who wants to remain in office would think twice about bucking a big-money interest's agenda—even to promote reforms that are certainly in the public's best interest and may have popular support. Chaos may prevent clarity, but money can prevent reelection.

Ultimately, here's where we end up. The insurance, pharma, and other health-related industries will resist reforms to the US healthcare system that are not in their own interests. Between the special-interest pressures and the partisan warfare, elected officials may make some attempts at reform (e.g., the ACA)—but probably not anything truly revolutionary. If choices about reform are left to these forces, we will have ceded control over our health to people whose primary motivations are corporate profit and political survival, not wellness and care.

But why would we cede this control? There are far more of us than there are of them. According to 2011 and 2012 data from the Kaiser Family Foundation's statehealthfacts.org website, there are nearly 835,000 active physicians in the United States, along with more than 180,000 nurse practitioners. There are more than 2.7 million registered nurses, and overall about 12 million people employed in some aspect of healthcare. As for the number of US healthcare consumers, it changes as the population clock ticks. But it's give or take 316 million people, because at some point in our lives, it's every one of us. If most providers believe the system should be changed and many consumers believe the system must be changed, then how can we *not* prevail? The answer: chaos. Partisan attacks and political rallies generate mind-numbing noise. What's reported, every hour on the hour, is the sound of noise, not critical if quiet facts.

We will only win if we can mobilize to demand what we need, want, and deserve—truly, the best healthcare system in the world.

Here are eight things we should do to work toward that goal:

1. We should eliminate fee-for-service.

2. We should replace it with a system that puts the patient first in all decision making, including end-of-life decisions. This system will have the means to honestly assess futility and, in compassionate collaboration with patients and loved ones, to appropriately remove support when there is nothing left to offer the patient except comfort care and preservation of dignity.

3. The new system should be "capitated," meaning that each member/patient will generate fixed revenue to hospitals and providers who

will then manage the costs of care within those fixed resources. It could be based regionally (as Canada operates its system by provinces) or nationally.

4. We should create metrics for clinical outcomes and quality of care, then reward hospitals and providers that meet the standards and pay less to those that don't. Hospitals and providers also should be held reasonably accountable for postdischarge outcomes to minimize the costly and unhealthy "revolving door" of readmissions soon after discharge.

5. We should mandate that *all* electronic medical records (EMR) systems speak the same language. This would simplify use of healthcare information when a patient is cared for in multiple facilities or systems and facilitate data sharing for assessment of outcomes and for access to healthcare information when a patient was cared for at another facility or system.

6. We should repeal the portion of Medicare Part D that prohibits competitive bidding for prices the government systems pay for drugs.

7. We should place providers in the top leadership and policymaking roles in health systems, with these mandated priorities: to focus first on patient outcomes achieved in a cost-efficient way, and second on business outcomes (read: profit for shareholders). Business experts are needed to manage the healthcare enterprise, but seasoned practitioners should have the final say on its policies and standards.

8. And finally, we should learn from the successes and failures of other nations' healthcare approaches and apply the findings to our own system.

I can recite this list of patient-centered, cost-conscious changes until I'm blue in the face. But none of it will go anywhere unless we, providers and patients, get behind it and push. Once we are resolved for change, we need to make our voices heard. On this issue, many of us have avoided engaging with government, considering it at least dysfunctional and obviously ineffective and, at worst, evil.

I agree that at times, government can be dysfunctional and inefficient. But I never would brand it as evil, because I've seen it do so much good. Through my work as a researcher, I have seen impressive, even noble efforts at the NIH, the CDC, the HRSA, and the FDA. I see Tony Fauci, who could be a president at any college or university in the nation, stay at his post at NIH's National Institute of Allergy and Infectious Diseases to make sure research into HIV and other infectious and rheumatologic diseases stays on course. Others at the NIH, CDC, and FDA with whom I have worked also could be making much more money (with fewer headaches) at an academic institution, in private practice, or with industry, but made the conscious decision to stay in government to make a difference.

In my dealings in healthcare policy, I've worked with brilliant and committed staffers at the Office of Management and Budget and on Capitol Hill. Like most Americans, I have flown on planes protected by the FAA, been shielded against security threats by the Departments of Defense and Homeland Security, and enjoyed trips to national treasures preserved by the Park Service. Within each of these government entities, where some might see bureaucrats, I see heroes: Americans serving their country, often with some degree of personal sacrifice.

So when I hear people like tax foe Grover Norquist—who famously said he'd like to shrink the government down to the size where he could drown it in a bathtub—I want to ask: Just who does he think "the government" is? It's *us!* It's our duty-bound representatives, put in office by our votes and supported by our tax dollars—and so by extension it's all of us, our relatives and coworkers and neighbors.

That fact was driven home for me in late November 2012, when I was invited to the White House observance of World AIDS Day. It was heady stuff, submitting my information for security clearance and getting instructions on where to enter the White House complex. The event was full of Washington luminaries. I was asked to speak about HIV treatment and care on a panel moderated by Rosie Perez, a member of the Presidential Advisory Council on HIV/AIDS and a television and movie star.

I was feeling a little out of place in the halls of power—until I met my fellow panelists. An AIDS foundation president. A leader of the National Black Gay Men's Advocacy Coalition. A young woman living with HIV. And me, an Alabama doctor. A rainbow of people from varied walks of life, gathered to do what proud Americans do: to serve in whatever way could help our nation. We weren't voted into doing it. We weren't lobbied into doing it. We were there because each of us, playing our part, is the essence of government in a representative democracy.

That's how it was in 1787, at the Constitutional Convention—a gathering of Continental Congress members and lawyers, to be sure, but also of planters and soldiers, educators and ministers and merchants. All of them helped create the blueprint for government in which each of them would have a role—as we have, today. They lived in a time of revolutionary chaos and uncertainty, but they did not yield to chaos. They sought the most noble aims and drafted the most noble document. Now, as then, *we* constitute the government. So if we really want to, we can influence what it does. It simply takes vision, focus, and will.

Making US healthcare both patient-centered and cost-efficient is a tall order. It hasn't been easy to make progress so far and it won't be easy from here. But it is necessary. Absolutely necessary. For the well being of us all.

———

Friday, April 26, 2013, we've organized events to salute the 1917 Clinic's twenty-fifth year in operation.

We begin with a six-hour scientific symposium. I feel like I'm hosting an ID class reunion, and I can't believe my good luck that so many past and present UAB eminences can attend. There's Eric Hunter, who once headed UAB's Center for AIDS Research and now heads the CFAR at Atlanta's Emory University. There's Michael Kilby, former medical director at the 1917 Clinic, now director of the Division of Infectious Diseases at the Medical University of South Carolina. There are my UAB colleagues Vicki Johnson (Virology Specialty Lab director), Paul Goepfert (Alabama Vaccine Research Center director), Michael "Mugs" Mugavero (CFAR deputy director), and Jim Raper. And, from my formative years in the Shaw-Hahn lab, there's George Shaw, now on faculty at the University of Pennsylvania. Beatrice Hahn wanted to be with us, but she's in Washington, D.C., being inducted into the National Academy of Science Institute of Medicine—one of the highest honors scientists in the United States can achieve—in recognition of her lifetime contribution to solving the mysteries of HIV. How fitting that Beatrice's induction to the IOM coincides with this day of celebration of the 1917 Clinic and UAB's Center for AIDS Research.

After UAB Vice President for Research Richard Marchase gives welcoming remarks to open our symposium, we spend the day reflecting on, in essence, what's been survived and what's been achieved.

George has titled his remarks "Discoveries from the UAB 1917 Clinic that have Changed the World"—and at risk of sounding arrogant, we do allow ourselves to revel in some hard-won victories. But mostly, we look with gratitude on the successes of the worldwide scientific community. Speakers acknowledge the work of Tony Fauci, Bob Gallo, the scientists at the Pasteur Institute, Paul Volberding, and on and on. With each successive speaker, I'm more aware of how the progress was possible only because the scientific community, the patient community, the pharmaceutical company community, and the government community all pulled together in a common cause.

After lunch, my cousin Mary speaks for her many fellow patients of the clinic. She offers thanks to "all of you who've forfeited sleep, and money, and fame, giving your lives to those of us who believed our lives were over."

Mary always knows exactly how to make me guffaw or weep, and this day is no exception. She jokes about initially resisting when her mother Marjorie urged her to consult with me: "I'd seen my cousin Michael. We'd been at weddings and funerals together. He seemed very nice. But I was in the care of New York City physicians with famous patient lists (and) terrific haircuts . . . Michael looked like he could be a junior high band instructor from Topeka."

Once the laughter stops, Mary concedes that she's glad she gave treatment here a try after all. "Two decades ago I came to UAB full of certainty and skepticism," she says. "I was certain about my own death; I was skeptical that Michael Saag, or any of you, could do anything about it. I've returned today as evidence that death did not have the last word on AIDS."

I choke up more than once during Mary's remarks, but especially at the end, when she turned toward me and said softly, "Thank you for my life."

———

Saturday, April 27, 2013. I am sitting in a front pew in the light-filled sanctuary of the Baptist Church of the Covenant in Birmingham, waiting for the start of an afternoon service led by two great friends of the 1917 Clinic: former chaplain Malcolm Marler and current chaplain Chris Hamlin, the former pastor of the 16th Street Baptist Church who led the service when Mary spoke there in 1993.

Sitting next to me in the front row is my cousin Mary. Sitting in the row immediately behind me are Amy, Andy and his wife, Brittany; my sisters, Terry and Barbara, my brother-in-law Greg, and my mom, The Big E. A few rows back: Jim Raper and Scott. As they'd say on Broadway, "the house is stacked."

As my eyes pan around the sanctuary, I see many more clinic staffers, present and past: Carol Linn, Patsy Barron, Gina Dobbs, Laura Secord, Joe Elmore, Michael Mugavero, Turner Overton. I see current patients—people recently enrolled in care, and people like Alan who have been in care for years.

As I gaze into the empty choir loft behind the podium, the more I look, the more I'm convinced I see others who were here earlier: Ones I could love but could not save. Brian . . . Michael . . . Jacob . . . Ed . . . Jim . . . Ben . . . Elliott . . . Granger. I see Cyndie and I hear her quiet prayer. Behind her, to the left, is that Eddie Saag—has my father somehow found this place, this day? From somewhere in the mist I hear a familiar voice say, "Mike, you did good"—that treasured compliment from my childhood construction crew buddy, Pitt.

We've gathered not to mourn but to celebrate. This worship service is the crowning event of the twenty-fifth anniversary weekend; it honors all the patients the clinic has served and all the staff who've worked so long, so hard, with such common purpose. When I imagined I was seeing all those dear departed patients in the choir loft, my eyes may have been playing tricks on me, but my heart was telling the truth. Everyone who figured in the clinic's first quarter century truly is there with me.

"It's important that we remember—not only for us as individuals, but for us as communities," my cousin Mary says when she rises to speak.

"There's a pan-African term, *abataka*, which means 'community.' But it also means oneness . . . shared traits and shared identity. It means belonging, in the sense that you and I belong to one another. *Abataka* reminds me that communities need history, and history needs memory. It helps me recognize that out of the most deadly epidemic in human history, you and I have been left with the gift of *abataka*, community. In the common experiences of brokenness and dying, we have found one another. In the agony we could not endure, we were held by those who understood."

After the service we walked en masse from the church's door to the 1917 Clinic two blocks away. It's a halfcentury since others walked these sidewalks under threat of fire hoses, billy clubs, racial taunts, and degrading curses. Today, we walk to celebrate the miracle and magic of science and compassion.

The strains of "Amazing Grace" have hardly faded when, in my mind, I hear the soft piano chords of John Lennon's *Imagine* playing in cadence to the sound of our marching feet. I have known and loved this song for so long that I don't so much hear the lyrics as feel them in my bones: that notion of no hell below or heaven above, just people living for today. It all seems right to me and true. There *is* amazing grace. It's what allows people like me to believe in change as vast and hopeful as John imagined. And if that belief earns me the label of dreamer . . . well, I'm in good company.

Had UAB and all these people left me alone, I would have failed. Together, we succeeded. Admittedly, we *were* all dreamers. Here and there, magic happened. But we were not the only ones. Despite the chaos, we found others who shared our dreams.

If we can tackle AIDS while it thrives under the shadow of bigotry and stigma, surely we can fix a broken healthcare system that's visible to all. Surely we can. We need to act *now*. We need to do what needs to be done with the same energy and persistence we applied to the AIDS epidemic, woven together as an inspired community—a medical neighborhood of providers and patients, researchers and activists, public servants and corporate citizens.

It isn't too late. I know because I still see the man I thought was Pitt sitting outside the VA. He's still lifting that Camel to the steel plate on his throat. He could still be saved. Surely he could.

What could we accomplish, all together? Just imagine.

Epilogue

hroughout this book, I've told stories of heroes in the war on AIDS as examples of how fortitude and perseverance can lead to victory, even when battling our dysfunctional healthcare system. As I readied this manuscript for the printer, I realized I needed to tell one more story, a truly inspirational account of personal commitment and courage. It's the story of Harry Wingfield.

In Chapter 9, I mentioned Harry, a songwriter and musician who had been fired from his job in UAB's theater department when his HIV-positive status became known. After participating in the L–697,661 study, Harry suffered additional bouts of *pneumocystis* pneumonia, the last of which, in 1995, was so severe that his family was called in to say good-bye. Fortunately, Harry survived that episode and went on to catch successive waves of new, more effective antiretroviral cocktails that ultimately returned him to good health.

Over the next few years, Harry continued to do well. He worked in his garden every day and was volunteering at the 1917 Clinic. Then, in 2002, the clinical trials research group at our clinic found itself in a crisis of sorts: The person who had managed the regulatory documents—Institutional Review Board paperwork, correspondence with pharmaceutical sponsors, and the like—had just resigned and left the office in a mess, with backed-up paperwork stacked on the desk and even the floor. Harry asked if he could take a shot at reorganizing the office, and we said, "Please do!"

In less than a month, Harry had revamped the entire operation. He submitted delinquent documents, filed stacks of papers into newly-created filing systems, and brought the entire operation into real time, responding to requests as they came in rather than shuffling them into stacks.

One afternoon Harry came to me with a concerned look on his face. "I have a dilemma," he said. "I've been on disability ever since the theater department fired me and I really would like to come off of disability and go to work . . . with you." We needed to fill the position in the regulatory office; Harry had more than proved his worth through the remarkable transformation he created there. "So what's the dilemma?" I asked.

Harry listed his concerns: "Well, what if I come off of disability and find I can't do the work long term? I have only been doing this a month, and I am pretty tired when I get home. What happens if I discover over time that I am really not up to it? I get all my health insurance through Medicare, and that requires me to have been on disabled status for two years. If I come to work for you, I lose that status. If I find I need to go back on disability because I can't sustain the effort, can I get back on Medicare?"

We had filed plenty of applications to put people *on* disability, but rarely were we asked by a patient to come *off* of disability! So I didn't have answers to Harry's questions at that moment, but I was determined to get them. I thanked him for his courage and desire to do this and promised him we would do everything possible to assure his success no matter how things turned out.

Working with the Social Security Administration, we were able to arrange for Harry to come off of disability with a path back to that status if he couldn't do the work. Harry came to work for us that summer and stayed for several years until he was hired away from us—by the UAB Institutional Review Board itself! They were so impressed with his organizational skills, attention to detail, work ethic, and knowledge of regulatory requirements that they stole him from us. I was never so pleased to lose a valued employee.

To me, this was one of our sweetest victories in the war on AIDS. So many others who were as sick as Harry never made it to the new life-saving drug cocktails. Among those who did survive to try newer drugs, many never regained enough function to go back to work full time. And even if they regained function, many lacked the courage to take on new careers and other challenges. Harry's story represents the triumph of science over an evil virus, the triumph of the Ryan White CARE Act over gaps in coverage, the triumph of flexibility over inertia in the Social Security system—and the triumph of a single individual's bravery over fear and uncertainty.

Above all, Harry's story is proof that we *can* improve healthcare in America by listening to our patients and putting their needs first. That's what we must remember, and what we must commit to, in this pivotal period for healthcare policy and reform. If we honor that commitment with reason and compassion, the results are bound to be positive.

Dr. Michael Saag received a BS in chemistry with honors from Tulane University and earned his medical degree with honors from the University of Louisville. During medical school, he served for three years on the Medical School Admissions Committee and received the Presley Martin Memorial Award for Excellence in Clinical Medicine. He completed his residency and infectious disease and molecular virology fellowship training at the University of Alabama at Birmingham. During his fellowship training, Dr. Saag made seminal discoveries in the genetic evolution of HIV in vivo. He evaluated isolates of virus obtained from individual patients at different periods in time and cloned and molecularly characterized these isolates to determine the degree of diversity of coexisting viral variants and to describe their evolution over time (*Nature*, 1988). While working with Dr. Dismukes, Dr. Saag designed and led a multicenter national AIDS clinical trial on the management of cryptococcal meningitis. This study included 194 patients and demonstrated the role of oral azole therapy in the treatment of this disorder in HIV-infected patients (*NEJM*, 1992). During the last six months of his fellowship, Dr. Saag conceived the concept of the 1917 Clinic, a comprehensive HIV outpatient clinic dedicated to the provision of comprehensive patient care in conjunction with the conduct of high quality clinic trials, basic science, and clinical outcomes research. Within the clinic structure, he established a clinical trials unit, a data management center, and a clinical specimen repository designed to support the activities of the newly established Center for AIDS Research at UAB. In essence, the clinic became a hub for the clinical, basic science, and behavioral science investigators within the center by creating a dynamic interface between the patients and the investigators.

Since the establishment of the clinic, Dr. Saag has participated in many studies of antiretroviral therapy and of novel treatments for opportunistic infections. He has published over 300 articles in peer-reviewed journals, including the first description of the use of viral load in clinical practice (*Science*, 1993), the first description of the rapid dynamics of viral replication (*Nature*, 1995), the first guidelines for use of viral load in practice (*Nature Medicine*, 1996), the first proof of concept of fusion inhibition as a therapeutic option (*Nature Medicine*, 1998), and directed the first inpatient studies of seven of the twenty-five antiretroviral drugs currently on the market (including indinavir, efavirenz, abacavir, and enfuvirtide). Dr. Saag has contributed over fifty chapters to medical textbooks, has served on the editorial board of *AIDS Research and Human Retroviruses*, coedited a textbook entitled *AIDS Therapy* (Churchill Livingston, now in its third edition), and currently serves as an editor of the *Sanford Guide to Antimicrobial Therapy* and the *Sanford Guide to HIV/AIDS Therapy*. He has served on the board of directors of the American Board of Internal Medicine (and as chair of the Infectious Disease Subspecialty Board), has twice served as a member of the HIV Disease Committee of the Medical Knowledge Self-Assessment Program for the American College of Physicians, and has served on the NIH Office of AIDS Research Advisory Council. Dr. Saag currently serves on the International AIDS Society-USA board of directors, is a past president of the HIV Medical Association, is a member of the HHS Guidelines Panel on Antiretroviral Therapy, and is on numerous state, local, and national committees. He was elected into the American Society of Clinical Investigation in 1997 and the Association of American Physicians in 2011. Among his other awards, Dr. Saag has received the Myrtle Wreath Award from Hadassah, was listed as one of the top ten cited HIV researchers by *Science* (1996), and has been listed as one of the "Best Doctors in America" since 1994. He received the Outstanding Medical Research Achievement Award from the AIDS Task Force of Alabama, an Excellence in Teaching Award from the Medical Association of the State of Alabama, was named a "Health Care Hero" by the *Birmingham Business Journal* (2003), received a Service Award from the AIDS Survival Project in Atlanta (2003), was a 2004 honoree of the Birmingham chapter of the National Conference on Community and Justice, was a recipient of the Birmingham Chamber of Commerce Spirit of Birmingham Award (2005), was a recipient of the Leonard Tow Humanism in Medicine Award (The

Arnold P. Gold Foundation), was a recipient of the UAB Alumni Society
Hettie Butler Terry Community Service Award (2007), and received four
Argus Awards for Best Lectures to the first-year medical students at UAB
in 2009 and three others in 2010, 2011, and 2013. In December 2010,
Dr. Saag was awarded the President's Medal of UAB, the highest honor
given at this institution. He is married to Amy Weil Saag, his wife of thirty-
six years, and they have three children, Andy (who is married to Brittany),
Harry, and Julie.